Signature SERIES

COREL® WORDPERFECT® 10

Nita Rutkosky
Pierce College at Puyallup
Puyallup, Washington

Nancy Graviett
St. Charles County Community College
St. Peters, Missouri

EMCParadigm

Editor	Desiree Faulkner
Proofreader	Judy Peacock
Indexer	Nancy Fulton
Text and Cover Designer	Jennifer Wreisner
Desktop Production	Desktop Solutions

Publishing Team—George Provol, Publisher; Janice Johnson, Director of Product Development; Tony Galvin, Acquisitions Editor; Lori Landwer, Marketing Manager; Shelley Clubb, Electronic Design and Production Manager.

Permissions—Material for selected documents has been excerpted from *Telecommunications: Systems and Applications for Business* by William Mitchell, Robert Hendricks, and Leonard Sterry, published by Paradigm Publishing, Inc.

Acknowledgments—The author and publisher wish to thank the following reviewer for her technical and academic assistance in testing exercises and assessing instructions: Mary Ruth Seefeldt, Hill College, Hillsboro, Texas.

Library of Congress Cataloging-in-Publication Data

Rutkosky, Nita Hewitt.
     Corel WordPerfect 10 / Nita Rutkosky, Nancy Graviett.
        p. cm. – (Signature series)
     Includes index.
     ISBN 0-7638-1634-5 (text)
        1. WordPerfect (Computer file). 2. Word processing. I. Title: Corel WordPerfect ten.
     II. Graviett, Nancy. III. Title IV. Signature series (Saint Paul, Minn.)

     Z52.5.W65 R846 2003
     652.5'5369–dc21

                                    2001059770

Text: ISBN 0-7638-1634-5
Order Number: 01579

© 2003 by Paradigm Publishing Inc.
            Published by **EMC**Paradigm
            875 Montreal Way
            St. Paul, MN 55102

            (800) 535-6865
            E-mail: educate@emcp.com
            Web site: www.emcp.com

Trademarks—Corel, WordPerfect, Grammatik, and TextArt are registered trademarks and QuickCorrect is a trademark of Corel Corporation. Microsoft and Windows are registered trademarks of Microsoft Corporation in the United States and other countries. Netscape Navigator is a trademark of Netscape. IBM is a registered trademark of IBM Corporation. Some of the product names and companies included in this book have been used for identification purposes only and may be trademarks or registered trademarks of their respective manufacturers and sellers. The authors, editor, and publisher disclaim any affiliation, association, or connection with, or sponsorship or endorsement by, such owners.

Care has been taken to provide accurate and useful information about the Internet capabilities of Corel® WordPerfect® 10. However, the authors, editor, and publisher cannot accept any responsibility for Web, e-mail, newsgroup, or chat room subject matter or content, or for consequences from any application of the information in this book, and make no warranty, expressed or implied, with respect to the book's content.

Printed in the United States of America
10 9 8 7 6 5 4 3 2

Contents

Contents

Introduction

When students prepare for a successful business career, they need to acquire the skills and qualifications essential to becoming a productive contributor to the business community. Microcomputer and information-processing systems are basic to all business offices, and most careers require a working knowledge of computers and computer software. One of the most popular uses of a microcomputer system is word processing—the creation of documents.

Word processing certainly belongs in the business world, but it is also a popular application for home computer use. People will want to learn word processing to write personal correspondence, keep personal records, provide support for a home-based business or cottage industry, write term papers and reports, and much more.

This textbook instructs students in the theories and practical applications of one of the most popular word processing programs—Corel® WordPerfect® 10. The text is designed to be used in beginning and advanced word processing classes and provides approximately 60 hours of instruction.

Text Structure

This textbook is divided into four units. The chapters within each unit contain the following:

- Performance Objectives, identifying the specific learning goals of the chapter.
- Introductory material, providing an overview of new concepts and features.
- Step-by-step intrachapter exercises at the computer, providing students with the opportunity to practice using the feature(s) presented in the chapter.
- Chapter Summary, reviewing the main points of the chapter.
- Commands Summary, listing the major commands learned in the chapter.
- Concepts Check, providing a knowledge self-check.
- Skills Check, offering computer skill assessment exercises that require students to complete exercises without step-by-step instruction.

Performance Assessments at the end of each unit focus on technical skills and writing skills.

- *Integrating Skills*. Practical computer simulation exercises that require students to make decisions about document preparation and formatting, providing ample opportunity to apply new features as well as to practice previously learned material.
- *Writing Solutions*. Writing activities that provide students with the opportunity to compose and format business documents, requiring the demonstration of problem-solving, critical, and creative abilities as well as hands-on computer skills.

Completing Computer Exercises

Some computer exercises in the chapters require students to download files from the Internet Resource Center. The files are contained in individual folders for each chapter. Detailed instructions on how to download and delete folders are provided in the "Getting Started" section that follows this section and, for added convenience, the instructions are repeated inside the front cover of the book.

Industry Standards from the SCANS Commission

This textbook covers important SCANS (Secretary's Commission on Achieving Necessary Skills) goals. The SCANS report was the result of a commission from the Department of Labor. The goal of the commission was to establish the interdisciplinary standards that should be required for all students. SCANS skill standards emphasize the integration of competencies from the areas of information, technology, basic skills, and thinking skills. The SCANS committee agreed that all curricula can be strengthened by emphasizing classroom work that is more authentic and relevant to learners, connecting context to content. Teaching in context helps students move away from subject-specific orientation to integrative learning that includes decision making, problem solving, and critical thinking. The concepts and applications material in each unit of this book has been designed to coordinate with and reflect this important interdisciplinary emphasis. In addition, learning assessment tools implement the SCANS standards. For example, the skill assessments at the end of each chapter reinforce acquired technical skills while providing practice in decision making and problem solving. The performance assessments at the end of each unit offer simulation exercises that require students to demonstrate their understanding of the major skills and technical features taught in the unit's chapters within the framework of critical and creative thinking. The addition of writing activities at the end of each unit makes it clear that students are not just producers, but editors and writers as well.

Learning Components Available with This Text

Signature Resource Center at www.emcp.com. The Signature Resource Center provides a wealth of Web-based resources for students and teachers, including course syllabus, study aids, vital Web links, numerous tests and quizzes, a wide variety of performance tests, and PowerPoint presentations.

Instructor's Guide. The Instructor's Guide is available on the Internet Resource Center and contains suggested course syllabus, grade sheets, and assignment sheets; comprehensive WordPerfect tests and answers for use as final exams; Supplemental Performance Assessments; model answers for all end-of-chapter and end-of-unit assessments. For each chapter, the Instructor's Guide also provides a summary of chapter content, Teaching Hints, and Reviewing Key Points answers.

Class Connection—Web Course Management Tool. The Class Connection is an online course management tool for traditional and distance learning, and is offered on both WebCT and Blackboard platforms. This product creates a personalized Web site for your course and provides supplementary course content, communication via e-discussions and online group conferences, and a testing and grading system. You will find these items will be preloaded on the course Web site: syllabus; assignments, quizzes, and tests; performance exams; course links; study aids; and supplementary course content.

Getting Started

As you work your way through this textbook, you will learn functions and commands for Corel WordPerfect 10. WordPerfect 10 is a word processing program. To operate the WordPerfect 10 program, you will need access to a computer.

Identifying Computer Hardware

The computer equipment you will use to operate the WordPerfect program is referred to as *hardware*. You will need access to a microcomputer system that should consist of the CPU, monitor, keyboard, printer, disk drives, and mouse. If you are not sure what equipment you will be operating, check with your instructor. The computer system displayed in figure G.1 consists of six components. Each component is discussed separately in the material that follows.

FIGURE
G.1 *Microcomputer System*

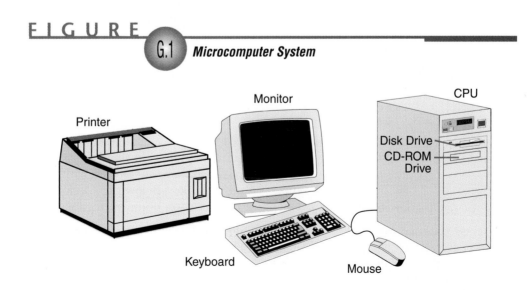

CPU

CPU stands for Central Processing Unit and is the intelligence of the computer. All the processing occurs in the CPU. Silicon chips, which contain miniaturized circuitry, are placed on boards that are plugged into slots within the CPU. An instruction given to the computer is processed through circuitry in the CPU.

Monitor

The monitor displays the information of a program and the text being input at the keyboard. The quality of display for monitors varies depending on the type of monitor and the type of resolution. Monitors also vary in size—generally from 14-inch size up to 21-inch size or larger.

Keyboard

The keyboard is used to input information into the computer. Keyboards for microcomputers vary in the number and location of the keys. Microcomputers have the alphabetic and numeric keys in the same location as the keys on a typewriter. The symbol keys, however, may be placed in a variety of locations, depending on the manufacturer. In addition to letters, numbers, and symbols, most microcomputer keyboards contain function keys, arrow keys, and a numeric keypad. Figure G.2 shows an enhanced keyboard.

F I G U R E *Microcomputer Enhanced Keyboard*

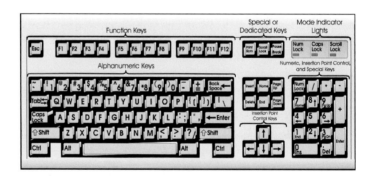

The 12 keys at the top of the enhanced keyboard, labeled with the letter F followed by a number, are called *function keys*. These keys can be used to perform functions within each of the suite programs. To the right of the regular keys is a group of *special* or *dedicated keys*. These keys are labeled with specific functions that will be performed when you press the key. Below the special keys are *arrow keys*. These keys are used to move the insertion point in the document screen.

In the upper right corner of the keyboard are three *mode indicator lights*. When certain modes have been selected, a light appears on the keyboard. For example, if you press the Caps Lock key, which disables the lowercase alphabet, a light appears next to Caps Lock. Similarly, pressing the Num Lock key will disable the special functions on the numeric keypad, which is located at the right side of the keyboard.

Disk Drives

Depending on the computer system you are using, WordPerfect 10 is installed on a hard drive or as part of a network system. Whether you are using WordPerfect on a hard drive or network system, you will need to have available a floppy disk drive. You will save documents you complete at the computer to folders on your disk in the floppy drive.

Printer

When you create a document in WordPerfect, it is considered *soft copy*. If you want a *hard copy* of a document, you need to print it. To print documents you will need to access a printer, which will probably be either a laser printer or an ink-jet printer. A laser printer uses a laser beam combined with heat and pressure to print documents, while an ink-jet printer prints a document by spraying a fine mist of ink on the page.

Mouse

Many functions in the WordPerfect program are designed to operate more efficiently with a *mouse*. A mouse is an input device that sits on a flat surface next to the computer. A mouse can be operated with the left or the right hand. Moving the mouse on the flat surface causes a corresponding mouse pointer to move on the screen. Figure G.1 shows an illustration of a mouse. For specific instructions on how to use a mouse, please refer to the "Using the Mouse" text later in this section.

Properly Maintaining Disks

You will be downloading chapter folders onto a 3.5-inch disk and then saving and opening files from this disk. To ensure that you will be able to retrieve information from the disk, you need to follow certain rules of disk maintenance. To properly maintain a 3.5-inch disk, follow these rules:

- Do not expose the disk to extreme heat or cold.
- Keep the disk away from magnets and magnetic fields. They can erase the information saved on the disk.
- Do not wipe or clean the magnetic surface of the disk.
- Keep the disk away from food, liquids, and smoke.
- Never remove the disk from the disk drive when the drive light is on.
- Carry the disk in a plastic case to prevent damage to the metal shutter.

The 3.5-inch disk on which you will open and save files must be formatted. Most likely, any disk you purchase will already be formatted. Formatting is a process that establishes tracks and sectors on which information is stored and prepares the disk to accept data from the disk operating system (and erases anything previously saved on the disk). If you are using a disk that is not formatted, check with your instructor on the steps needed to format it.

Using the Mouse

WordPerfect can be operated using a keyboard or it can be operated with the keyboard and a mouse. The mouse may have two or three buttons on top, which are tapped to execute specific functions and commands. To use the mouse, rest it on a flat surface or a mouse pad. Put your hand over it with your palm resting on top of the mouse and your wrist resting on the table surface. As you move the mouse on the flat surface, a corresponding pointer moves on the screen.

When using the mouse, there are four terms you should understand—*point*, *click*, *double-click*, and *drag*. When operating the mouse, you may need to *point* to a specific command, button, or icon. Point means to position the mouse pointer on the desired item. With the mouse pointer positioned on the desired item, you may need to *click* a button on the mouse. Click means quickly tapping a button on the mouse once. To complete two steps at one time, such as choosing and then executing a function, *double-click* a mouse button. Double-click means to tap the left mouse button twice in quick succession. The term *drag* means to press and hold the left mouse button, move the mouse pointer to a specific location, and then release the button.

Using the Mouse Pointer

The mouse pointer will change appearance depending on the function being performed or where the pointer is positioned. The mouse pointer may appear as one of the following images:

The mouse pointer appears as an I-beam (called the *I-beam pointer*) in the document screen and can be used to move the insertion point or select text.

The mouse pointer appears as an arrow pointing up and to the left (called the *arrow pointer*) when it is moved to the Title bar, Menu bar, or one of the toolbars at the top of the screen or when a dialog box is displayed. For example, to open a new document with the mouse, you would move the I-beam pointer to the <u>F</u>ile option on the Menu bar. When the I-beam pointer is moved to the Menu bar, it turns into an arrow pointer. To make a selection, position the tip of the arrow pointer on the <u>F</u>ile option and then click the left mouse button. At the drop-down menu that displays, make selections by positioning the arrow pointer on the desired option and then clicking the left mouse button.

The mouse pointer becomes a double-headed arrow (either pointing left and right, pointing up and down, or pointing diagonally) when performing certain functions such as changing the size of a picture or sizing a frame.

In certain situations, such as moving a picture or clip art image, the mouse pointer becomes a four-headed arrow. The four-headed arrow means that you can move the object left, right, up, or down.

When a request is being processed or when a program is being loaded, the mouse pointer may appear with an hourglass beside it. The hourglass image means "please wait." When the process is completed, the hourglass image is removed.

The mouse pointer displays as a hand with a pointing index finger in certain functions such as Help and indicates that there is more information available about the item.

Choosing Commands

Once a program is open, several methods can be used to choose commands. A command is an instruction that tells the program to do something. You can choose a command with one of the following methods:

- Click a toolbar button with the mouse.
- Choose a command from a menu.
- Use shortcut keys.
- Use a shortcut menu.

Choosing Commands on Toolbars and Property Bars

WordPerfect provides several toolbars and property bars containing buttons for common tasks. Generally, two bars are visible on the screen (unless your system has been customized). One is called the WordPerfect 10 Toolbar (referred to as just the Toolbar in this text); the other is referred to as the Main property bar. To choose a command from either bar, position the tip of the arrow pointer on a button and then click the left mouse button. For example, to print the document currently displayed in the document screen, position the tip of the arrow pointer on the Print button on the WordPerfect 10 Toolbar and then click the left mouse button.

Choosing Commands on the Menu Bar

The Menu bar, located toward the top of the WordPerfect screen, contains a variety of options you can use to perform functions and commands on data. Functions are grouped logically into options, which display on the Menu bar. For example, features to work with files (documents) are grouped in the File option. Either the mouse or the keyboard can be used to make choices from the Menu bar or to make a choice at a dialog box.

To use the mouse to make a choice from the Menu bar, move the I-beam pointer to the Menu bar. This causes the I-beam pointer to display as an arrow pointer. Position the tip of the arrow pointer on the desired option and then click the left mouse button.

To use the keyboard, press the Alt key to make the Menu bar active. Options on the Menu bar display with an underline below one of the letters. To choose an option from the Menu bar, key the underlined letter of the desired option, or move the insertion point with the left or right arrow keys to the option desired, and then press Enter. This causes a drop-down menu to display. For example, to display the

File drop-down menu shown in figure G.3 using the mouse, position the arrow pointer on File on the Menu bar and then click the left mouse button. To display the File drop-down menu with the keyboard, press the Alt key and then key the letter F for File.

G.3 *File Drop-Down Menu*

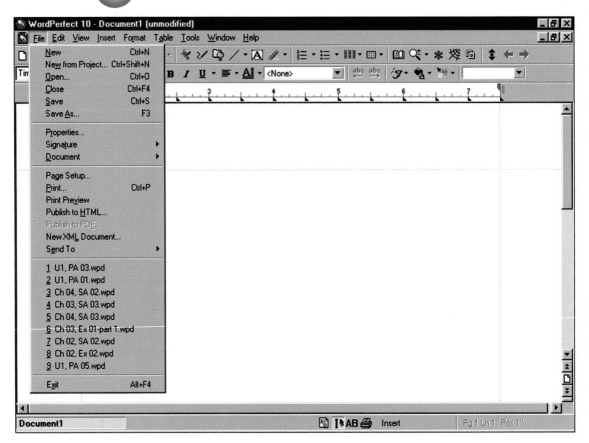

Choosing Commands from Drop-Down Menus

To choose a command from a drop-down menu with the mouse, position the arrow pointer on the desired option and then click the left mouse button. At the drop-down menu that displays, move the arrow pointer down the menu to the desired option, and then click the left mouse button.

To make a selection from the drop-down menu with the keyboard, key the underlined letter of the desired option. Once the drop-down menu displays, you do not need to hold down the Alt key with the underlined letter. If you want to close a drop-down menu without making a choice, click in the document screen outside the drop-down menu, or press the Esc key twice.

Some menu options may be gray shaded (dimmed). When an option is dimmed, that option is currently not available. For example, if you choose the Table option on the Menu bar, the Table drop-down menu displays with dimmed options including Row/Col Indicators and SpeedFormat.

Some menu options are preceded by a check mark. The check mark indicates that the option is currently active. To make an option inactive (turn it off) using the mouse, position the arrow pointer on the option and then click the left mouse button. To make an option inactive (turn it off) with the keyboard, key the underlined letter of the option.

If an option from a drop-down menu displays followed by an ellipsis (...), a dialog box will display when that option is chosen. A dialog box provides a variety of options to let you specify how a command is to be carried out. For example, if you choose File and then Print, the Print dialog box displays as shown in figure G.4. Or if you choose Format and then Font from the Menu bar, the Font Properties dialog box displays as shown in figure G.5.

FIGURE

G.4 **Print Dialog Box**

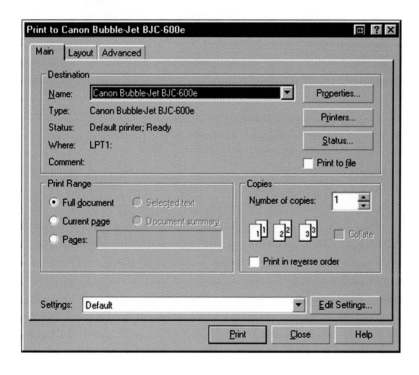

G.5 *Font Properties Dialog Box*

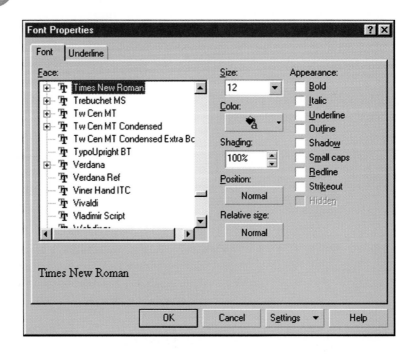

Some dialog boxes provide a set of options. These options are contained on separate tabs. For example, the Font Properties dialog box shown in figure G.5 contains a tab at the top of the dialog box with the word Font on it. Another tab displays to the right of the Font tab. The tab that displays in the front is the active tab. To make a tab active using the mouse, position the arrow pointer on the desired tab and then click the left mouse button. If you are using the keyboard, press Ctrl + Tab. For example, to change the tab to Underline in the Font dialog box, click Underline, or press Ctrl + Tab.

To choose options from a dialog box with the mouse, position the arrow pointer on the desired option and then click the left mouse button. If you are using the keyboard, press the Tab key to move the insertion point forward from option to option. Press Shift + Tab to move the insertion point backward from option to option. You can also hold down the Alt key and then press the underlined letter of the desired option. When an option is selected, it displays with a dark blue background, surrounded by a dashed box called a *marquee*, or with the insertion point positioned inside a text box.

A dialog box contains one or more of the following elements: text boxes, list boxes, check boxes, option buttons, spin boxes, and command buttons.

Text Boxes

Some options in a dialog box require text to be entered. For example, the boxes to the right of the Find what and Replace with options at the Find and Replace dialog box shown in figure G.6 are text boxes. In a text box, you key text or edit existing text. Edit text in a text box in the same manner as normal text. Use the left and right arrow keys on the keyboard to move the insertion point without deleting text and use the Delete key or Backspace key to delete text.

FIGURE

G.6 *Find and Replace Dialog Box*

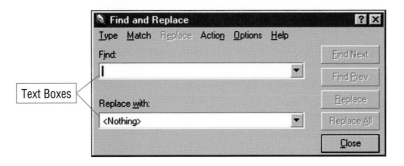

Text Boxes

List Boxes

Some dialog boxes, such as the Bullets & Numbering dialog box shown in figure G.7, may contain a list box. The list at the right side of the dialog box contains a list of outline choices. To make a selection from a list box with the mouse, move the arrow pointer to the desired option and then click the left mouse button.

FIGURE

G.7 *Bullets & Numbering Dialog Box*

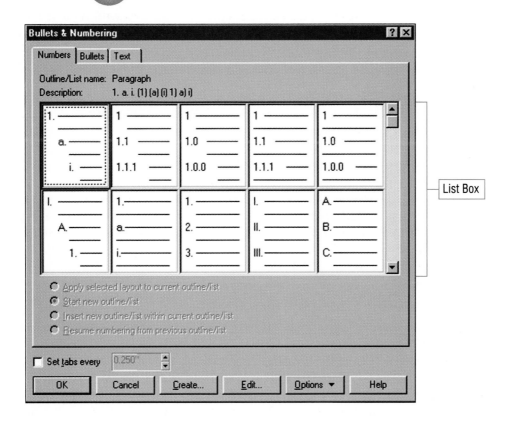

List Box

Some list boxes, such as the one in the Bullets & Numbering dialog box, may contain a scroll bar. This scroll bar will display at the right side of the list box (a vertical scroll bar) or at the bottom of the list box (a horizontal scroll bar). Either a vertical scroll bar or a horizontal scroll bar can be used to move through the list if the list is longer than the box. To move down through a list on a vertical scroll bar, position the arrow pointer on the down-pointing triangle and hold down the left mouse button. To scroll up through the list in a vertical scroll bar, position the arrow pointer on the up-pointing triangle and hold down the left mouse button. To move through a list with a horizontal scroll bar, click the left-pointing triangle to scroll to the left of the list or click the right-pointing triangle to scroll to the right of the list.

In some dialog boxes where there is not enough room for a list box, lists of options are inserted in a drop-down list box. Options that contain a drop-down list box display with a down-pointing triangle. For example, the Size option at the Font Properties dialog box shown in figure G.5 contains a drop-down list. To display the list, click the down-pointing triangle to the right of the Size option box. If you are using the keyboard, press Alt + S.

Check Boxes

Some dialog boxes contain options preceded by a box. A check mark may or may not appear in the box. The Font dialog box shown in figure G.5 displays a variety of check boxes within the Appearance section. If a check mark appears in the box, the option is active (turned on). If there is no check mark in the check box, the option is inactive (turned off). Any number of check boxes can be active. For example, in the Font Properties dialog box, you can insert a check mark in any or all of the boxes in the Appearance section and these options will be active.

To make a check box active or inactive with the mouse, position the tip of the arrow pointer in the check box and then click the left mouse button. If you are using the keyboard, press Alt + the underlined letter of the desired option.

Option Buttons

In the Print dialog box shown in figure G.4, the options in the Page range section are preceded by option buttons (also referred to as *radio buttons*). Only one option button can be selected at any time. When an option button is selected, a dark circle displays in the button.

To select an option button with the mouse, position the tip of the arrow pointer inside the option button and then click the left mouse button. To make a selection with the keyboard, hold down the Alt key and then press the underlined letter of the desired option.

Spin Boxes

Some options in a dialog box contain measurements or numbers that can be increased or decreased. These options are generally located in a spin box. For example, the Paragraph Format dialog box shown in figure G.8 contains a variety of spin boxes located after the First line indent, Left margin adjustment, and Right margin adjustment options. To increase a number in a spin box, position the tip of the arrow pointer on the up-pointing triangle to the right of the desired option, and then click the left mouse button. To decrease the number, click the down-pointing triangle. If you are using the keyboard, press Alt + the underlined letter of the desired option and then press the up arrow key to increase the number or the down arrow key to decrease the number.

G.8 **Paragraph Format Dialog Box**

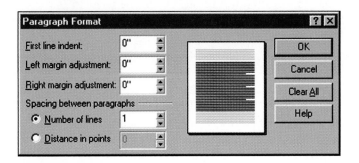

Command Buttons

In the Find and Replace dialog box shown in figure G.6, the buttons at the right of the dialog box are called *command buttons*. A command button is used to execute or cancel a command. Some command buttons display with an ellipsis (...). A command button that displays with an ellipsis will open another dialog box. To choose a command button with the mouse, position the arrow pointer on the desired button and then click the left mouse button. To choose a command button with the keyboard, press the Tab key until the desired command button contains the marquee and then press the Enter key.

Choosing Commands with Shortcut Keys

At the left side of a drop-down menu is a list of options. At the right side, shortcut keys for specific options may display. For example, the shortcut keys to save a document are Ctrl + S and are displayed to the right of the Save option at the File drop-down menu shown in figure G.3. To use shortcut keys to choose a command, hold down the Ctrl key, key the letter for the command, and then release the Ctrl key.

Choosing Commands with QuickMenus

WordPerfect includes QuickMenus that contain commands related to the item with which you are working. A QuickMenu appears right where you are working in the document. To display a QuickMenu, click the *right* mouse button. For example, if the insertion point is positioned in a paragraph of text in a document, clicking the *right* mouse button will cause the QuickMenu shown in figure G.9 to display in the document screen.

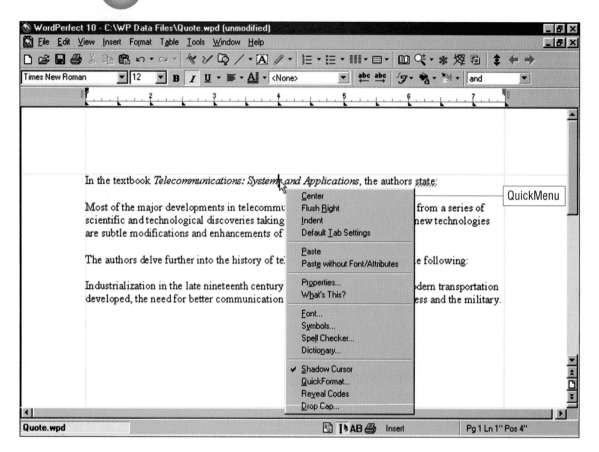

To select an option from a QuickMenu with the mouse, click the desired option. If you are using the keyboard, press the up or down arrow key until the desired option is selected and then press the Enter key. To close a QuickMenu without choosing an option, click anywhere outside the QuickMenu or press the Esc key.

Completing Computer Exercises

Some computer exercises in this textbook require that you open an existing file. Exercise files are located at the Internet Resource Center (IRC) located at www.emcp.com. The files you need for each chapter are saved in individual folders. The IRC icon will appear on the first page of a chapter to indicate that there are student data files to download for that chapter. If this icon does not appear, there are no student data files to download. Three chapters do not have any data files to download. They are chapter 1, chapter 8, and chapter 12. Before beginning a chapter, create a chapter folder on your student data disk and then download the necessary data files from the Internet Resource Center to your student data disk. You will still need to create a chapter folder for those chapters without student data files to download. After completing exercises in a chapter, delete the chapter folder before creating a new chapter folder and downloading the appropriate data files.

Downloading Data Files

1. Open WordPerfect 10.

2. Insert a formatted 3.5-inch disk in the floppy disk drive.

3. Click the Open button on the WordPerfect 10 Toolbar.

4. At the Open File dialog box, click the down-pointing triangle at the right side of the Look in list box.

5. At the drop-down list that displays, click the drive where your disk is located.

6. On the Open File Menu bar, click File, point to New, and then click Folder to create a new chapter folder.

7. In the text box at the right of the folder icon, key the name of the appropriate chapter.

8. Click Close to close the Open File dialog box.

9. Connect to the Internet and go to www.emcp.com.

10. At the EMCParadigm home page, click on *College Division*.

11. In the Quick Links Task Pane at the right side of the screen, click on *Internet Resource Centers*.

12. In the Computer Applications section, click *Signature Series*.

13. In the Signature Series box that displays, click the *Student* link next to Signature WordPerfect 10.

14. Click the down-pointing triangle next to *Choose a Resource* and then select *Student Data Files* from the drop-down list. (You may need to scroll down the list to find this option.)

15. Click *View Student Data Files*.

16. Click the chapter for which you want to download files.

17. At the File Download dialog box, make sure the *Save this file to disk* option is selected and then click OK.

18. At the Save As dialog box, click the down-pointing triangle at the right side of the Save in list box.

19. At the drop-down list that displays, click the drive where your disk is located.

20. In the list box, double-click the folder you created in steps 6 and 7 and then click Save.

21. At the Download complete dialog box, click Close and then close the browser.

Deleting a Folder

Before downloading student data files for a chapter onto your disk, delete any pervious chapter folders. Do this by completing the following steps:

1. Open WordPerfect 10.

2. Insert your disk in the floppy disk drive.

3. Click the Open button on the WordPerfect 10 Toolbar.

4. At the Open File dialog box, click the down-pointing triangle at the right side of the Look in list box.

5. At the drop-down list that displays, click the drive where your disk is located.

6. Click the chapter folder in the list box.

7. Click the Delete button on the Open File dialog box toolbar.

8. At the message asking if you want to remove the folder and all its contents, click Yes.

9. Click the Close button to close the Open File dialog box.

Browsing the Internet

The Internet is a network of networks, a group of computers connected throughout the world. It began as a government project in 1969; then, only four computers were networked to allow researchers in various sites to work together. Since then, the Internet has grown tremendously, to thousands of computers and millions of users. Anyone can connect their computer to the Internet with a modem and an Internet Service Provider. The Internet serves many purposes for users today, including electronic mail (e-mail), chat rooms, transferring files from computer to computer, and accessing any kind of information on the Internet.

In this section, you will be completing several exercises that require you to visit locations and search for information on the Internet. To do this, you will need the following:

1. A modem or network connection to a server with Internet access.

2. Browser software installed and configured. (This section will explore the Internet using Internet Explorer 5.5.)

3. An Internet Service Provider account.

Using Internet Explorer

Double-click the Internet Explorer icon on the Windows desktop to open the program. The default home page is displayed when the program opens. Figure W.1 displays the IE window with the Corel's Web site as the default home page.

FIGURE

W.1 *Internet Explorer Window*

The Internet Explorer window contains many features similar to a Corel WordPerfect window. These features are described in figure W.2.

FIGURE

W.2 *Internet Explorer Features*

Feature	Description
Title Bar	Displays the name of the Web page followed by the name of the program.
Menu Bar	Contains a list of options for using and customizing Internet Explorer.
Toolbar	Contains buttons for commonly used features such as navigating, searching, and printing.
Address Bar	Displays the address of the current Web site.
Status Indicator	The animated Microsoft logo moves to show a Web page is being loaded.
Web Page Window	Displays the contents of the current Web page.
Status Bar	Displays information about the connection progress and the percentage of information that has been transferred.

The Internet Explorer toolbar contains buttons for navigating the Internet. The buttons and a description of each button are included in figure W.3.

FIGURE

W.3 *Internet Explorer Toolbar*

Click this button	Named	To do this
Back	Back	Navigates to the last visited Web page.
Forward	Forward	Navigates to the next Web page.
Stop	Stop	Abandons linking to a Web page.
Refresh	Refresh	Reloads the current Web page.
Home	Home	Navigates to the default home page.
Search	Search	Displays the Search pane.
Favorites	Favorites	Displays a list of interesting places on the Internet including those the user identifies.
History	History	Displays a list of recently visited Web pages.
Mail	Mail	Allows you to send and receive E-mail.
Print	Print	Prints the current Web page.

Locating URLs on the Internet

Uniform Resource Locators, referred to as URLs, are the method used to identify locations on the Internet. The format of a URL is http://server-name.path. The first part of the URL, *http://*, identifies the protocol. The letters *http* stand for Hypertext Transfer Protocol, which is the protocol or language used to transfer data within the World Wide Web. The colon and slashes separate the protocol from the server name. (You typically do not need to key the "http://" when entering a Web address in a Web browser.)

The server name is the second component of the URL. For example, in the URL *http://www.corel.com*, the server name is identified as corel. The last part of the URL specifies the domain to which the server belongs. For example, *.com* refers to "commercial" and establishes that the URL is a commercial company. Other examples of domains include *.edu* for "educational," *.gov* for "government," and *.org* for an "organization." Some examples of URLs display in figure W.4.

FIGURE

W.4 *Example URLs*

URL	Connects to
http://www.corel.com	Corel Corporation home page
http://www.emcp.com	EMCParadigm Publishing home page
http://www.stchas.edu	St. Charles Community College home page
http://lcweb.loc.gov	The Library of Congress home page
http://www.pbs.org	Public Broadcasting Service home page

exercise 1

Exploring the Web

1. Make sure you are connected to the Internet and then double-click the Internet Explorer icon on the Windows desktop to open the browser. (Your instructor will give you any additional instructions for connecting to the Internet.)
2. View the NASA Web site by completing the following steps:
    a. Key **www.nasa.gov** in the text box on the Address bar and press the Enter key. In a few seconds, you will see the home page for NASA as shown below. (Web sites are changing constantly—the page may vary from what you see below.)

b. Spend a few minutes reading the information on the NASA home page. Scroll through the page by clicking the down-pointing triangle on the vertical scroll bar.

3. Navigate to the home page for USA Today by completing the following steps:
    a. Select the current URL by clicking the left mouse button in the Address bar text box.
    b. Key **www.usatoday.com** and then press the Enter key.
    c. Spend a few minutes reading the information on the USA Today home page. Scroll through the page by clicking the down-pointing triangle on the vertical scroll bar.

4. Close Internet Explorer by clicking <u>F</u>ile and then <u>C</u>lose.

Using Hyperlinks

Text displayed in a different color and underlined indicates text that has been identified as a *hyperlink*. A hyperlink allows you to link or connect to another item from your current location. To use a hyperlink, position the mouse pointer on the desired hyperlink until the mouse pointer turns into a hand and then click the left mouse button.

The Internet Explorer toolbar contains a Back and a Forward button. If you click a hyperlink, clicking the Back button will display the previous Web page or location. If you click the Back button and then would like to go back to the hyperlink, click the Forward button. By clicking the Back button, you can back your way out of any hyperlinks and return to the Internet Explorer window.

In exercise 2, you will be using Internet Explorer to access the Internet, locate specific home pages, and then use hyperlinks to display specific information. (Web pages are changing constantly so some of the instructions in exercise 2 and other exercises in this chapter may need slight modification.)

Back

Forward

exercise 2

Exploring the Web and Using Hyperlinks

1. Make sure you are connected to the Internet and then double-click the Internet Explorer icon on the Windows desktop to open the browser. (Your instructor will give you any additional instructions for connecting to the Internet.)
2. View the home page for Southwest Airlines at **www.iflyswa.com**.
3. Navigate to another page linked to this home page using a hyperlink by completing the following steps:
    a. Scroll down the Southwest Airlines page until you see the underlined text *WHAT'S NEW*.

b. Position the arrow pointer on *WHAT'S NEW* until the pointer turns into a hand and then click the left mouse button.

Step 3b

c. In a few moments, a page will display providing information on current company activities. (This page is updated regularly.)

d. Scroll through this page until you find a hyperlink that interests you and then click the hyperlink.

e. After viewing information on the current page, click the Back button. This returns you to the company activities page. (Notice when you return to the previous page that the hyperlink text has changed color. This identifies the pages you have already viewed.)

f. Click the Back button again. This returns you to the Southwest Airlines home page.

4. View the United States Postal Service Web site at **www.usps.com**.

5. When the United States Postal Service home page displays, click the *Calculate Postage* hyperlink.

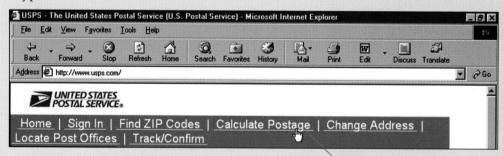

Step 5

6. At the Domestic Calculator page, click *A Package*.

7. Key the following text in the specified text boxes:

a. Key **63362** in the From ZIP Code text box.

b. Key **98031** in the To ZIP Code text box.

c. Key **1** in the Pounds text box in the Weight Information section.

8. Scroll down to the bottom of the page and then click the Continue button.

9. View the results of the Domestic Calculator.

10. Click the Print button located on the Internet Explorer toolbar to send the cost results to the printer.

11. Click the Back button until the Southwest Airlines home page is displayed.

12. Click File and then Close to close Internet Explorer.

Searching for Information on the Internet

In the previous exercises, you navigate the Web by keying URLs, which is a fast way to move from site to site. Often, however, you will access the Web to search for information without knowing the URL.

A phenomenal amount of information is available on the Internet. Searching through all of that information to find the specific information you need may be an overwhelming task. Software programs, called *search engines*, have been created to help you search more quickly and easily for the desired information. There are many search engines available on the Internet, each offering the opportunity to search for specific information. As you use different search engines, you may find you prefer one over the others.

Using the Search Pane

Search engines are valuable tools to assist a user in locating information on a topic by simply keying a few words or a short phrase. Internet Explorer has a built-in search engine accessed by clicking the Search button. The Search pane displays at the left side of the window as shown in figure W.5. To search using this pane, select a category in which your search topic is included, add key words in the text box to search for on the Web, and then press Enter or click the Search button. Click the *X* in the upper right corner of the pane to close it.

Search

FIGURE

W.5 **Internet Explorer Search Pane**

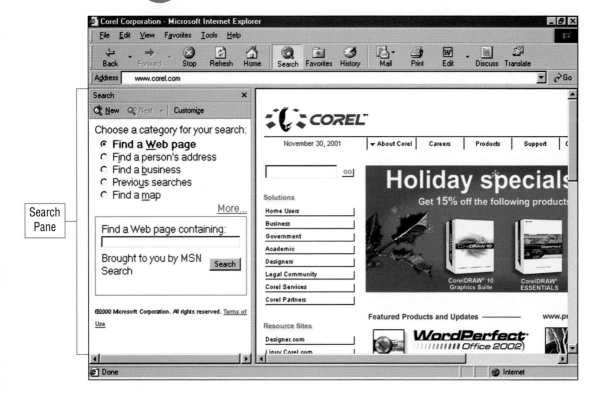

exercise 3

Conducting a Search Using the Search Pane

1. Open Internet Explorer.
2. Search for information about manatees by completing the following steps:
   a. Click the Search button on the toolbar.
   b. At the Search pane, click the Find a <u>W</u>eb page category for the search.
   c. Click in the Find a Web page containing text box and then key **manatee**.
   d. Click the Search button. (The results will display as hyperlinks.)
3. Click on the *Manatees of Florida* hyperlink. The Web page will display to the right of the Search pane.
4. Browse the site and then click the *Miami Seaquarium* hyperlink in the Search pane. (You may need to scroll down to see this link.)
5. Close the Search pane by clicking the *X* in the upper right corner of the pane. The Web page automatically resizes to fill the window.
6. Click the Back button to return to the Manatees of Florida home page.
7. Close Internet Explorer.

Step 3

Using Search Engines

There are many other search engines available on the Internet, some of which are displayed in figure W.6. Each offers the opportunity to search for specific information, but may yield some different results.

FIGURE *Popular Search Engines*

Search Engine	URL
Ask Jeeves	www.aj.com
Excite	www.excite.com
Google	www.google.com
Infoseek	www.infoseek.com
Lycos	www.lycos.com
Yahoo	www.yahoo.com

To search for information using a search engine you would follow these basic steps:

1. Open Internet Explorer.

2. Enter the URL for the search engine.

3. At the search engine home page, key a word or phrase in the Search text box and then click the button that begins the search.

4. The search engine will return (display) a list of Web sites that have the key word or phrase in the index. Scroll through the list and read the short descriptions. Use the hyperlink to browse pages that may contain the information you are seeking.

The World Wide Web contains millions of pages covering a huge variety of subjects. In order to narrow your results to those most likely contain relevant information, it is important to limit your search with specific key words. Plan your search carefully; begin with the main topic and then narrow it down as much as possible to reduce the number of sites you have to browse to find the information you want. You might choose to search Google for information for an upcoming fishing trip to Canada. A search with *fishing* and *Canada* generates about 677,000 results. If you narrow the search by adding the word *Ontario*, it reduces the number of results to about 144,000; this is still too large a list to browse for information. Narrow the search one more time using *Lake Minnetonka* and the number of results is reduced to about 237, a more manageable number to begin looking for information. Your results may vary with the same search performed using a different search engine.

Some search engines recognize search operators to assist in finding documents containing specific information. These search operators are explained in figure W.7.

FIGURE

 W.7 *Search Operators*

Operator	Function
Plus sign (+)	Find Web pages that contains all of the words preceded by a plus sign. Do not space between the symbol and the word.
Minus sign (-)	Find Web pages that do not contain any words immediately preceded by a minus sign. Do not space between the symbol and the word.
Quotation marks (" ")	Enclose a series of terms in quotation marks to find Web pages containing all of the terms in that specific order.

In addition, some search engines recognize Boolean operators to help narrow a search. These operators are explained in figure W.8.

FIGURE

W.8 *Boolean Operators*

Operator	Function
AND	Find Web pages that contains all of the words joined by AND.
OR	Find Web pages that contains at least one of the words joined by OR.
NOT	Find Web pages that contain the word before NOT, but not the word after.

To determine the appropriate syntax in the search engine you are using, use the *Advanced Search* link on the search engine home page. It will provide detailed directions for limiting your Web search. Be sure to view this page for each search engine because they do vary.

exercise

Using Search Engines to Locate Information on the Web

1. Open Internet Explorer.
2. Search for information about The Butchart Gardens using the Google search engine by completing the following steps:
   a. Key **www.google.com** in the Address bar and press Enter.
   b. Key **Butchart Gardens** in the text box and then click the Google Search button or press Enter.
   c. When the list of sites meeting your search criteria appears, write down the total number of sites found by Google.
3. Perform a new search for information about The Butchart Gardens that doesn't include information on tours using the Google search engine by completing the following steps:
   a. Key **Butchart Gardens -tour** in the text box and then press Enter.
   b. When the list of sites meeting your search criteria appears, write down the total number of sites found by Google.
4. Close Internet Explorer.

UNIT one

CREATING AND PREPARING DOCUMENTS

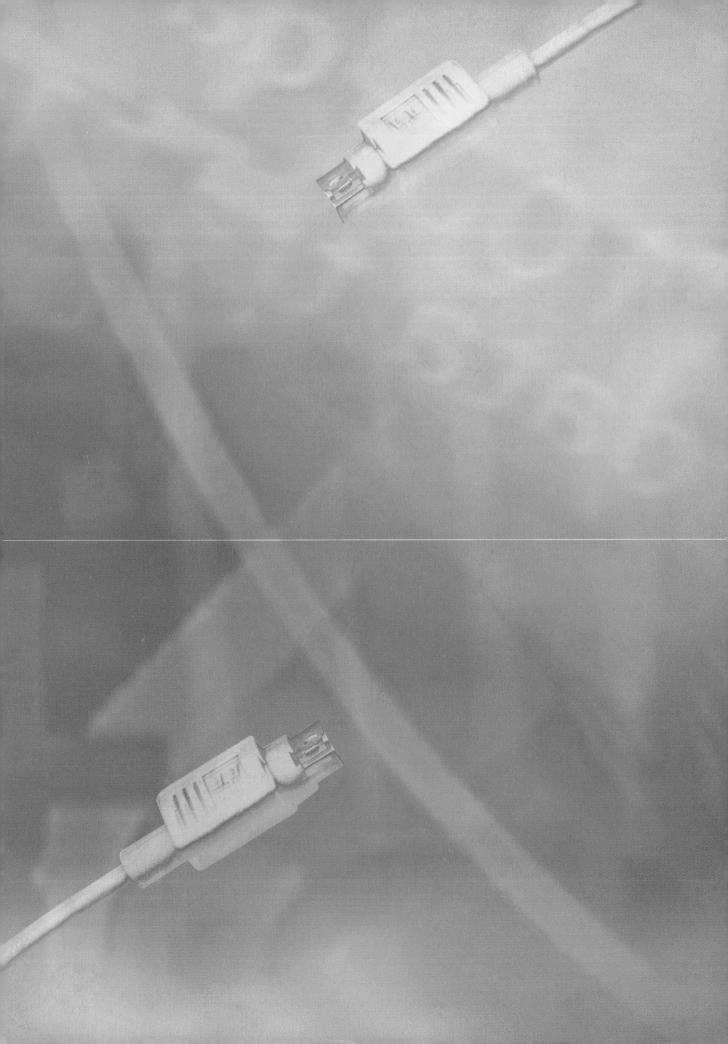

Creating, Saving, and Printing Corel WordPerfect 10 Documents

PERFORMANCE OBJECTIVES

Upon successful completion of chapter 1, you will be able to:
- Open WordPerfect 10
- Create, save, close, name, open, and print a Corel WordPerfect 10 document
- Exit WordPerfect 10 and Windows

(Note: There are no data files to download for this chapter.)

You will be learning to operate a software program called Corel WordPerfect 10 on a microcomputer system. In this chapter, you will learn how to create, save, close, open, and print a document.

Creating a WordPerfect Document

Eight basic steps are completed when creating a document in WordPerfect. The steps are

1. Opening the program
2. Keying (typing) the information to create the document
3. Saving the document on the disk
4. Proofreading the document and making any necessary edits (changes)
5. Saving the revised document on the disk
6. Printing a hard copy of the document
7. Closing the document
8. Exiting the program

In this chapter, you will be provided with the information to complete all of the steps except 4, which will be covered in chapter 2. As you work your way through this chapter, you will complete several exercises to practice the steps.

Opening WordPerfect

The steps to open WordPerfect may vary depending on the system setup. Generally, to open WordPerfect, you would complete the following steps:

1. Turn on the computer. (This may include turning on the CPU, the monitor, and possibly the printer.)

2. After a few moments, the Windows desktop shown in figure 1.1 displays (your screen may vary). At the Windows desktop, position the arrow pointer on the Start button on the Taskbar, and click the left mouse button. This causes the pop-up menu shown in figure 1.2 to display.

FIGURE

1.1 *Windows 98 Desktop*

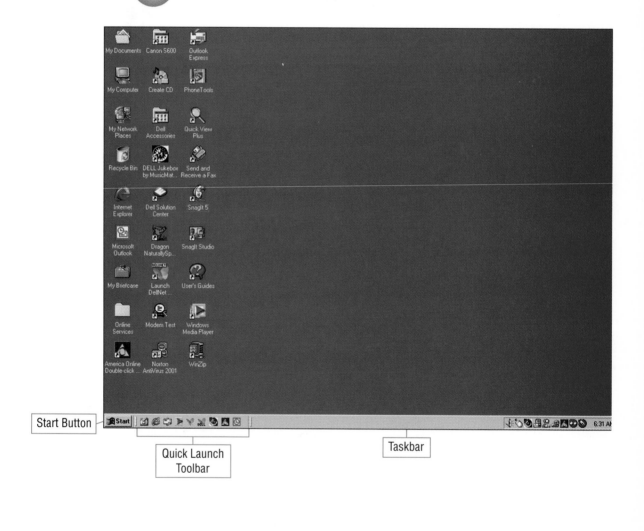

Start Button

Quick Launch Toolbar

Taskbar

1.2 *Startup Pop-Up Menu*

3. Position the arrow pointer on *Programs*, then *WordPerfect Office 2002* (you do not need to click the left mouse button). This should cause another menu to display to the right of the first pop-up menu.

4. Move the arrow pointer to *Corel WordPerfect 10* and click the left mouse button.

The steps for opening WordPerfect on your computer system may vary from these instructions. If necessary, ask your instructor for specific steps to open WordPerfect.

Identifying the Parts of the Document Window

When you open WordPerfect, you will be presented with a screen that looks similar to the one shown in figure 1.3. This screen is referred to as the document window.

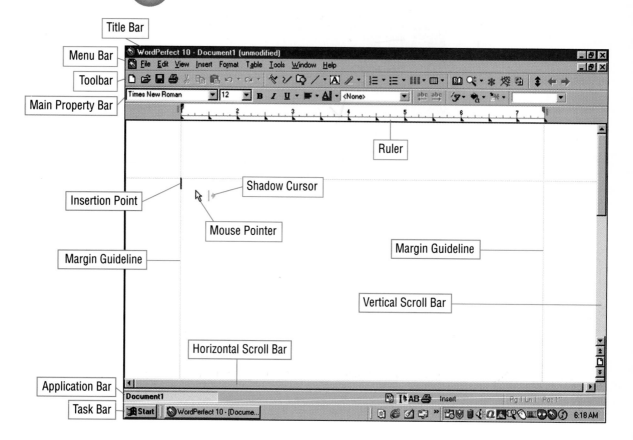

Title Bar

The top line of the document window is referred to as the *Title bar*. When you first open WordPerfect, a new document window displays named Document1. The word *unmodified* displays after the document name indicating that nothing has been entered or modified in the document. As soon as you begin keying (typing) text, the word *unmodified* disappears from the Title bar.

When a document is completed, it can be saved with a new name. If you open a previously saved document in the document window, the document name is displayed in the Title bar.

Menu Bar

The second line of the document window is called the *Menu bar*. The Menu bar contains a list of options that are used to customize a WordPerfect document. WordPerfect functions and features are grouped into menu options located on the Menu bar.

1.4 *File Drop-Down Menu Displaying Keyboard Shortcuts*

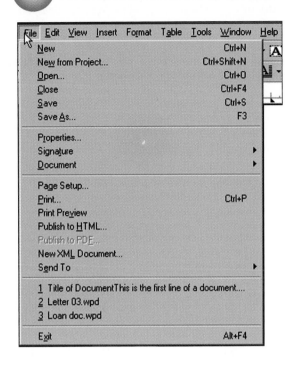

File	Edit	View	Insert	Format	Table	Tools	Window	Help
New							Ctrl+N	
New from Project...							Ctrl+Shift+N	
Open...							Ctrl+O	
Close							Ctrl+F4	
Save							Ctrl+S	
Save As...							F3	
Properties...								
Signature							▶	
Document							▶	
Page Setup...								
Print...							Ctrl+P	
Print Preview								
Publish to HTML...								
Publish to PDF...								
New XML Document...								
Send To							▶	
1 Title of DocumentThis is the first line of a document....								
2 Letter 03.wpd								
3 Loan doc.wpd								
Exit							Alt+F4	

As shown in figure 1.4, some options display a keyboard shortcut to the right of the menu option item. This keyboard shortcut can be used to access the same feature.

Toolbar

WordPerfect includes a *Toolbar* that contains icons of common features. An *icon* is a picture or an image that represents a function. With this Toolbar, you can use the mouse to execute certain commands quickly. For example, clicking the button containing an image of an open folder (called the Open button) will cause the Open File dialog box to display.

Open

WordPerfect provides *QuickTip*, which is a small box containing a brief description of the function of a button on the Toolbar (and other bars). To view a QuickTip, position the arrow on a button on the Toolbar. After approximately one second, the QuickTip displays below the button in a yellow box. (The color of the box may vary.)

Main Property Bar

The row of options below the Toolbar is called the *Main property bar*. Drop-down lists and icons for performing common functions are contained on the Main property bar. WordPerfect provides over 20 different property bars, which automatically change to reflect the function or feature with which you are working. If there is not a property bar specific to the function or feature you are working with, the Main property bar will remain.

Ruler

Below the Main property bar, a *Ruler* may display. If the Ruler is not displayed, click the View menu and then Ruler. The Ruler is used to set margins, indents, and tabs. You will learn more about the Ruler in future chapters.

Insertion Point

The blinking vertical bar located approximately an inch below the Ruler and at the left side of the document window is called the *insertion point* (also referred to as the *cursor*). The insertion point indicates the location where the next character entered at the keyboard will appear.

The insertion point is positioned in the portion of the window called the *editing window* where text is entered, edited, and formatted.

Mouse Pointer

When the mouse pointer is positioned on a bar (such as the Title bar, Menu bar, Main property bar, and so on), it displays as an *arrow* pointing up and to the left (referred to as the "arrow pointer"). When the mouse pointer is positioned over text in a document, it displays as an *I-beam* (referred to as the "I-beam pointer").

Shadow Cursor

As you move the mouse pointer in white space in the document window, a *shadow cursor* will display near the mouse pointer (see figure 1.3). The shadow cursor is a thin gray line that identifies exactly where the insertion point will be positioned when you click the left mouse button. Position the shadow cursor where you want the insertion point located and click the left mouse button. This moves the insertion point to the tab position closest to the shadow cursor. As the shadow cursor moves in a document, it moves to preset tabs.

The display of the shadow cursor will change depending on where it is positioned. In most locations in the document window, the shadow cursor displays as a thin gray vertical bar followed by a right-pointing gray arrow. This arrow specifies text alignment. The right-pointing arrow indicates that the text will be left aligned. Position the shadow cursor in the middle of the document window and it will display with a left-pointing and a right-pointing arrow. Move the shadow cursor to the right margin and the shadow cursor displays with a left-pointing arrow indicating the text will be right aligned.

Scroll Bars

The gray-shaded bars along the right side and bottom of the document window are called *scroll bars*. Use the scroll bars to view various sections of a document. Additional information on the scroll bars is presented in chapter 2.

Application Bar

The gray bar located immediately above the Taskbar is called the *Application bar*. The Application bar displays the following:

- The name of any open document(s)
- A button for turning the shadow cursor on/off
- A button for turning caps lock on/off
- A button to display the Print dialog box
- A button to change from Insert to Typeover mode
- The current cursor location

Taskbar

The *Taskbar*, which is part of the Windows operating system, displays along the bottom of the screen. The Start button, by default, displays at the left side of the Taskbar and the current time displays at the right side. The name of any open program(s) displays to the right of the Start button. If more than one program is open at the same time, you can switch between open programs by clicking the program button on the Taskbar.

Word Wrap

As you key text, you do not need to press the Enter key at the end of each line. WordPerfect automatically wraps text to the next line based on the right margin setting. A word is wrapped to the next line if it begins before the right margin and continues past it. The only times you need to press Enter are to end a paragraph, create a blank line, or end a short line.

QuickCorrect

WordPerfect contains a feature called *QuickCorrect* that automatically corrects certain words as they are being keyed. For example, if you key *adn* instead of *and*, QuickCorrect corrects it when you press the spacebar after the word. There are over 150 words that QuickCorrect will automatically correct. QuickCorrect also changes formatting by correcting capitalization errors (cAPS lOCK is replaced with Caps Lock), changing quotation marks (" is replaced with "), and replacing numbers with superscript ordinals (1st is replaced with 1st).

Spell-As-You-Go

The WordPerfect *Spell-As-You-Go* feature automatically inserts red slashmarks below words that are not contained in the Spelling dictionary or not automatically corrected by QuickCorrect. This may include misspelled words, proper names, some terminology, and some foreign words. If you key a word not recognized by the Spelling dictionary, red slashmarks will appear as soon as you press the spacebar. If the word is correct, you can leave it as keyed. If the word is incorrect, you have two choices—you can backspace over the word using the Backspace key and key it correctly, or you can right-click the word and click the correct spelling in the pop-up menu (if available).

For example, if you key the word *aplication* and then press the spacebar, WordPerfect inserts red slashmarks below the word. To correct it, position the mouse pointer (displays as the I-beam pointer) on any character in the word *aplication*, click the *right* mouse button, and then click *application* at the pop-up menu that displays. If WordPerfect inserts red slashmarks below a proper name such as *Weinburg* that is spelled correctly, you can either leave it (the red slashmarks will not print) or position the I-beam pointer on any character in the name, click the *right* mouse button, and then click Skip in Document option at the pop-up menu.

Sentence Punctuation

WordPerfect uses *Times New Roman* as the default typeface. Times New Roman is a proportional typeface. (You will learn more about typefaces in chapter 6.) When keying text in a proportional typeface, space once (not twice) after end-of-sentence punctuation such as a period, a question mark, or an exclamation point, and after a colon. Proportional typefaces are set closer together and extra white space at the end of a sentence or after a colon is not needed.

Completing Computer Exercises

At the end of sections within chapters and at the end of chapters, you will be completing hands-on exercises at the computer. These exercises will provide you with the opportunity to practice the functions and commands presented. The skill assessment exercises at the end of each chapter include general directions. If you do not remember how to perform a particular function, refer to the text or the Commands Summary at the end of each chapter.

Downloading Data Files

In several exercises in each chapter you will be opening documents that you have downloaded from the Internet Resource Center. The IRC icon on the first page of a chapter will inform you that you must download files for that chapter. (Note that this chapter does not have any student files to download.) Before beginning each chapter, create a chapter folder on your floppy disk, download the student files, if any, for that chapter from the Internet Resource Center, and then make that folder the active folder. Detailed steps on how to download files from the Internet Resource Center to your floppy disk are presented in the *Getting Started* section. Abbreviated steps are printed on the inside front cover of this textbook. Before you begin exercise 1, create the *Chapter 01* folder on your disk.

Changing the Default Folder

In this and the remaining chapters in the textbook, you will be saving documents. More than likely, you will want to save documents to your student data disk. To save and open documents on your data disk, you will need to specify the drive where your disk is located as the default folder. Unless your computer system has been customized, WordPerfect defaults to the hard drive (usually C) or the network drive. Once you specify the drive where your data disk is located, WordPerfect uses this as the default folder until you exit the WordPerfect program. The next time you open WordPerfect, you will need to specify again the drive where your disk is located.

You can change the default folder at the Open File dialog box or the Save File dialog box. To change the folder to the *Chapter 01* folder on the disk in drive A at the Open File dialog box, you would complete the following steps:

1. Click the Open button on the Toolbar (the second button from the left).

2. At the Open File dialog box, click the down-pointing triangle at the right side of the Look in text box.

3. From the drop-down list that displays, click *3½ Floppy (A:)*.

4. Double-click Chapter 01 that displays in the list box.

5. Click the Close button located at the bottom right side of the dialog box.

Keying and Saving a WordPerfect Document

At the clear WordPerfect editing window, you can begin keying information to create a document. A document is any information you choose; for instance, a letter, a memo, a report, a term paper, and a table are all documents.

Saving a Document

When you have created a document, the information will need to be saved on your disk. When a document is keyed for the first time and is displayed in the editing window, it is only temporary. If you turn off the computer or if the power goes off, you will lose the information and have to rekey it. Only when you save a document on a disk or drive is it saved permanently. Every time you open WordPerfect, you will be able to bring a saved document back to the editing window.

A variety of methods can be used to save a document, such as the following:

- Click the Save button on the Toolbar.
- Click <u>F</u>ile and then <u>S</u>ave.
- Press Ctrl + S.

Save

To save a document with the Save button, you would complete the following steps:

1. Position the arrow pointer on the Save button on the Toolbar and then click the left mouse button.

2. At the Save File dialog box, an Auto-suggest file name is highlighted in the File <u>n</u>ame text box and can be accepted by clicking <u>S</u>ave or pressing Enter. To replace the Auto-suggest file name, key a name in the File <u>n</u>ame text box (as shown in figure 1.5) and click <u>S</u>ave or press Enter.

3. Click the <u>S</u>ave button located in the bottom right corner of the dialog box.

FIGURE

1.5 *Save File Dialog Box*

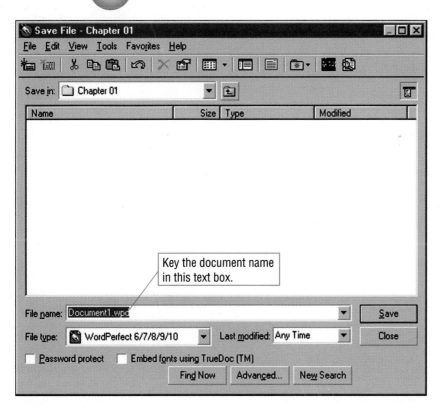

Key the document name in this text box.

To save a document using the Menu bar, you would open the Save File dialog box by clicking the <u>F</u>ile menu with your left mouse button and then click <u>S</u>ave. The keyboard shortcut Ctrl + S will also open the Save File dialog box. Steps 2 and 3 from above remain the same with both methods.

As you can see, there are several methods of completing the same process. In this textbook, the focus will be placed on the steps that are the easiest or the fastest. For most features, instructions for using the mouse will be presented. You may find that you prefer other options. At times, you may want to explore other options not presented in this text for completing steps or procedures.

Naming a Document

A WordPerfect document name can be up to 255 characters and spaces, including the drive letter and any folder names. File names cannot include any of the following:

forward slash (/)	question mark (?)
backslash (\)	quotation mark (")
greater-than sign (>)	colon (:)
less-than sign (<)	semicolon (;)
asterisk (*)	pipe symbol (|)

WordPerfect automatically adds the extension *.wpd* to the file name.

Canceling a Command

If a drop-down menu is displayed on the document screen, it can be removed with the mouse or keyboard.

- If you are using the mouse, position the mouse pointer on the document screen (outside the drop-down menu), and then click the left mouse button.
- If you are using the keyboard, press the Alt key.
- Press the Esc key twice; the first time will remove the drop-down menu and the second will deselect the option on the Menu bar.

If a dialog box obstructs your view of the document, click on the blue title bar, hold down the left mouse button, and drag the dialog box to a new position. Several methods can be used to remove a dialog box from the editing window.

- If you are using the mouse, position the mouse pointer on the Cancel command button, and click the left mouse button.

Close

- Click the Close button containing an *X* in the upper right corner of the dialog box.
- If you are using the keyboard, press the Esc key.

Closing a Document

When a document is saved, it is on the disk and remains in the editing window. To remove the document from the editing window, click File, Close; or click the Close button in the right corner of the Menu bar. (Be sure to use the *X* on the Menu bar; the Close button on the Title bar will close the WordPerfect program.) When you close a document, the document is removed and a new, blank editing window is displayed. At this editing window, you can open a previously saved document, create a new document, or exit the WordPerfect program.

Creating a Document

1. Follow the instructions in the chapter to open Windows and Corel WordPerfect 10.
2. At the clear editing window, change the default folder to the drive where your student data disk is located (if necessary, ask your instructor) by completing the following steps:
   a. Click the Open button on the Toolbar.

b. At the Open File dialog box, click the down-pointing triangle at the right side of the <u>L</u>ook in text box.

c. From the drop-down list that displays, click *3½ Floppy (A:)* (this may vary on your system). If *3½ Floppy (A:)* is not visible, click the up-pointing triangle at the right side of the drop-down list until it displays.

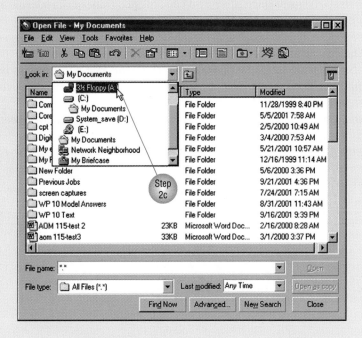

d. Double-click the *Chapter 01* folder that displays in the list box.

e. Click the Close button in the bottom right corner of the dialog box.

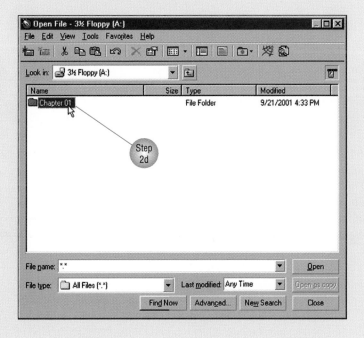

3. At the clear editing window, key the text in figure 1.6. Your line endings may differ from what you see in figure 1.6. If you make a mistake while keying and Spell-As-You-Go inserts red slash marks below your text, backspace over the incorrect word using the Backspace key and then rekey the correct text. (Don't worry about doing a lot of correcting since you will learn more about editing a document in chapter 2.) Remember to space only once after end-of-sentence punctuation while keying the text.

4. When you are done keying the text, save the document and name it Ch 01, Ex 01 (for chapter 1, exercise 1) by completing the following steps:
   a. Click the Save button on the Toolbar.
   b. At the Save dialog box, key **Ch 01, Ex 01** in the File name text box. (Key a zero when naming documents, not the letter *O*. In this textbook, the zero (0) displays thinner than a letter *O*.)
   c. Click the Save button in the bottom right corner of the dialog box or press Enter.

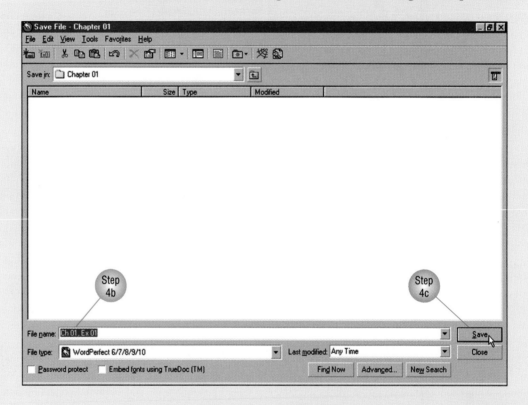

5. Close Ch 01, Ex 01 by clicking File and then Close or clicking the Close button (the button containing the *X*) located at the right edge of the Menu bar.

1.6   **Exercise 1**

The field of telecommunications has been expanding rapidly in the past few decades. In a textbook written by William Mitchell, Robert Hendricks, and Leonard Sterry, the authors state that telecommunications systems are destined to become as common in the workplace of the nineties as typewriters were in the offices of the sixties.

The authors also state that people entering the job market now and in the future will need to understand the basics of telecommunications technology and its applications. This fundamental knowledge will prepare workers to accept and use the new products that result from each advance in technology.

Opening and Printing a Document

When a document has been saved, it can be opened at the Open File dialog box. To open a previously saved document, you would complete the following steps:

1. Click the Open button on the Toolbar.

2. Double-click the file name to be opened.

Open

When a document is opened, it is displayed in the editing window where you can make changes. Whenever changes are made to a document, you must save the document again to save the changes.

To print a document, you can display the Print dialog box by clicking File and then Print or clicking the Print button on the Toolbar. Before displaying the Print dialog box, be sure the printer is turned on.

Print

Opening, Printing, and Closing a Document

1. At a clear editing window, open the document named Ch 01, Ex 01 by completing the following steps:
    a. Click the Open button on the Toolbar.
    b. At the Open dialog box, position the arrow pointer on *Ch 01, Ex 01*, and then double-click the left mouse button.

    Step 1a

    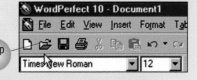

2. Print Ch 01, Ex 01 by completing the following steps:
    a. Click the Print button on the Toolbar.

    Step 2a

    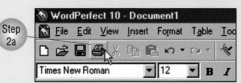

b. At the Print dialog box, click the <u>P</u>rint button located at the bottom of the dialog box.

3. Close Ch 01, Ex 01 by clicking the Close button located at the right side of the Menu bar.

Step 2b

Exiting WordPerfect and Windows

When you are finished working with WordPerfect and have saved all necessary information, exit WordPerfect by clicking <u>F</u>ile, E<u>x</u>it or clicking the Close button located at the right edge of the Title bar. After exiting Corel WordPerfect 10, exit Windows by completing the following steps:

1. Click the Start button on the Taskbar.

2. At the pop-up menu, click Sh<u>u</u>t Down.

3. At the Shut Down Windows dialog box, make sure <u>S</u>hut down is selected, and then click OK. (Check with your instructor before performing this step.)

Creating a Document and Exiting WordPerfect

1. At a clear editing window, key the information shown in figure 1.7. (Correct any errors highlighted by Spell-As-You-Go as they occur and remember to space once after end-of-sentence punctuation.)

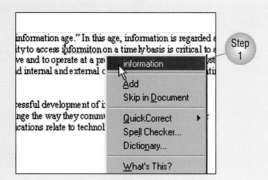

Step 1

2. Save the document and name it Ch 01, Ex 03 by completing the following steps:
   a. Click the Save button on the Toolbar.
   b. At the Save dialog box, key **Ch 01, Ex 03** in the File name text box.
   c. Click the Save button or press Enter.

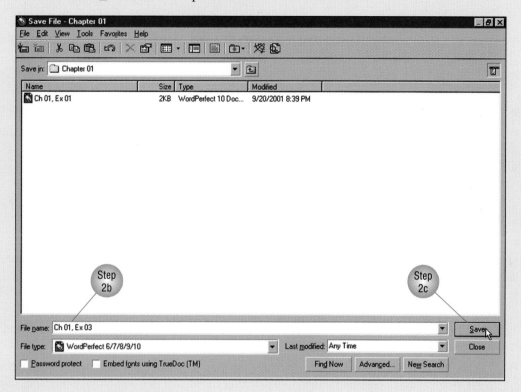

3. Print Ch 01, Ex 03.
4. Close the document by clicking File and then Close or clicking the Close button at the right side of the Menu bar.
5. Exit WordPerfect 10 and Windows by completing the following steps:
   a. Click File and then Exit.
   b. At the Windows desktop, click the Start button on the Taskbar, and then click Shut Down. At the Shut Down Windows dialog box, click OK.

FIGURE

1.7 *Exercise 3*

We are living in what is called the "information age." In this age, information is regarded as a company asset or resource. The ability to access information on a timely basis is critical to an organization's ability to be competitive and to operate at a profit. Business information systems that integrate software, hardware, and internal and external communication links are continually being developed and refined.

There are many obstacles to the successful development of integrated systems. First and foremost is how to get people to change the way they communicate information. Other obstacles to improving telecommunications relate to technology.

CHAPTER summary

➤ The Title bar is located at the top of the screen and displays the name of the current document.

➤ The Menu bar is the second line on the screen and contains a list of commands used to customize a WordPerfect document.

➤ The Toolbar is located below the Menu bar and displays icons of common features.

➤ The Main property bar is located below the Toolbar and contains pull-down lists and buttons for performing common functions.

➤ The Ruler may display below the Main property bar. Use it for setting margins, indents, and tabs.

➤ The insertion point appears as a blinking vertical bar and indicates the position of the next character entered in the editing window.

➤ The mouse pointer displays on the screen as an arrow pointing up and to the left (called the arrow pointer) or as an I-beam (called the I-beam pointer). As the mouse pointer is moved on a document screen, a shadow pointer (thin gray line followed by a right-pointing arrow) displays. The shadow pointer indicates where the insertion point will be positioned when the left mouse button is clicked.

➤ The scroll bars appear as gray-shaded bars along the right side and bottom of the document window; they are used to quickly scroll through a document.

➤ The Application bar, positioned below the horizontal scroll bar, displays the names of any open documents; contains buttons for turning on/off the shadow cursor, turning caps lock on/off, displaying the Print dialog box, and turning Insert on/off; and displays the current location of the insertion point.

➤ WordPerfect automatically wraps text to the next line as you key information.

➤ WordPerfect's QuickCorrect feature will automatically correct certain errors as soon as you press the spacebar. For example, if you key *adn* and then press the spacebar, QuickCorrect will automatically change the word to *and*.

➤ The Spell-As-You-Go feature will insert red slashmarks below words that are not found in the Spelling dictionary.

➤ In order to save on or open documents from your data disk, the default folder should be changed. Do this at the Open File or Save File dialog box.

➤ Document names can include a maximum of 255 characters and spaces, including the drive letter and folder name. The name can contain letters, numbers, and spaces.

➤ Drop-down menus and dialog boxes can be removed from the editing window with the mouse or the keyboard.

➤ Dialog boxes can be moved within the editing window by clicking and dragging on the title bar of the dialog box.

➤ A document can be printed by displaying the Print dialog box and then clicking the Print button at the bottom of the dialog box. To display the Print dialog box, click the Print button on the Toolbar or click File and then Print.

➤ You should always exit Corel WordPerfect 10 and Windows before turning off the computer.

COMMANDS summary

Opening WordPerfect

1. Turn on the computer.
2. At the Windows screen, click the Start button on the Taskbar, point to *Programs*, then to *WordPerfect Office* 2002, and then click *WordPerfect 10*.

Saving a Document

1. Click the Save button on the Toolbar or click File and then Save.
2. At the Save dialog box, key the name of the document.
3. Click the Save button or press Enter.

Changing the Default Folder

1. Click the Open button on the Toolbar.
2. At the Open dialog box, click the down-pointing triangle at the right side of the Look in text box.
3. From the drop-down list, click *3½ Floppy (A:)*.
4. Double-click the desired folder that displays in the list box.
5. Click the Close button located at the bottom right side of the dialog box.

Opening a Document

1. Click the Open button on the Toolbar.
2. At the Open dialog box, double-click the document name.

Printing a Document

1. Open the document.
2. Click the Print button on the Toolbar.
3. At the Print dialog box, click the Print button located at the bottom of the dialog box.

Exiting WordPerfect

1. Be sure all needed documents have been saved.
2. Click the Close button at the right edge of the Title bar or click File and then Exit.

CONCEPTS check

Matching: On a blank sheet of paper, indicate the letter of the term that matches each description.

- Ⓐ Application bar
- Ⓑ Close
- Ⓒ Exit
- Ⓓ FastTip
- Ⓔ Insertion point
- Ⓕ Main property bar
- Ⓖ Menu bar
- Ⓗ QuickCorrect
- Ⓘ QuickTip
- Ⓙ Scroll bar
- Ⓚ Shadow cursor
- Ⓛ Spell-As-You-Go
- Ⓜ Taskbar
- Ⓝ Title bar
- Ⓞ Toolbar

1. This bar displays icons of common features.

2. This bar contains a list of commands used to customize a WordPerfect document.

3. This bar contains pull-down lists and buttons for performing common functions.

4. Position the arrow pointer on a button on the Toolbar and this appears after approximately one second.

5. This is located at the top of the WordPerfect screen and displays the name of the currently open document.

6. This feature inserts red slashmarks below words not contained in the Spelling dictionary.

7. This displays as a vertical bar and indicates the position of the next character entered in the editing window.

8. The current location of the insertion point is displayed at the right side of this bar.

9. This WordPerfect feature automatically corrects certain words that are keyed incorrectly.

10. One method for exiting WordPerfect is to click this button (displays with an *X*), located at the right side of the Title bar.

11. Using the mouse, position this where you want the insertion point to be positioned, and then click the left mouse button.

SKILLS check

Assessment 1

1. Load Windows and then open Corel WordPerfect 10.
2. At a clear editing window, change the default folder to the drive where your student data disk is located. (Check with your instructor to see if this step is necessary.)
3. Key the text in figure 1.8. Correct any errors highlighted by Spell-As-You-Go as they occur and remember to space once after end-of-sentence punctuation.
4. Save the document and name it Ch 01, SA 01.
5. Print Ch 01, SA 01.
6. Close Ch 01, SA 01.

FIGURE

1.8 Assessment 1

For more than 100 years, the U.S. public telephone system has provided the means to transmit information via voice. In the past 30 years, the public telephone system, designed for voice transmission, has also provided the means for transmitting data. Currently, 80 to 85 percent of the traffic over telephone lines is voice. Within the next few years, data traffic over the public telephone system is expected to exceed voice traffic.

Traditionally, the signals sent over the telephone system were sent as analog waves, which are fine for voice transmission. The signals for information transmitted from computers used for business applications are sent as digits that have only two values, 0 or 1.

A series of 0s and 1s is used to represent letters, numbers, sounds, values, symbols, and format codes. Since the telephone system transmits information as an analog wave, a modem (MOdulator/DEModulator) is needed to convert digits into analog waves. The modem adds to the cost of transmitting data over the public telephone system.

Assessment 2

1. At a clear editing window, change the default folder to the drive where your student disk is located. (Check with your instructor to determine if this step is necessary.)
2. Key the text in figure 1.9. Correct any errors highlighted by Spell-As-You-Go as they occur and remember to space once after end-of-sentence punctuation.
3. Save the document and name it Ch 01, SA 02.
4. Print and then close Ch 01, SA 02.

FIGURE

1.9 *Assessment 2*

Early mainframe computers consisted of a centralized system. Most computer systems resided in a separate room and were operated by a few highly trained individuals. For many companies, computers represented a large investment. The centralized organization required employees to bring individual requests to the computer room for processing.

The advent of microcomputers brought substantial computing power to the desktop. This capability was in direct contrast to the centralized mainframe computing of the past. Individual computers that operate with little or no central control are called distributed computing systems. Distributed computing allows desktop computers to perform many of the tasks formerly only available on mainframe computers.

Editing a Document

PERFORMANCE OBJECTIVES

Upon successful completion of chapter 2, you will be able to:
- **Move the insertion point within a WordPerfect document**
- **Select text in a document**
- **Edit a document**
- **Use the Help feature**

Chapter 02

Many documents that are created need to have changes made to them. These changes may include adding text, called *inserting*, or removing text, called *deleting*.

To move the insertion point without interfering with text, you can use the mouse, the keyboard, or the mouse combined with the keyboard.

Moving within a WordPerfect Document

WordPerfect offers several methods of moving within a document. These methods are

1. Using Autoscroll
2. Using the mouse
3. Using the keyboard
4. Using page icons
5. Using the Go To command

Each of these methods is explained in this chapter.

Using Autoscroll

The Autoscroll feature allows you to scroll through a document without using the scroll bars. The Autoscroll button is located on the Toolbar.

Click once on the Autoscroll button using the left mouse button. Your insertion point is temporarily hidden and the Autoscroll icon appears on the document window. Without pressing either mouse button, drag your mouse in the direction you want to scroll. Notice the direction the arrow is pointing on the Autoscroll

Autoscroll

button. This is the direction in which you are moving. To turn off Autoscroll, click once with the left mouse button, click the Autoscroll button on the Toolbar, or press any key on the keyboard.

Using the Mouse

The mouse can be used to point quickly to a specific location in your document. Simply move the arrow pointer to the desired location and click once with the left mouse button.

Scrolling with the Mouse

In addition to moving the insertion point to a specific location, the mouse can be used to move the display of text in the editing window. This is referred to as *scrolling*. Scrolling in a document changes the text displayed in the document window, but does not move the insertion point.

You can use the mouse in conjunction with the *vertical* and *horizontal scroll bars*. Using the scroll bars changes your view of the page but does not change the location of the insertion point. Figure 2.1 shows a document window with the scroll bars and elements of the scroll bars identified. The vertical scroll bar appears to the right of the document window; the horizontal scroll bar appears at the bottom of the document window, above the Application bar.

FIGURE

2.1 *Scroll Bars*

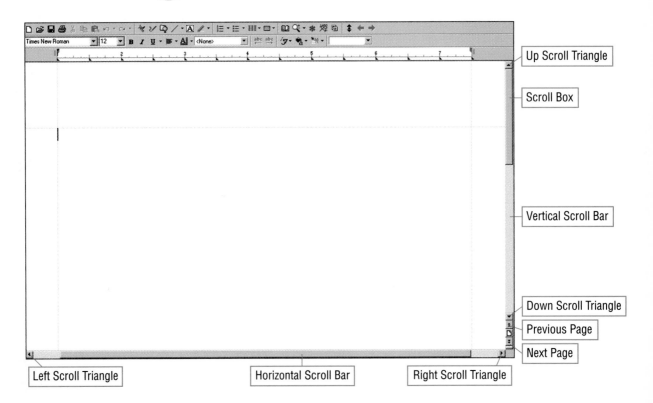

Up Scroll Triangle

Scroll Box

Vertical Scroll Bar

Down Scroll Triangle

Previous Page

Next Page

Left Scroll Triangle

Horizontal Scroll Bar

Right Scroll Triangle

Each scroll bar offers several methods of scrolling. These methods are

- Clicking on the arrows pointing up/down or left/right. Each click moves you one line at a time.
- Clicking in the area directly above or below the scroll box. This moves you up or down one screen at a time.
- Clicking on the scroll box. The *scroll box* indicates the location of the text in the editing window in relation to the entire document. This box moves along the vertical scroll bar as you move through a document. By clicking and dragging on the scroll box, you can reposition the text in the editing window. Remember, however, that scrolling does not change the location of your cursor. To scroll to the beginning of the document, drag the scroll box to the top of the scroll bar. To move to the end of the document, drag the scroll box to the bottom of the scroll bar.

Using the Keyboard

To move the insertion point with the keyboard, use the arrow keys located to the right of the regular keyboard. The keypad is marked with left, right, up, and down arrows that will move the insertion point as long as the Num Lock feature is not active.

Pressing the up or down arrow keys moves the cursor up or down one line. Other keys move the insertion point in the direction indicated on the key. You can also move the insertion point to a specific location in a document by using one of the commands shown in figure 2.2.

F I G U R E

2.2 *Insertion Point Movement Commands*

To move insertion point	Press
One character left	←
One character right	→
One line up	↑
One line down	↓
To end of a line	End
To beginning of a line	Home
Up one screen	Page Up
Down one screen	Page Down
To beginning of previous page	Alt + Page Up
To beginning of new page	Alt + Page Down
To beginning of document	Ctrl + Home
To end of document	Ctrl + End

Previous Page

Next Page

Using Page Icons

The *Previous page* and *Next page* buttons, also known as page icons, allow you to scroll to either the previous page or the next page. These buttons are located at the bottom of the vertical scroll bar.

Using the Go To Command

If you know the page number of the location to which you want to move, you can click <u>E</u>dit and then <u>G</u>o To or press Ctrl + G. This opens the Go To dialog box. Key the desired page number and press Enter. Figure 2.3 shows the Go To dialog box.

F I G U R E

2.3 *Go To Dialog Box*

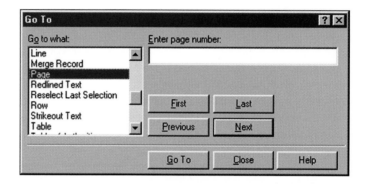

Inserting Text

Once you have created a document, you may want to insert information you forgot or have since decided to include. At the default WordPerfect editing window, the Insert mode is on. The word *Insert* is displayed toward the right side of the Application bar. With Insert on, anything you key will be inserted in the document rather than taking the place of existing text.

If you want to insert or add something, leave Insert on. However, if you want to key over existing text, turn Insert off by pressing the Insert key. When you press the Insert key, the word *Typeover* (rather than Insert) displays on the Application bar. To turn Insert back on, press the Insert key again. You can also click *Insert* on the Application bar and Insert changes to Typeover. Click *Typeover* to change back to Insert. *Caution: Be careful to turn Insert back on when you are finished using Typeover.*

Deleting Text

When you edit a document, you may want to delete (remove) text. You may want to delete just one character or several lines. WordPerfect offers the deletion commands shown in figure 2.4.

FIGURE

2.4 *Deletion Commands*

To delete	Press
Character immediately to the right of insertion point	Delete
Character immediately to the left of insertion point	←Backspace
Word where insertion point is positioned	Ctrl + ←Backspace
Text to the end of the line	Ctrl + Delete

Splitting and Joining Paragraphs

By inserting or deleting, paragraphs of text can be split or joined. To split a large paragraph into two smaller paragraphs, position the insertion point on the first letter that will begin the new paragraph, and then press Enter once or twice. The first time you press Enter, the text is moved to the next line. If you want to create a blank line between paragraphs, press the Enter key again.

To join two paragraphs into one, you need to delete the spaces between them. To do this, position the insertion point on the first character of the second paragraph, and then press the Backspace key until the paragraphs join. More than likely, you will need to then press the spacebar to separate the sentences. You can also join two paragraphs together by positioning the insertion point one space past the period at the end of the first paragraph and then pressing the Delete key until the paragraphs join. When you join the two paragraphs, the new paragraph will be automatically adjusted.

Saving a Document with Save As

In chapter 1, you learned to save a document with the Save button on the Toolbar or the Save option from the File drop-down menu. The File drop-down menu also contains a Save As option. The Save As option is used to save a previously created document with a new name or to save it in a new location.

For example, suppose you created and saved a document named Memo, and then later open it. If you save the document again with the Save button on the Toolbar or the Save option from the File drop-down menu, WordPerfect will save the document with the same name, replacing the previous version. You will not be prompted to key a name for the document. This is because WordPerfect assumes that when you use the Save option on a previously saved document, you want to save it with the same name.

If you open the document named Memo, make some changes to it, and then want to save it with a new name or save it in a new location, you must use the Save As option. When you use the Save As option, WordPerfect displays the Save As dialog box where you can key a new name for the document. To save the document to a new location, click the drop-down arrow next to the Save in text box and point to the desired location. To save a document with Save As, click File and then Save As.

In many of the computer exercises in this text, you will be asked to open a document from your student data disk, and then save it with a new name. You will be instructed to use the Save <u>A</u>s option to do this.

(Before completing computer exercises, delete the Chapter 01 *folder on your disk. Next, download the* Chapter 02 *data files from the Internet Resource Center to the* Chapter 02 *folder you have created on your disk, and then make* Chapter 02 *the active folder.)*

Editing a Document

1. Open Para 06.
2. Save the document with Save <u>A</u>s and name it Ch 02, Ex 01.

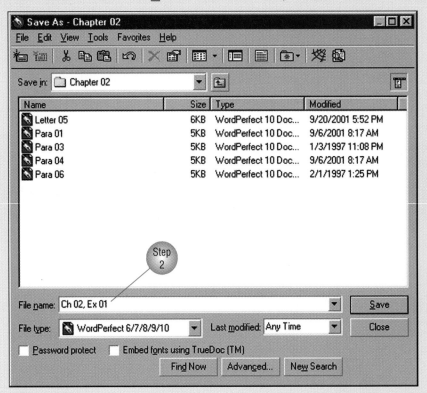

3. Make the changes indicated by the proofreaders' marks shown in figure 2.5. (Proofreaders' marks are listed and described in appendix A at the end of this textbook.)
4. Save the document with the same name (Ch 02, Ex 01) by clicking the Save button on the Toolbar.

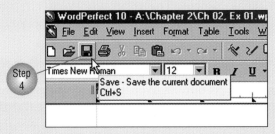

5. Print and then close Ch 02, Ex 01.

One obstacle to smooth communications has to do with standards. ~~A procedure becomes standard through common practice.~~ A person can pick up a phone anywhere and call someone nearly anywhere in the world and if both people speak the same language, they can communicate.

Conversely, not all computers made by manufacturers are able to communicate with each other This is because they speak different languages. Before communication can occur, special equipment is needed to "translate" the message. Solutions are being developed to correct these and other communication obstacles. There are other operations that depend on system of telecommunications.

Most major hotel chains, for example, can book reservations from any location in the United States, and increasingly from anywhere in the world. Airlines also use a one-location reservation service This gives customers the convenience of booking round-trip vacations before they ever leave home. These are just a few ways business and industry use telecommunications to gain a sharp competitive edge. To remain competitive, even the smallest businesses are finding themselves entering the telecommunications technology market. ~~Their aim is to increase customer satisfaction and their profit margins.~~

Selecting Text

Once a specific amount of text is selected, you can delete the text or perform other WordPerfect functions involving the selected text.

Selecting Text with the Mouse

The mouse can be used to select varying amounts of text. When text is selected, it displays in reverse video on the document window as shown in figure 2.6. For example, if the document window displays with a white background and black characters, selected text will display as white characters on a black background.

2.6 *Selected Text*

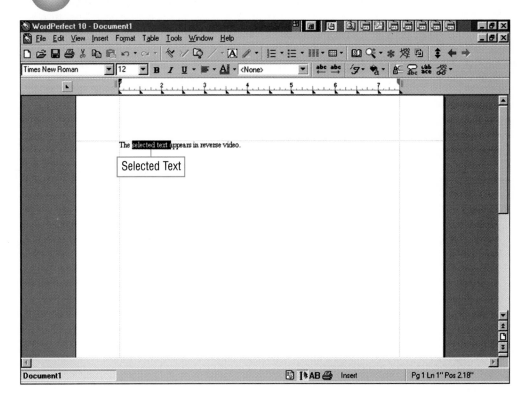

You can use the mouse to select a word, sentence, paragraph, or an entire document. Figure 2.7 indicates the steps to follow to select various amounts of text. To select certain amounts of text such as a line, the instructions in the figure tell you to click in the selection bar. The selection bar is the space at the left side of the document window between the left edge of the screen and the vertical guide line. When the arrow pointer is positioned in the selection bar, the pointer turns into an arrow pointing up and to the right (instead of to the left).

F I G U R E

2.7 *Selecting with the Mouse*

To select	Complete these steps using the mouse
A word	Double-click anywhere in the word.
A sentence	Triple-click anywhere in the sentence.
Multiple lines	Click and drag in selection bar to the left of the lines.
A paragraph	Double-click in selection bar next to the paragraph or quadruple-click anywhere in the paragraph.
Multiple paragraphs	Click and drag in selection bar to the left of the paragraphs.

To select an amount of text other than a word, sentence, or paragraph, position the I-beam pointer on the first character of the text to be selected, hold down the left mouse button, drag the I-beam pointer to the last character of the text to be selected, and then release the mouse button. You can also position the I-beam on the first character of the text to be selected, hold down the Shift key and click on the last character to be selected. Everything in between will be selected. To delete selected text, press the Delete key. To deselect text, position the mouse pointer outside the selected text, and then click the left mouse button.

Selecting Text with the Edit Menu

The Edit drop-down menu contains an option that lets you select a sentence, paragraph, page, or the entire document. Position your cursor in the desired sentence, paragraph, or page and then click Edit, point to Select, and choose from Sentence, Paragraph, Page, or All.

Selecting and Deleting Text

1. Open Letter 05.
2. Save the document with Save As and name it Ch 02, Ex 02.
3. Delete the name, *Mr. Gerald Koch*, and the department, *CIS Department*, using the mouse by completing the following steps:
   a. Position the I-beam pointer on the *M* in *Mr.* (in the address).
   b. Hold down the left mouse button and then drag the arrow pointer down until *Mr. Gerald Koch* and *CIS Department* are selected.
   c. Release the left mouse button.
   d. Press the Delete key.
4. With the insertion point positioned at the left margin on the line above *San Mateo Community College*, key the name **Ms. Aleta Sauter**.

   December 3, 2003

   Step 3b

   Mr. Gerald Koch
   CIS Department
   San Mateo Community College
   4122 Sierra Nevada Drive
   Burlingame, CA 94110

5. Change the salutation from *Dear Mr. Koch* to *Dear Ms. Sauter*.
   a. Click in the selection bar to the left of *Dear Mr. Koch*.
   b. When *Dear Mr. Koch:* is selected, key **Dear Ms. Sauter:** to replace the selected text.
6. Delete the reference line, *Re: Telecommunications Course*, by completing the following steps:
   a. Triple-click anywhere in the reference line to select it.
   b. Press the Delete key.
   c. Press the Backspace key twice to delete the extra space.

7. Delete the first sentence in the first paragraph using the Edit drop-down menu by completing the following steps:
   a. Click anywhere in the sentence *The Western Computer Technology conference we attended last week was very educational for me.*
   b. Click Edit, point to Select, and then click Sentence.
   c. Press the Delete key.
8. Delete the first sentence in the second paragraph (*The interest in the class has been phenomenal.*) by completing the following steps:
   a. Triple-click the left mouse button anywhere in the sentence to select it.
   b. Press the Delete key.
9. Delete the third paragraph in the letter using the Edit menu by completing the following steps:
   a. Click anywhere in the third paragraph (the paragraph that begins *The instructor for the course…*).
   b. Click Edit, point to Select, and then click Paragraph.
   c. Press the Delete key.
10. Save, print, and then close Ch 02, Ex 02.

Using the Undo and Redo Options

Undo

Redo

If you make a mistake and delete text that you did not intend to delete, or if you change your mind after deleting text and want to retrieve it, you can use the Undo option. The Undo option will undo the last function entered at the keyboard. Following are some examples of how the Undo feature works:

- If you just changed the left and right margins, clicking the Undo button on the Toolbar or clicking Edit and then Undo will cause the new (or added) margin codes to be removed from the document.

- If you just turned on bold, clicking the Undo button on the Toolbar or clicking Edit and then Undo causes the bold codes to be removed from the document.

- If you just keyed text in the document, clicking the Undo button on the Toolbar or clicking Edit and then Undo causes the text to be removed. WordPerfect removes text to the beginning of the document or up to the point where text had been deleted previously in the document.

The Redo option will reverse the last Undo action. To do this, click the Redo button on the Toolbar or click Edit and then Redo.

If you want to undo an action performed earlier, click the Undo/Redo History option at the Edit drop-down menu. With the Undo/Redo History option, you can reverse up to 300 actions in a document. To undo or redo a previous action, click

Edit and then Undo/Redo History. This causes the Undo/Redo History dialog box to display as shown in figure 2.8. The contents of this dialog box will vary depending on what type of action has been performed in the document. Actions that have been performed in the document are displayed at the left side of the dialog box in the Undo list box. Any actions that have been redone are displayed in the Redo list box at the right side of the dialog box.

FIGURE

2.8 *Undo/Redo History Dialog Box*

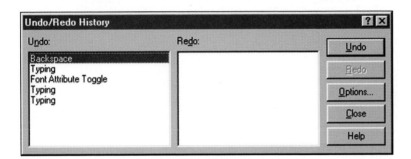

To undo or redo two or more actions, select the item to be undone or redone. This causes any actions listed above the selected item to also be selected. With the items selected, click the Undo button or the Redo button. Click the Options button to display the Undo/Redo Options dialog box. At this dialog box, you can specify the number of Undo or Redo items (from 0 to 300) you want to maintain. (The more actions you maintain, the more system resources you are using. If you are running low on memory, change this to a smaller number.) After selecting items to be undone or redone at the Undo/Redo History dialog box, click the Close button to return to the document.

The down-pointing triangle next to the Undo and Redo buttons will display the history for each, but the options at the right side of the dialog box are not included. If you are not changing any options, select the item to be undone or redone in this list.

Deleting and Restoring Text

1. Open Para 01.
2. Save the document with Save As and name it Ch 02, Ex 03.
3. Make the following changes to the document:
   a. Move the insertion point to the end of the document.
   b. Press the Backspace key until the last three words of the document (*cluttering your desk.*) are deleted.

c. Undo the deletion by clicking the Undo button on the Toolbar.

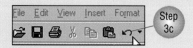

Step 3c

d. Select the first sentence in the first paragraph and then delete it.

Step 3d

Telecommunications will have a tremendous impact on the office of the twenty-first century. Picture yourself in the year 2000. You arrive at your office to meet the challenges of a new day. As you look around at the workstations, you notice that each has a multi-function display terminal for voice, data, and video applications. You recall that just a short time ago, only selected workers had terminals, and they were used primarily for text and data manipulation activities. That has changed dramatically.

e. Select the second paragraph in the document and then delete it.
f. Click the Undo button on the Toolbar. (This redisplays the second paragraph in the document.)
g. Click the Undo button on the Toolbar. (This redisplays the first sentence in the first paragraph.)
h. Click the Redo button on the Toolbar. (This removes the first sentence in the first paragraph.)

Step 3h

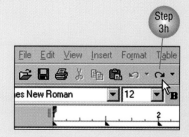

4. Save, print, and then close Ch 02, Ex 03.

Using Help

WordPerfect's Help feature is an on-screen reference manual containing information about all WordPerfect functions and commands. To display the Help Topics dialog box shown in figure 2.9, click Help and then Help Topics. At the Help Topics dialog box, click the Contents tab. The options in the list box contain information (or instructions) about performing the action described. For example, double-click *Welcome to WordPerfect 10* and WordPerfect will display a list of categories. Double-clicking a category will cause a further list of WordPerfect features to appear. Click an item in this list and then click the Display button and you will be presented with a summary describing how to use the new feature. Complete exercises 4 and 5 to practice using the Help feature.

2.9 *Help Topics Dialog Box*

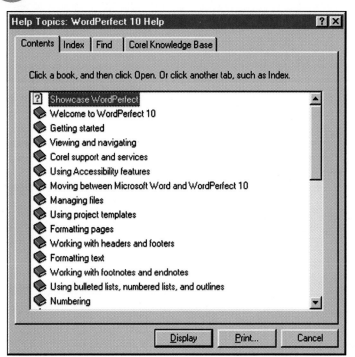

exercise

Using Help

1. At a clear editing window, learn what is new with Corel WordPerfect 10 by completing the following steps:

   a. Click Help and then Help Topics.

   b. At the Help Topics dialog box, make sure the Contents tab is selected. (If not, click the Contents tab.)

   c. Double-click *Welcome to WordPerfect 10* in the list box.

   d. Double-click *What's new in WordPerfect 10* in the list box and then double-click *What's different in WordPerfect 10*.

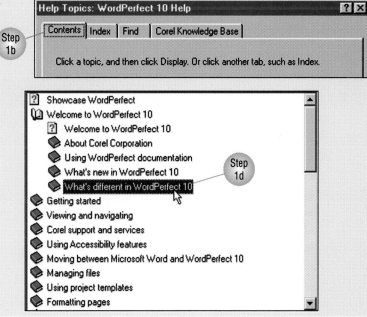

e. Read the information that displays in the Corel WordPerfect Help dialog box.
    (Press the down arrow key or scroll with the scroll bar to view all the information.)
2. After reading the information in the Corel WordPerfect Help dialog box, click the
    Close button (contains an *X*) that displays in the upper right corner of the dialog box.

Click the Index tab at the Help Topics dialog box and an index displays in the
list box as shown in figure 2.10. Using the Help Topics dialog box with the Index
tab selected is often easier than looking through the dialog box with the Contents
tab selected since you can enter different phrases into the text box.

F I G U R E

2.10 *Help Topics Dialog Box with Index Tab Selected*

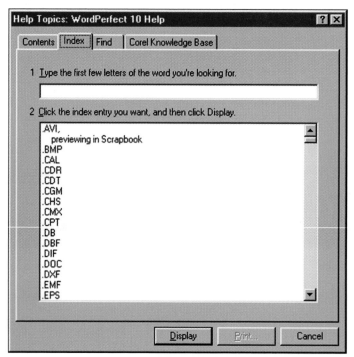

Using the Index Feature in WordPerfect's Help

1. At a clear editing window, use WordPerfect's Help feature to read about italics by
    completing the following steps:
    a. Click <u>H</u>elp and then <u>H</u>elp Topics.
    b. At the Help Topics dialog box, click the Index tab.
    c. At the Help Topics dialog box with the Index tab selected, key **italic**, and then
        click the <u>D</u>isplay button.
    d. Read the information on the italic feature that displays in the WordPerfect Help
        dialog box.
2. After reading the information on the italic feature, click the Close button (contains an
    X) that displays in the upper right corner of the dialog box.

CHAPTER summary

➤ The insertion point can be moved throughout the document without interfering with text by using Autoscroll, the mouse, the keyboard, or the mouse combined with the keyboard. The insertion point can be moved by character, word, screen, or page and from the first to the last character in a document.

➤ Use the horizontal/vertical scroll bars and the mouse to scroll through a document. Use the scroll box to determine insertion point location in an editing window.

➤ By default, the Insert mode is on so text can be easily inserted in a document. The Insert mode can be turned on and off with the Insert key or by clicking Insert on the Application bar. When Insert has been turned off, the message *Typeover* displays on the Application bar. When Insert is on, *Insert* displays on the Application bar.

➤ Text can be deleted by character, word, line, several lines, or partial page using specific keys or by selecting text.

➤ To split a paragraph into two, position the insertion point on the first letter that will begin the new paragraph, and then press Enter once or twice. To join two paragraphs into one, position the insertion point on the first character of the second paragraph, and then press the Backspace key until the paragraphs join.

➤ The Save <u>A</u>s option is used to save a previously created document with a new name.

➤ A specific amount of text can be selected using the mouse. This text can then be deleted or manipulated in other ways using WordPerfect commands.

➤ The Undo option will undo the last function entered at the keyboard or delete text that was just entered. WordPerfect retains the last 300 actions in temporary memory. These actions are listed in the Undo/Redo History dialog box.

➤ WordPerfect's Help feature is an on-screen reference manual containing information about WordPerfect functions and commands.

COMMANDS summary

Command	Mouse	Keyboard
Display the Go To dialog box	<u>E</u>dit, <u>G</u>o To	Ctrl + G
Delete character immediately to the right of insertion point		Delete
Delete character immediately to the left of insertion point		Backspace
Delete word where insertion point is positioned		Ctrl + Backspace
Delete text to the end of the line		Ctrl + Delete
Save	<u>F</u>ile, <u>S</u>ave	Ctrl + S
Save As	<u>F</u>ile, Save <u>A</u>s	

Select text	Position the I-beam pointer at the beginning of text to be selected, hold down the left mouse button, drag the I-beam pointer to the end of text to be selected, then release the button	
Select a word	Position the I-beam pointer within the word, then double-click the left mouse button	
Select a sentence	Position the I-beam pointer within the sentence, then triple-click the left mouse button	
Select a paragraph	Position the I-beam pointer within the paragraph, quickly click the mouse button four times or double-click in the selection bar	
Undo	Edit, Undo; or click Undo button on the Toolbar	Ctrl + Z
Redo	Edit, Redo; or click Redo button on the Toolbar	Ctrl + Shift + Z
Undo/Redo History	Edit, Undo/Redo History; or click the down-pointing arrow next to the Undo/Redo buttons	
Help	Help, Help Topics	F1

CONCEPTS check

Matching: On a blank sheet of paper, indicate the letter of the term that matches each description.

Ⓐ Autoscroll
Ⓑ Backspace
Ⓒ Ctrl +Home
Ⓓ Delete
Ⓔ Help

Ⓕ Help Topics
Ⓖ Insert
Ⓗ Redo
Ⓘ Save
Ⓙ Save As

Ⓚ Toolbar
Ⓛ Undo
Ⓜ Undo/Redo History dialog box

1. Press this key on the keyboard and the word *Insert* on the Application bar changes to *Typeover*.

2. Press this key to delete text immediately to the left of the insertion point.

3. Use this option from the File drop-down menu to save the currently displayed document with a different name.

4. Press this key to delete the character immediately to the right of the insertion point.

5. Press these keys to move the insertion point to the first character in the document.

6. When text is selected, certain buttons become active on this bar.

7. Click this button on the Toolbar to reverse the last Undo.

8. Choose this option from the Help drop-down menu to display a panel of topics to help you complete WordPerfect functions.

9. This dialog box displays a list of functions that have been performed and that can be undone.

10. Press this button to scroll through your document without using the scroll bars.

11. This is the name for the on-screen reference manual containing information about all of the WordPerfect functions and commands.

SKILLS check

Assessment 1

1. Open Para 03.
2. Save the document with Save As and name it Ch 02, SA 01.
3. Make the changes indicated by the proofreaders' marks in figure 2.11.
4. Save, print, and then close Ch 02, SA 01.

FIGURE

2.11 *Assessment 1*

In defending or prosecuting individuals, an attorney must research cases ~~very~~ extensively. ~~This~~ research is based on precedents established in cases ~~having~~ already ~~been~~ resolved before the courts. Many volumes of law books are available to search for the information needed. ~~A number of companies have taken volumes of law manuals and recorded them electronically.~~

In conventional law practice, hundreds of hours are devoted to checking the indexes for the source of facts and figures and finding the pages that contain the information.

Being able to access information quickly eliminates wasted time. Attorneys are now able to conduct much of their research electronically by using databases developed for legal research. Attorneys at their law firms pay a monthly fee to access these databases, plus a per-minute charge for the electronic searches.

All the attorney needs is a computer terminal (such as a microcomputer), communication software, and a modem (a device that converts computer signals that travel over a telephone line). To use the electronically stored database of information, the attorney dials the telephone number of the computer that contains the database and as soon as the connection is made, the attorney enters ~~some~~ key words related to the information needed.

~~In a matter of seconds~~ the computer electronically searches for the information and sends a message back to the attorney noting the information's location. The attorney can ~~then~~ either direct the computer to display this information on the screen or go back to the hard copy volumes of the law books to complete the research.

Assessment 2

1. Open Para 04.
2. Save the document with Save As and name it Ch 02, SA 02.
3. Make the changes indicated by the proofreaders' marks in figure 2.12.
4. Save, print, and then close Ch 02, SA 02.

F I G U R E

2.12 *Assessment 2*

Picture
Imagine yourself in the year 2005. ~~You arrive at your office to meet the challenges of a new day.~~ As you look around your office at the workstations, you notice that each has a multifunction display terminal for voice, data, and video applications.

No ¶
You recall that just a short time ago, only selected workers had terminals. and /lc They were used primarily for text and data manipulation ~~functions and~~ activities.

The movement of documents and information has also changed. Incoming correspondence ~~that is~~ not transmitted electronically to your workstation is converted to a digitized format via laser scanners. and /lc This is input into the electronic filing system.

No ¶
You can access the information from your terminal and choose which to act upon at your convenience. An added bonus is that you don't have a pile of papers ~~sitting around~~ cluttering your desk. Another challenge is the ability to create documents by dictating to your terminal through a feature called voice-activated display. This feature allows you to view dictation on your terminal for editing and revising. You also have the option of dictating or using your hand-manipulated input device to make corrections.

~~Everything you dictate is run through an electronic dictionary and a grammar and syntax validator before the final draft is distributed. If you mistakenly dictate "you is" instead of "you are," the grammar and syntax validator corrects it.~~

CHAPTER 3

Formatting Text

As you work with WordPerfect, you will learn a number of commands and procedures that affect how the document appears when printed. The appearance of a document in the editing window and how it looks when printed is called the *format*. Formatting may include such elements as all caps, line spacing, margin settings, even or uneven margins, tabs, bolding, underlining, and much more. WordPerfect contains a number of features that can be used to affect the appearance or layout of a line of text. Three common line features are centering, line spacing, and justification.

Creating Text in All Caps

To key text in all uppercase letters, press the Caps Lock key. The Caps Lock key is a toggle key—press the key once to activate the Caps Lock feature, and press it again to turn it off.

Using the Tab Key

The WordPerfect program contains a variety of default settings. A *default* is a preset standard or value that is established by the program. One default setting in WordPerfect is a Ruler that contains tab settings every one-half inch. In a later chapter, you will learn how to change the default tab settings. For now, use the default tab settings to indent text from the left margin. To indent text, press the Tab key. The Tab key on a microcomputer keyboard is generally located above the Caps Lock key.

Formatting Text

Formatting can be applied to accentuate text, elicit a particular feeling about the text, or draw the reader's eyes to a particular word or phrase. There are a variety of ways that text can be accentuated such as bolding, italicizing, and underlining. Text can be **bolded**, *italicized*, or <u>underlined</u> with buttons on the Main property bar, shortcut commands, or options at the Font dialog box. In this chapter, you will learn to bold, italicize, and underline with buttons on the Main property bar and shortcut commands. The Font dialog box is discussed in chapter 6.

Bolding Text

The Bold button on the Main property bar or the shortcut command Ctrl + B can be used to bold text. When text is bolded, it appears darker than surrounding text in the editing window and also on the printed page. Text can be bolded as it is being keyed, or existing text can be bolded. To bold text as it is being keyed, click the Bold button on the Main property bar or press Ctrl + B. Key the text to be bolded and then click the Bold button again or press Ctrl + B. If you prefer, you can just press the right arrow key on the keyboard to turn off bold.

B

Bold

In exercise 1 and other exercises in this text, you will be required to create memos. Please refer to appendix B at the end of this text for the correct placement and spacing of a traditional-style memo. Unless otherwise instructed by your teacher, use this format when creating memos. The initials of the person keying the memo usually appear at the end of the document. In this text, the initials will appear in the exercises as *xx*. Key your initials where you see *xx*. Identifying document names in correspondence is a good idea because it lets you find and open the document quickly and easily at a future date. In this text, the document name is identified after the reference initials. Before printing any exercises, always proofread the document and correct any errors.

Text that has already been keyed in a document can be formatted as bold text by selecting the text first and then clicking the Bold button on the Main property bar or pressing Ctrl + B.

(Before completing computer exercises, delete the Chapter 02 *folder on your disk. Next, download the* Chapter 03 *data files from the Internet Resource Center to the* Chapter 03 *folder you have created on your disk, and then make* Chapter 03 *the active folder.)*

Bolding Text

1. At a clear editing window, key the memo shown in figure 3.1 in the traditional-style memo format. Use Caps Lock to key the memo headings—*DATE*, *TO*, *FROM*, and *SUBJECT*. To align the information after *DATE:*, key **DATE:**, press Tab, and then key **November 15, 2002**. (Press Tab after the other headings to align them properly. You will need to press Tab twice after *TO:*.) Bold the monetary amounts as shown in the memo as they are being keyed by completing the following steps:
   a. Press Ctrl + B.
   b. Key the monetary amount.

DATE: November 15, 2002

TO: All School Principals

FROM: Pat Windslow, Superintendent

SUBJECT: BOARD OF EDUCATION MEETING

Two decisions were made at the Board of Education meeting last night that I would like to bring to your attention. The board members passed a recommendation to set a Maintenance and Operation levy for February 2003. The estimated collection for 2002 is **$4,500,000**

Step 1b

   c. Press Ctrl + B (or press the right arrow key).
2. Save the memo and name it Ch 03, Ex 01.
3. With Ch 03, Ex 01 still displayed in the editing window, select and bold the words *Maintenance and Operations* in the first paragraph by completing the following steps:
   a. Using the mouse, position the I-beam pointer on the *M* in *Maintenance*, hold down the left button, drag the I-beam pointer to the end of *Operations*, and then release the mouse button.
   b. With *Maintenance and Operations* selected, click the Bold button on the Main property bar, and then click outside the selected text to deselect it.
4. Select and bold the following text in the memo:
   a. *Assistant Superintendent for Support Services* in the second paragraph.
   b. The heading *DATE:*.
   c. The heading *TO:*.
   d. The heading *FROM:*.
   e. The heading *SUBJECT:*.
5. Save, print, and then close Ch 03, Ex 01.

FIGURE

3.1 *Exercise 1*

DATE: November 15, 2002

TO: All School Principals

FROM: Pat Windslow, Superintendent

SUBJECT: BOARD OF EDUCATION MEETING

Two decisions were made at the Board of Education meeting last night that I would like to bring to your attention. The board members passed a recommendation to set a Maintenance and Operations levy for February 2003. The estimated collection for 2002 is **$4,500,000** and the estimated collection for 2003 is **$4,850,000**. These estimates are based on a levy rate of **$4.20** for each **$1,000** assessed value.

The Assistant Superintendent for Support Services reported that the District will save **$9,100** annually if heat pumps are installed in 23 portable buildings. The board members awarded an **$85,450** bid to Gemini Mechanics to install the pumps. You will be notified when portables at your school will be upgraded.

xx:Ch 03, Ex 01

Displaying the Reveal Codes Window

There are special codes embedded in the text that are not visible; these codes tell WordPerfect where to start and stop bold. To display the bold codes, you must display a special window called *Reveal Codes*. At the Reveal Codes window, you can view the format changes that have been made to a document. To display the Reveal Codes window, click <u>V</u>iew and then Reveal <u>C</u>odes or press Alt + F3.

In Reveal Codes a gray bar is inserted toward the bottom of the screen. Above the gray bar, the text displays normally. Below the gray bar, text displays with formatting codes added. Figure 3.2 shows a document with Reveal Codes displayed.

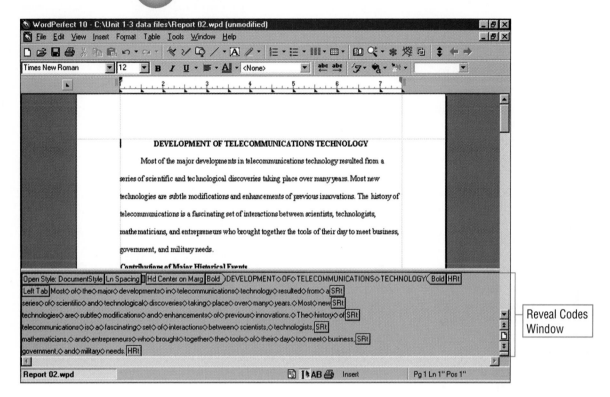

Reveal Codes
Window

The insertion point appears above the gray bar as a blinking vertical bar. Below the gray bar, the insertion point displays as a red rectangle. The insertion point can be moved through text with the insertion point movement keys.

Codes and text can be deleted in Reveal Codes with the regular deletion commands or with the mouse. The Reveal Codes insertion point cannot be positioned on a code. Instead, the Reveal Codes insertion point moves to the left or right side of a code. To delete a code with the Backspace key, position the Reveal Codes insertion point (the red rectangle) immediately to the right of the code to be deleted, and then press the Backspace key. To delete a code with the Delete key, position the Reveal Codes insertion point immediately to the left of the code to be deleted, and then press the Delete key. To remove a code with the mouse, position the arrow pointer on the code to be removed. Hold down the left mouse button, drag the code into the editing window, and then release the mouse button.

Special codes appear in Reveal Codes that identify functions and commands. Some of the lines of text in figure 3.2 end with the code SRt. This code indicates a soft return, which is the end of a line created by word wrap. The code HRt identifies a hard return and indicates that the Enter key has been pressed. In Reveal Codes, the code Bold identifies the beginning of the bold text and the code Bold identifies the end of bold text. If after bolding text you change your mind, display Reveal Codes, and then delete one of the bold codes. Because bold codes are paired codes, when one code is deleted, its pair is automatically deleted.

Removing Bold Codes

1. Open Ch 03, Ex 01.
2. Save the document with Save As and name it Ch 03, Ex 02.
3. Remove the bold codes from the heading *DATE:* by completing the following steps:
   a. Make sure the insertion point is immediately to the left of the *D* in *DATE:*.
   b. Display the Reveal Codes window by clicking <u>V</u>iew and then Reveal <u>C</u>odes.
   c. Position the insertion point immediately to the right of the Bold code and then press the Backspace key. (This will delete the on code as well as the off code.)
4. Complete similar steps to delete the bold codes from the heading *TO:*.
5. Remove the bold codes from the heading *FROM:* by completing the following steps:
   a. Move the insertion point to the *F* in *FROM:*.
   b. Position the arrow pointer on the Bold code on the left side of *FROM:*.
   c. Hold down the left mouse button.
   d. Drag the arrow pointer into the editing window and then release the mouse button.
6. Complete similar steps to delete the bold codes from the heading *SUBJECT:*.
7. Remove the Reveal Codes window by pressing Alt + F3.
8. Change the document name after your initials from Ch 03, Ex 01 to Ch 03, Ex 02.
9. Save, print, and then close Ch 03, Ex 02.

> TO: Hd Left Ind | Hd Left Ind | All◇School◇Princ
> HRt
> Bold ❚ FROM (Bold): Hd Left Ind | Pat◇Wind
> HRt
> Bold) SUBJECT (Bold): Hd Left Ind | BOARD◇
> HRt

Step 5a

Italicizing Text

Italic

WordPerfect's italic feature can be used in documents to emphasize specific text such as the names of published works. Text can be italicized using the Italic button on the Main property bar or using the shortcut command Ctrl + I. To italicize text as it is being keyed, click the Italic button on the Main property bar or press Ctrl + I. Key the text to be italicized, and then click the Italic button again or press Ctrl + I. You can also just press the right arrow key. Text that has already been keyed in a document can be italicized by selecting the text first.

Text formatted with italics will appear in italics on the screen. In Reveal Codes, the code Italic identifies the beginning of italicized text and the code Italic identifies the end of italicized text.

Italicizing Text

1. Open Bibliography.
2. Save the document with Save As and name it Ch 03, Ex 03.
3. Select and italicize the book title *Telecommunications in Today's Businesses* by completing the following steps:

a. Using the mouse, position the I-beam pointer on the *T* in *Telecommunications*, hold down the left button, drag the I-beam pointer to the end of *Businesses*, and then release the mouse button.

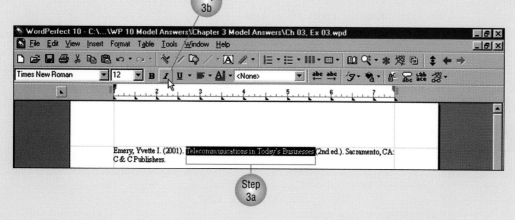

b. With *Telecommunications in Today's Businesses* selected, click the Italic button on the Main property bar.
4. Click outside the selected text to deselect it.
5. Select and italicize the following book titles in the document:
    a. *Technological Advancements* in the second paragraph.
    b. *Computer Systems and Applications* in the third paragraph.
    c. *The Changing Business Office* in the fourth paragraph.
6. Press Enter twice following the end of the last line. Key the text shown in figure 3.3. Italicize the text shown as it is being keyed by completing the following steps:
    a. Press Ctrl + I.
    b. Key the text.
    c. Press Ctrl + I (or press the right arrow key).
7. Save, print, and then close Ch 03, Ex 03.

FIGURE

3.3   *Exercise 3*

Collier, Samuel G. (2000). *Technology: Educating Our Children* (pp. 56-78). Montpelier, VT: Maple Leaf Publishers.

Kitamura, Toshiki (2001). *Managing the Technology Classroom*. Boston, MA: Harbor Publishing House.

Underlining Text

Underline

Text can be underlined using the Underline button on the Main property bar or the shortcut command Ctrl + U. To underline text as it is being keyed, click the Underline button on the Main property bar or press Ctrl + U. Key the text to be underlined and then click the Underline button again or press Ctrl + U. You can also just press the right arrow key.

Text that has already been keyed in a document can be underlined by selecting the text first and then clicking the Underline button on the Main property bar or pressing Ctrl + U. In Reveal Codes, the [Und] code identifies the beginning of underlined text and the code [Und] identifies the end of underlined text.

exercise 4

Underlining Text

1. Open Ch 03, Ex 03.
2. Save the document with Save As and name it Ch 03, Ex 04.
3. Delete all italic codes from the titles.
4. Select and underline the title *Telecommunications in Today's Businesses* by completing the following steps:
    a. Using the mouse, position the I-beam pointer on the *T* in *Telecommunications*, hold down the left button, drag the I-beam pointer to the end of *Businesses*, and then release the mouse button.
    b. With *Telecommunications in Today's Businesses* selected, click the Underline button on the Main property bar.

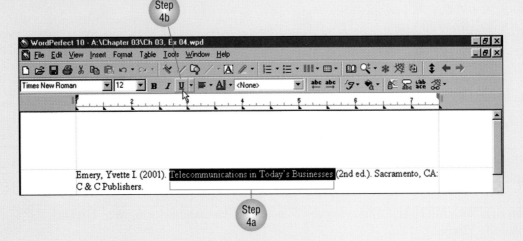

Step 4b

Step 4a

   c. Click outside the selected text to deselect it.
5. Select and underline the title *Technological Advancements* in the second paragraph.
6. Select and underline the title *Computer Systems and Applications* in the third paragraph.
7. Select and underline the title *The Changing Business Office* in the fourth paragraph.
8. Select and underline the title *Technology: Educating Our Children* in the fifth paragraph.
9. Select and underline the title *Managing the Technology Classroom* in the sixth paragraph.
10. Press Enter twice following the end of the last line. Key the text in figure 3.4.

11. Underline the text shown as it is being keyed by completing the following steps:
    a. Press Ctrl + U.
    b. Key the text.
    c. Press Ctrl + U (or press the right arrow key).
12. Save, print, and then close Ch 03, Ex 04.

FIGURE

3.4 *Exercise 4*

Caprin, Heidi L. (1999). <u>The Business Educator</u>. Dallas, TX: Longhorn Publishing.

Centering Text

Text can be centered between the left and right margins with the shortcut command Shift + F7, with an option at the Format menu, or with the shadow cursor.

In Reveal Codes, the code `Hd Center on Marg` identifies the beginning and the code `HRt` identifies the end of centered text.

exercise 5

Bolding and Centering Text

1. At a clear editing window, key the text shown in figure 3.5 centered and bolded by completing the following steps:
   a. Key the first line by completing the following steps:
      1) Press Shift + F7.
      2) Press Ctrl + B (this turns on bold).
      3) Key **CIS 120, TELECOMMUNICATIONS**.
      4) Press Enter twice.
   b. Key the second line by completing the following steps:
      1) Click Format, point to Line, and then click Center.
      2) Key **Monday through Thursday**.
      3) Press Enter twice.
   c. Key the remaining lines following steps similar to those in steps 1a or 1b.
   d. After keying the last line, **Room 428**, press Ctrl + B to turn off bold.
2. Save the document and name it Ch 03, Ex 05.
3. Print and then close Ch 03, Ex 05.

CIS 120, TELECOMMUNICATIONS

Monday through Thursday

9:00 - 10:10 a.m.

Room 428

Using QuickMenus

WordPerfect contains a number of *QuickMenus* that help speed up the customizing and formatting of text. QuickMenus are pop-up menus that display when you click the *right* button on the mouse. The QuickMenu that displays depends on the position of the mouse pointer when you click the right button. A different QuickMenu will display when you position the mouse pointer at each of the following positions and then click the *right* mouse button:

- between the left margin and the edge of the screen
- the editing window
- a table
- a graphic figure or line
- the Toolbar, Main property bar, Application bar, Ruler, or scroll bars

A QuickMenu can be used to center text between the left and right margins. To use the QuickMenu, you would complete the following steps:

1. Position the arrow pointer anywhere in the editing window (except the area between the edge of the screen and the left margin).

2. Click the right button on the mouse.

3. At the QuickMenu shown in figure 3.6, position the arrow pointer on Center, and then click the left mouse button.

3.6 *QuickMenu*

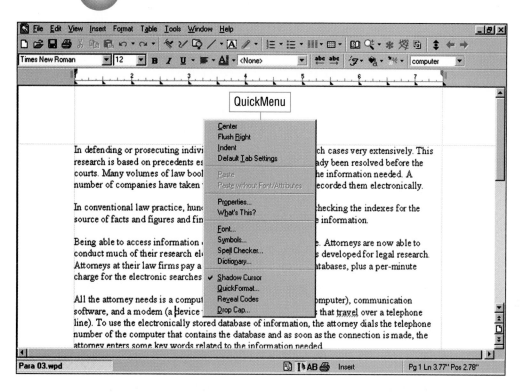

Centering Text with a QuickMenu

1. At a clear editing window, key the document shown in figure 3.7 using a QuickMenu by completing the following steps:

   a. Position the arrow pointer anywhere in the editing window (except the area between the edge of the screen and the left margin).

   b. Click the *right* button on the mouse.

   c. At the QuickMenu, position the arrow pointer on Center and then click the left button.

   d. Key **Chief Executive Officer, Chris Hedegaard**.

   e. Press Enter.

   f. Complete similar steps to center the remaining four lines.

2. After keying all lines in the document, save it and name it Ch 03, Ex 06.

3. Print and then close Ch 03, Ex 06.

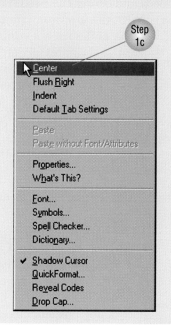

Step 1c

FIGURE

3.7 *Exercise 6*

Chief Executive Officer, Chris Hedegaard
Vice President, Robert Freitas
Vice President, Richard Dudley
Vice President, Glenna Wykoff
Vice President, Laura Culver

Centering Text at a Specific Position

The Center feature can be used to center text at a specific position on the line other than at the midpoint (or half way) between the left and right margin settings.

When text is centered at a specific position, the code `Hd Center on Pos` displays in Reveal Codes. The center on position feature can be useful for centering a heading over a column of text.

exercise 7

Centering Text at a Specific Location

1. Open Column 01.
2. Save the document with Save As and name it Ch 03, Ex 07.
3. Bold and center the heading *Directors* over the text by completing the following steps:
   a. With the insertion point located on the first line in the document (this line is blank and does not contain text), press the spacebar until the insertion point is located at approximately Position 2.6". (Check the right side of the Application bar; your position measurement may vary slightly.)
   b. Press Shift + F7 to access the Center command. (This does not move the insertion point—it tells WordPerfect to center text at Position 2.6".)
   c. Press Ctrl + B to turn on bold or click the Bold button on the Main property bar.
   d. Key **Directors**.
   e. Press Ctrl + B or click the Bold button on the Main property bar to turn off bold.
4. Save, print, and then close Ch 03, Ex 07.

Changing Line Spacing

By default, WordPerfect's word wrap feature single-spaces text. Occasionally, you may want to change to another spacing, such as one and a half or double. Change line spacing at the Line Spacing dialog box shown in figure 3.8. To display this dialog box, click Format, point to Line, and then click Spacing.

You can enter whole numbers, decimal numbers, or fractions. You can key up to six numbers after the decimal point; however, WordPerfect will only carry the number to three decimal places.

FIGURE

3.8   *Line Spacing Dialog Box*

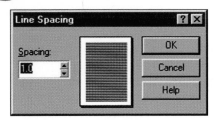

When changes are made to line spacing, a code is inserted in the document that can be seen in Reveal Codes. The line spacing code is inserted at the beginning of the paragraph where the insertion point is located. Line spacing changes affect text from the location of the code to the end of the document or until another line spacing code is encountered. If a line spacing code is deleted, line spacing reverts to the default setting of single spacing or to the setting of a previously placed line spacing code. If line spacing in a document is changed to double, the code would appear in Reveal Codes as `Ln Spacing: 2.0`. To see the number after Ln Spacing, the insertion point must be positioned immediately left of the code; otherwise, the code appears as `Ln Spacing`. You can also display the number in the code using the mouse. To do this, position the arrow pointer on the code, and then click the left mouse button.

exercise 8

Changing Line Spacing to 1.5 at the Line Spacing Dialog Box

1. Open Memo 01.
2. Save the document with Save As and name it Ch 03, Ex 08.
3. Change the line spacing to 1.5 for the body of the memo by completing the following steps:

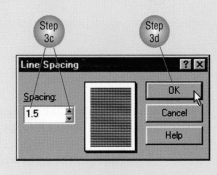

a. Position the insertion point on any character in the first paragraph of the memo.
b. Click Format, point to Line, and then click Spacing.
c. Click the up-pointing triangle at the right side of the Spacing text box until *1.5* displays in the text box.
d. Click OK or press Enter to close the dialog box.
4. View the line spacing code in Reveal Codes by completing the following steps:
a. If Reveal Codes is turned off, click View and then Reveal Codes.

b. In the Reveal Codes window, position the arrow pointer on the Ln Spacing code and then click the left mouse button. (This should expand the code to display the number *1.5*.)

c. After viewing the code, turn off the display of Reveal Codes.

5. Save, print, and then close Ch 03, Ex 08.

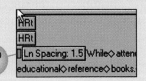

Changing Justification

Justification

By default, WordPerfect justifies text evenly at the left margin but leaves the text near the right margin uneven. This is referred to as *left justification*. A variety of methods are available for changing justification including shortcut commands; the Justification button on the Main property bar; and the Format, Justification side menu. Figure 3.9 illustrates the different paragraph justifications.

F I G U R E

3.9 *Paragraph Justifications*

Left Justified Text

Center Justified Text

Right Justified Text

Fully Justified Text

In addition to the four paragraph justifications shown in figure 3.9, you can also fully justify all lines of text in paragraphs. The difference between *Full* justification and *All* justification is that All will justify to both margins all lines of text in a paragraph, including short lines, while Full will not justify the last line of text in a paragraph to the right margin.

To make changes to justification with the Format menu, click Format and then point to Justification. At the side menu that displays as shown in figure 3.10, click the desired justification. The justification you select will stay in effect until another justification code is encountered.

3.10 *Justification Side Menu*

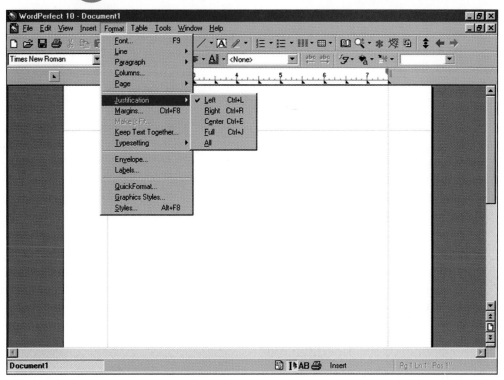

exercise 9

Changing Justification Using Menu Options

1. Open Para 03.
2. Save the document with Save As and name it Ch 03, Ex 09.
3. Change to center justification using the Format, Justification side menu by completing the following steps:
   a. Position the insertion point on any character in the first paragraph.
   b. Click Format, point to Justification, and then click Center.
4. Save, print, and then close Ch 03, Ex 09.

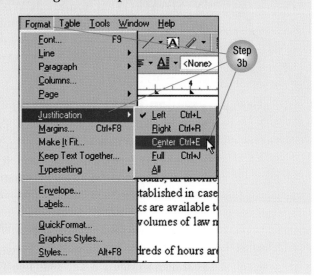

Justification changes can also be made with the Justification button on the Main property bar. To display the justification options, click the Justification button.

exercise 10

Changing Justification with the Justification Button

1. Open Para 03.
2. Save the document with Save As and name it Ch 03, Ex 10.
3. Change the justification to full for all lines by completing the following steps:
   a. Position the insertion point anywhere in the first paragraph.
   b. Click the Justification button on the Main property bar.
   c. Click *All* at the drop-down list.
4. Save, print, and then close Ch 03, Ex 10.

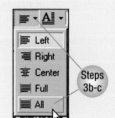

Steps 3b-c

When a change is made to justification, WordPerfect inserts the code at the beginning of the paragraph where the insertion point is positioned. Changes to justification take effect from the location of the code to the end of the document or until another justification code is encountered.

Changing the Viewing Mode

WordPerfect has more than one viewing mode. You have been using the default viewing mode, which is Page. You can also change the viewing mode to Draft, Two Pages, or Preview in Browser.

Viewing in the Page Mode

The Page mode, which is the default, displays a document in what is considered WYSIWYG (What You See Is What You Get). All aspects of a document display, such as headers, footers, page numbers, and watermarks. Because all elements of a document are displayed, the Page mode is slower than the Draft mode. If the viewing mode has been changed and you want to return to the Page mode, click View and then Page.

Viewing in the Draft Mode

The viewing mode can be changed to the Draft mode by clicking View and then Draft. In the Draft mode, text displays as it will appear when printed; however, special elements such as headers, footers, page numbers, and watermarks will not display. Because special elements are not displayed, the Draft mode is faster than the Page mode.

Viewing in the Two-Pages Mode

In the Two-Pages viewing mode, two pages of a document are displayed side by side as shown in figure 3.11. The Two-Pages mode is useful for viewing the position of elements on pages. You can edit in Two-Pages mode but doing so is not practical. You may want to switch to Two-Pages mode to see how elements are positioned and then switch to Draft or Page mode to make any changes.

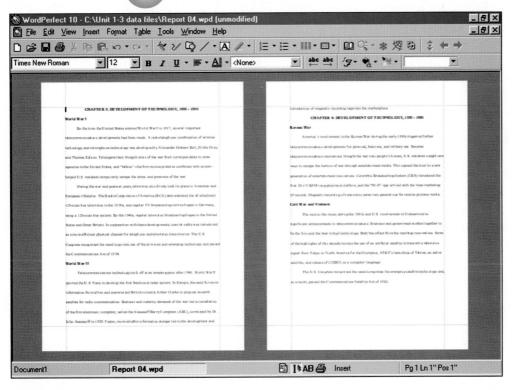

3.11 *Two-Pages Viewing Mode*

Preview in Browser Mode

If you intend to place your document on the World Wide Web, previewing your page in the browser will show you how your document will appear in your default browser. To close the preview, click <u>F</u>ile and then <u>C</u>lose or use the *X* in the upper right corner of the window.

Changing the Zoom Ratio

In the Draft or Page viewing modes, you can change the size of text and document elements displayed on the screen. By default, the document is displayed at approximately 100% of the size of the document when printed. This ratio can be changed with the <u>Z</u>oom option from the <u>V</u>iew drop-down menu or with the Zoom button on the Toolbar. When you click <u>V</u>iew and then <u>Z</u>oom, the Zoom dialog box shown in figure 3.12 displays.

Zoom

3.12 *Zoom Dialog Box*

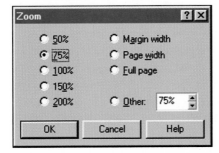

To decrease the display of the document, choose a percentage lower than 100%. To increase the display, choose a percentage higher than 100%. If you choose Margin width at the Zoom dialog box, the document displays so that all text and graphics between the left and right margins are visible. Choose Page width to display the entire document between the left and right edges of the page. If you choose Full page, the entire current page is displayed. With the Other option from the Zoom dialog box, you can decrease or increase the percentage from 25% to 400%. The same zoom options are available by clicking the Zoom button located toward the right side of the Toolbar.

exercise 11

Changing the Viewing Mode and the Zoom Ratio

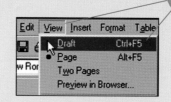

Step 2a

1. Open Report 04.
2. Make the following view changes:
   a. Change the view to Draft by clicking View and then Draft.
   b. Move the insertion point to the end of the document page by page.
   c. Move the insertion point to the beginning of the document and then change the view to Two Pages by clicking View and then Two Pages. Your screen should look similar to the one shown below.

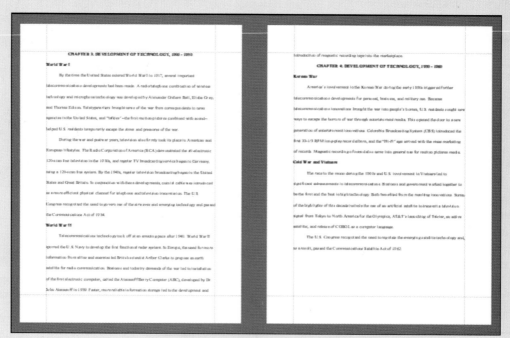

   d. Make sure the insertion point is located at the beginning of the document and then change the view to a preview in your browser by clicking View and then Preview in Browser.
   e. Move the insertion point to the end of the document page by page and then close the browser.

f. Move the insertion point to the beginning of the document and then change the view to Draft.
g. Change the Zoom option to 75% by completing the following steps:
    1) Click <u>V</u>iew and then <u>Z</u>oom.
    2) At the Zoom dialog box, click <u>7</u>5%. To do this, position the tip of the arrow pointer inside the circle before <u>7</u>5%, and then click the left mouse button.
    3) Click OK or press Enter.
h. Change the Zoom option to Margin Width using the Zoom button by completing the following steps:
    1) Click the Zoom button on the Toolbar.
    2) At the drop-down list that displays, click *Margin Width*.
i. Change the Zoom option to Full Page by completing steps similar to those in 2h.
j. Change the Zoom option back to the default of 100%.
3. Close Report 02 without saving it.

Using the PerfectExpert

The PerfectExpert can provide directions on how to complete WordPerfect functions. Click <u>H</u>elp on the Menu bar and then click Perfect<u>E</u>xpert. The PerfectExpert panel displays at the left side of the screen as shown in figure 3.13. Use buttons on the PerfectExpert panel to learn how to complete specific tasks. You can also display the PerfectExpert panel by clicking the PerfectExpert button located at the right side of the Toolbar.

PerfectExpert

FIGURE

3.13 **PerfectExpert Panel**

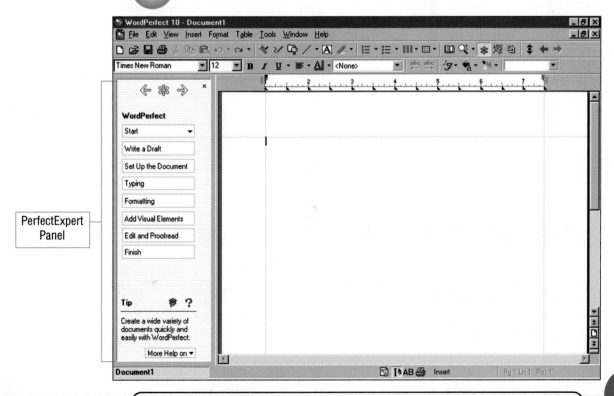

PerfectExpert Panel

Click a button on the PerfectExpert panel and another list of options or a dialog box will display. If another list of options displays, you can return to the original PerfectExpert panel by clicking the Back button. This button is located at the top of the PerfectExpert panel and contains a left-pointing arrow.

In exercise 12, you will be using the PerfectExpert to help you add numbers to selected paragraphs of text. Consider experimenting with other options available in the PerfectExpert panel.

Using the PerfectExpert to Add Numbers to Text

1. Open Para 02.
2. Save the document with Save As and name it Ch 03, Ex 12.
3. Use the PerfectExpert to add numbers to selected paragraphs by completing the following steps:
   a. Click the PerfectExpert button on the Toolbar. (This displays the PerfectExpert panel at the left side of the screen.)

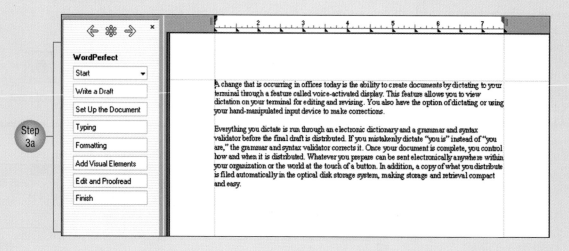

   b. Click Edit on the Menu bar, point to Select, and then click All to select the entire document.
   c. With the text selected, click the Typing button in the PerfectExpert panel.
   d. Click the Add Bullet/Number List button that displays in the PerfectExpert panel.
   e. At the Bullets & Numbering dialog box with the Number tab selected, click the first numbering option and then click OK. (This inserts numbers before the two paragraphs.)
   f. Deselect the text by clicking in the editing window outside the selected text.
   g. Remove the PerfectExpert panel by clicking the PerfectExpert button on the Toolbar.
4. Save, print, and then close Ch 03, Ex 12.

CHAPTER summary

➤ To key text in all uppercase letters, press the Caps Lock key.

➤ The default or preset tab setting is one tab set every one-half inch. Press the Tab key to move the insertion point to the next tab to the right.

➤ Text can be bolded, italicized, or underlined with buttons on the Main property bar, shortcut commands, or options at the Font dialog box. When text has been bolded, italicized, or underlined, special codes are inserted in the document. These codes can be viewed in the Reveal Codes window.

➤ To bold, italicize, or underline existing text, select the text first, and then click the necessary button on the Main property bar or press the shortcut command that will apply the desired formatting.

➤ Three common line alignment features are centering, line spacing, and justification.

➤ Text can be centered between the left and right margins or at a specific position.

➤ QuickMenus are pop-up menus that display when you click the *right* mouse button.

➤ The default line spacing, which is single, can be changed at the Line Spacing dialog box. A line spacing code is inserted at the beginning of the paragraph where the insertion point is located.

➤ Justification determines how text will be aligned when it is printed. The five possible settings are left (which is the default setting); center; right; full; and all lines. A justification code is inserted at the beginning of the paragraph where the insertion point is located.

➤ Four viewing modes are available in WordPerfect: Page (the default), Draft, Two Pages, and Preview in Browser.

➤ By default, a document displays at approximately 100% of the size it will be when printed. This ratio can be increased or decreased with the Zoom option from the View drop-down menu or the Zoom button on the Toolbar.

➤ Choose the PerfectExpert option from the Help drop-down menu or click the PerfectExpert button on the Toolbar and a PerfectExpert panel displays at the left side of the screen. Use buttons on this panel to help complete a variety of WordPerfect functions.

COMMANDS summary

Command	Mouse	Keyboard
Turn on/off Bold	Click the Bold button on the Main property bar	Ctrl + B
Turn on/off Reveal Codes	View, Reveal Codes	Alt + F3
Turn on/off Italics	Click the Italic button on the Main property bar	Ctrl + I
Turn on/off Underline	Click the Underline button on the Main property bar	Ctrl + U
Center text		Shift + F7
Change to single spacing	Format, Line, Spacing, 1	Ctrl + 1
Change to double spacing	Format, Line, Spacing, 2	Ctrl + 2
Change Zoom Ratio	View, Zoom	
Change to Justify Center	Format, Justification; or click the Justification button on the Main property bar	Ctrl + E
Change to Justify Full	Format, Justification; or click the Justification button on the Main property bar	Ctrl + J
Change to Justify Left	Format, Justification; or click the Justification button on the Main property bar	Ctrl + L
Change to Justify Right	Format, Justification; or click the Justification button on the Main property bar	Ctrl + R
Display the PerfectExpert panel	Help, PerfectExpert; or click the PerfectExpert button on the Toolbar	

CONCEPTS check

Completion: On a blank sheet of paper, indicate the correct term, symbol, or command for each item.

1. Press this key to indent the insertion point to the next tab stop to the right

2. This code in Reveal Codes indicates the beginning of underlined text.

3. Existing text can be italicized only if this is done first.

4. This is the shortcut command to underline text.

5. This symbol is inserted in the document each time a line of text is ended by word wrap.

6. This code HRt in Reveal Codes indicates that this key has been pressed.

7. The insertion point displays as this in the Reveal Codes window.

8. This code appears in Reveal Codes before centered text.

9. At this justification setting, all lines in a paragraph, including short lines, align at the left and right margins.

10. This is the default justification type.

11. To see the number after a line spacing code in Reveal Codes, the insertion point must be positioned on this side of the code.

12. This is the name of the pop-up menu that displays when you click the right mouse button.

13. Four viewing modes are available in WordPerfect: Page, Two Pages, Draft, and this.

14. Choose this option from the Help drop-down menu to display a panel of buttons to help you complete WordPerfect functions.

SKILLS check

Assessment 1

1. Open Memo 01.
2. Save the document with Save As and name it Ch 03, SA 01.
3. Make the following changes to the document:
   a. Move the insertion point to the first letter of the body of the memo and change the line spacing to 1.5.
   b. Display Reveal Codes and delete the underline codes from the publication titles *The ABCs of Integrated Learning* and *Total Quality Management in the Education Environment*.
   c. Select and italicize the publication titles *The ABCs of Integrated Learning* and *Total Quality Management in the Education Environment*.
   d. Select and bold the following text:
      1) The headings *DATE:*, *TO:*, *FROM:*, and *SUBJECT:*.
      2) *Tuesday, November 16* in the third paragraph.
      3) *7:00 p.m. to 8:00 p.m.* in the third paragraph.
   e. Insert your initials at the end of the document where you see *xx*. Change the document name after your initials from Memo 01 to Ch 03, SA 01.
4. After keying the document, move the insertion point to the beginning of the document, and then change justification to full.
5. Save, print, and then close Ch 03, SA 01.

Assessment 2

1. At a clear editing window, key the memo shown in figure 3.14. Bold the text as shown. Use the Center command, Shift + F7, to center the dates.
2. After keying the document, move the insertion point to the beginning of the first paragraph, and then change justification to full.
3. Save the memo and name it Ch 03, SA 02.
4. Print and then close Ch 03, SA 02.

FIGURE

3.14 *Assessment 2*

DATE: May 6, 2003

TO: All College Staff

FROM: James Vaira, Training and Education

SUBJECT: WORDPERFECT CLASSES

Tampa Community College employees will have the opportunity to complete training in Corel WordPerfect 10. This training is designed for current users of WordPerfect who want to become familiar with the changes in the new version. The WordPerfect classes will be held in Room 200 from 9:00 a.m. to 11:00 a.m. on the following days:

Wednesday, May 21
Thursday, May 22
Tuesday, June 3
Thursday, June 5

Room 200 contains 15 computers; therefore, each training session is limited to 15 employees. Preregistration is required. To register, please call Training and Education at extension 6552.

xx:Ch 03, SA 02

Assessment 3

(Note: In this exercise and other exercises in the text, you will be required to create business letters. Please refer to appendix B at the end of this text for the correct placement and spacing of elements in a block-style business letter.)

1. At a clear editing window, key the business letter shown in figure 3.15. Bold, center, and italicize the text as shown.
2. Save the letter and name it Ch 03, SA 03.
3. Print and then close Ch 03, SA 03.

FIGURE

3.15 *Assessment 3*

January 14, 2003

Mr. Anthony Maloney
Tampa Community College
6100 Park Drive
Tampa, FL 33610

Dear Mr. Maloney:

The first meeting of the members of the **Outcomes Assessment Project (OAP)** was held yesterday, January 13. As you know from our conversations, the purpose of the project is to determine a process for assessing the success of graduating students as well as determining if college programs are meeting the needs of the business community. At the meeting, the members agreed that the top priority for the project is to develop a survey instrument.

With your expertise in project management, we feel you can provide us with needed information to begin the project. Our next meeting will be held at St. Petersburg College on the following day:

Wednesday, February 5, 2003
1:30 to 3:00 p.m.
Room 104

If you can attend this meeting, please call me at (813) 555-9660, extension 1335, to determine specific topics. The input you can provide the project members will be invaluable.

Very truly yours,

Dawn Perez, Coordinator
Outcomes Assessment Project

xx:Ch 03, SA 03

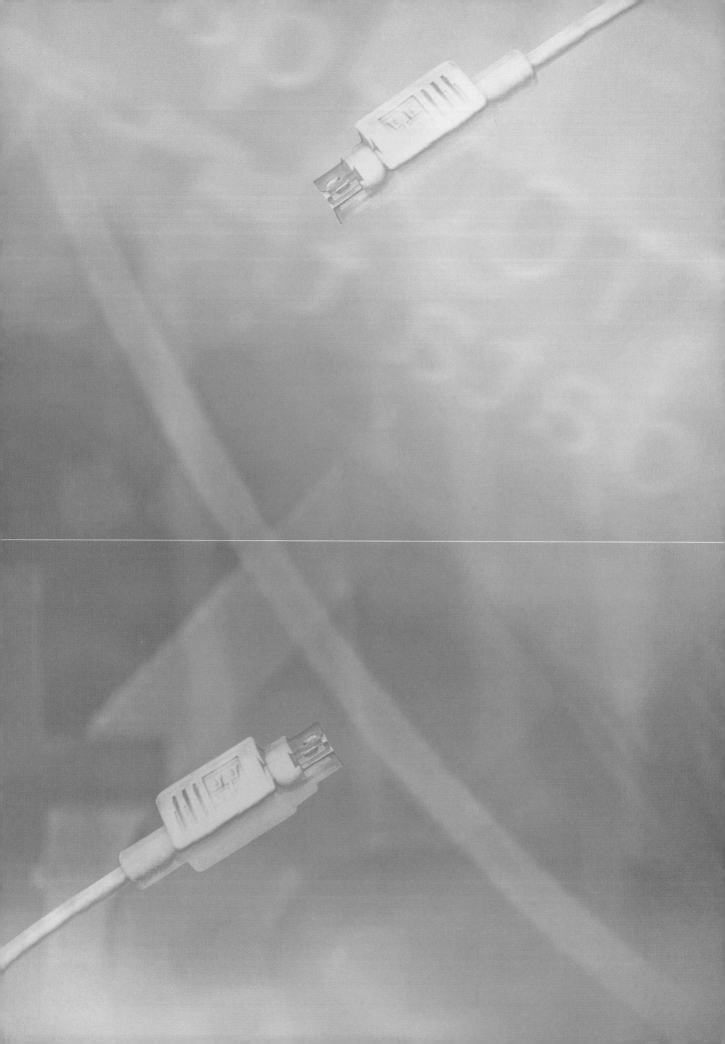

CHAPTER 4

Formatting Documents

PERFORMANCE OBJECTIVES

Upon successful completion of chapter 4, you will be able to:
- Change margins in a document
- Indent text in paragraphs
- Create numbered and bulleted paragraphs
- Turn on/off the Widow/Orphan feature
- Insert page breaks
- Center text vertically on a page
- Insert page numbering in a document

Chapter 04

When you begin creating a document, WordPerfect provides default left, right, top, and bottom margins of 1 inch. When text is keyed and the insertion point reaches the right margin, WordPerfect automatically wraps text down to the next line. A standard piece of paper is 8.5 inches wide and 11 inches long. With the one-inch default margins, WordPerfect begins the printed text 1 inch from the top left corner of the paper and ends 1 inch from the bottom right corner of the paper. Therefore, an actual printed text line is 6.5 inches and 9 vertical inches are available for text to be printed on a standard page.

As you create a long document, you will notice when the insertion point nears Line 9.65", a page break is inserted at the next line in the document. The line below the page break is the beginning of page 2. While WordPerfect's default settings break each page near Line 9.65", several features can affect the location of page breaks.

Changing Margins

Even though the default margins may be appropriate for many documents, there will be occasions when you need to increase or decrease margin settings. You can change the margins at the Page setup dialog box, or the left and right margins with the Ruler.

As with justification codes, margin changes take effect from the location of the code to the end of the document or until another margin code is encountered. When left or right margin settings are changed, a code is inserted in the document at the beginning of the paragraph where the insertion point is positioned. Top and bottom margin codes are inserted at the beginning of the page where the insertion point is located. For example, if the insertion point is located in the middle of page 3 when the top and bottom margins are changed, the codes are inserted at the beginning of page 3. If you want top and bottom margins to affect the entire document, position the insertion point on page 1 before displaying the Page setup dialog box with the Page Setup tab selected. While in Reveal Codes, you can display the Page setup dialog box by positioning the arrow pointer on the margin code and double-clicking the left mouse button.

In addition to the code changing top and/or bottom margins, WordPerfect inserts a Delay code at the beginning of the document. The code at the beginning of the document indicates that formatting has been added to the document that is delayed until the code is encountered. The number after the word *Delay* identifies which Delay code it relates to within the document. If you delete either of the Delay codes, the other is removed.

If you want to delete a margin code, display Reveal Codes and do one of the following:

- Position your cursor to the right of the code and press Backspace.
- Position your cursor to the left of the code and press Delete.
- Drag the code out of the Reveal Codes window.

If all margin codes are deleted, margins will revert back to the default of 1 inch or to the last margin setting.

Changing Margins at the Page Setup Dialog Box

Margins can also be changed at the Page setup dialog box. Click Format and then Margins; Format, point to Page, and then click Page Setup; or File, Page Setup to display the dialog box shown in figure 4.1.

4.1 *Page Setup Dialog Box*

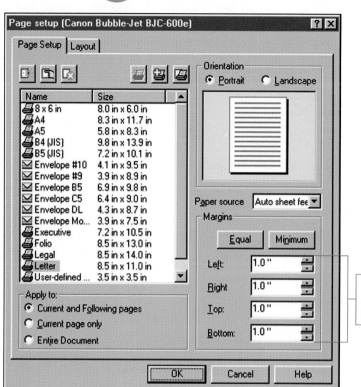

Select the Page Setup tab and click in either the Top, Bottom, Left, or Right margin box and key a new value. You can enter the value in whole numbers, decimals, or fractions. You can also click either the up- or down-pointing arrow in these boxes to scroll to a value.

Changing Margins with the Ruler

WordPerfect provides a Ruler that, together with the mouse, can be used to change margins and tabs. If the Ruler is not displayed, you can display it by clicking View and then Ruler. The Ruler, shown in figure 4.2, displays below the Main property bar.

4.2 *Ruler*

First Line Indent

Left Margin Marker

Right Margin Marker

The left margin marker displays at the left side of the Ruler above the one-inch mark as identified in figure 4.2. The right margin marker displays at the right side of the Ruler above the 7.5-inch mark. To change the left margin in a document using the Ruler, you would position the arrow pointer on the left margin marker, hold down the left mouse button, drag the margin marker to the desired location, and then release the button. Change the right margin in a document using the Ruler by completing similar steps.

By positioning your mouse in the white area above the Ruler and clicking the right mouse button, you can display a QuickMenu, from which you can also change top, bottom, left, and right margins.

(Before completing computer exercises, delete the Chapter 03 *folder on your disk. Next, download the* Chapter 04 *data files from the Internet Resource Center to the* Chapter 04 *folder you have created on your disk, and then make* Chapter 04 *the active folder.)*

exercise

Changing Margins

1. Open Para 02.
2. Save the document with Save As and name it Ch 04, Ex 01.
3. Change the top and bottom margins to 1.5 inches by completing the following steps:
   a. Click Format and then Margins.
   b. At the Page setup dialog box with the Page Setup tab selected, click the up-pointing triangle at the right side of the Top text box until 1.5" displays.
   c. Click the up-pointing triangle at the right side of the Bottom text box until 1.5" displays.
   d. Click OK or press Enter.
4. Change the left and right margins to 1.75 inches using the Ruler by completing the following steps:
   a. If the Ruler is not visible, turn it on by clicking View and then Ruler.

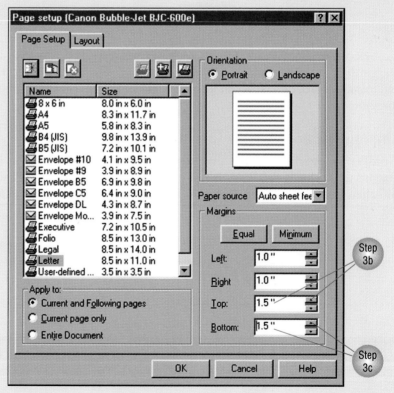

70

Chapter Four

b. Position the tip of the arrow pointer on the left margin marker.

c. Hold down the left mouse button, drag the margin marker to the right until *Left Margin 1.75"* displays, and then release the mouse button.

d. Position the tip of the arrow pointer on the right margin marker.

e. Hold down the left mouse button, drag the margin marker to the left until *Right Margin 1.75"* displays, and then release the mouse button.

5. Save, print, and then close Ch 04, Ex 01.

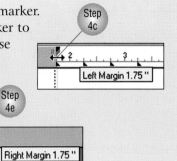

Indenting Text

A variety of options are available to force text to wrap to a tab setting instead of the left margin, including

- Indenting all lines of a paragraph from the left margin
- Indenting all lines of a paragraph on both sides (called double indenting)
- Indenting all lines except the first line (called a hanging indent)

To create these formats, use shortcut keys, the Ruler, or options from the Paragraph Format dialog box.

Indenting the First Line of a Paragraph

You can indent the first line of a paragraph by pressing the Tab key or with an option from the Paragraph Format dialog box.

If you use the Tab key to indent the first line of a paragraph, the insertion point is indented to the first tab setting, which is, by default, 0.5 inch. When you press the Tab key, a code, Left Tab, is inserted in the document and can be seen in Reveal Codes.

If you want to indent the first line of text to a specific measurement (other than tab settings), or if you want the first line of all paragraphs indented, use the Paragraph Format dialog box shown in figure 4.3. Changes made at the Paragraph Format dialog box affect every paragraph in the document from the location of the code to the end of the document or until another indent code is encountered.

4.3 *Paragraph Format Dialog Box*

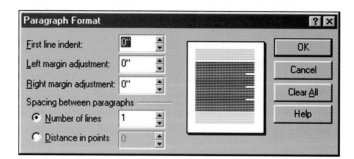

exercise 2

Indenting Paragraphs to a Specific Measurement

1. Open Para 04.
2. Save the document with Save As and name it Ch 04, Ex 02.
3. Indent the first line of each paragraph 0.25 inch by completing the following steps:
   a. Make sure the insertion point is positioned at the beginning of the first paragraph.
   b. Click Format, point to Paragraph, and then click Format.
   c. At the Paragraph Format dialog box, key **0.25** in the First line indent text box.
   d. Click OK or press Enter.
4. Save, print, and then close Ch 04, Ex 02.

Indenting Text from the Left Margin

Text in a paragraph can be indented to a tab setting or to a specific measurement from the left margin. When text is indented, all lines in the paragraph are indented to the tab or specific measurement. This is different from pressing the Tab key, which only indents the current line. The indentation is canceled by pressing Enter.

To indent all text in a paragraph to a tab setting, use one of the following methods:

- Press F7 at the beginning of the paragraph.
- Click Format, point to Paragraph, and then click Indent.
- Display a QuickMenu by right-clicking at the beginning of a paragraph and selecting Indent.

exercise 3

Indenting Paragraphs

1. Open Memo 02.
2. Save the document with Save As and name it Ch 04, Ex 03.
3. Indent the second paragraph in the document (containing the book title) to the first tab setting using the shortcut command by completing the following steps:
   a. Position the insertion point at the beginning of the second paragraph.
   b. Press F7.
4. Indent the third paragraph in the document to the first tab setting using the Format drop-down menu by completing the following steps:
   a. Position the insertion point at the beginning of the third paragraph.
   b. Click Format, point to Paragraph, and then click Indent.
5. Indent the fourth paragraph in the document to the first tab setting using a QuickMenu by completing the following steps:
   a. Position the insertion point at the beginning of the fourth paragraph.
   b. Position the I-beam pointer on the insertion point and then click the *right* mouse button.
   c. At the QuickMenu that displays, click Indent.
6. Indent the fifth paragraph in the document by completing steps similar to those in steps 3, 4, or 5.
7. Insert your initials at the end of the document where you see *xx*. Change the document name after your initials from Memo 02 to Ch 04, Ex 03.
8. Save, print, and then close Ch 04, Ex 03.

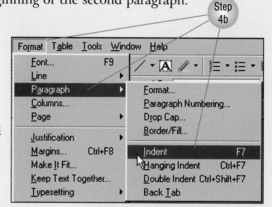

Step 4b

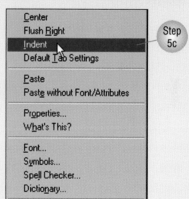

Step 5c

Indenting Text from the Left and Right Margins

A paragraph that you want visually set off from other text in a document or a paragraph containing a quotation can be indented from the left as well as the right margin. Indenting from the left and right margins gives a paragraph a balanced look. You can indent text from both sides by choosing one of the following methods:

- Press Ctrl + Shift + F7. Each time you press this key combination, the text is indented to the next tab stop.

- Click Format, point to Paragraph, and then click Double Indent.

exercise 4

Indenting Text from Both Margins and Returning to the Default

1. Open Quote.
2. Save the document with Save As and name it Ch 04, Ex 04.
3. Indent the second paragraph 0.5 inch from the left and right margins by completing the following steps:
    a. Position the insertion point at the beginning of the second paragraph.
    b. Click Format, point to Paragraph, and then click Format.
    c. At the Paragraph Format dialog box, select the *0"* that displays in the Left margin adjustment text box, and then key **0.5**.
    d. Select the *0"* that displays in the Right margin adjustment text box and then key **0.5**.
    e. Click OK or press Enter.
4. Return the left and right margin adjustments to 0" for the third paragraph by completing the following steps:
    a. Position the insertion point at the beginning of the third paragraph.
    b. Click Format, point to Paragraph, and then click Format.
    c. At the Paragraph Format dialog box, select the *0.500"* that displays in the Left margin adjustment text box, and then key **0**.
    d. Select the *0.500"* that displays in the Right margin adjustment text box and then key **0**.
    e. Click OK or press Enter.
5. Indent the fourth paragraph in the document to the first tab setting from the left and right margins by completing the following steps:
    a. Position the insertion point at the beginning of the fourth paragraph.
    b. Press Ctrl + Shift + F7.
6. Save, print, and then close Ch 04, Ex 04.

Step 3c

Step 3d

Paragraph Format   ? ☒

First line indent: 0"

Left margin adjustment: 0.500"

Right margin adjustment: 0.500"

Spacing between paragraphs

   ⦿ Number of lines   1

   ◯ Distance in points   0

OK   Cancel   Clear All   Help

Creating Hanging Indent Paragraphs

With WordPerfect's Hanging Indent feature, you can create paragraphs such as bibliographic entries where the first line begins at the left margin, but the second and all subsequent lines in the paragraph are indented to the first tab setting. Figure 4.4 shows an example of a hanging indent paragraph.

4.4 *Hanging Indent Paragraph*

This paragraph demonstrates the hanging indent feature in WordPerfect 10. Create a hanging indent with the shortcut command Ctrl + F7, click Format, point to Paragraph, and then click Hanging Indent, or use options at the Paragraph Format dialog box.

To create a hanging indent, choose one of the following methods:
- Position the cursor at the beginning of the paragraph and press Ctrl + F7.
- Click Format, point to Paragraph, and then click Hanging Indent.

When you create a hanging indent paragraph with the shortcut command or the Paragraph option from the Format drop-down menu, special codes are inserted in the document at the location of the insertion point.

When using the Paragraph Format dialog box to create a hanging indent, key a negative number in the First line indent text box and then key a positive number in the Left margin adjustment text box.

If you use the Paragraph Format dialog box or the Ruler to indent text in a paragraph, each paragraph is indented from the location of the code to the end of the document or until another code is encountered.

exercise

Creating Hanging Indents on Single Paragraphs

1. Open Bibliography.
2. Save the document with Save As and name it Ch 04, Ex 05.
3. Hang-indent the first paragraph by completing the following steps:
   a. Make sure the insertion point is positioned at the beginning of the first paragraph.
   b. Press Ctrl + F7.
4. Indent the remaining paragraphs by completing the following steps:
   a. Make sure the insertion point is positioned at the beginning of the second paragraph.
   b. Click Format, point to Paragraph, and then click Format.
   c. At the Paragraph Format dialog box, key **-0.5** in the First line indent text box.
   d. Select the current measurement in the Left margin adjustment text box and then key **0.5**.
   e. Click OK or press Enter
5. Select and then italicize the title of the publication in each paragraph.
6. Save, print, and then close Ch 04, Ex 05.

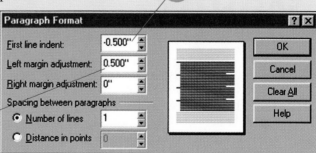

Inserting Numbers and Bullets with the Bullets & Numbering Dialog Box

Numbers or bullets can be inserted in a document with options at the Bullets & Numbering dialog box with the appropriate tab selected as shown in figure 4.5. To display this dialog box, click Insert and then Outline/Bullets & Numbering. A variety of numbers and bullet styles are available.

FIGURE

4.5 *Bullets & Numbering Dialog Box*

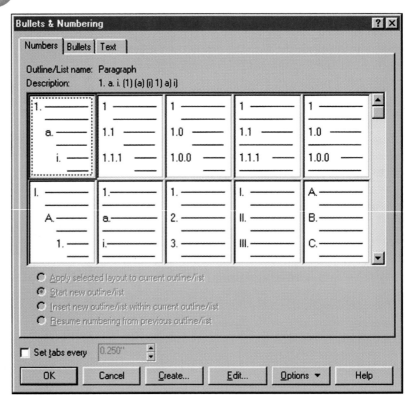

exercise 6

Inserting Bullets Using the Bullets & Numbering Dialog Box

1. Open Para 03.
2. Save the document with Save As and name it Ch 04, Ex 06.
3. Insert bullets before each of the paragraphs by completing the following steps:
   a. Select the entire document using the mouse.
   b. Display the Bullets & Numbering dialog box by clicking Insert and then Outline/Bullets & Numbering.
   c. At the Bullets & Numbering dialog box, click the Bullets tab.

d. Click the box containing the check marks. (This is the third box from the left in the bottom row.)

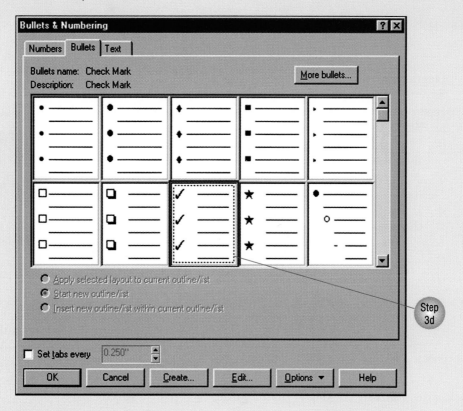

e. Click OK or press Enter.
f. If necessary, click outside the selected area to deselect the text.
4. Save, print, and then close Ch 04, Ex 06.

Inserting Bullets and Numbers with Buttons

In addition to the Bullets & Numbering dialog box, numbers and bullets can be inserted in a document with the Numbering button on the Toolbar and bullets can be inserted with the Bullets button.

Numbering

Click the Numbering button on the Toolbar and WordPerfect inserts the number *1* followed by a period at the left margin and moves the insertion point to the first tab setting. You can change the numbering method by clicking the down-pointing triangle at the right side of the Numbering button. This causes a palette of numbering styles to display. Click the desired style and the first number (or letter) is inserted at the left margin and the insertion point is moved to the first tab setting. Use similar steps to insert or change bullets in a document.

Bullets

exercise 7

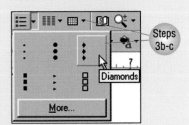

Inserting Bullets with the Bullets Button

1. Open Para 04.
2. Save the document with Save As and name it Ch 04, Ex 07.
3. Insert bullets before each of the paragraphs by completing the following steps:
   a. Select the entire document using the mouse.
   b. Click the down-pointing triangle at the right side of the Bullets button on the Toolbar.
   c. At the palette of bullet choices that displays, click the diamonds (last symbol at the right in the first row).
   d. If necessary, click outside the selected area to deselect the text.
4. Save, print, and then close Ch 04, Ex 07.

Keeping Text Together on a Page

The Keep Text Together dialog box, shown in figure 4.6, contains three options you can use to keep a certain number of lines together on a page—Widow/Orphan, Block protect, and Conditional end of page. With these features, you can control where page breaks occur in a document. Display the Keep Text Together dialog box by clicking Format and then Keep Text Together.

F I G U R E

4.6 *Keep Text Together Dialog Box*

Click this option to turn on the Widow/Orphan feature.

Turning on Widow/Orphan

In a long document, you will want to avoid creating widows or orphans. A *widow* is the last line of a paragraph that appears at the top of a page. An *orphan* is the first line of a paragraph that appears at the bottom of a page.

WordPerfect contains a feature that lets you control whether widows or orphans appear in a document. This feature, called Widow/Orphan, is turned off by default. At this setting, WordPerfect inserts page breaks without considering whether a widow or orphan has occurred. When this feature is turned on, WordPerfect takes the first line of a paragraph to the next page or breaks the page a line sooner so that a minimum of two lines of a paragraph fall at the top of a page.

To turn on the Widow/Orphan feature, display the Keep Text Together dialog box, and then click the check box in the Widow/Orphan section. To turn off the Widow/Orphan feature, complete similar steps to remove the check mark in the Widow/Orphan check box.

Turning on the Widow/Orphan Feature

1. Open Report 01.
2. Save the report with Save As and name it Ch 04, Ex 08.
3. Make sure the insertion point is located somewhere on page 1 and then turn on the Widow/Orphan feature by completing the following steps:
   a. Click Format and then Keep Text Together.
   b. At the Keep Text Together dialog box, click the check box in the Widow/Orphan section (this inserts a check mark).
   c. Click OK or press Enter.
4. Save, print, and then close Ch 04, Ex 08.

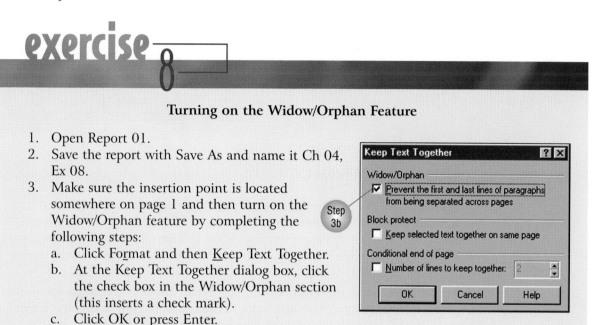

Step 3b

Keep Text Together

Widow/Orphan
☑ Prevent the first and last lines of paragraphs from being separated across pages

Block protect
☐ Keep selected text together on same page

Conditional end of page
☐ Number of lines to keep together: 2

OK   Cancel   Help

Protecting Selected Text

With the second option from the Keep Text Together dialog box, Block protect, you can tell WordPerfect to protect selected text from being divided by a page break. For example, you might want to keep a list of numbered items together on a page.

Preventing Page Breaks within a Selected Block

1. Open Report 01.
2. Save the report with Save As and name it Ch 04, Ex 09.
3. Make sure the insertion point is located at the beginning of the document and then change the left, right, top, and bottom margins to 1.5 inches.
4. Select the paragraph and the items preceded by bullets toward the end of the first page by completing the following steps:
   a. Position the insertion point at the left margin of the line that begins *The advantages of light wave systems...*.
   b. Select the lines of text through *relative low cost*.
   c. Click Format and then Keep Text Together.

d. At the Keep Text Together dialog box, click the check box in the Block protect section (this inserts a check mark).
e. Click OK or press Enter.
f. Deselect the text by pressing F8 or clicking the arrow pointer outside the selected area.

5. Save, print, and then close Ch 04, Ex 09.

Step 4d

Inserting Hard Page Breaks

WordPerfect's default settings break each page after approximately Line 9.65". If you have turned on the Widow/Orphan feature or changed the top or bottom margins, page breaks may vary. Even with these features, however, page breaks may occur in undesirable locations. To remedy these occurrences, you can insert your own page break.

In the Draft mode, the WordPerfect page break displays as a single line across the screen. The page break you insert displays as a double line across the screen. The default page break is called a *soft page break* and a page break you insert is called a *hard page break*. Soft page breaks automatically adjust if text is added to or deleted from a document. A hard page break does not adjust. If text is added to or deleted from a document with a hard page break, check the break to determine whether it is still in a desirable location.

To insert a page break, move the insertion point to the position where you want the page to break, click Insert and then New Page; or press Ctrl + Enter. Always check page breaks in a document; some require a judgment call that only you can make.

Inserting Page Breaks

1. Open Report 01.
2. Save the report with Save As and name it Ch 04, Ex 10.
3. Insert a hard page break at the line beginning *The speed at which information...* by completing the following steps:
   a. Position the insertion point at the left margin of the line beginning *The speed at which information...* (toward the end of the first page).
   b. Click Insert and then New Page; or press Ctrl + Enter.
4. Insert a hard page break at the left margin of the line beginning *Computing and telecommunications...* (toward the end of the second page).
5. Save the report again with the same name (Ch 04, Ex 10).
6. Print and then close Ch 04, Ex 10.

Centering Text Vertically on the Page

With WordPerfect's centering page(s) option, you can center text vertically on the current page and/or subsequent pages. You may, for example, want to center vertically the title page of a report, a short letter or memo, a table, or an illustration.

With options from the Center Page(s) dialog box, shown in figure 4.7, you can center text vertically on only the page where the insertion point is positioned or center text on current and subsequent pages. To display the Center Page(s) dialog box, click Format, point to Page, and then click Center.

FIGURE

4.7 *Center Page(s) Dialog Box*

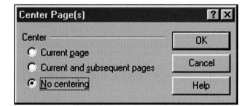

exercise 11

Centering Text Vertically

1. At a clear editing window, key the text shown in figure 4.8. Center and bold the text as indicated. Press the Enter key the number of times indicated.
2. Center the text vertically on the page by completing the following steps:
   a. With the insertion point positioned anywhere in the page, click Format, point to Page, and then click Center.
   b. At the Center Page(s) dialog box, click Current page.

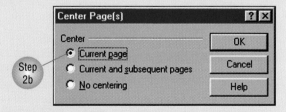

Step 2b

   c. Click OK or press Enter.
3. Save the document and name it Ch 04, Ex 11.
4. Print and then close Ch 04, Ex 11.

HISTORY OF TELECOMMUNICATIONS
press Enter 15 times
by Ramona Salas
press Enter 15 times
CIS 120
November 14, 2002

Inserting Page Numbering

WordPerfect, by default, does not print page numbers on a page. For documents such as one-page memos and letters, this is appropriate. For longer documents, however, page numbers may be needed. WordPerfect includes several options for numbering pages in documents. Page numbers can appear in a variety of locations on the page and can be turned on and off in the same document.

Numbering Pages in a Document

When page numbering is turned on in a document, WordPerfect inserts a page numbering code at the beginning of the page where the insertion point is located. If you want page numbering to appear on all pages of the document, position the insertion point somewhere on page 1. Turn on page numbering by clicking Format, point to Page, and then click Numbering. This displays the Select Page Numbering Format dialog box shown in figure 4.9.

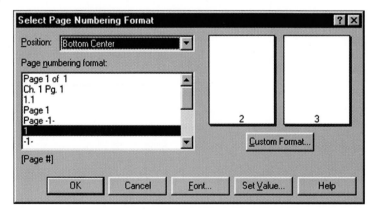

When a document includes page numbering, WordPerfect subtracts two lines from the total number of lines printed on a page. One line is subtracted for the page number and the other to separate the page number from text. Page numbers appear on the screen in Page and Two-Pages view, but not Draft view.

Suppressing Page Numbering

WordPerfect includes a feature that lets you suppress page numbering on specific pages. This is different from turning page numbering off. When you turn page numbering off, it stays off until the document ends or until numbering is turned back on. With the Suppress dialog box, the page number is turned off for that specific page and turned back on again for the other pages. To suppress a page number on a specific page, position the insertion point anywhere on that page, then click Format, point to Page, and then click Suppress. This displays the Suppress dialog box shown in figure 4.10. To suppress page numbering, click Page numbering at the Suppress dialog box, and then click OK or press Enter.

F I G U R E

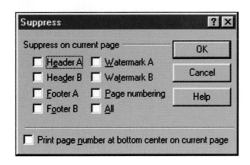

4.10 **Suppress Dialog Box**

The Print page number at bottom center on current page option from the Suppress dialog box can be used to print the page number at the bottom center of the first page of a title page or report. The remaining page numbers will appear in the location identified at the Select Page Numbering Format dialog box.

exercise 12

Numbering Pages at the Bottom Right and Suppressing Page Numbering

1. Open Report 02.
2. Save the report with Save As and name it Ch 04, Ex 12.
3. With the insertion point positioned anywhere on the first page, turn on the Widow/Orphan feature.
4. With the insertion point positioned anywhere on the first page, turn on page numbering and number pages at the bottom right of the page by completing the following steps:
   a. Click Format, point to Page, and then click Numbering.

b. At the Select Page Numbering Format dialog box, click the down-pointing triangle at the right side of the Position text box.

c. Click *Bottom Right* at the drop-down list that displays.

d. Click OK or press Enter.

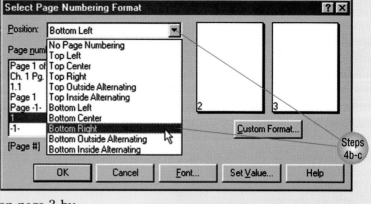

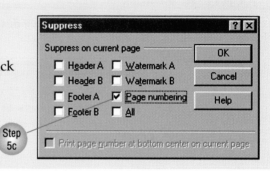

5. Suppress page numbering on page 3 by completing the following steps:

a. Position the insertion point anywhere on page 3.

b. Click Format, point to Page, and then click Suppress.

c. At the Suppress dialog box, click Page numbering.

d. Click OK or press Enter.

6. Save, print, and then close Ch 04, Ex 12.

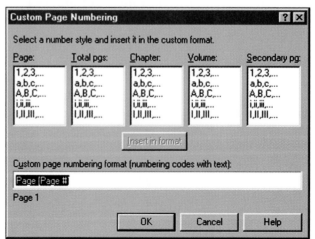

Changing the Page Numbering Method

When page numbering is turned on in a document, WordPerfect uses Arabic numbers (1, 2, 3, and so on). With the Custom Format button from the Select Page Numbering Format dialog box, you can change this numbering method to

- Lowercase letters (a, b, c)
- Uppercase letters (A, B, C)
- Lowercase Roman numerals (i, ii, iii)
- Uppercase Roman numerals (I, II, III)

These choices are offered at the Custom Page Numbering dialog box shown in figure 4.11

FIGURE

4.11 *Custom Page Numbering Dialog Box*

Custom Page Numbering

Select a number style and insert it in the custom format.

Page:	Total pgs:	Chapter:	Volume:	Secondary pg:
1,2,3,...	1,2,3,...	1,2,3,...	1,2,3,...	1,2,3,...
a,b,c,...	a,b,c,...	a,b,c,...	a,b,c,...	a,b,c,...
A,B,C,...	A,B,C,...	A,B,C,...	A,B,C,...	A,B,C,...
i,ii,iii,...	i,ii,iii,...	i,ii,iii,...	i,ii,iii,...	i,ii,iii,...
I,II,III,...	I,II,III,...	I,II,III,...	I,II,III,...	I,II,III,...

Insert in format

Custom page numbering format (numbering codes with text):

Page [Page #]

Page 1

OK   Cancel   Help

Adding Accompanying Text

At the Custom Page Numbering dialog box, text can be included with the page number. For example, the word *Page* can be included before the page number, such as *Page 3*. Or, a section heading can be included with the page number, such as *Outcomes Assessment - 5*. Just key the text you want in the C̲ustom page numbering format (numbering codes with text): text box. If you want accompanying text to appear before the page number, press the left arrow key, and then key the accompanying text. If you want the accompanying text to follow the page number, press the right arrow key, and then key the accompanying text.

Adding Additional Page Numbering

Additional page numbering options are available in WordPerfect. In addition to the method described earlier, other options are explained below:

- Secondary page numbering lets you add a second page numbering level. Periodicals or journals sometimes number every page consecutively for the year while also numbering each page within an issue. For this situation, you can use the regular numbering method for the consecutive numbering for the year and the secondary method for the numbering within the individual issue. Secondary page numbers operate exactly like page numbers. Page numbers and secondary page numbers increment automatically.

- With chapter and volume numbering, you can include chapter or volume numbers in a document. For example, if a document contains three chapters, you can have the page numbering list the chapter number as well as the page number. Chapter and volume numbers do not increment automatically like page numbers and secondary page numbers. You must increment them manually.

CHAPTER summary

➤ The one-inch default left, right, top, and bottom margins can be changed by dragging the margin guidelines, or at the Page setup dialog box with the Page Setup tab selected. Margins can be set by whole inches as well as by tenths and hundredths of inches.

➤ When margin settings are changed, codes such as `Lft Mar: 1.5"` and `Rgt Mar: 1.5"` display in Reveal Codes. Margin codes appear at the beginning of the paragraph in which the insertion point was located when the margins were changed.

➤ To indent the first line of a paragraph by a specific measurement (other than tab settings), use the Paragraph Format dialog box or the first-line indent marker on the Ruler.

➤ The Indent feature will indent text from the left margin to the first tab setting or to a specific measurement.

➤ The Double Indent feature will indent text from both the left and right margins.

➤ The first line of a hanging indent paragraph begins at the left margin and the rest of the paragraph is indented.

➤ Use the Bullets & Numbering dialog box to easily insert bullets or numbers in a document.

➤ Click the Numbering button on the Toolbar to insert numbering in a document. Click the down-pointing triangle at the right side of the Numbering button to display a palette of numbering styles.

➤ Click the Bullets button on the Toolbar to insert bullets in a document. Click the down-pointing triangle at the right side of the Bullets button to display a palette of bullets.

➤ WordPerfect inserts a page break at approximately 10 inches from the top of the page. With the default one-inch top and bottom margins, this allows a total of 9 inches of text to be printed on a standard page.

➤ The Keep Text Together dialog box contains three options you can use to keep a certain number of lines together on one page: Widow/Orphan, Block protect, and Conditional end of page.

➤ If an automatic page break (soft page break) occurs in an undesirable location, you can insert a page break (hard page break). A page break inserted manually in a document is called a hard page break and appears in Draft mode as a double line across the screen.

➤ To center text vertically on one page or on all pages in a document, use the options at the Center Page(s) dialog box. The text will look centered in the Page and Two-Pages viewing modes, but not the Draft mode.

➤ WordPerfect includes several options at the Select Page Numbering Format dialog box. The page numbers in a document can be placed in different locations on the page turned on and off, or the format of the page numbering can be changed.

➤ These options are also available at the Select Page Numbering Format dialog box: changing the page number, changing from Arabic to Roman numerals, adding text to the page number, adding a secondary page number, and numbering chapter and volume.

COMMANDS summary

Command	Mouse	Keyboard
Change margins	Format, Margins; or Format, Page, Page Setup; or File, Page Setup; or drag the margin marker to desired location	Ctrl + F8
Indent the first line of a paragraph	Format, Paragraph, Format	Tab Key
Indent from the left margin	Format, Paragraph, Indent	F7
Indent from both margins	Format, Paragraph, Double Indent	Ctrl + Shift + F7
Create a hanging indent	Format, Paragraph, Hanging Indent	Ctrl + F7
Apply bullets to a list	Insert, Outline/Bullets & Numbering; or click the Bullets button on the Main property bar	
Apply numbers to a list	Insert, Outline/Bullets & Numbering; or click the Numbers button on the Main property bar	
Display the Keep Text Together dialog box	Format, Keep Text Together	
Insert page break	Insert, New Page	Ctrl + Enter
Display the Center Page(s) dialog box	Format, Page, Center	
Display the Select Page Numbering Format dialog box	Format, Page, Numbering	
Display the Suppress dialog box	Format, Page, Suppress	

CONCEPTS check

Matching: On a blank sheet of paper, provide the correct letter or letters that match each definition.

- (A) 1 inch
- (B) 11 inches
- (C) 11.5 inches
- (D) 7.5 inches
- (E) 8.5 inches
- (F) 9 inches
- (G) Center Page(s) dialog box
- (H) Ctrl + Enter

- (I) Hanging indent paragraph
- (J) Indenting first line of a paragraph
- (K) Indenting text from both margins
- (L) Indenting text from left margin
- (M) Orphan
- (N) Shift + Enter
- (O) Widow

1. Could be used for creating a bibliography.

2. Used when inserting long quotations in a document.

3. Length of a standard piece of paper.

4. Default top and bottom margins.

5. Total inches of printed vertical text on a page.

6. Press these keys on the keyboard to insert a hard page break in a document.

7. This is the term for the last line of a paragraph that appears at the top of a page.

8. Center text vertically on a page with options at this dialog box.

Completion: On a blank sheet of paper, indicate the correct term, symbol, or command for each item.

1. This is the width in inches of a standard piece of paper.

2. This is the default left and right margin settings.

3. This is the width of the default line for text.

4. This dialog box contains options for changing margins.

5. The margin code would be found here in relation to a paragraph.

6. This is the keyboard command to indent a paragraph from the left margin.

7. This is the keyboard command to indent a paragraph from the left and right margins.

8. This keyboard command will create a hanging indent paragraph.

SKILLS check

Assessment 1

1. At a clear editing window, change the left and right margins to 1.25 inches, and then key the document shown in figure 4.12. Bold and center the text as indicated.
2. After keying the document, move the insertion point back to the beginning of the document, and then change the justification to full.
3. Save the document and name it Ch 04, SA 01.
4. Print and then close Ch 04, SA 01.

FIGURE

4.12 *Assessment 1*

EXPANSION AND ENHANCEMENT

OF LOCAL AND WIDE AREA NETWORKS

The foundation of the national telecommunications network is the publicly owned telephone network. This network, which was originally designed, installed, and operated by AT&T and local independent telephone companies to provide traditional voice messaging services, now offers a multitude of information services, including

1. **Electronic Mail/Message Systems.** Individuals have an electronic mailbox in a computer that is accessed via a computer terminal such as a microcomputer.

2. **Voice Mail.** The primary difference in electronic mail/message systems and voice mail is the input/output device, which is a telephone rather than a computer.

3. **Value Added Networks.** These are special services provided by telecommunications companies in addition to transferring information, such as storing information for delivery at a later time, providing security features so that no one is able to intercept the information, and selecting alternative routes for transmitting that help reduce costs.

4. **Expanded Voice Services.** Examples include voice mail, voice responses to answer phones and direct callers to specific departments, and systems that provide callers with an electronic voice response to questions such as weather information, bank balances, and time of day.

5. **Database Services.** Examples include airline reservation systems that allow individuals to reserve seats on flights.

6. **Data Networking.** This includes the connection of computers within a complex, such as a school, or connecting computers at distant sites, such as two schools located in separate areas, for the purpose of exchanging data.

Assessment 2

1. At a clear editing window, make the following changes:
   a. Change the left and right margins to 1.5 inches.
   b. Change the line spacing to double (2).
2. Key the document shown in figure 4.13. Bold, center, and italicize text as indicated. Apply a hanging indent to the paragraphs as shown.
3. Center the document vertically on the page.
4. Save the document and name it Ch 04, SA 02.
5. Print and then close Ch 04, SA 02.

F I G U R E

4.13 *Assessment 2*

BIBLIOGRAPHY

Brickman, Andrew C. (2001). "Networking Computers." *Power Computing*, (pp. 10-14). Omaha, NE: Myers-Townsend Publishing Company.
Daughtery, Megan A. (2000). "Managing a Local Area Network." *Computer Technologies*, (pp. 19-23). Jacksonville, FL: Macadam Publishers.
Layug, Angela M. (1999). "Wireless LANs." *Business Offices of the 90s*, (pp. 31-45). Denver, CO: Mile-High Publishing International.
Owen, Kerry H. (2001). "Interconnecting Internal LANs." *Network Management*, (pp. 22-31). Fairbanks, AK: Marsh & Monroe Press.

Assessment 3

1. Open Report 04.
2. Save the report with Save As and name it Ch 04, SA 03.
3. With the insertion point positioned at the beginning of the document, make the following changes:
   a. Change the top, left, and right margins to 1.5 inches.
   b. Turn on the Widow/Orphan feature.
   c. Number pages at the bottom center of each page.
4. Insert a hard page break at the line that contains the heading *CHAPTER 4: DEVELOPMENT OF TECHNOLOGY, 1950 - 1960*.
5. Select the heading *World War II* (toward the end of the first page) and three lines of text below the heading and identify the lines as a block to be protected.
6. Save, print, and then close Ch 04, SA 03.

PERFORMANCE Assessments

CREATING AND PREPARING DOCUMENTS

INTEGRATING SKILLS

In this unit, you have learned to create, edit, and save WordPerfect 10 documents using selection techniques, undo and redo features, text formatting features, the Reveal Codes window, QuickMenu features, line spacing options, justification options, help features, margin and indent features, keep text together options, and page numbering features.

(Before completing computer exercises, delete the Chapter 04 *folder on your disk. Next, download the* Unit 01 *data files from the Internet Resource Center to the* Unit 01 *folder you have created on your disk, and then make* Unit 01 *the active folder.)*

Assessment 1 one

1. At a clear editing window, key the text shown in figure U1.1 in an appropriate memo format with the following specifications:
   a. Change the view to Draft mode.
   b. Change the left and right margins to 1.5 inches.
   c. Double-indent the second paragraph.
   d. Save the memo and name it U01, PA 01.
   e. Print and then close U01, PA 01.

DATE: November 10, 2003

TO: Pat Windslow, Superintendent

FROM: Jocelyn Cook, Assistant Superintendent

SUBJECT: RESERVOIR REPAIR

As you requested, I called Jack Manuel, president of the Alderton Water Company. He explained about the problem with the spring and reservoir that serve Leland Elementary School. During our conversation, he stated:

Continued on next page

According to the contract between the District and Alderton Water Company, the District must pay $10,000 toward the repair of the reservoir.

I contacted the District's attorney and asked her to review the documentation referred to by Mr. Manuel. She will call me next week with her impressions.

xx:U01, PA 01

FIGURE U1.1 • Assessment 1

Assessment 2
two

1. At a clear editing window, key the bibliography shown in figure U1.2 with the following specifications:
   a. Bold and center the title as shown.
   b. Italicize the text in the bibliography as shown.
   c. Create a hanging indent for each paragraph.
   d. After keying the bibliography, move the insertion point to the beginning of the first entry, and then change the justification to full.
   e. Center the document vertically on the page.
2. Save the document and name it U01, PA 02.
3. Print and then close U01, PA 02.

BIBLIOGRAPHY

Anspaugh, Janeen A. (2002). *Communications for the New Century* (pp. 23-32). New York, NY: Liberty Press.

Davis, Jared M. (2003). *Preparing International Business Documents*. Vancouver, British Columbia, Canada: Maple Leaf Publishing.

Geiger, Ricardo J. (2002). *Communicating Internationally* (pp. 6-14). Sacramento, CA: Mainstay Publishing House.

Nakagawa, Lisa M. (2001). *Managing Conflict*. New Orleans, LA: Sutherland & Gaines Publishing.

FIGURE U1.2 • Assessment 2

Assessment 3

1. At a clear editing window, key the letter shown in figure U1.3 in an appropriate business letter format. Double-indent the paragraphs as indicated.
2. Save the letter and name it U01, PA 03.
3. Print and then close U01, PA 03.

November 24, 2003

Mr. and Mrs. Paul Schadt
2311 Northeast 41st Street
St. Charles, MO 63303

Dear Mr. and Mrs. Schadt:

You are invited to participate in our mortgage life insurance plan that could leave your family a home without house payments. We recommend this program for our home loan customers because it provides important protection at an affordable price.

 While there are many types of insurance, only mortgage life insurance is designed exclusively to pay off the mortgage balance if you were to die.

Even if you already have a life insurance plan, you will want to consider mortgage life insurance as a low-cost, attractive supplement.

 Because so many households rely on two wage earners to make mortgage payments, we have selected a plan that can insure a second person at HALF-PRICE.

I think you will agree that this protection is almost a necessity, but you may be concerned about cost. We have carefully chosen a plan that can fit your budget. We are pleased to offer this important customer service and encourage you to apply today, while it is available at these attractive rates. To apply, please call 1-800-555-3255.

Sincerely,

Jonathon Baker
Insurance Products Manager

xx:U01, PA 03

FIGURE U1.3 • Assessment 3

1. At a clear editing window, key the document shown in figure U1.4.
2. Save the document and name it U01, PA 04.
3. Print and then close U01, PA 04.

DENVER MEMORIAL HOSPITAL

MANAGER OF EMPLOYEE TRAINING

General Description

The *Manager of Employee Training* is responsible for planning, implementing, maintaining, and evaluating employee training and education programs for Denver Memorial Hospital. The manager is also responsible for coaching and counseling individual employees.

Characteristic Duties

♦ Assists Director of the Employee Training Department in the administration, data analysis, feedback, and planned change strategies in response to results of employee relation survey.

♦ Performs in-depth analysis of education and training needs of all support and diagnostic services.

♦ Develops, implements, and evaluates educational programs and services within and across all non-nursing units in the hospital.

♦ Coordinates the design and implementation of all non-nursing education and training programs in collaboration with internal and external resources.

♦ Recognizes and participates in the organizational and departmental customer service/employee relations action plan programs.

Minimum Qualifications

♦ Master's Degree in Nursing or equivalent.

♦ Certification in area of nursing specialty and continuing education desired.

♦ Minimum three (3) years of supervision experience.

♦ Minimum two (2) years of educational experience.

FIGURE U1.4 • Assessment 4

Assessment 5

1. Open Report 05.
2. Save the document with Save As and name it U01, PA 05.
3. Make the following changes to the report:
   a. Change the line spacing to double (2). Delete all extra lines in the report so there is only a double space between all lines.
   b. Change top and bottom margins to 1.25 inches.
   c. Change the left and right margins to 1.5 inches.
   d. Turn on the Widow/Orphan feature.
   e. Insert page numbers in the top right corner of each page of the document.
   f. Suppress the page numbering on page 1.
   g. Apply block protection to keep the heading *Application Methodology* and the first line of the paragraph following it on the same page.
4. Save, print, and then close U01, PA 05.

WRITING SOLUTIONS

The following activities give you the opportunity to practice your writing skills along with demonstrating an understanding of some of the important WordPerfect features you have mastered in this unit. In planning the documents, remember to shape the information according to the writing purpose and the audience. Use correct grammar, appropriate word choices, and clear sentence constructions.

Assessment 6

Situation: You are Dione Landers of Landers & Associates. Compose a letter to Steven Ayala, Director of the Training and Education Department at Denver Memorial Hospital, 900 Colorado Boulevard, Denver, CO 80202, that includes the following information:

- Confirmation of a one-day training session on telephone systems and techniques to be held on Wednesday, March 26, 2003, from 9:00 a.m. to 4:30 p.m.

- The training topics, which include

      Handling incoming calls
      Transferring calls
      Telephone etiquette
      Articulation and pronunciation
      Handling stressful calls

Save the letter and name it U01, PA 06. Print and then close U01, PA 06.

Assessment 7

Situation: You are Jocelyn Cook, Assistant Superintendent for Omaha City School District. Compose a memo to Jennifer Stanford that includes the following information:

- Her application for a principal internship has been accepted.
- You would like to schedule an interview with her in your office on either of the following dates and times: Tuesday, May 20, 2003, at 3:00 p.m. or Wednesday, May 21, 2003, at 1:30 p.m.

Save the memorandum and name it U01, PA 07. Print and then close U01, PA 07.

UNIT two

MANAGING AND ENHANCING DOCUMENTS

CHAPTER 5

Managing Documents

PERFORMANCE OBJECTIVES

Upon successful completion of chapter 5, you will be able to:

- **Create a folder**
- **Copy, move, rename, delete, and print documents**
- **Use the QuickFinder feature**
- **Create document summaries**

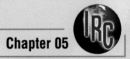

Chapter 05 IRC

Almost every business maintains a filing system. The system may consist of documents, folders, and cabinets; or it may be a computerized filing system where information is stored on tapes and disks. Whatever kind of filing system a business uses, daily maintenance of files is important to a company's operation. Maintaining files can include such activities as copying, renaming, and moving documents, creating folders, and deleting documents. These types of functions can be completed at the Open File, Save As, or Insert File dialog boxes.

Displaying Document Information

The Open File, Save As, and Insert File dialog boxes contain many of the same options. The Open File dialog box is shown in figure 5.1. The Save As and Insert File dialog boxes are similar in appearance.

5.1 *Open File Dialog Box*

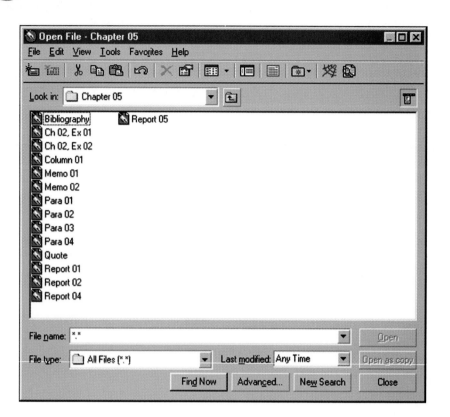

A toolbar displays toward the top of the Open File dialog box. This toolbar contains buttons for managing documents and folders and for changing the display of the dialog box. A menu bar is also available at the Open File dialog box. To display the dialog box Menu bar, click the Toggle Menu On/Off button located at the far right side of the dialog box in the same horizontal position as the Look in text box.

Toggle Menu
On/Off

The Look in option displays the current folder. Below the Look in option is an alphabetical list of the documents in the current folder. Document names with numbers are alphabetized before document names with letters. For example, Memo 01 would come before Memo A. To change to a different drive, click the down-pointing triangle at the right of the Look in text box and then click the desired disk drive. Once you are looking in the right drive, you can double-click on a folder within that drive to display its contents.

Go back one
folder level

If the disk drive displayed is the correct drive, but you need to see the folders one level above the current folder, click the Go back one folder level button at the right of the Look in text box.

The File name text box displays just below the list box. You can open a document by keying the document name in the File name text box, or clicking once on the file name and then clicking Open.

The File type text box allows you to choose what type of documents you want displayed in the list box. By default, WordPerfect will display all documents in the folder. Click the down-pointing triangle at the right side of the File type text box and choose the appropriate document extension. If you select *.*, all documents will be displayed.

In chapter 1, you learned how to change the default folder with the Look in option. In this chapter, you will be moving back and forth between the student data disk in drive A and the hard drive or network drive. If necessary, your instructor will provide you with instructions on which drive and folder to select when completing some of the exercises in this chapter.

Creating a Folder

Documents are usually filed electronically based on a system where similar types of documents are stored together. For example, all of the memos might be stored together in a folder named *Memos*.

Once you start using a word processor to create a large number of files, you will want to devise your own system of storing the documents in folders that will make them easy to locate. A new folder can be created at the Open File, Save As, or Insert File dialog boxes. To create a folder, you would complete the following steps:

1. Display the Open File, Save As, or Insert File dialog box.

2. With the folder from which you want to branch on the left side of the dialog box, right-click in an empty area on the right side, point to New, and then click Folder.

3. Type a name for the folder. Names can be up to 255 characters long and may include spaces, numbers, and some special characters. Press Enter when finished naming the folder.

exercise

Creating a Folder

1. Create two folders named *Letters* and *Memos* on your student data disk by completing the following steps:
   a. Display the Open File dialog box.
   b. Make *Chapter 05* on your disk the active folder.
   c. Position the arrow pointer in any white area of the list box and then click the *right* mouse button.

d. At the shortcut menu that displays, point to <u>New</u> and then click <u>F</u>older.

e. At the New Folder text box, key **Letters** and then press Enter.

f. Complete steps similar to those in 1c through 1e to create a second folder named *Memos*.

2. Click the Close button to close the Open File dialog box.

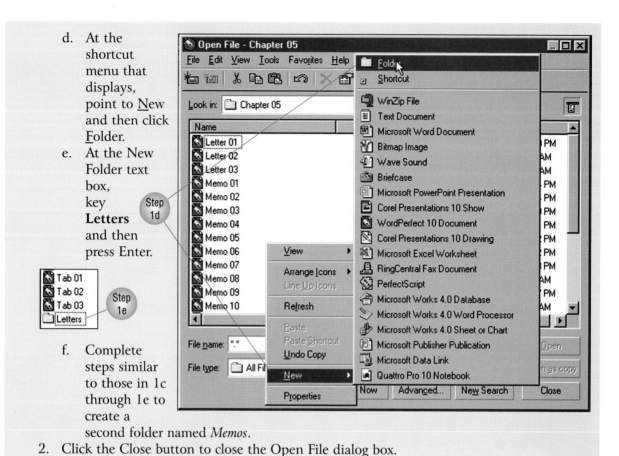

Selecting Documents

Document management tasks can be performed on one document at a time, or you can select several documents and copy, move, delete, or print them all at once. Figure 5.2 explains how to select documents.

FIGURE

5.2 *Selecting Documents*

To select documents that are	Do this
Single documents	Position the pointer on the document name and click the left mouse button.
Adjacent documents	Click the first document name, hold down the Shift key, and then click on the last document name.
Non-adjacent documents	Click the first document name, hold down the Ctrl key, click the second document name, and, while continuing to hold the Ctrl key, keep clicking until all the documents are selected.

Copying a Document

A toolbar displays at the Open File, Save As, and Insert File dialog boxes. With the Copy and Paste buttons on the Toolbar, or using the right mouse button after selecting documents, you can make an exact copy of a document and save it on the same disk, on another disk, or into another folder. If you copy a document to the same folder, WordPerfect will give the duplicate copy the name "Copy of xxx" (where *xxx* is the original document name). If you copy a document to another folder or drive, it can retain its original name. To copy a document, you would complete these steps:

Copy

Paste

1. Select the file to be copied.
2. Click the Copy button on the Toolbar.
3. Change to the destination folder.
4. Click the Paste button on the Toolbar.

Alternatively, you can right-click on the document name after it is selected, and choose Copy or Paste from the shortcut menu that appears.

Copying Documents

1. Copy Memo 01 to the *Memos* folder by completing the following steps:
   a. Display the Open File dialog box with the *Chapter 05* folder active.
   b. Select the document named *Memo 01* in the list box.
   c. Click the Copy button on the dialog box Toolbar.

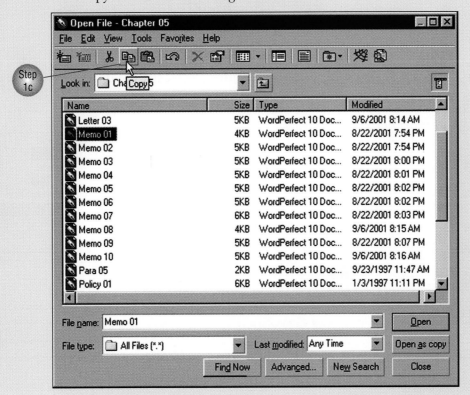

d. Change to the *Memos* folder by double-clicking the folder named *Memos* in the list box.

e. Click the Paste button on the dialog box Toolbar.

f. Return to the previous list of documents. Do this by clicking the Go back one folder level button (located at the right of the Look in text box).

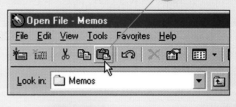

Step 1e

2. Copy the remaining memo documents all at the same time to the *Memos* folder by completing the following steps:

a. Click the document named *Memo 02*.

b. Hold down the Shift key and then click *Memo 10*. (This will select all of the documents starting at Memo 02 and ending at Memo 10.)

c. Move the arrow pointer inside the selected group of documents and then click the *right* mouse button.

d. At the shortcut menu that displays, click Copy.

e. Change to the *Memos* folder by double-clicking the folder named *Memos* in the list box.

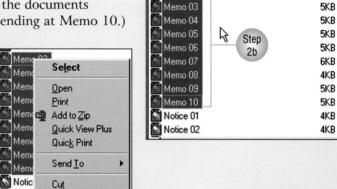

Step 2b

Step 2d

f. Position the arrow pointer in any white area of the list box and then click the *right* mouse button.

g. At the shortcut menu that displays, click Paste.

h. Click the Go back one folder level button (located at the right of the Look in text box) to return to the previous list of documents.

3. Copy two letters into the same folder (Chapter 05) by completing the following steps:

a. Click the document *Letter 01*.

b. Hold down the Ctrl key and then click *Letter 03*. (This will select only the documents Letter 01 and Letter 03.)

c. Position the arrow pointer over one of the selected documents and then click the *right* mouse button.

d. At the shortcut menu that displays, click Copy.

e. Deselect the documents by clicking in any white area in the list box.

f. Click the *right* mouse button in a white area in the list box and then click Paste at the shortcut menu.

g. Scroll through the list of document names to view the copied document names *Copy of Letter 01* and *Copy of Letter 03*.

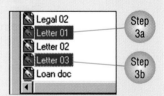

Step 3a

Step 3b

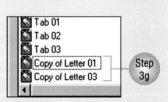

Step 3g

4. Click the Close button to close the Open File dialog box.

Cutting and Pasting Documents

If you decide that a document needs to be moved to a different folder or drive, select the document, and then click the Cut button on the dialog box Toolbar. Change to the folder or drive where you want to move the document and then click the Paste button on the dialog box Toolbar.

Cut

Cutting and Pasting Documents

1. Move Copy of Letter 01 and Copy of Letter 03 to the *Letters* folder by completing the following steps:
    a. Display the Open File dialog box with the *Chapter 05* folder active.
    b. Select the two documents *Copy of Letter 01* and *Copy of Letter 03*.
    c. Click the Cut button on the dialog box Toolbar.

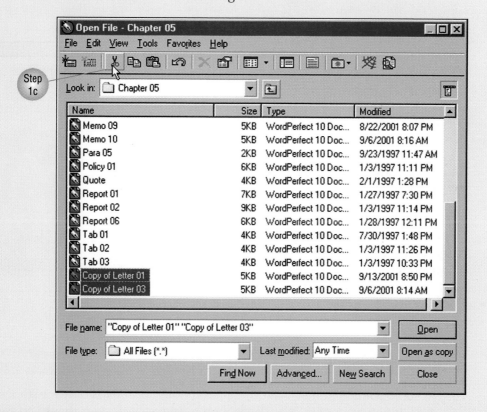

Step 1c

    d. Change to the *Letters* folder by double-clicking the folder named *Letters* in the list box.
    e. Click the Paste button on the dialog box Toolbar.
    f. Click the Go back one folder level button to return to the previous list of document names.
2. Close the Open File dialog box.

Renaming Documents

At the Open File, Save As, or Insert File dialog boxes, you can use the Rename option from the shortcut menu to give a document a different name and keep it in the same folder.

To use the Rename option, select the document. Position the arrow pointer over the selected document, click the *right* mouse button, and then click Rename at the shortcut menu. Key the new name. Depending on your system configuration, you may need to add the extension *.wpd* to the end of the document name. The extension *.wpd* stands for WordPerfect document and is the default extension for WordPerfect documents.

Renaming a Document

1. Rename a document located in the *Letters* folder by completing the following steps:
   a. Display the Open File dialog box with *Chapter 05* the active folder.
   b. Change to the *Letters* folder by double-clicking *Letters* in the list box.
   c. Click *Copy of Letter 01*.
   d. Position the arrow pointer over the selected document and then click the *right* mouse button.
   e. At the shortcut menu that displays, click Rename.
   f. Key **Denver Memorial Hospital** and then press Enter. (You may need to add the extension *.wpd*. If this is the case, key **Denver Memorial Hospital.wpd** and then press Enter.)
2. Complete steps similar to those in steps 1c through 1e to rename the document Copy of Letter 03 to *Facilities Dept at DMH*. (If you need to add an extension, key **Facilities Dept at DMH.wpd**.)
3. Click the Go back one folder level button to return to the previous list of document names.
4. Close the Open File dialog box.

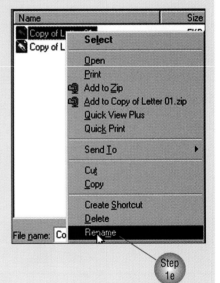

Deleting a Document

At some point, you may want to delete certain documents on your student data disk. If you work with WordPerfect on a regular basis, you should establish a system for deleting documents. The system you choose depends on the work you are doing.

To delete a document or multiple documents, display the Open File, Save As, or Insert File dialog box. Select the document(s) to be deleted and then click the Delete button on the dialog box Toolbar. You can also click the *right* mouse button and then click Delete at the shortcut menu. At the Confirm File Delete dialog box, make sure the correct document name is displayed and then click Yes.

Delete

Documents deleted from the floppy disk are deleted permanently. Documents deleted from the hard drive are sent to the Windows Recycle Bin. The Recycle Bin can become full very quickly and you should empty it on a periodic basis to free up space on your hard drive. To empty the Recycle Bin, right-click the *Recycle Bin* icon located at the left side of the Windows desktop and choose Empty Recycle Bin from the shortcut menu.

To restore a file from the Recycle Bin, open the Recycle Bin window by double-clicking the Recycle Bin icon located at the left side of the Windows desktop. Select the file(s) to be restored. Position the arrow pointer over the selected file(s), click the *right* mouse button, and then click Restore. The file(s) will be restored to its original folder.

Deleting Documents

1. Delete the document Denver Memorial Hospital in the *Letters* folder by completing the following steps:
   a. Display the Open File dialog box with *Chapter 05* the active folder.
   b. Change to the *Letters* folder.
   c. Click the document named *Denver Memorial Hospital*.
   d. Click the Delete button on the dialog box Toolbar.
   e. At the Confirm File Delete dialog box, make sure the correct document name is displayed and then click Yes.

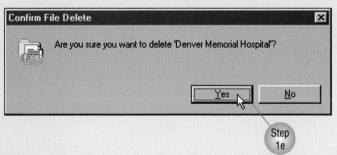

2. Delete the document Facilities Dept at DMH in the *Letters* folder by completing the following steps:
   a. Click the document named *Facilities Dept at DMH*.
   b. Position the arrow pointer on the selected document and then click the *right* mouse button.
   c. At the shortcut menu that displays, click Delete.
   d. At the Confirm File Delete dialog box, make sure the correct document name is displayed and then click Yes.
3. Return to the previous list of document names.
4. Delete multiple documents by completing the following steps:
   a. Display the Open File dialog box.
   b. Click *Para 05*.
   c. Hold down the Shift key and then click *Quote*. (This should select the documents Para 05, Policy 01, and Quote. If not, hold down the Ctrl key and click on each of these documents.)

     d.   Click the Delete button on the dialog box Toolbar.

     e.   At the question asking if you are sure you want to delete the documents, click Yes.

5. Close the Open File dialog box.

Deleting a Folder and Its Contents

A folder can be removed (deleted) from the disk or drive in the same manner that a document is deleted.

Deleting a Folder and Its Contents

1. Delete the *Letters* folder and its contents by completing the following steps:

    a.   Display the Open File dialog box with *Chapter 05* the active folder.

    b.   Click the *Letters* folder in the list box.

    c.   Click the Delete button on the dialog box Toolbar.

    d.   At the Confirm Folder Delete dialog box, make sure the *Letters* folder name is displayed and then click Yes.

2. Remove the *Memos* folder and its contents by completing steps similar to those in 1b through 1d.

3. Close the Open File dialog box.

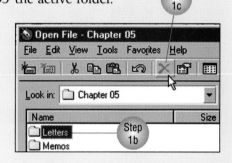

Viewing a Document's Properties

Properties

Information about a document such as the type, location, and size can be displayed at the Properties dialog box. To display the Properties dialog box, display the Open File, Save As, or Insert File dialog box and select the desired document. Click the Properties button on the dialog box Toolbar. At the Properties dialog box, you can choose to archive (back up) a document the next time you run a backup program; protect a document from being modified or deleted by clicking Read-only; hide a document in the file lists; and/or identify documents as part of the computer's operating system. Figure 5.3 shows the Properties dialog box for the document named *Para 01*.

5.3 *Properties Dialog Box*

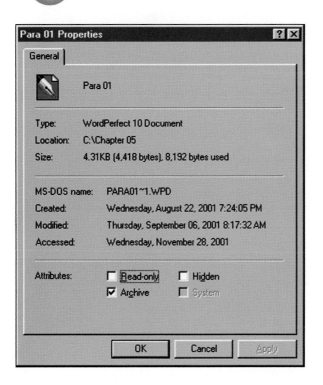

Printing a Document

In chapter 1, you learned to print documents with the Print button on the Toolbar or at the Print dialog box. In addition to these methods, you can also print a document or multiple documents with the Print option from the shortcut menu. To do this, click the document(s) to be printed, position the arrow pointer on any of the documents to be printed, click the *right* mouse button, and then click Print at the shortcut menu.

Printing a Document List

At times, you may want a hard copy of folder contents as an index of the documents that are stored in the folder. To print the list of documents, display the Open File, Save As, or Insert File dialog box. At the dialog box Menu bar, click File, and then click Print File List at the drop-down menu. At the Print File List dialog box shown in figure 5.4, make any needed changes, and then click OK.

5.4 *Print File List Dialog Box*

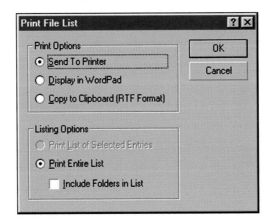

exercise 7

Printing a List of Documents

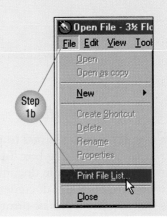

1. Complete the following steps to print a list of the documents in the *Chapter 05* folder on the student data disk:
   a. Display the Open File dialog box with *Chapter 05* the active folder.
   b. Click File on the dialog box Menu bar and then click Print File List at the drop-down menu.
   c. At the Print File List dialog box, click OK.
2. Close the Open File dialog box.

Step 1b

Viewing a Document

Preview

With the Preview button on the Open File, Save As, or Insert File Toolbar, you can view a document without bringing it to the editing window. This feature is useful if you are looking for a particular document but cannot remember what it was named.

When you click the Preview button on the dialog box Toolbar, the document is inserted in a window at the right side of the dialog box as shown in figure 5.5. You can use the mouse with the up, down, left, or right scroll triangles to view different parts of the document. To view the text as it appears on the page, click the *right* mouse button anywhere inside the Preview window and then click Page View. To remove the Preview window, click the Preview button on the dialog box Toolbar.

5.5 *Preview Window*

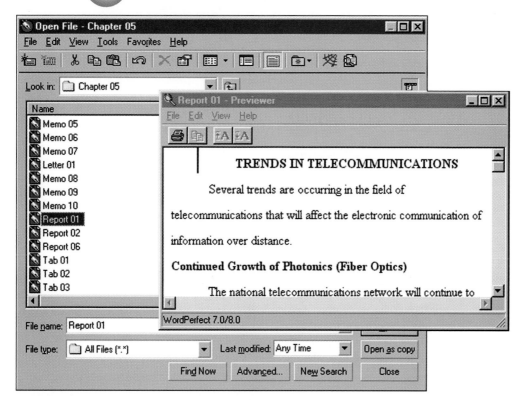

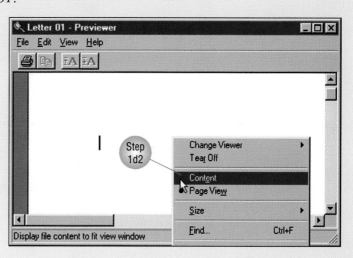

exercise 8

Viewing Documents at the Open File Dialog Box

1. Complete the following steps to view Letter 01:
   a. Display the Open File dialog box with *Chapter 05* the active folder.
   b. Click the document *Letter 01*.
   c. Click the Preview button on the dialog box Toolbar.
   d. Change the view of the Preview text to the page view of the letter by completing the following steps:
      1) Move the arrow pointer inside the Preview window and then click the *right* mouse button.
      2) At the shortcut menu that displays, click Content.

e. Use the horizontal and vertical scroll bars to scroll through the document and view it.
2. Remove the Preview window by clicking the Preview button.
3. Close the Open File dialog box.

Changing Display Options

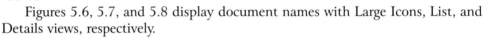

The way document names are displayed in the Open File, Save As, or Insert File dialog boxes can be altered to display large file icons, small file icons, a list of document names, or all file details. The list can be changed by clicking the down-pointing triangle on the Views button on the dialog box Toolbar and selecting the appropriate view.

Views

Figures 5.6, 5.7, and 5.8 display document names with Large Icons, List, and Details views, respectively.

F I G U R E

5.6 *Large Icons View*

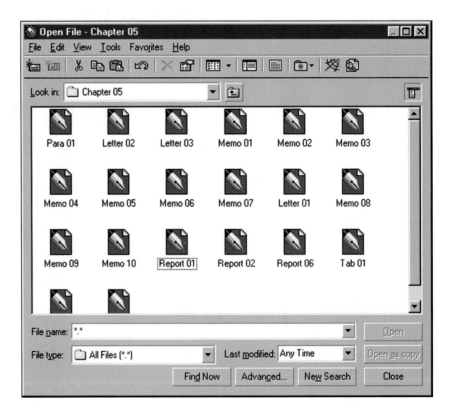

FIGURE

5.7 List View

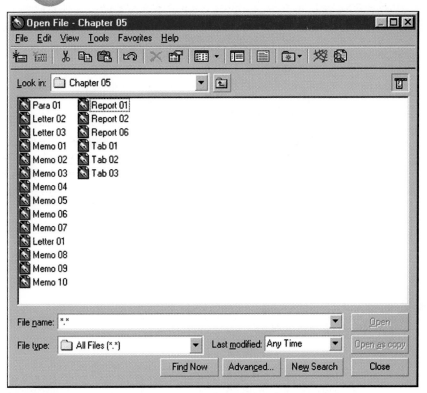

FIGURE

5.8 Details View

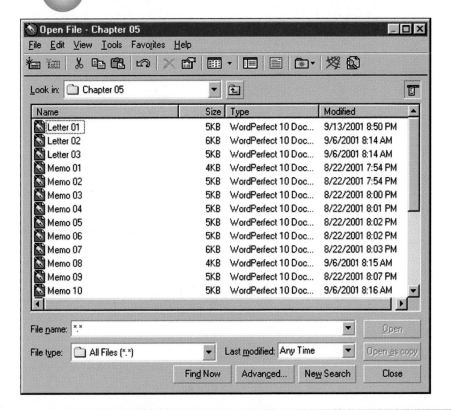

Whatever setting you choose will stay in effect until you choose another display setting.

Using QuickFinder

With WordPerfect's QuickFinder feature you can search a folder or specific files within a folder for a particular word pattern. This is useful in locating certain documents when you cannot remember the document name, but you can remember a unique word or words contained in the document.

To use QuickFinder, display the Open File, Save As, or Insert File dialog box. Specify in the Look in text box the drive or folder you want to search, key a specific word or phrase in the File name text box, and then click the Find Now button. For example, if you want to find all documents containing the name *Ayala*, you would key **Ayala** in the File name text box and then click the Find Now button.

You can use special operators to locate more than one word. For example, you can search for all documents that contain the name *Ayala* and the name *Lam* by using the & operator. Figure 5.9 shows example operators that can be used and the results the search would return.

FIGURE

5.9 *Example Operators*

Operator inserted	QuickFinder will find documents
Dearing&Windslow	containing Dearing and Windslow
Dearing|Windslow	containing Dearing or Windslow
!Dearing	that do not contain Dearing
Dearing!Windslow	containing Dearing but not Windslow
Carey..Dearing	containing Carey followed by Dearing
(computer literacy program)	containing all three words in any order

In addition to the operators in figure 5.9, you can use the asterisk (*) symbol to indicate a combination of letters or the question mark (?) to indicate one character. For example, you can key **educa*** in the File name text box and QuickFinder will search documents for words that begin with *educa* and end with any combination such as education, educating, and educated. If you key **probabl?** in the File name text box, QuickFinder will search documents for words that begin with *probabl* and end with any one character (such as probable and probably).

Once you have specified the search text in the File name text box, click the Find Now button. QuickFinder searches the specified folder for the text and then displays documents containing the specified text in the list box. Figure 5.10 shows the results of a search for documents containing the words *Denver Memorial Hospital*.

5.10 *QuickFinder Search Results*

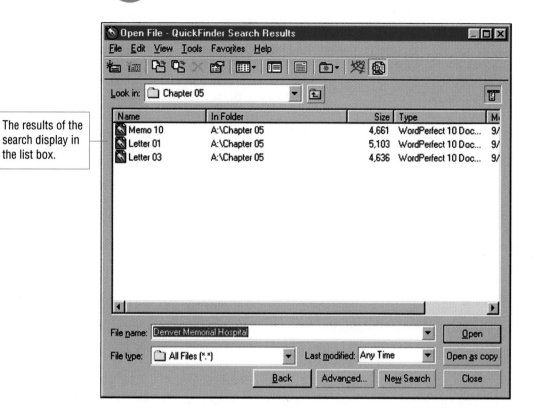

The results of the search display in the list box.

Once the search results are listed in the dialog box, you can perform any of the file management tasks learned in this chapter on the documents. You can also choose to open a document by selecting the document and then clicking the Open button located toward the bottom of the dialog box or by double-clicking the document name.

(Note: Check with your instructor if the QuickFinder feature is unavailable; it may need to be installed.)

Finding Documents Containing Specific Words

1. At a clear editing window, search for documents on your student data disk containing the words *Denver Memorial Hospital* by completing the following steps:
   a. Display the Open File dialog box with *Chapter 05* the active folder.
   b. Key **Denver Memorial Hospital** in the File name text box.

c. Click the Fin**d** Now button.

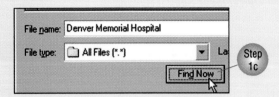

d. When the search results are displayed in the list box, print a list of documents by completing the following steps:
   1) If the dialog box Menu bar is not visible, display it by clicking the Toggle Menu On/Off button located at the far right side of the dialog box in the same horizontal position as the **L**ook in text box.
   2) Select the documents in the list box. (To do this, click the first document in the list, hold down the Shift key, and then click the last document in the list.)
   3) Click **F**ile and then Print File **L**ist.
   4) At the Print File List dialog box, click OK.
2. Close the Open File dialog box.

Inserting Information at the Properties Dialog Box

To help you manage your documents, WordPerfect provides the Properties dialog box shown in figure 5.11. Use the Properties dialog box with the Summary tab selected to provide information about a document such as the document's creation date and time, the author, the subject, key words, and an abstract of the document. Display the Properties dialog box by clicking **F**ile and then P**r**operties.

F I G U R E

5.11 *Properties Dialog Box with Summary Tab Selected*

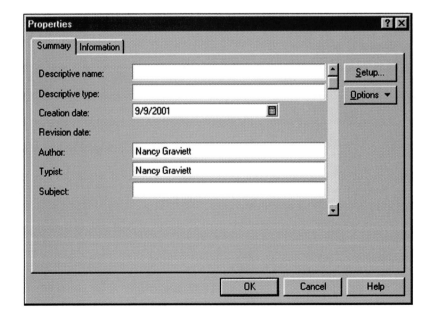

From the Summary tab in the Properties dialog box, you can enter the following information:

- Descriptive name
- Descriptive type
- Creation date
- Revision date
- Author

- Typist
- Subject
- Account
- Keywords
- Abstract

You may need to use the vertical scroll bar on the right side of the dialog box to see all the options.

Note that some information is displayed automatically by WordPerfect. You can change this information by typing in new information.

Using Properties Options

If you click the Options button at the Properties dialog box (with the Summary tab selected), a drop-down menu of options displays. With these options you can do the following:

Print Summary: By default, a summary does not print with the document. To print a summary, click Options and then Print Summary.

Delete Summary From Document: A summary can be deleted from a document. To do this, click Options and then Delete Summary From Document. At the Delete document summary? query, click Yes.

Extract Information From Document: At the Properties dialog box, click Options and then Extract Information From Document. WordPerfect will retrieve pertinent information from the document and display it in the summary. WordPerfect searches the current document and inserts the first 400 characters of the document after the Abstract option. WordPerfect also looks for a subject in the document. WordPerfect looks for text after the letters *RE:*. If it does not find these letters, WordPerfect will look for the first heading in a document. This information will be inserted after the Subject option.

Save Summary As New Document: By default, the summary will be attached to the current document. If you want to save the summary as a separate document, click Options and then Save Summary As New Document. At the Save Document Summary dialog box, key a name for the document and then click Save or press Enter.

Inserting Information at the Properties Dialog Box

1. Open Report 01.
2. Save the report with Save As and name it Ch 05, Ex 10.
3. Insert information at the Properties dialog box for Ch 05, Ex 10 by completing the following steps:
   a. Click File and then Properties.
   b. At the Properties dialog box, make sure the Summary tab is selected.

c. Key **Trends in Telecommunications** in the Descriptive name text box.
d. Press the Tab key. This moves the insertion point to the next field, Descriptive type.
e. Key **Report** in the Descriptive type text box.
f. Press the Tab key twice. This moves the insertion point to the Author field.
g. Key your first and last name in the Author text box.
h. Press the Tab key. This moves the insertion point to the Typist field.
i. Key your initials in the Typist text box.

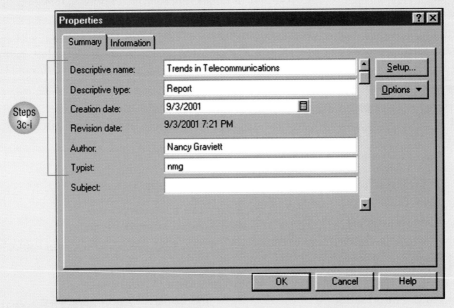

j. Click <u>O</u>ptions and then click <u>E</u>xtract Information From Document.
k. Click <u>O</u>ptions and then click <u>P</u>rint Summary.
l. Click OK to close the Properties dialog box.

4. Save and then close Ch 05, Ex 10.

CHAPTER summary

➤ Some of the activities involved in disk and document maintenance are creating folders; cutting, copying, and pasting documents; and deleting documents.

➤ Three dialog boxes will allow you to do all of the activities listed above. These dialog boxes are Open File, Save As, and Insert File.

➤ Several file management choices are available at any of the three dialog boxes, either by using buttons on the dialog box Toolbar, options from the dialog box Menu bar, or by accessing the shortcut menu with the *right* mouse button, including the following:

♦ Copy can make an exact copy of a document and save it on the same disk, on another disk, or into another folder.

♦ Cut can place a document in another folder or drive.

♦ Rename allows the name of a document to be changed.

♦ Delete will remove unneeded documents.

♦ Properties allows instructions to be given regarding archiving, backing up documents, and so on.

♦ The Print option offers an additional method for printing documents.

♦ The Print File List from the File drop-down menu prints a hard copy of a folder's contents.

♦ Clicking New and then Folder creates new folders or subfolders.

➤ Click the Preview button on the Open File, Save As, or Insert File dialog box Toolbar to view a document without bringing it to the editing window.

➤ Use WordPerfect's QuickFinder feature to search a folder or specific documents for a particular word pattern.

➤ For each document, you can insert specific information about the document at the Properties dialog box. This information includes the document's creation date and time, the author, the subject, key words, and an abstract of the document.

COMMANDS summary

Command	Mouse
Copy/Paste document	Select item, click the Copy button, move to new file location, click the Paste button
Cut/Paste document	Select item, click the Cut button, move to new file location, click the Paste button
Select adjacent files	Select the first item to be selected, hold down the Shift key, click the left mouse button on the file name of the last file to be selected

Select non-adjacent files	Select the first item to be selected, hold down the Ctrl key, click the left mouse button on the file name of each additional file to be selected
See folders one level above current folder	Click the Go back one folder level button
Rename a document	Right-click the file name, select Rename, key new name
Delete file or folder	Select item, click the Delete button
View document properties	Select desired document, click the Properties button
Print a document list	Display the Open File dialog box, click File, Print File List
Preview a document	Display the Open File dialog box, click the Preview button
Change display options	Display the Open File dialog box, click the View menu, and select the option; or click the Views button and select the option

CONCEPTS check

Completion: On a blank sheet of paper, indicate the right term, symbol, or command.

1. Most document maintenance functions can be performed at these three dialog boxes.

2. To print a list of documents in a specific folder, click Print File List from this drop-down menu.

3. This is the button you click to move from one folder to the folder above it.

4. Click this button at the Open File dialog box to view a document without bringing it to the editing window.

5. Click this button at the Open File dialog box to display information about documents such as the size and type of a document and the last date the document was modified.

6. Click this button at the Open File dialog box to display the dialog box Menu bar.

7. With this feature you can search a folder or specific documents within a folder for a particular word pattern.

8. Key this in the File name text box at the Open File dialog box to find documents containing the words *Workplace Literacy* or *Ayala*.

9. Key this in the File name text box at the Open File dialog box to find documents that do not contain the words *Workplace Literacy*.

10. WordPerfect automatically inserts certain details about a document in this dialog box with the Summary tab selected.

SKILLS check

Assessment 1

1. Display the Open File dialog box.
2. If necessary, make the *Chapter 05* folder the active folder.
3. Create a new folder named *Student Letters*.
4. Copy Letter 01, Letter 02, and Letter 03 to the *Student Letters* folder.
5. With the *Student Letters* folder the active folder, rename the following documents:
   a. *Letter 01* to *Correspondence 01* (or *Correspondence 01.wpd*)
   b. *Letter 02* to *Correspondence 02* (or *Correspondence 02.wpd*)
   c. *Letter 03* to *Correspondence 03* (or *Correspondence 03.wpd*)
6. Print the *Student Letters* folder file list.
7. Return to the previous list of document names.
8. Delete the *Student Letters* folder and its contents.
9. Close the Open File dialog box.

Assessment 2

1. Display the Open File dialog box and then delete all documents that begin with the word *Tab*.
2. Close the Open File dialog box.

Assessment 3

1. Display the Open File dialog box.
2. Search for all documents on the student data disk that contain the words *trends in telecommunications*.
3. When the list of documents displays, print the file list.
4. Close the Open File dialog box.

Assessment 4

1. Open Report 02.
2. Save the document with Save As and name it Ch 05, SA 04.
3. Insert information about the document at the Properties dialog box with the Summary tab selected. (You determine the information for the options.)
4. Print the summary information.
5. Close Ch 05, SA 04.

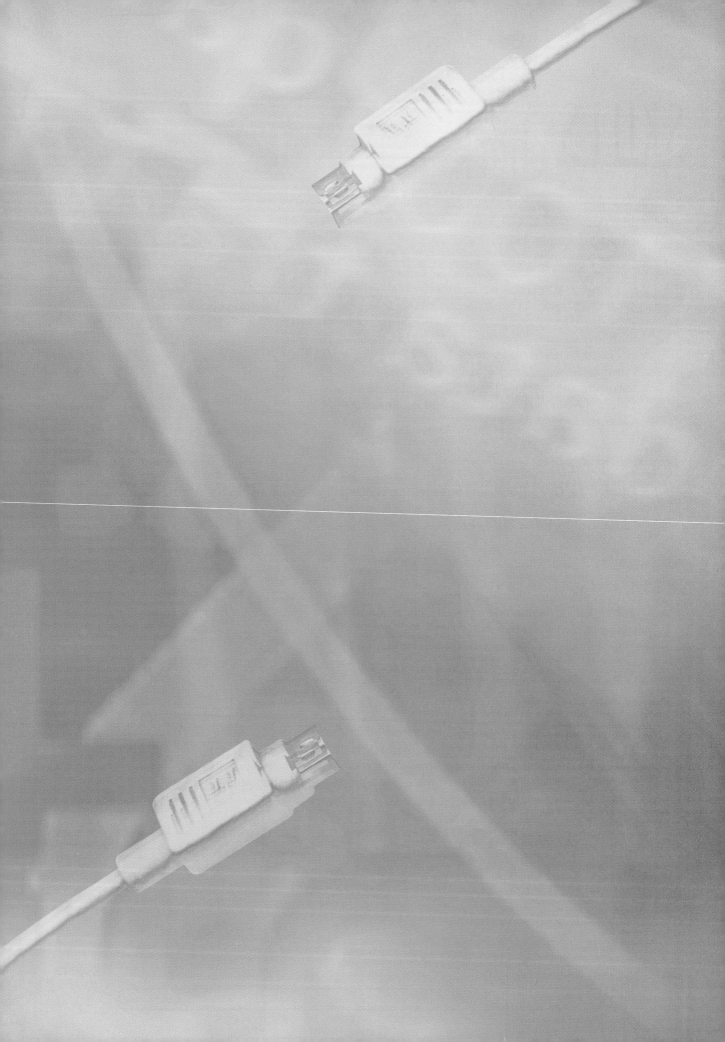

6

Changing Fonts

The default font for WordPerfect is Times New Roman. Other fonts may be available depending on the printer you are using. The number of fonts available ranges from a few to several hundred. A font consists of three parts: typeface, type size, and type style.

Choosing a Typeface

A typeface is a set of characters with a common design and shape. Typefaces may be decorative, blocked, or plain. Typefaces are either monospaced or proportional. WordPerfect refers to typeface as font face.

A *monospaced* typeface allots the same amount of horizontal space for each character. Courier is an example of a monospaced typeface. *Proportional* typefaces allot a varying amount of space for each character. The space allotted is based on the width of the character. For example, the lowercase *i* will take up less space than the uppercase *M*.

Proportional typefaces are divided into two main categories: *serif* and *sans serif*. A serif is a small line at the end of a character stroke. Traditionally, a serif typeface is used in documents that are text intensive (documents that are mainly text) because the serifs help move the reader's eyes across the page. Examples of serif typefaces are shown in figure 6.1.

6.1 *Serif Typefaces*

Bookman Old Style
Galliard BT

Goudy Old Style
Times New Roman

A sans serif typeface does not have serifs (sans is French for *without*). Sans serif typefaces are often used for headlines and advertisements that are not text intensive. Examples of sans serif typefaces are shown in figure 6.2.

FIGURE

6.2 *Sans Serif Typefaces*

Arial
Futura Bk BT

Tahoma
Verdana

Choosing a Type Size

Proportional typefaces can be set in different sizes. The size of proportional type is measured vertically in units called *points*. A point is approximately ½2 of an inch. The higher the point size, the larger the characters. Examples of different point sizes in the Arial typeface are shown in figure 6.3.

FIGURE

6.3 *Different Point Sizes in Arial*

8-point Arial

12-point Arial

18-point Arial

24-point Arial

Choosing a Type Style

Within a typeface, characters may have a varying style. The standard style of the typeface is referred to as *Regular*. There are four main categories of type styles— Regular, Bold, Italic, and Bold Italic. These four main type styles are displayed in figure 6.4.

F I G U R E

6.4 *Four Main Type Styles*

Arial (Regular)	Times New Roman (Regular)
Arial Bold	**Times New Roman Bold**
Arial Italic	*Times New Roman Italic*
Arial Bold Italic	***Times New Roman Bold Italic***

The term *font* describes a particular typeface in a specific style and size. Some examples of fonts are 10-point Arial, 12-point Tahoma Bold, 12-point Garamond Italic, and 14-point Times New Roman Bold Italic.

Choosing a Font

The printer that you are using has built-in fonts. These fonts can be supplemented with cartridges and/or soft fonts. The fonts you have available with your printer depend on the specific printer you are using, the amount of memory installed with the printer, and the supplemental fonts you have. Soft fonts are available as software. The Corel WordPerfect 10 program comes with additional fonts that were loaded during installation.

Using the Font Dialog Box

The fonts available with your printer are displayed in the Face list box at the Font Properties dialog box with the Font tab selected, also known as the Font dialog box. You can use several methods to display the Font dialog box as shown in figure 6.5, including:

- Click Format and then Font.
- Display a QuickMenu and then click Font.
- Double-click a Font code in Reveal Codes.

6.5 *Font Dialog Box*

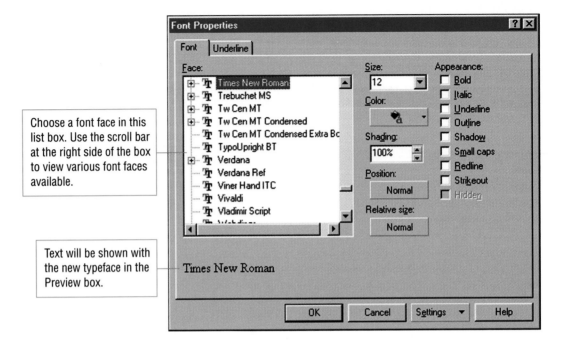

Choose a font face in this list box. Use the scroll bar at the right side of the box to view various font faces available.

Text will be shown with the new typeface in the Preview box.

Font Face

The Face list box at the Font dialog box displays the typefaces (font faces) available with your printer. Figure 6.5 shows the typefaces available with a popular laser printer (the fonts displayed with your printer may vary from those shown).

An icon displays before the typefaces in the Face list box. The printer icon identifies a built-in font provided with your printer. The *TT* icon identifies soft fonts. WordPerfect provides a number of TrueType soft fonts that are identified with the *TT* icon. The TrueType fonts are graphically generated while printer fonts are printer generated. Graphically generated fonts take longer to print than printer-generated fonts.

To change to a different typeface, select the desired typeface, and then click OK or press Enter. You may need to scroll through the list to display the desired typeface. To do this, click the up-pointing or down-pointing triangle at the right side of the Face list box. You can also move quickly to a particular typeface by pressing the first letter or first few letters of the typeface on the keyboard. For example, to move quickly to the Galliard BT typeface, you would display the Font dialog box and then press the letter *g*. The first typeface beginning with the letter *g* is displayed and selected in the Face list box.

When the typeface is changed, WordPerfect inserts a code in the document at the position of the insertion point. For example, the code to change the typeface to Arial would appear as Font: Arial. When different typefaces are selected, the Preview box at the bottom of the Font dialog box displays the appearance of the selected font.

The WordPerfect 10 Preview box will display your document text rather than sample text to show the effects of the new font selection. This feature is called *Real-Time Preview*. If you have text selected (highlighted) when opening the Font dialog box, the selected text will be shown with the new typeface in the Preview box. If no text is selected, the word in which the cursor is located is displayed in the Preview box. If your cursor is on a blank line, the text following the blank line is displayed.

Changing Margins and Typeface

1. Open Para 02.
2. Save the document with Save As and name it Ch 06, Ex 01.
3. With the insertion point positioned at the beginning of the document, change the left and right margins to 1.5 inches.
4. Change the typeface to Garamond by completing the following steps:
    a. With the insertion point positioned at the beginning of the document, display the Font dialog box by clicking Format and then Font.
    b. At the Font dialog box, key the letter **g**. (This displays and selects the first typeface beginning with the letter *g*.)
    c. Click *Garamond* in the list to select it. (Skip this step if it is already selected. If Garamond is not available, choose a similar serif typeface such as Galliard BT.)

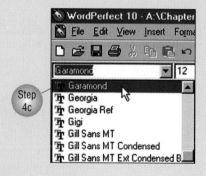

Step 4c

    d. Click OK or press Enter.
5. Save, print, and then close Ch 06, Ex 01.

In addition to using the Font dialog box to select a typeface, you can use the Font Face button on the Main property bar. When you click the down-pointing triangle at the right of the Font Face button, a drop-down menu displays as shown in figure 6.6 (your drop-down menu may vary). To select a typeface, position the arrow pointer on the desired typeface, and then click the left mouse button. Scroll through the list using the up- or down-pointing triangles or key the first letter (or letters) of the desired typeface.

Font Face

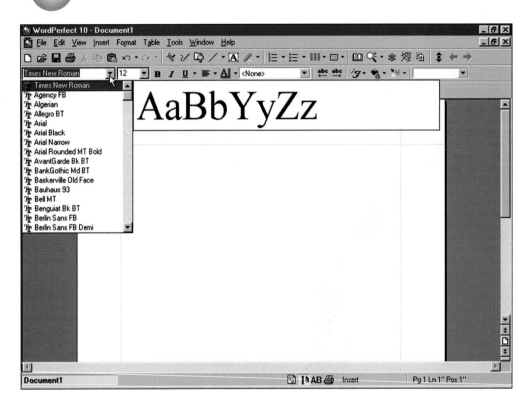

Font Size

The Size list box at the Font dialog box displays a variety of common type sizes. Decrease point size to make text smaller or increase point size to make text larger. Change the font size by clicking the down-pointing triangle next to the Size text box and selecting the desired size in the list box. You can also select the current size in the Size text box and then key the desired size.

exercise 2

Changing the Typeface and Size

1. Open Para 04.
2. Save the document with Save As and name it Ch 06, Ex 02.
3. With the insertion point positioned at the beginning of the document, change the font to 10-point Bookman Old Style using the Font dialog box by completing the following steps:
    a. With the insertion point positioned at the beginning of the document, display the Font dialog box by clicking Format and then Font.

b. At the Font dialog box, click the up-pointing triangle at the right side of the Face list box until Bookman Old Style displays and then click it. (If Bookman Old Style is not available, choose another serif typeface such as Garamond.)

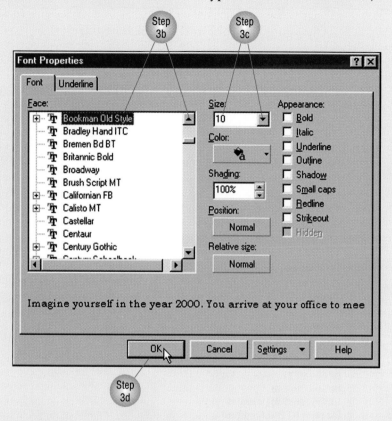

c. Change the Font size option to 10. To do this, click the down-pointing triangle next to the Size text box and select *10* from the list box.
d. Click OK or press Enter.
4. Save, print, and then close Ch 06, Ex 02.

In addition to the Font dialog box, you can use the Font Size button on the Main property bar to change type size. To change the type size with this button, click the down-pointing triangle at the right of the Font Size button and then click the desired type size at the drop-down list.

Font Size

Appearance

The Appearance section of the Font dialog box contains a variety of options that can be used to create different character styles. In chapter 3, you learned to bold, underline, and italicize text with shortcut commands or buttons on the Main property bar. The shortcut commands or buttons on the Main property bar are probably the easiest to use. However, if you want to specify a variety of character styles, you can use the Font dialog box.

Changing the Font and Character Style

1. Open Report 06.
2. Save the document with Save As and name it Ch 06, Ex 03.
3. With the insertion point positioned at the beginning of the document, change the font to 12-point Garamond. (If Garamond is not available, choose another serif typeface such as Charter BT.)
4. Bold and italicize the last six lines in the report by completing the following steps:
   a. Select the last six lines in the report (*increased random access memory* through *increased cycle speeds*).
   b. Display the Font dialog box.
   c. At the Font dialog box, click Bold in the Appearance section.

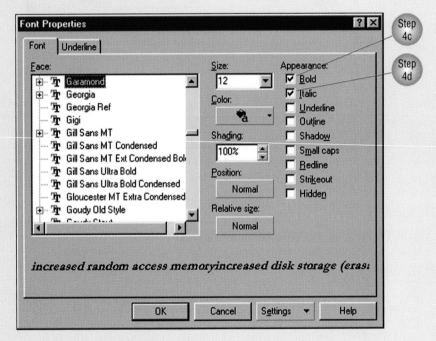

   d. Click Italic in the Appearance section.
   e. Click OK or press Enter.
   f. Deselect the text.
5. Save, print, and then close Ch 06, Ex 03.

Use the <u>R</u>edline option from the Font dialog box to identify text that is added to a legal document. When text is added to a legal document, it may print in red, print with a shaded background, or print a vertical bar in the left margin. The appearance of redlined text is printer dependent. How redlined text appears when printed can be changed at the Redline dialog box shown in figure 6.7. To display the Redline dialog box, click <u>F</u>ile, point to <u>D</u>ocument, and then click Redline Method.

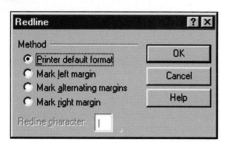

At the Redline dialog box, the default setting is Printer default format. You can also choose to mark redlined text at the left margin of the document, alternating margins, or the right margin. If you choose Mark left margin or Mark right margin, you can change the Redline character from the default of a vertical line (|) to any other symbol with the Redline character option at the bottom of the dialog box. WordPerfect will insert a redline mark at the left or right margin of a line where text has been added to a document. If you choose Mark alternating margins as the redlining method, WordPerfect will insert a redline mark at the left margin for even pages and at the right margin for odd pages. If your printer supports shaded background and text is redlined in a document, it will look like this:

This is Redlined text.

With the Strikeout option from the Font dialog box, you can identify text that needs to be deleted from a document. Strikeout prints text with a line of hyphens running through it. This feature has practical application for some legal documents in which deleted text must be retained in the document. The hyphens indicate that the text has been deleted. Strikeout text looks like this:

~~This is Strikeout text~~.

Using Strikeout and Redline

1. Open Legal 01.
2. Save the document with Save As and name it Ch 06, Ex 04.
3. Make the following changes to the document:
   a. With the insertion point positioned at the beginning of the document, change the font to 12-point Galliard BT.
   b. Select the last sentence in the second paragraph (the one that begins *A default judgment is one where the plaintiff...*), and identify it for strikeout by completing the following steps:
      1) Select the sentence.
      2) Display the Font dialog box.
      3) Click Strikeout in the Appearance section.
      4) Click OK or press Enter.

c. In the third paragraph, add the words *or a representative of the law firm* at the end of the sentence (but before the period) that reads *If you do so, the demand must be in writing and must be served upon the person signing this summons.* as redlined text by completing the following steps:

    1) Position the insertion point immediately to the left of the period at the end of the sentence.

    2) Turn on redlining by completing the following steps:

        a) Display the Font dialog box.

        b) Click <u>R</u>edline in the Appearance section.

        c) Click OK or press Enter.

    3) Press the spacebar and then key **or a representative of the law firm**.

4. Save, print, and then close Ch 06, Ex 04.

Position

When you click the Normal button at the <u>P</u>osition section of the Font dialog box, a drop-down menu displays with three options—Normal, Superscript, and Subscript.

With the *Superscript* option, you can create text that is raised slightly above the line. Some mathematical expressions are written with superscript numbers. For example, the mathematical expression 4 to the second power is written as 4^2. You can create a superscript as you key text or you can superscript selected text.

With the *Subscript* option from the Font dialog box, you can create text that is lowered slightly below the line. Some chemical formulas require the use of subscripted characters. For example, the formula for water is written as H_2O. You can create a subscripted character as you key text or you can subscript selected text.

 exercise

Creating Superscript and Subscript Numbers

1. At a clear editing window, key the memo shown in figure 6.8 in an appropriate memo format with the following specifications:

    a. Change the left and right margins to 1.5 inches.

    b. Indent and italicize text as indicated.

    c. Create the superscripted numbers in the memo by completing the following steps:

        1) Key text to the point where superscripted text is to appear.

        2) Display the Font dialog box.

        3) At the Font dialog box, click Normal at the <u>P</u>osition section.

        4) At the drop-down menu that displays, click Superscript.

        5) Click OK or press Enter.

        6) Key the superscripted text.

        7) Display the Font dialog box.

        8) At the Font dialog box, click Superscript.

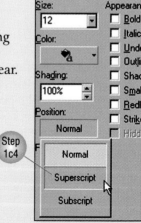

Step 1c4

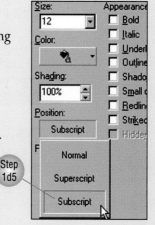

9) At the drop-down menu that displays, click Normal.
10) Click OK or press Enter.
d. Create the subscripted numbers in the memo by completing the following steps:
   1) Key the text in the memo.
   2) Select the text to be subscripted.
   3) Display the Font dialog box.
   4) Click Normal at the Position section.
   5) At the drop-down menu that displays, click Subscript.
   6) Click OK or press Enter.
2. Save the memo and name it Ch 06, Ex 05.
3. Print and then close Ch 06, Ex 05.

FIGURE

6.8 *Exercise 5*

DATE: June 2, 2003; TO: Thomas Scannell; FROM: Barbara Jaech; SUBJECT: STATISTICAL ANALYSIS

The research and analysis you are conducting on medical health care is very important to the project planning. As you complete your analysis, please address the following areas:

1.   What is the relationship between the indices C, D, and I to both r^1 and r^2?

2.   What is the improvement when $r^1 = .55$ and r^2 is nearly .79?

3.   What is the main effect on the scores of X_1, X_2, and X_3?

When these areas have been addressed, please give me a copy of the analysis.

xx:Ch 06, Ex 05

Relative Size

The Relative size option at the Font dialog box contains a drop-down menu with a variety of size options. The size options are used to change the size of the type based on the size of the font in the document. The selections change the size of the current font by the following percentages:

Fine = 60%
Small = 80%
Large = 120%
Very Large = 150%
Extra Large = 200%

Some printers support only a few point sizes. If your printer does not support the exact point size selected, WordPerfect tries to choose and print an approximate size.

Changing point size with a Relative size option from the Font dialog box allows changes to be made easily to text in the document. If the size of the font is changed, any type with relative size options attached is automatically updated. Also, if the typeface is changed, the size options will apply to the new typeface.

exercise 6

Changing the Font and Relative Size

1. Open Report 06.
2. Save the document with Save As and name it Ch 06, Ex 06.
3. Make the following changes to the document:
   a. With the insertion point positioned at the beginning of the document, change the font to 12-point Galliard BT. (If Galliard BT is not available, choose another serif typeface such as Garamond.)
   b. Change the relative size of the title *TRENDS IN TELECOMMUNICATIONS* to Very large by completing the following steps:
      1) Select the title *TRENDS IN TELECOMMUNICATIONS*.
      2) Display the Font dialog box.
      3) Click Normal at the Relative size section.
      4) At the drop-down menu that displays, click Very large.

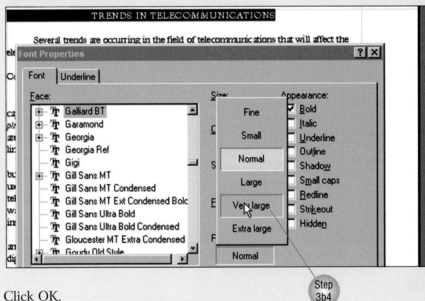

Step 3b4

   5) Click OK.
   c. Select the heading *Continued Growth of Photonics (Fiber Optics)* and then change the relative size to Large.
   d. Select the heading *Microcomputer Trends in the Nineties* and then change the relative size to Large.
   e. Deselect the heading.
4. Save, print, and then close Ch 06, Ex 06.

Underline

When underlining is turned on, WordPerfect will underline spaces between words but not spaces caused by pressing the Tab key. With Underline options from the Font Properties dialog box with the Underline tab selected, also known as the Underline dialog box, you can tell WordPerfect whether or not you want spaces between words and/or spaces created with the Tab key underlined. Figure 6.9 displays the Underline dialog box.

FIGURE 6.9 *Underline Dialog Box*

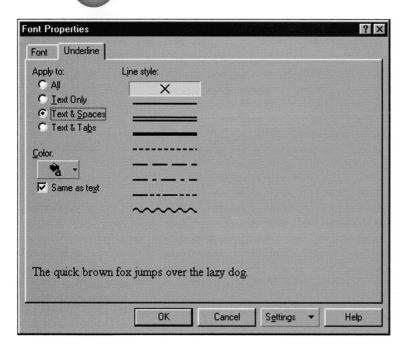

Color

To change the text color, click the Color button at the Underline dialog box. This causes a palette of color choices to display. At this palette, click the desired color. You can also display a palette of text color choices by clicking the Font Color button on the Main property bar.

Font Color

If you click the Color button at the Underline dialog box or the Font Color button on the Main property bar and then click More at the palette of color choices, the Select Color dialog box displays. At this dialog box, you can select color models and values.

Formatting with QuickFormat

You can use WordPerfect's QuickFormat feature to quickly copy fonts and attributes or paragraph formatting already applied to text to different locations in the document. To use QuickFormat, position the insertion point on a character containing the desired character or paragraph formatting, turn on QuickFormat, and then select text to which you want the character and/or paragraph formatting applied. When

QuickFormat

you turn on QuickFormat, the arrow pointer displays with a paint roller attached (similar to the paint roller that displays on the button on the Toolbar). To turn on QuickFormat, click the QuickFormat button on the Toolbar or click Format and then QuickFormat.

When you are done formatting with QuickFormat, turn it off by clicking the QuickFormat button on the Toolbar or clicking Format and then QuickFormat. You can also just key text to turn off the QuickFormat feature.

The QuickFormat dialog box (figure 6.10) can also be displayed with a QuickMenu. To do this, position the arrow pointer anywhere in the editing window (except the top, bottom, left, or right margins), click the *right* mouse button, and then click QuickFormat.

FIGURE

6.10 *QuickFormat Dialog Box*

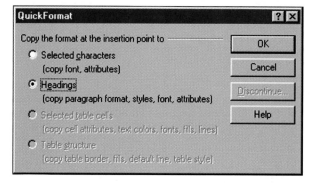

exercise 7

Formatting Text with QuickFormat

1. Open Report 06.
2. Save the document with Save As and name it Ch 06, Ex 07.
3. Select the title *TRENDS IN TELECOMMUNICATIONS* and then change the relative size to Large.
4. Use QuickFormat to change the two headings in the report to Large by completing the following steps:
   a. Position the insertion point on any character in the title *TRENDS IN TELECOMMUNICATIONS*.
   b. Click the QuickFormat button on the Toolbar.
   c. At the QuickFormat dialog box, make sure Headings is selected and then click OK or press Enter.
   d. Click once on the heading *Continued Growth of Photonics (Fiber Optics)* (this will select the entire heading and apply the Large formatting).
   e. Click once on the heading *Microcomputer Trends in the Nineties*.
   f. Click the QuickFormat button on the Toolbar to turn off the QuickFormat feature.
5. Save, print, and then close Ch 06, Ex 07.

Using WordPerfect Character Sets

The WordPerfect program includes character sets you can use to create special letters and symbols. WordPerfect provides over 1,500 characters and symbols. Depending on the printer you are using, some or all of these symbols will be available. These symbols are grouped into 15 character sets. Each character set contains different types of symbols. For example, character set 4 contains typographic symbols and character set 6 contains mathematic and scientific symbols.

Inserting a Symbol in a Document

You can insert a symbol in a document with the Symbol option from the Insert menu or the shortcut command Ctrl + W.

When you click Insert and then Symbol, or press Ctrl + W, the Symbols dialog box displays as shown in figure 6.11. At the Symbols dialog box, use the arrow pointer on the scroll bar to display the desired symbol, and then click the symbol. This inserts a dotted box around the symbol and inserts the character set and symbol number in the Number text box. Click the Insert and Close button to close the dialog box and insert the symbol in the document.

FIGURE

6.11 **Symbols Dialog Box**

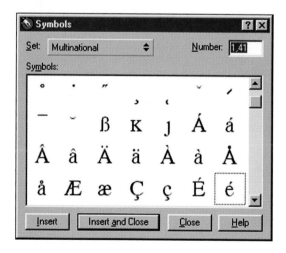

At the Symbols dialog box, you can click the Insert button to insert the symbol in the document and not close the dialog box. This might be useful if you are inserting more than one symbol in the document at the same time. You can also key the character set number and the symbol number in the Number text box. For example, if you want to insert a copyright symbol in the document and you know the character set number is 4 and the symbol number is 23, you would key 4,23 in the Number text box.

When a symbol is inserted in a document, a code can be seen in Reveal Codes. For example, if you chose the paragraph symbol ¶ (4,5) at the Symbols dialog box, the code displays in Reveal Codes.

Changing the Character Set

At the Symbols dialog box, you can change the character set with the <u>S</u>et option. This changes the display of symbols in the viewing box. To do this, click the button displayed immediately at the right of <u>S</u>et. This causes a pop-up menu to display with character set options. At this pop-up menu, click the desired character set. After changing the character set, click a symbol, and then click the Insert <u>a</u>nd Close button to close the Symbols dialog box and insert the symbol in the document.

Inserting Special Symbols

1. At a clear editing window, key the memo shown in figure 6.12 in an appropriate memo format with the following specifications:
    a. Change the left and right margins to 1.5 inches.
    b. Complete the following steps to create the special symbols:
        1) Click Symbol from the <u>I</u>nsert menu.
        2) At the Symbols dialog box, key the character set number, a comma, and the symbol number, and then press Enter. Use the following numbers at the Symbols dialog box to insert the special symbol:

é	=	1,41
ñ	=	1,57
°	=	6,36
®	=	4,22

2. Save the document and name it Ch 06, Ex 08.
3. Print and then close Ch 06, Ex 08.

FIGURE

6.12 **Exercise 8**

DATE: February 18, 2003; TO: Maggie Hénédine; FROM: Joni Kapshaw; SUBJECT: DISTRICT NEWSLETTER

The layout for the March newsletter looks great! I talked with Anita Nuñez about the figures. She explained how we can rotate the image inside the box by 90°, 180°, and 270°. As soon as she shows me how to do this, I will pass on the information to you.

Anita plans to offer an informal workshop on some of the graphic capabilities of Corel WordPerfect®. She plans to discuss customizing box borders, inserting shaded fill, rotating and scaling images, and creating drop shadow boxes. If you want her to address any other topics, please give me a call by the end of this week.

xx:Ch 06, Ex 08

CHAPTER summary

➤ A font consists of three parts: typeface, type style, and type size. WordPerfect refers to these three parts as font face, font style, and font size.

➤ A typeface is a set of characters with a common design and shape. Typefaces are either monospaced or proportional. A monospaced typeface allots the same amount of horizontal space for each character. A proportional typeface allots a varying amount of space for each character.

➤ The type size of proportional typefaces is a vertical measurement. The higher the point size, the larger the characters.

➤ Real-Time Preview allows you to view your font changes before applying the changes to your document.

➤ A type style is a variation of style within a certain typeface. The standard style is regular. Other type styles include bold, italic, and bold italic.

➤ At the Font dialog box you can change the typeface and/or the type size and see examples of the text as you make each change. You can also create different character styles such as bold, underline, double underline, and italic or a combination of these styles.

➤ Other options available at the Font dialog box include Outline, Shadow, Small caps, Redline, Strikeout, Superscript, and Subscript.

➤ Also available at the Font dialog box are options to change the relative type size of the current font, the mode of underlining, and the color choices for color printing.

➤ The QuickFormat feature lets you quickly copy fonts and attributes or paragraph formatting already applied to text.

➤ Corel WordPerfect includes character sets you can use to create special letters and symbols.

COMMANDS summary

Command	Mouse	Keyboard
Display the Font dialog box	Format, Font	F9
Turn on QuickFormat	Format, QuickFormat; or click the QuickFormat button on the Toolbar	
Display the Symbols dialog box	Insert, Symbol	Ctrl + W

CONCEPTS check

Matching: On a blank sheet of paper, indicate the correct letter that matches each numbered item.

Ⓐ Arial
Ⓑ bold
Ⓒ font
Ⓓ Garamond
Ⓔ italic
Ⓕ points
Ⓖ proportional
Ⓗ regular

Ⓘ sans serif
Ⓙ serif
Ⓚ subscript
Ⓛ superscript
Ⓜ Times New Roman
Ⓝ type size
Ⓞ type style
Ⓟ typeface

1. Examples of different type styles.

2. A small line at the end of a character stroke.

3. A particular typeface in a specific style and size.

4. A set of characters with a common design and shape.

5. Text that is lowered slightly below the regular line of text.

6. The size of proportional type is measured vertically in units called this.

7. Examples of different typefaces.

8. Text that is raised slightly above the regular line of text.

Completion: On a blank sheet of paper, indicate the correct term, command, or number for each item.

1. The typefaces available with your printer are displayed in this box at the Font dialog box.

2. The common font sizes are displayed in this box at the Font dialog box.

3. This option lets you show which text has been deleted from a document.

4. This option lets you identify text that is added to a legal document.

5. This choice in the Relative size option box changes the size of the current font to twice its normal size.

6. The feature that allows you to see your changes before applying them is called this.

SKILLS check

Assessment 1

1. At a clear editing window, display the Font dialog box. Change the font to 24-point Garamond and turn on the Shadow appearance option. (If Garamond is not available, choose another serif typeface.)
2. Key the text centered as shown in figure 6.13.
3. Save the document and name it Ch 06, SA 01.
4. Print and then close Ch 06, SA 01.

FIGURE

6.13 *Assessment 1*

Intensive Care Unit
Respiratory Therapy Techniques
Tuesday, May 20, 2003
1:00 - 3:30 p.m., Room 430

Assessment 2

1. Open Legal 02.
2. Save the document with Save As and name it Ch 06, SA 02.
3. Make the following changes to the document:
   a. Change the relative size of the title *IN DISTRICT COURT NO. 4, PIERCE COUNTY STATE OF WASHINGTON* to Large.
   b. Following the proofreaders' marks displayed in figure 6.14, identify the text that is deleted with the Strikeout option from the Font dialog box, and then identify the text that is added with the Redline option from the Font dialog box.
4. Save, print, and then close Ch 06, SA 02.

6.14 *Assessment 2*

IN DISTRICT COURT NO. 4, PIERCE COUNTY
STATE OF WASHINGTON

STATE OF WASHINGTON)
                   Plaintiff,) NO. NUMBER

vs.) **NOTICE OF APPEARANCE**
) **AND DEMAND FOR**
) **INFORMATION**

NAME1,)
                Defendant.)
_____)

TO: **CLERK OF DISTRICT COURT**, AND TO THE **PROSECUTING ATTORNEY**:

    YOU AND EACH OF YOU ~~will~~ please take notice that Coburn, Raintree & Thompson hereby appear in the above entitled action on behalf of the Defendant, NAME1, *as attorneys of record* and hereby enter a plea of **NOT GUILTY**, waive arraignment, ~~the Sixty Day Rule~~ and make the following demands:

1.   That the trial of this matter be heard by jury;

2.   That the undersigned *attorney* be furnished with full information concerning the test ~~or tests~~ of blood alcohol content that ~~were~~ *was* submitted to by the Defendant, NAME1 ~~, if any, and a copy of the alcohol influence report form;~~

3.   That the undersigned *attorney* be advised as to whether or not a videotape was taken of the Defendant, NAME1;

4.   That the breathalyzer operator be present at the time of trial; however, the Defendant, NAME1, may waive this request at a subsequent date ~~upon the satisfactory examination of the inspection data heretofore requested.~~

    DATED this _____ day of _____, 2003.

_____
LESLIE COBURN
of Coburn, Raintree & Thompson
Attorneys for Defendant

Assessment 3

1. At a clear editing window, key the memo shown in figure 6.15 in an appropriate memo format with the following specifications:
   a. Change the left and right margins to 1.5 inches.
   b. Change the font to 12-point Garamond (or a similar serif typeface).
   c. Indent, italicize, superscript, and subscript text as indicated.
2. Save the memo and name it Ch 06, SA 03.
3. Print and then close Ch 06, SA 03.

6.15 *Assessment 3*

DATE: June 16, 2003; TO: Barbara Jaech; FROM: Thomas Scannell; SUBJECT: STATISTICAL ANALYSIS

I have been running an analysis on the areas mentioned in your June 2 memo. Completing the computations has brought up the following questions:

1. With smaller section ratios of r^1 and r^2 (.10 to .25)^1, what will be the yield increase?

2. What is the interaction effect on the scores of X_1, X_2, and X_3?

I will try to report on the findings to these questions by the end of next week.

xx:Ch 06, SA 03

Using Writing Tools

PERFORMANCE OBJECTIVES

Upon successful completion of chapter 7, you will be able to:
- **Complete a spelling check on text in a document using Spell Checker**
- **Display synonyms and antonyms for specific words using the Thesaurus**
- **Improve the grammar of text in a document using Grammatik**
- **Find and replace specific text or formatting in a document**

Chapter 07

WordPerfect includes writing tools to help create a thoughtful and well-written document. One of these writing tools, Spell Checker, finds misspelled words and offers replacement words. It also finds duplicate words and irregular capitalizations. Another tool, Thesaurus, provides a list of synonyms and antonyms for words. Grammatik can help you create a well-written document, but it does not replace the need for human proofreading.

Using Spell Checker

In chapter 1, you learned about the Spell-As-You-Go feature, which automatically inserts red slash marks below words that are not recognized by WordPerfect and might be misspelled, and provides you with a menu of suggested replacements and other options if you click the *right* mouse button over the error. You may prefer to work with Spell-As-You-Go turned off and perform one spelling check when the document is complete. To turn off Spell-As-You-Go, click <u>T</u>ools, point to Proofread, and then click <u>O</u>ff. Spell-As-You-Go will remain turned off until you turn it on again. To turn it back on, click <u>T</u>ools, point to <u>P</u>roofread, and then click Spell-<u>A</u>s-You-Go.

Spell Checker works mainly with two word lists—a user word list and a main word list (containing more than 100,000 words). In addition to these two word lists, a document-specific word list is automatically attached to a document where you can add words that are specific to the current document only and that you want Spell Checker to skip.

When a spell check is run, Spell Checker first checks the words in the document against words in the default user word list. If a match is not found, Spell Checker looks for the word in the main word list. Additional word lists can be purchased and used with Spell Checker for specific industries (medical, legal, scientific, and so on).

What Spell Checker Can Do

Spell Checker operates by comparing each word in a document with words in the user word list and the main word list. If there is a match, Spell Checker moves on to the next word. If there is no match for the word, Spell Checker will stop and highlight the word for correction if it fits one of the following situations:

- a possible misspelled word if the spelling does not match any word that exists in the word lists
- typographical errors such as transposed letters
- double word occurrences (such as *and and*)
- irregular capitalization (such as *COlumbus*)
- some proper names
- jargon and some technical terms

Spell Checker may not stop at all proper names. For example, Spell Checker would assume the first name *Robin* is spelled correctly and pass over it because Robin would appear in the word lists as a type of bird.

What Spell Checker Cannot Do

Spell Checker will not do the following:

- Highlight words that are spelled correctly but used incorrectly.
- Check grammar.
- Eliminate the need for proofreading.

Spell Checking a Document

Spell Checker

Before using Spell Checker, save the current document or open an existing document. To begin Spell Checker, click <u>T</u>ools and then <u>S</u>pell Checker; or click the Spell Checker button on the Toolbar. This causes the Writing Tools dialog box with the Spell Checker tab selected to display as shown in figure 7.1.

FIGURE

7.1 *Writing Tools Dialog Box with the Spell Checker Tab Selected*

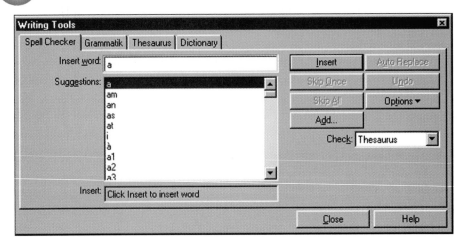

By default, the Writing Tools dialog box displays in the bottom half of the editing window and the Title bar for the dialog box is not visible. If you want to display the Title bar for the Writing Tools dialog box, position the mouse pointer in the gray area of the dialog box at the right side of the tabs until the pointer turns into a four-headed arrow. Hold down the left mouse button, drag the dialog box up slightly until an outline border displays, and then release the mouse button. Figure 7.1 displays the Writing Tools dialog box with the Title bar displayed. If the dialog box has not been moved, it will be larger and the Title bar will not be visible.

Using Command Buttons

The Writing Tools dialog box with the Spell Checker tab selected contains several command buttons that display at the right side of the box. These buttons are described in figure 7.2.

F I G U R E

7.2 **Command Buttons**

Command Button	Function
Start	If the automatic start has been disabled, click the Start button to begin spell checking. When Spell Checker discovers a word not contained in its word lists, the word is selected and replacements are suggested.
Replace	When suggestions are offered, choose the replacement word and click Replace to insert the new word into your document.
Skip Once/Skip All	Select Skip Once to skip that occurrence of the highlighted word. Select Skip All to skip all occurrences of the highlighted word.
Add	Click the Add button to add a highlighted word to your user word list. Spell Checker will not highlight the word again (in the current and future documents).
Auto Replace	Selecting this will add the word to the QuickCorrect word list. To do this, make sure the proper spelling is inserted in the Replace with text box and then click Auto Replace.
Undo	Click this to reverse the last replacement made.
Options	Click this button to display the drop-down menu shown in figure 7.3. Check marks indicate that an option is active. To deactivate an option, click the left mouse button on the option.

7.3 *Spell Checker Options Drop-Down Menu*

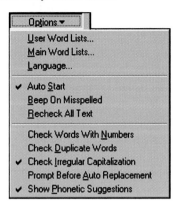

Editing in Spell Checker

When spell checking a document, you can temporarily leave the Writing Tools dialog box, make corrections in the document, and then resume spell checking. To do this, move the I-beam pointer to the location in the sentence where the change is to occur, and then click the left mouse button. Make changes to the sentence and then click the Resume button in the Writing Tools dialog box (previously the Start button).

exercise

Completing a Spelling Check

1. Open Memo 03.
2. Save the memo with Save As and name it Ch 07, Ex 01.
3. Perform a spelling check by completing the following steps:
   a. Click the Spell Checker button on the Toolbar.
   b. Spell Checker highlights the word *Mai*. This name is spelled properly so click the Skip All button.

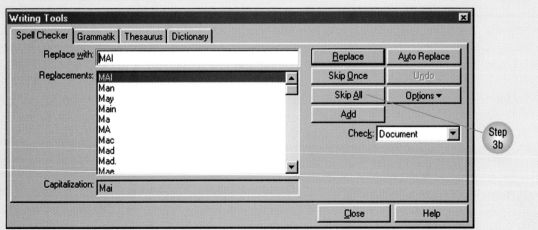

c. Spell Checker highlights the word *Ayala*. This name is spelled properly so click the Skip All button.
d. Spell Checker highlights the word *idenified*. The proper spelling is displayed in the Replace with text box so click the Replace button.

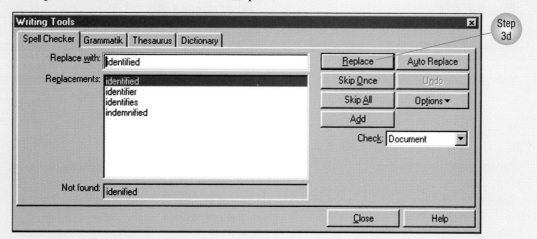

e. Spell Checker highlights the word *reqiured*. The proper spelling is displayed in the Replacements list box. Move the arrow pointer to the correct spelling (*required*) and then double-click the left mouse button.
f. Spell Checker highlights *departmnts*. Move the arrow pointer to the correct spelling (*departments*) and then double-click the left mouse button.
g. Spell Checker highlights the word *hte*. Click the correct spelling (*the*) in the Replacements list box and then click the Replace button.
h. Spell Checker highlights the word *tmies*. The correct spelling is selected in the Replacements list box so click the Replace button.
i. Spell Checker highlights the word *ncesary* and gives no suggestions. Correct *ncesary* in the Replace with text box by moving the insertion point and keying the letters **e** and **s** in the appropriate location in the word and then clicking the Replace button. (The correct spelling is *necessary*.)
j. Spell Checker highlights *xx:Memo*. Leave this as written by clicking the Skip Once button.
k. At the *Spell check completed. Close Spell Checker?* query, click Yes or press Enter.
4. Save, print, and then close Ch 07, Ex 01.

Customizing Spell Check Options

Use the Check list box and the Options button to change options that affect the way the Spell Checker operates.

> **Check**: By default, Spell Checker will check the entire document, no matter where the insertion point is positioned. Options available from this feature are listed in figure 7.4.

7.4 *Spell Checker Check List Box*

To check this	Do or choose this
Entire document	Choose *Document* in the Check list box.
Specified number of pages	Choose *Number of Pages* in the Check list box and then specify how many.
Current page	Choose *Page* in the Check list box.
Paragraph	Choose *Paragraph* in the Check list box.
Selected text	Select the text before activating Spell Checker.
Current sentence	Choose *Sentence* in the Check list box.
From current point to end of document	Choose *To End of Document* in the Check list box.
Current word	Choose *Word* in the Check list box.

Options: As previously mentioned, click the Options button at the Writing Tools dialog box with the Spell Checker tab selected and a drop-down menu displays with options for customizing a spelling check. These are described in figure 7.5.

7.5 *Spell Checker Options Drop-Down Menu*

Option	Meaning
Auto Start	Spell checking starts automatically if this option is checked. Deselect Auto Start to turn feature off.
Beep On Misspelled	When turned on, you will hear a beep when a misspelled word is found.
Recheck All Text	Select this to have Spell Checker recheck the document.

Continued on next page

Option	Meaning
Check Words With Numbers	Select this to have Spell Checker highlight all words that contain numbers. If you wish Spell Checker to ignore words that contain numbers, deselect this option.
Check Duplicate Words	Select this option to have Spell Checker highlight double words, such as *Dan Schneider and and I went on a picnic.*
Check Irregular Capitalization	Select this option to check words that may have irregular capitalization.
Prompt Before Auto Replacement	If this option is selected, WordPerfect will prompt you before QuickCorrect replaces words as you type.
Show Phonetic Suggestions	Turned on by default, this feature will display similar-sounding words to the word not found.

Working with User Word Lists

A user word list is a list of words or phrases that you want Spell Checker to skip, replace, or display alternatives for. Examples of words that you might want included in a user word list are proper names of individuals, technical jargon specific to your business, or acronyms that you use consistently.

You can add, create, or delete user word lists, or edit words or phrases in the default user word list using the Options button in the Writing Tools dialog box.

Adding, Creating, or Removing User Word Lists

A user word list can be added, created, or removed. To do this, click the Options button in the Writing Tools dialog box. At the drop-down menu that displays, click User Word Lists. This displays the User Word Lists dialog box as shown in figure 7.6.

7.6 *User Word Lists Dialog Box*

To add a user word list, click the Add List button, key a name for the user word list, and then click the Open button. The new list will appear in the list box with an X in a box beside it. The extension *.uwl* is automatically added to the end of the document name.

Add the word or phrase you want WordPerfect to skip in the Word/phrase text box by moving the I-beam pointer to the text box and then clicking the left mouse button. Key the text and then click the Add Entry button.

To remove a word list, select the user word list file name in the User word lists list box and then click the Remove List button. Removing a user word list only removes it from the spell checking scan sequence. The file is not deleted from the hard drive.

exercise 2

Changing Spell Checking Options and Adding Words to the User Word List

1. Open Letter 01.
2. Save the letter with Save As and name it Ch 07, Ex 02.
3. Change spell checking options and then perform a spelling check by completing the following steps:
   a. Click the Spell Checker button on the Toolbar.
   b. When Spell Checker selects *Loren*, click the Options button.

c. At the Options drop-down menu, click Check Duplicate Words to turn off this option.

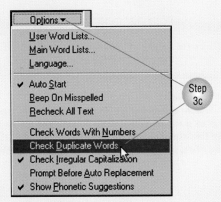

d. Click the Options button again.
e. At the Options drop-down menu, click Beep On Misspelled to turn on this option.
f. Click the Add button to add this name to the user list.
g. When Spell Checker selects *leter*, click *letter* in the Replacements list box and then click the Replace button.
h. As Spell Checker selects other words for correction, replace misspelled words with the proper spelling, make corrections to irregular capitalizations, and tell Spell Checker to skip proper names.
i. When the spell check is completed, click Yes or press Enter.
4. Proofread the letter and make corrections to mistakes not selected by Spell Checker.
5. Save and print Ch 07, Ex 02.
6. Change the Spell Checker options back to the default by completing the following steps:
a. Click the Spell Check button on the Toolbar.
b. When asked if you want to close Spell Checker, click No.
c. At the Writing Tools dialog box with the Spell Checker tab selected, click the Options button.
d. At the Options drop-down menu, click Check Duplicate Words. (This turns the feature back on.)
e. Click the Options button again.
f. At the Options drop-down menu, click Beep On Misspelled. (This turns the feature off.)
g. Click the Close button.
7. Close Ch 07, Ex 02.

Using Thesaurus

WordPerfect offers a Thesaurus program that can be used to find *synonyms* and *antonyms* for words. Synonyms are words that have the same or nearly the same meaning. Antonyms are words that have the opposite meaning.

To use Thesaurus, open the document containing the word for which you want to find synonyms and/or antonyms. Position the insertion point next to any character in the word, click Tools, and then click Thesaurus. This displays the Writing Tools dialog box with the Thesaurus tab selected similar to the one shown in figure 7.7. The dialog box in figure 7.7 displays synonyms and antonyms for the word *award*.

7.7 *Writing Tools Dialog Box with the Thesaurus Tab Selected*

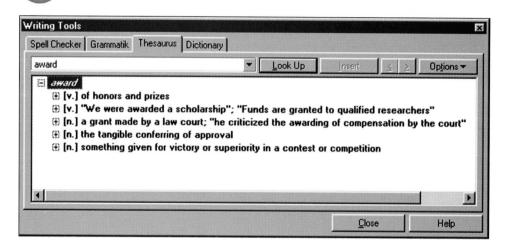

Definitions for the word will display in the list box in the Writing Tools dialog box. Several possible definitions are offered. Click on the plus sign next to the definition that most closely matches your need. Alternative words for the definition you selected appear.

Thesaurus Options

The Writing Tools dialog box with the Thesaurus tab selected contains several options you can access through list boxes and command buttons.

Using List Boxes

To see the remaining definitions for *award* using the mouse, move the arrow pointer to the down-pointing triangle and hold down the left mouse button. To move back through the list, move the arrow pointer to the up-pointing triangle and hold down the left mouse button.

Using Command Buttons

The Writing Tools dialog box with the Thesaurus tab selected contains three command buttons that display at the top right side of the box. If you find an appropriate synonym or antonym for a word, insert the desired word in the document by clicking it in the list box and then clicking the Replace button. For example, to replace *award* with *grant*, click the plus sign next to the appropriate definition. In this case the appropriate definition is *"We were awarded a scholarship"; "Funds are granted to qualified researchers"*. Click *grant* and then click the Replace button.

If you open the Writing Tools dialog box with the Thesaurus tab selected when the insertion point is not positioned on or near a word, the Replace button changes to the Insert button. In addition, the Replace with text box is changed to the Insert text box. The insertion point will be positioned in the Insert text box. Key the word you want to look up and press Enter or click the Look Up button. To insert one of the suggested words in the current document, click the desired word and then click the Insert button.

Click the Options button at the Writing Tools dialog box with the Thesaurus tab selected and a drop-down menu displays as shown in figure 7.8.

FIGURE

7.8 *Thesaurus Options Drop-Down Menu*

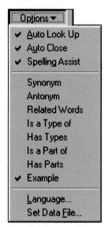

Figure 7.8 illustrates the default options that are active when you open the Thesaurus. An option is active if there is a check mark beside it. To deactivate an option, click the option. This removes the check mark. To reactivate the option after it has been deactivated, follow the same procedure you used to remove the check mark. Figure 7.9 explains the options available at the Options drop-down menu.

FIGURE

7.9 *Thesaurus Options Drop-Down Menu*

Click this	*To do this*
Auto Look Up	The Thesaurus will automatically look up the word at the insertion point when the dialog box is opened.
Auto Close	When active, the Writing Tools dialog box automatically closes when the Replace button is clicked.
Spelling Assist	This displays spelling suggestions when you key a word the Thesaurus does not recognize in the Replace with text box.
Synonym	Select this option to display synonyms for the specified word.
Antonym	Select this option to display antonyms for the specified word.
Related Words	This displays words with a similar meaning to the specified word.

Continued on next page

Click this	To do this
Is a Type of	This displays the category in which the word falls, like *cat* is a type of *feline*.
Has Types	This displays the different categories in which the word can be broken into, like *car* has types including *cab* and *sportscar*.
Is a Part of	This displays the whole item to which the word is a section, like a *lock* is part of a *door* or *gate*.
Has Parts	This displays the sections that make up the word, like a *car* has parts including a *windshield wiper* and *transmission*.
Language	If you have installed other language modules, you can direct the Thesaurus to look up words in other languages. To change to a different language, click Language at the Options drop-down menu. At the Language dialog box that displays, click the desired language in the Language list box and then click OK.
Set Data File	If you have installed other Thesaurus files, use this option to choose the data file you want to work with.

 **exercise 3**

Using Thesaurus to Replace Words

1. Open Memo 02.
2. Save the memo with Save As and name it Ch 07, Ex 03.
3. Change the word *several* in the first paragraph to *numerous* using Thesaurus by completing the following steps:
   a. Position the insertion point in the word *several*.
   b. Click Tools and then Thesaurus.
   c. Click the plus sign next to the first definition and then click the plus sign next to *Related Words*.

d. At the list that displays, click *numerous* and then click the <u>R</u>eplace button.

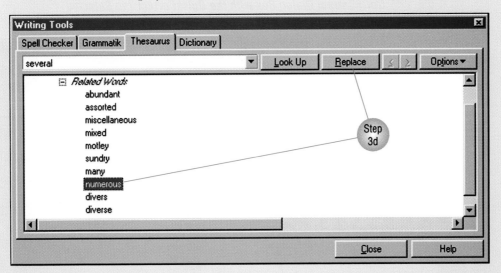

4. Follow similar steps to change the first occurrence of *purchase* in the last paragraph to *buy*.
5. Save, print, and then close Ch 07, Ex 03.

Using QuickCorrect

As mentioned in chapter 1, WordPerfect includes a feature called QuickCorrect that automatically corrects certain words as they are being keyed. For example, if you key *adn* instead of *and*, QuickCorrect automatically corrects it when you press the spacebar after the word. There are numerous automatic corrections that can be seen in the QuickCorrect dialog box. To display the QuickCorrect dialog box with the QuickCorrect tab selected as shown in figure 7.10, click <u>T</u>ools and then QuickCorrect. At the QuickCorrect dialog box, use the vertical scroll bar in the list box to view the entire list of words, symbols, and numbers that WordPerfect will correct.

7.10 *QuickCorrect Dialog Box with the QuickCorrect Tab Selected*

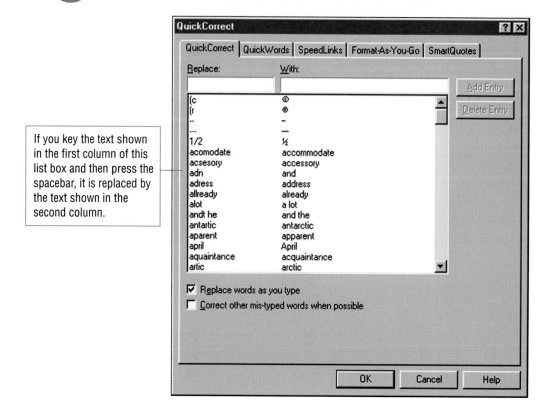

If you key the text shown in the first column of this list box and then press the spacebar, it is replaced by the text shown in the second column.

Adding Words to QuickCorrect

Commonly misspelled words or typographical errors can be added to QuickCorrect. In addition, technical words you use frequently, or your company name, can be added to QuickCorrect. The following are two examples of ways to use QuickCorrect.

- If you consistently key *oopen* instead of *open*, you can add *oopen* to QuickCorrect and tell it to correct *oopen* as *open*.

- If you work for a company called *Pharmacological Institute of America,* you may wish to add the abbreviation *pia* and have it replaced with your full company name. Using QuickCorrect in this manner decreases errors. Make sure the abbreviation you enter is not an actual word.

To add an entry to QuickCorrect, key the misspelling or abbreviation in the Replace text box, key the correct spelling in the With text box, and then click the Add Entry button.

Entries in QuickCorrect can be deleted. To delete an entry, select the entry in the list box at the QuickCorrect dialog box and then click the Delete Entry button. WordPerfect will ask you to confirm the deletion; select Yes.

By default, QuickCorrect will automatically replace text. You can turn automatic replacement off by removing the check mark from the Replace words as you type check box that displays toward the bottom of the QuickCorrect dialog box.

Changing QuickCorrect Options

The QuickCorrect feature can be customized with options from the QuickCorrect dialog box with various tabs selected. Click the Format-As-You-Go tab and the QuickCorrect dialog box displays as shown in figure 7.11.

F I G U R E

7.11 *QuickCorrect Dialog Box with the Format-As-You-Go Tab Selected*

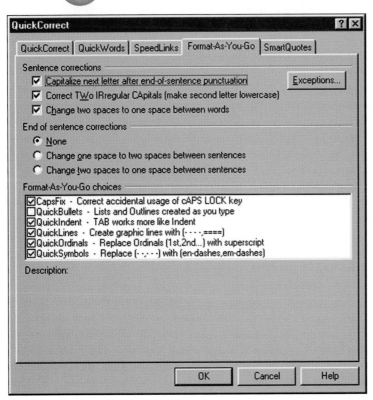

The QuickCorrect dialog box with the Format-As-You-Go tab selected contains a variety of options that can be active or inactive. An option is active if a check mark appears in the check box or if a black dot appears in the radio button preceding it.

The Sentence corrections section of the dialog box contains three options for specifying what capitalizations you want QuickCorrect to make. Insert a check mark in the options you want active and remove the check mark from those you want inactive. The End of sentence corrections section contains three choices: None, Change one space to two spaces between sentences, and Change two spaces to one space between sentences. The default is None. Click one of the other options if you want QuickCorrect to correct how many spaces are inserted after punctuation at the end of a sentence.

The Format-As-You-Go choices list box contains options to alter the automatic formatting that is applied to text as you type. If you are not sure what a formatting item does, such as QuickLines, click the item. This causes a description of what the item does to display toward the bottom of the dialog box.

Click the SmartQuotes tab at the QuickCorrect dialog box and the dialog box displays as shown in figure 7.12.

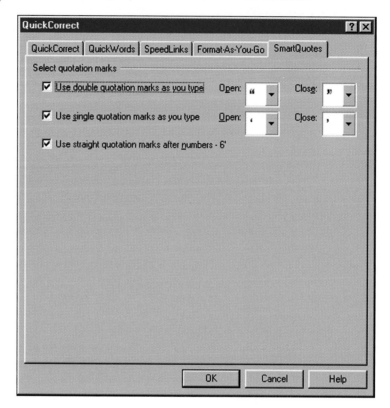

7.12 *QuickCorrect Dialog Box with SmartQuotes Tab Selected*

By default, QuickCorrect will automatically change straight quotation marks to open and closed quotation marks and use a straight quotation mark after numbers. If you do not want a SmartQuote option active, remove the check mark.

exercise

Editing QuickCorrect Entries

1. At a clear editing window, add words to QuickCorrect by completing the following steps:
    a. Click Tools and then QuickCorrect.
    b. At the QuickCorrect dialog box with the QuickCorrect tab selected, make sure the insertion point is positioned in the Replace text box. (If not, click inside the Replace text box.)

c. Key **efficiancy**.
d. Press the Tab key.
e. Key **efficiency**.
f. Click the <u>A</u>dd Entry button.
g. With the insertion point positioned in the <u>R</u>eplace text box, key **facters**.
h. Press the Tab key.
i. Key **factors**.
j. Click the <u>A</u>dd Entry button.
k. With the insertion point positioned in the <u>R</u>eplace text box, key **tele**.
l. Press the Tab key.
m. Key **telecommunications**.
n. Click the <u>A</u>dd Entry button.
o. Click the OK button to close the QuickCorrect dialog box.

2. Key the text shown in figure 7.13. (Key the text exactly as shown. QuickCorrect will correct the words as you key.)

3. Save the document and name it Ch 07, Ex 04.

4. Print Ch 07, Ex 04.

5. Delete the words you added to QuickCorrect by completing the following steps:
   a. Click <u>T</u>ools and then QuickCorrect.
   b. At the QuickCorrect dialog box with the QuickCorrect tab selected, click *efficiancy* in the list box. (You will need to scroll down the list box to display *efficiancy*.)
   c. Click the <u>D</u>elete Entry button.
   d. At the dialog box asking if you want to delete the entry, click <u>Y</u>es.

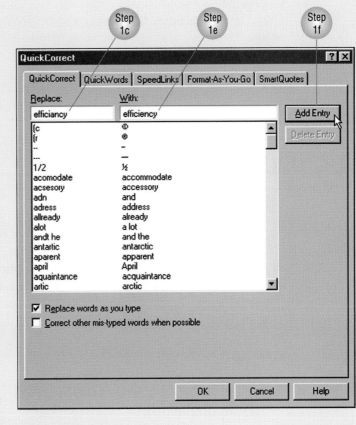

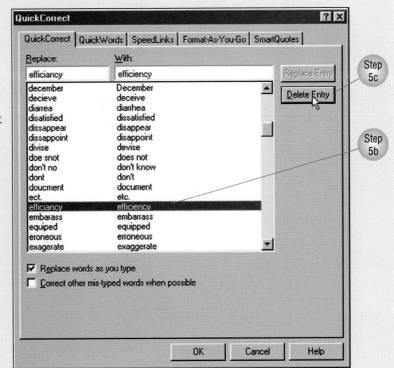

FIGURE

7.13 *Exercise 4*

You consider several important facters before deciding which new tele management system you should purchase. You thoroughly study cost, efficiancy, quality, time, and ease of use. You use these facters to evaluate every tele application in terms of how well it solves a specific business problem. Later, you will be asked to rate proposed tele systems using the facters of cost, efficiancy, quality, time, and ease of use.

Using Grammatik

WordPerfect includes a grammar-checking program called Grammatik. The Grammatik program searches a document for incorrect grammar, style, punctuation, and word usage. Like Spell Checker, Grammatik does not find every error in a document and may stop at correct phrases. Grammatik can help you create a well-written document, but it does not replace the need for human proofreading.

Editing a Document with Grammatik

To check a document with Grammatik, you would open the document to be checked and then click <u>T</u>ools and then <u>G</u>rammatik; or press Alt + Shift + F1. Grammatik automatically starts checking the document and stops at the first error. When Grammatik selects an error, you can correct it or skip the error. When Grammatik is done checking the document, a box displays with the query *Grammar check completed. Close Grammatik?* At this message, click <u>Y</u>es.

When you click <u>T</u>ools and then <u>G</u>rammatik, the Writing Tools dialog box with the Grammatik tab selected displays when a possible error is encountered. The text related to the possible error is selected in the document and the dialog box contents will vary depending on the type of error that Grammatik has found. When Grammatik selects an error, possible replacement words may be displayed in the Re<u>p</u>lacements list box in the dialog box. These replacement words can be used to quickly correct the error.

In addition to the Re<u>p</u>lacements list box, Grammatik may also rewrite the sentence containing an error and place that sentence in the New sentence text box. If the rewritten sentence is correct, click the <u>R</u>eplace button and Grammatik will replace the original sentence with the rewritten sentence and then continue searching for errors. If you want Grammatik to use a different word in the Replacements list box when writing the sentence, click the desired word. Grammatik then rewrites the sentence using the selected word and displays it in the New sentence text box. When Grammatik selects an error in a document, the rule class for the error is displayed in the Rule name text box below the New sentence text box.

Making Replacements

When Grammatik detects an error, it tries to include replacement words in the Replacements list box and displays a rewritten sentence in the New sentence text box. If you want to replace the selected sentence with the suggested sentence, click the Replace button. If there is more than one replacement option in the Replacements list box, click the desired replacement option and then click the Replace button.

If you want to leave the text as written and not make a correction, click the Skip Once or Skip All button. If you click the Skip Once button, Grammatik will ignore the selected phrase for the current occurrence only. If you click the Skip All button, Grammatik will ignore the selected phrase for the rest of the document.

If Grammatik stops at a possible error and does not offer a replacement or the offered replacements are not acceptable, you can edit the error. To do this, position the I-beam pointer in the editing window at the location of the error, and then click the left mouse button. Make the necessary corrections and then click the Resume button to continue grammar checking.

Checking for Errors with Grammatik

1. Open Memo 08.
2. Save the document with Save As and name it Ch 07, Ex 05.
3. Complete a grammar check with Grammatik by completing the following steps:
    a. Click Tools and then Grammatik.
    b. Grammatik selects *Vanderburg*. This proper name is spelled correctly so click the Skip Once button.

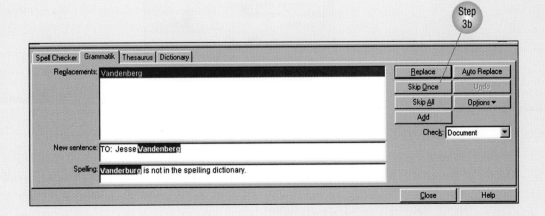

c. Grammatik selects *likes* and displays the rule class *Incorrect Verb Form* with the advice, *Words like would require that the following verb be in the base verb form.* The word *like* is displayed in the Replacements list box, so click the Replace button.

d. Grammatik selects *a computer literacy programs* and displays the rule class *Noun Phrase* with the advice, *A is not usually used with a plural noun such as programs.* Grammatik suggests two possible corrections in the Replacements list box. Click *a computer literacy program* in the Replacements list box and then click the Replace button.

e. Grammatik selects *compare* and displays the rule class *Subject-Verb Agreement* with the advice, *If it is the subject of the verb compare, try making them agree in number.* The word *compares* is displayed in the Replacements list box, so click the Replace button.

f. Grammatik selects *08* and displays the rule class *Number Style* with the advice *Spell out whole numbers in this range, even as part of larger numbers ("eight million").* Since this is the document identification in the initial line, click the Skip Once button.

g. At the *Grammar check completed. Close Grammatik?* query, click Yes.

4. Save, print, and then close Ch 07, Ex 05.

Changing Checking Styles

Grammatik provides a number of checking styles for various documents. To change the checking style, click the Options button and then click Checking Styles at the drop-down menu. This causes the Checking Styles dialog box to display as shown in figure 7.14. Choose the desired checking style in the list box. For the formal checking styles such as Formal Memo or Letter, Technical or Scientific, and Documentation or Speech, Grammatik checks a document using most rules of grammar. If you choose a less formal style such as Informal Memo or Letter, Advertising, or Fiction, Grammatik uses fewer grammar rules when checking a document.

FIGURE

7.14 *Checking Styles Dialog Box*

Customizing Grammatik

When you click the Options button at the Writing Tools dialog box with the Grammatik tab selected, a drop-down menu displays. You have already learned about the Checking Styles option. Other options available at the Options drop-down menu are described in figure 7.15.

FIGURE

7.15 *Grammatik Options Drop-Down Menu*

Use this option	To do this
Turn On Rules	If a rule has been turned off, turn it back on by clicking this option.
Save Rules	Save the rules that have been turned off as a new checking style.
User Word Lists	Add, delete, or edit words in the default user word list, or select a different word list for Grammatik to use while proofreading your document.
Language	Select a different language to use for proofreading. The dictionary files for the other language must be installed for this option to work.
Analysis	Choose this option to view parts of speech, a parse tree, or statistics for the entire document.
Auto start	Grammatik starts proofreading the document as soon as you click Tools, then Grammatik if this option is checked.
Prompt Before Auto Replacement	If QuickCorrect is activated, Grammatik will prompt you before it makes an automatic replacement if this option is checked.
Suggest Spelling Replacements	Grammatik will offer alternative words for the selected word in the Replacements list box if this option is checked.
Check Headers, Footers, Footnotes	Instructs Grammatik to proofread all headers, footers, and footnotes in the current document if this option is checked.

Changing Checking Options

If you click the down-pointing triangle at the right side of the Check text box at the Writing Tools dialog box with the Grammatik tab selected, a list box displays with the following options: Document, Number of Pages, Page, Paragraph, Selected Text, Sentence, To End of Document, and Word. The default setting is Document. Choose one of the other options to control how much of the document you want to check with Grammatik.

Using Grammar-As-You-Go

In chapter 1, you learned about the Spell-As-You-Go feature, which automatically inserts red slash marks below words that are misspelled, and provides you with a menu of suggested replacements and other options if you click the *right* mouse button over the error. WordPerfect also includes a Grammar-As-You-Go feature, which will automatically insert blue slash marks below words or phrases that might contain incorrect grammar or usage.

The Grammar-As-You-Go feature is turned off by default. To turn it on, click Tools, point to Proofread, and then click Grammar-As-You-Go. When the Grammar-As-You-Go feature is turned on, blue slash marks will be inserted below words or phrases that may contain incorrect grammar or usage. To correct the grammar, position the I-beam pointer over the blue slash marks and then click the *right* mouse button. At the pop-up menu that displays, click the word or phrase that will correct the problem. You can also click the Skip option if you want the word or phrase left as written. If you need more information, click the Grammatik option and the Writing Tools dialog box with the Grammatik tab selected will display as explained earlier in this chapter.

To turn off the Grammar-As-You-Go feature, click Tools, point to Proofread, and then click Off.

exercise 6

Using Grammar-As-You-Go

1. At a clear editing window, turn on the Grammar-As-You-Go feature by clicking Tools, point to Proofread, and then click Grammar-As-You-Go.
2. Key the business letter shown in figure 7.16 in an appropriate business letter format.
3. After keying the letter, correct the grammar errors selected by the Grammar-As-You-Go feature. (These are the words or phrases that display with blue slash marks below.)
4. Save the document and name it Ch 07, Ex 06.
5. Print and then close Ch 07, Ex 06.
6. Turn off the Grammar-As-You-Go feature by clicking Tools, point to Proofread, and then click Off.

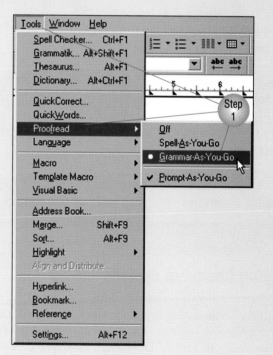

February 19, 2003

Ms. Lola Albright
ES Communications
4311 Sterling Avenue
Denver, CO 69500

Dear Ms. Albright:

The next meeting of the board of directors for Community Outreach will be held March
3. I looks forward to hearing your presentation. Jason Hanson indicated that you need
photocopies of your presentation for all board members. Please send the printed
presentation to Jason or I by early next week. We will make sure the presentation is
photocopied for the board members. After you're presentation, we hope to finalize the
fund-raising plan for next year.

Sincerely,

Katie Bradshaw

xx:Ch 07, Ex 06

Finding and Replacing Text

With WordPerfect's Find and Replace feature, you can look for a specific word(s) or
code(s) within a document. When WordPerfect finds the word(s) or code(s), you
can replace, edit, or delete the word(s) or code(s). With Find and Replace, you can:

- Correct a misspelled word by searching for it and replacing it throughout
  a document with the correct spelling.
- Use abbreviations for common phrases when entering text and then
  replace the abbreviations with the actual text later.
- Set up standard documents with generic names and replace them with
  other names to make personalized documents.
- Find and replace format codes.

When you click Edit and then Find and Replace, the Find and Replace dialog
box shown in figure 7.17 displays. In the Find text box, enter the string for which
you are searching. A search string can be up to 80 characters in length and can
include spaces. After you have completed a find and replace, the Find text box will

default to the previous search string. Alternatively, clicking the down-pointing triangle at the right of the Find text box will display a list of previously searched-for words. Search for the same word(s) again by clicking it in the drop-down list.

FIGURE

7.17 *Find and Replace Dialog Box*

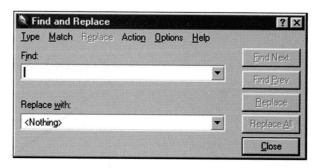

Click in the Replace with text box and then enter the string with which you want the search string replaced. You can also click the down-pointing triangle at the right of the Replace with text box to display a list of words you have replaced previously. At the drop-down list, click the words you want inserted in the Replace with text box.

A find and replace begins at the position of the insertion point. You can find and replace a search string from the location of the insertion point to the beginning of the document or from the insertion point to the end of the document.

The Find and Replace dialog box contains five command buttons at the right side. These buttons are described in figure 7.18.

FIGURE

7.18 *Find and Replace Command Buttons*

Button	Function
Find Next	Tells WordPerfect to find the next occurrence of the search string.
Find Prev	Tells WordPerfect to search from the insertion point to the previous occurrence of the search string.
Replace	Tells WordPerfect to replace the currently selected search string and find the next occurrence of the string.
Replace All	Tells WordPerfect to replace every occurrence of the search string from the location of the insertion point to the end of the document or the beginning of the document, depending on which direction you are searching.

exercise 7

Using Find and Replace

1. Open Report 08.
2. Save the document with Save As and name it Ch 07, Ex 07.
3. Find all occurrences of *SSL* and replace with *Space Systems Laboratory* by completing the following steps:
   a. Position the insertion point at the beginning of the document.
   b. Click Edit and then Find and Replace.
   c. At the Find and Replace dialog box, key **SSL** in the Find text box.
   d. Press the Tab key to move the insertion point to the Replace with text box.
   e. Key **Space Systems Laboratory**.
   f. Click the Replace All button.
   g. At the box saying that 12 occurrences have been replaced, click the OK button.
   h. Click the Close button to close the Find and Replace dialog box.
4. Save, print, and then close Ch 07, Ex 07.

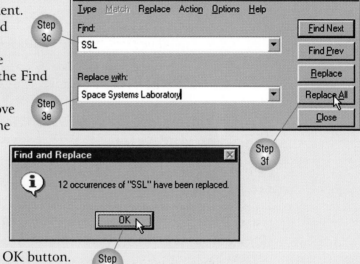

If you want to confirm each replacement before it is made, click the Find Next button or the Find Prev button. When WordPerfect stops at the first occurrence of the search string, click the Replace button if you want to replace the search string.

Customizing Find and Replace

The Find and Replace dialog box contains a menu bar with six options—Type, Match, Replace, Action, Options, and Help. Use options from this menu bar to customize a find and replace.

Changing Type Options

If you click Type at the Find and Replace dialog box Menu bar, a drop-down menu displays with the options Text, Word Forms, and Specific Codes. The default setting is Text. Use this setting when searching for text.

Click the Word Forms option to find and replace words based on the root form of the word. For example, you can search for the word form *buy* and WordPerfect will find words that match the root form such as *buys, buying,* and *bought* and replace them with the correct tense of the root form of the word in the Replace with text box.

exercise 8

Using the Word Forms Option

1. Open Para 05.
2. Save the document with Save As and name it Ch 07, Ex 08.
3. Find all forms of *prepare* and replace with *create* by completing the following steps:
   a. With the insertion point at the beginning of the document, click Edit and then Find and Replace.
   b. At the Find and Replace dialog box, key **prepare** in the Find text box.
   c. Press the Tab key to move the insertion point to the Replace with text box and then key **create**.
   d. Click Type and then Word Forms.
   e. Click the Replace All button.
   f. At the box saying that 3 occurrences have been replaced, click the OK button.
   g. Remove the check mark from the Word Forms option by clicking Type and then Word Forms.
   h. Click the Close button to close the Find and Replace dialog box.
4. Save, print, and then close Ch 07, Ex 08.

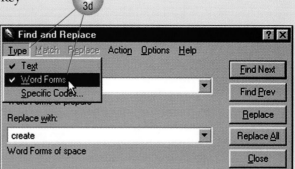

Use the Specific Codes option from the Type drop-down menu to find a code that has been assigned a specific value. For example, instead of telling WordPerfect to search for a Ln Spacing code, which would find any line spacing code, you can specify a 1.5 line spacing code.

When you click Specific Codes, the Specific Codes dialog box shown in figure 7.19 displays.

FIGURE 7.19 Specific Codes Dialog Box

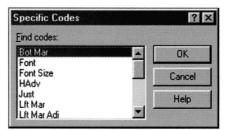

This dialog box contains a list of specific codes. To choose a specific code, click the desired code in the Find codes list box and then click OK or press Enter. When you make a choice from this dialog box, WordPerfect displays a dialog box where you enter the specific value.

Changing Match Options

With the <u>M</u>atch drop-down menu options shown in figure 7.20, you can specify what you want WordPerfect to match. When finding a search string, WordPerfect will stop at occurrences that match the search string. For example, if you enter the string *her* in the F<u>i</u>nd text box, WordPerfect stops at *there, hers, rather,* and so on. If you want to find a specific word such as *her*, click <u>W</u>hole Word at the <u>M</u>atch drop-down menu. With this option selected, WordPerfect will stop at any occurrence of the specific word *her*. This includes any occurrence of *her* that ends in punctuation. You can also tell WordPerfect to find a whole word by keying a space followed by the word and then another space in the F<u>i</u>nd text box. This, however, causes WordPerfect to skip any word that is followed by punctuation.

F I G U R E

7.20 *Match Drop-Down Menu*

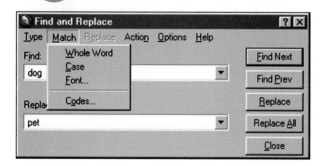

If you enter lowercase text as the search string, WordPerfect will match any case of the text. For example, if you enter *robin* as the search string, WordPerfect will find *robin, Robin,* or *ROBIN* (or any other combination of uppercase and/or lowercase letters). If you want WordPerfect to find only those occurrences that exactly match the search string, click <u>C</u>ase at the <u>M</u>atch drop-down menu.

With the <u>F</u>ont option from the <u>M</u>atch drop-down menu, you can find a specific typeface, type size, or type style. When you click <u>F</u>ont from the <u>M</u>atch drop-down menu, the Match Font dialog box shown in figure 7.21 displays.

F I G U R E

7.21 *Match Font Dialog Box*

At the Match Font dialog box, identify the font, font style, point size, and/or attributes, and then click OK or press Enter.

With the Codes option from the Match drop-down menu, you can find codes within a document. When you click Codes, the Codes dialog box shown in figure 7.22 displays in the upper right corner of the editing window.

FIGURE

7.22 *Codes Dialog Box*

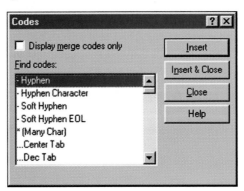

The Codes dialog box contains an extensive list of codes. Select the desired code and then click the Insert button. This inserts the code in the Find text box. More than one code can be inserted in the Find text box. When the code or codes have been inserted in the Find text box, close the Codes dialog box by clicking the Close button or click the Insert & Close button when inserting the last code. (The Codes dialog box will disappear when the search begins.)

With the Find and Replace feature, you can also find codes and replace them with other codes. For example, you can search for all double indent codes and replace them with hanging indent codes.

Finding and Replacing Codes

1. Open Report 08.
2. Save the document with Save As and name it Ch 07, Ex 09.
3. Find all Hd Left Ind codes and replace with Hd Left/Right Ind codes by completing the following steps:
   a. Position the insertion point at the beginning of the document.
   b. Click Edit and then Find and Replace.
   c. At the Find and Replace dialog box, click Match and then Codes.
   d. At the Codes dialog box, select *Hd Left Ind*, and then click Insert. (You must scroll down through the list to find the *Hd Left Ind* code.)
   e. Click in the Replace with text box. (Make sure that no text displays in the Replace with text box.)

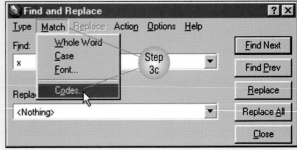

Changing Replace Options

When the Find and Replace dialog box is first displayed, the Replace option on the dialog box Menu bar is dimmed. This option will become available and display in black when the insertion point is positioned in the Replace with text box. When you click Replace on the Find and Replace dialog box Menu bar, a drop-down menu displays with the options Case, Font, and Codes. These are the same options you have available at the Match drop-down menu.

Changing Options

If you click Options on the Find and Replace dialog box Menu bar, the drop-down menu shown in figure 7.23 displays. The default setting is Include Headers, Footers, etc. in Find. At this setting, WordPerfect searches all parts of a document for the search string including such features as headers, footers, footnotes, endnotes, and graphic elements.

F I G U R E

7.23 *Options Drop-Down Menu*

If you click Begin Find at Top of Document, WordPerfect will begin the search at the beginning of the document no matter where the insertion point is positioned. At the Wrap at Beg./End of Document setting, WordPerfect will search from the position of the insertion point to the end of the document and then search from the beginning of the document to the position of the insertion point. If you select text and then display the Find and Replace dialog box, the Limit Find Within Selection option is automatically selected. At this setting, WordPerfect will only search the selected text.

Use the Limit Number of Changes option to tell WordPerfect that you want only *x* number of changes made. For example, if you want only the first four occurrences of the search text replaced with the replacement text, you would click

Options and then Limit Number of Changes. This causes the Limit Number of Changes dialog box to display. At this dialog box, you would key **4** in the Limit changes to text box and then click OK; or press Enter. When you complete the find and replace, WordPerfect only replaces the first four occurrences.

Conducting a Find and Replace

1. Open Report 08.
2. Save the document with Save As and name it Ch 07, Ex 10.
3. Find the *Ln Spacing: 2.0* code and replace it with *Ln Spacing: 1.5* by completing the following steps:
   a. Click Edit and then Find and Replace.
   b. At the Find and Replace dialog box, click Type and then Specific Codes.
   c. At the Specific Codes dialog box, click the down-pointing triangle at the right side of the Specific Codes list box until *Ln Spacing* is visible and then click *Ln Spacing*.
   d. Click OK.
   e. At the Find and Replace Line Spacing dialog box, click the down-pointing triangle after the Replace with option box until the number in the option box displays as *1.5*.
   f. Click the Find Prev button. (The line spacing code is positioned before the location of the insertion point.)
   g. Click the Replace button.
   h. At the box with the message that the specific code is not found, click No.
   i. Click the Close button. (Turn on the display of Reveal Codes and notice the insertion point is positioned in front of the new line spacing code.)
4. Find and delete all bold codes except the bold codes around the title *IDENTIFICATION OF CI* and the subheadings *Requirements During Development* and *Requirements for Operations/Maintenance* by completing the following steps:
   a. Position the insertion point at the beginning of the document.
   b. Click Edit and then Find and Replace.
   c. At the Find and Replace dialog box, click Match and then Codes.
   d. At the Codes dialog box, click *Bold On* in the Find codes list box. (You will need to scroll through the list to display this code.)
   e. Click the Insert & Close button.
   f. Make sure there is no text or codes in the Replace with text box. If there is, select it and then delete it.
   g. Click the Find Next button.
   h. WordPerfect stops at the first *Bold On* code at the beginning of the title. (You will not be able to see the insertion point.) You do not want to delete this code, so click the Find Next button.
   i. WordPerfect stops at the next occurrence of the *Bold On* code (at the heading *Introduction*; you will not be able to see the insertion point). You want this code removed, so click the Replace button.
   j. Continue finding *Bold On* codes. Click the Find Next button if you do not want to delete the code or click the Replace button if you do. (Remember, do not replace the *Bold On* code for the subheadings *Requirements During Development* and *Requirements for Operations/Maintenance*.)
   k. Click the Close button to close the Find and Replace dialog box.
5. Save, print, and then close Ch 07, Ex 10.

CHAPTER summary

➤ Spell Checker is a spell-checking program that consists mainly of two word lists—a main word list and a user word list. In addition, a document-specific word list is automatically attached to a document where you can add words that are specific only to that document that you want the Spell Checker to skip.

➤ Spell Checker will not identify words that are spelled correctly but used incorrectly, nor does it identify misspellings that match other words in its word lists. Spell Checker cannot check grammar or usage.

➤ After correcting a misspelled word, Spell Checker automatically corrects all future occurrences of that error within the document.

➤ Among other options in the Writing Tools dialog box with the Spell Checker tab selected, you can instruct Spell Checker to check the following: a word, a sentence, a paragraph, a page, a specific number of pages, to the end of the document from the insertion point location, or the entire document.

➤ Spell Checker may identify some proper names as misspelled. Frequently used proper names or other terms can be added to the user word list.

➤ You can add, create, or delete user word lists or edit words or phrases in the default user word list at the User Word Lists dialog box.

➤ The Thesaurus can be used to find synonyms and antonyms for words in a document.

➤ Use the command buttons in the Writing Tools dialog box with the Thesaurus tab selected to replace a word, look up synonyms and antonyms for another word, or specify Thesaurus options.

➤ QuickCorrect automatically corrects specific words as they are keyed. Add words to or delete words from QuickCorrect at the QuickCorrect dialog box. Display this dialog box by clicking Tools and then QuickCorrect.

➤ WordPerfect includes a grammar-checking program called Grammatik. With Grammatik you can check the grammar, style errors, and spelling errors in a document.

➤ When Grammatik detects a possible error, it tries to include replacement words or sentences in the Replacements list box. You can incorporate these replacements in the document, click the Skip Once or Skip All button, or edit the document yourself.

➤ Grammatik uses a default checking style of Quick Check. This can be changed with options at the Checking Styles dialog box.

➤ With the Grammar-As-You-Go feature, blue slash marks will be inserted below words or phrases that might contain incorrect grammar or usage.

➤ Use the Find and Replace feature to quickly locate a search string such as word(s) and/or code(s) and replace the search string with other words or codes.

➤ The text and/or codes you search for is called a search string and can be up to 80 characters in length.

➤ The Find and Replace dialog box contains a menu bar with six options—Type, Match, Replace, Action, Options, and Help. Each option has a drop-down menu that allows you to customize your search.

➤ WordPerfect will search for specific formatting codes and replace them with other codes. Codes that are turned on and off, such as bold and underline, can be deleted in this manner but cannot be replaced with another code.

➤ If the search string is entered in lowercase letters, WordPerfect will find all occurrences of the string that contain lowercase or uppercase letters. If you want WordPerfect to find only those occurrences that exactly match the search string, click Case at the Match drop-down menu.

➤ To search for format codes, use the Codes option from the Match drop-down menu or the Specific Codes option from the Type drop-down menu.

COMMANDS summary

Command	Mouse	Keyboard
Display the Spell Checker	Tools, Spell Checker; or click the Spell Checker button on the Toolbar	Ctrl + F1
Display the Thesaurus	Tools, Thesaurus	Alt + F1
Display the QuickCorrect dialog box	Tools, QuickCorrect	Ctrl + Shift + F1
Display Grammatik	Tools, Grammatik	Alt + Shift + F1
Turn on Grammar-As-You-Go	Tools, Proofread, Grammar-As-You-Go	
Display the Find and Replace dialog box	Edit, Find and Replace	

CONCEPTS check

Completion: On a blank sheet of paper, indicate the correct term, command, or number for each item.

1. Begin spell checking a document by clicking this button on the Toolbar.

2. Click QuickCorrect from this drop-down menu to display the QuickCorrect dialog box.

3. If during a spelling check you temporarily leave the Spell Checker dialog box, click this button in the dialog box to continue spell checking.

4. These are words with opposite meanings.

5. These are words with similar meanings.

6. This feature automatically corrects certain words as they are being keyed.

7. Click this option on the Menu bar and then click Grammatik to display the Writing Tools dialog box with the Grammatik tab selected.

8. Click this button at the Writing Tools dialog box with the Grammatik tab selected and then click Checking Styles at the drop-down menu to change the checking style.

9. If you are preparing a technical document, choose this checking style at the Writing Tools dialog box with the Grammatik tab selected.

10. Turn on the Grammar-As-You-Go feature by clicking Tools, pointing to this option, and then clicking Grammar-As-You-Go.

11. Click this button at the Find and Replace dialog box to replace all occurrences of the search string with the replacement text.

12. Click this button at the Find and Replace dialog box to search for the next occurrence of the search string without replacing the current text.

13. Enter the search string in this case and WordPerfect will find all occurrences of the string in uppercase and lowercase.

14. If you want WordPerfect to find only those occurrences that exactly match the search string, click this option at the Match drop-down menu.

SKILLS check

Assessment 1

1. Open Letter 03.
2. Save the letter with Save As and name it Ch 07, SA 01.
3. This letter overuses the words *manage* (in various forms), *efficient*, and *efficiently*. Use Thesaurus to make changes to some of the occurrences of *manage*, *managing*, and/or *managed* to make the letter read better. Also, use Thesaurus to make changes to one or two of the occurrences of *efficient* and/or *efficiently*.
4. Save, print, and then close Ch 07, SA 01.

Assessment 2

1. At a clear editing window, add the following entries to QuickCorrect:
   a. Key **dtp** in the Replace text box and **desktop publishing** in the With text box.
   b. Key **prouduce** in the Replace text box and **produce** in the With text box.
2. Key the text shown in figure 7.24. (Key the text exactly as shown. QuickCorrect will correct the words as you key.)
3. Save the document and name it Ch 07, SA 02.
4. Print and then close Ch 07, SA 02.
5. Delete *dtp* and *prouduce* from QuickCorrect.

FIGURE

7.24 *Assessment 2*

In the graphic arts world, dtp is considered a prepress technology, that is, the dtp system itself is generally not used to prouduce the final multiple copies of a publication, but rather to prouduce masters for reproduction. Because it is relatively inexpensive and user-friendly, dtp has put the power of professional-quality publishing in the hands of many who are not publishing professionals. Some speak out against this trend and point to the flood of poorly designed publications produced by inexperienced publishers.

Assessment 3

1. Open Memo 09.
2. Save the document with Save As and name it Ch 07, SA 03.
3. Change the checking style and check the grammar of the document by completing the following steps:
   a. Click Tools and then Grammatik.
   b. When Grammatik stops at *Mortensen*, change the checking style to Formal Memo or Letter and then click the Skip All button to leave Mortensen as written.
   c. When Grammatik selects *prevelance*, change it to the correct spelling.
   d. When Grammatik selects *have*, replace it with *has*.
   e. When Grammatik selects *a moderately high prevalence of latex allergies has been noted*, change it to *we have noted a moderately high prevalence of latex allergies*.
   f. When Grammatik selects *prevelance*, change it to the correct spelling.
   g. When Grammatik selects *rate for health care workers are*, change it to *rate for health care workers is*.
   h. When Grammatik selects *reason for this difference are*, change it to *reason for this difference is*.
   i. When Grammatik selects *09*, click the Skip Once button.
   j. At the *Grammar check completed. Close Grammatik?* query, click No.
   k. Change the checking style back to the default of Quick Check and then close the Writing Tools dialog box.
4. Save, print, and then close Ch 07, SA 03.

Assessment 4

1. Open Legal 02.
2. Save the document with Save As and name it Ch 07, SA 04.
3. Complete the following find and replaces:
   a. Find all occurrences of *NAME1* and replace with *ELENA C. TREECE*.
   b. Find the one occurrence of *NUMBER* and replace with *D-4311*.
   c. Find all *Bold On* codes and delete them except the following:
      1) *IN DISTRICT COURT NO. 4, PIERCE COUNTY, STATE OF WASHINGTON* (displays on two lines)
      2) *DATED*
      3) *LESLIE COBURN*
   d. Find all *Hd Left/Right Ind* indent codes and replace with *Hd Left Ind* codes.
4. Save, print, and then close Ch 07, SA 04.

Manipulating Tabs

When you work with a document, WordPerfect offers a variety of default settings such as margins and line spacing. One WordPerfect default is tab settings every 0.5 inch. In some situations, these default tab settings are appropriate; in others, you may want to create your own tab settings. There are two methods for clearing and setting tabs. Tabs can be cleared and set at the Ruler or at the Tab Set dialog box.

Manipulating Tabs on the Ruler

The Ruler can be used, together with the mouse, to clear, set, and move tabs. If the Ruler is not displayed as shown in figure 8.1, click View and then Ruler. You can also display the Ruler by pressing Alt + Shift + F3.

FIGURE

8.1   *Ruler*

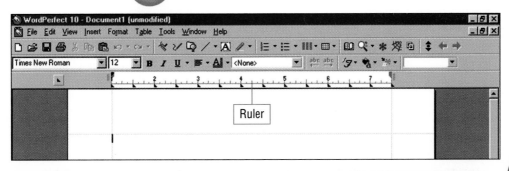

The Ruler, by default, contains left tabs every 0.5 inch. This is indicated by the left triangles below the numbers. At this setting, text aligns at the left edge of the tab setting. The other types of tabs that can be set are Center, Right, and Decimal. The columns displayed in figure 8.2 show text aligned at different tabs. Text in the first column was keyed at a left tab. The second column was keyed at a center tab, the third column at a right tab, and the fourth column at a decimal tab.

F I G U R E

8.2 **Types of Tabs**

Left	Center	Right	Decimal
Ashe	Maine	Augusta	5.313
Ferdinand	New Hampshire	Concord	134.7
Kalinsky	Vermont	Montpelier	1,772.875

To display the types of tabs available, position the arrow pointer on any tab icon on the Ruler and then click the *right* mouse button. This causes a pop-up menu to display as shown in figure 8.3.

F I G U R E

8.3 **Tab Pop-Up Menu**

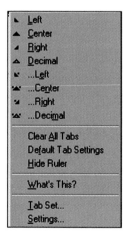

The four types of tabs can also be set with dot leaders. Leaders are useful in a table of contents or other material where you want to direct the reader's eyes across the page. Figure 8.4 shows an example of leaders. The text in the first column was keyed at a left tab. The text in the second column was keyed at a right tab with dot leaders.

FIGURE 8.4 *Leaders*

British Columbia	Victoria
Alberta	Edmonton
Saskatchewan	Regina
Manitoba	Winnipeg
Ontario	Toronto
Quebec	Montreal

Clearing Tabs

Before setting tabs, you will more than likely want to clear the default tabs. Figure 8.5 illustrates several methods of clearing tabs.

FIGURE 8.5 *Clearing Tabs*

To clear	*Do this*
One Tab from the Ruler	Position the arrow pointer on the tab to be cleared, hold down the left mouse button, and drag the tab into the editing window.
All Tabs from the Ruler	Position the arrow pointer on a tab icon on the Ruler, click the *right* mouse button, and then select Clear All Tabs.
To Clear Multiple Tabs	Position the arrow below the numbers on the Ruler and to the left of the first tab to be cleared. Hold down the Shift key and drag to the right until all tabs are selected. Using the left mouse button, drag the tabs to be cleared into the editing window.

Setting Tabs

To set a left tab on the Ruler, position the tip of the arrow pointer at the position on the Ruler where you want the tab set, and then click the left mouse button. To set a tab other than a left tab, position the tip of the arrow pointer on a tab icon, and then click the *right* mouse button. At the Tab pop-up menu that displays, move the arrow pointer to the desired tab type, and then click the left mouse button. After changing the tab type, set the tab on the Ruler in the normal manner. If you change the type of tab at the Tab pop-up menu, the type stays changed until you change it again or until you exit WordPerfect.

Setting Tabs on the Ruler

1. At a clear editing window, create the document shown in figure 8.6 by completing the following steps:
   a. Key the heading **FINANCE DEPARTMENT** centered and bolded.
   b. Press Enter two times.
   c. Set left tabs at the 2.5-inch mark on the Ruler and the 4.75-inch mark by completing the following steps:
      1) Make sure the Ruler is displayed. (If not, click View and then Ruler.)
      2) Position the arrow pointer on a tab icon on the Ruler, click the *right* mouse button, and then click Clear All Tabs.
      3) Position the arrow pointer just below the 2.5-inch mark on the Ruler and then click the left mouse button.
      4) Position the arrow pointer just below the 4.75-inch mark on the Ruler and then click the left mouse button.
   d. Key the text in columns as shown in figure 8.6. Press the Tab key before keying each column entry. (Make sure you press Tab before keying the text in the first and second columns.)
2. Save the document and name it Ch 08, Ex 01.
3. Print and then close Ch 08, Ex 01.

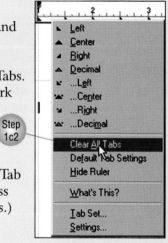

Step
1c2

FIGURE

8.6 *Exercise 1*

FINANCE DEPARTMENT

Patient Accounts	Julius Ramo
Admitting	Simone Watanabe
Medical Records	Marina Pasquale
Payroll	James Fairbanks

Setting Tabs with Dot Leaders on the Ruler

1. At a clear editing window, key the document shown in figure 8.7 by completing the following steps:
   a. Key the heading **NURSING DEPARTMENT** centered and bolded.
   b. Press Enter three times.

    c. Change the line spacing to double (2).

    d. Set a left tab at the 2.5-inch mark on the Ruler and a right tab with dot leaders at the 6-inch mark by completing the following steps:

       1) If necessary, turn on the display of the Ruler.

       2) Position the tip of the arrow pointer on a tab icon, click the *right* mouse button, move the arrow pointer to Clear <u>A</u>ll Tabs, and then click the left mouse button.

       3) Position the arrow pointer just below the 2.5-inch mark on the Ruler and then click the left mouse button.

       4) Position the tip of the arrow pointer on the tab icon on the Ruler, click the *right* mouse button and then click ...Right.

       5) Position the arrow pointer just below the 6-inch mark on the Ruler and then click the left mouse button.

    e. Key the text in columns as shown in figure 8.7. Press the Tab key before keying each column entry. (Make sure you press Tab before keying the text in the first and second columns.)

2. Change the tab type back to left by positioning the arrow pointer on a tab icon, clicking the *right* mouse button, and then clicking <u>L</u>eft.

3. Save the document and name it Ch 08, Ex 02.

4. Print and then close Ch 08, Ex 02.

FIGURE

8.7   *Exercise 2*

NURSING DEPARTMENT

Intensive Care Unit .... Terrie Mamaud

Emergency Room .... Kimberly Goetz

Labor and Delivery .... Ola Busching

Coronary Care Unit .... Thomas Heusers

Surgical Unit .... Bernice Light

Medical Services .... Bethany Mortensen

Pediatrics .... Tina Vitali

Moving Tabs

After a tab has been set on the Ruler, it can be moved to a new location. To move a single tab, position the tip of the arrow pointer on the tab icon to be moved, hold down the left mouse button, drag the icon to the new location on the Ruler, and then release the mouse button. To move several tabs at once, select the tabs first and then move them in the same manner as a single tab.

Moving Tabs

1. Open Ch 08, Ex 02.
2. Save the document with Save As and name it Ch 08, Ex 03.
3. Move the tab settings so there is more space between the columns by completing the following steps:
   a. Move the insertion pointer to the line containing *Intensive Care Unit*.
   b. Position the arrow pointer on the left tab icon at the 2.5-inch mark, hold down the left mouse button, move the arrow pointer to the left until it is located below the 2-inch mark, and then release the mouse button.
   c. Position the arrow pointer on the right tab icon with dot leaders at the 6-inch mark, hold down the left mouse button, drag the arrow pointer to the right until it is located below the 6.5-inch mark, and then release the mouse button.
4. Center the document vertically on the page. (Use the Current page option from the Center Page(s) dialog box.)
5. Save, print, and then close Ch 08, Ex 03.

Manipulating Tabs with the Tab Set Dialog Box

The Tab Set dialog box shown in figure 8.8 can be used to complete such tasks as clearing a tab or tabs and setting a variety of tabs at precise measurements. Several methods can be used to display the Tab Set dialog box including the following:

- Click Format, point to Line, and then click Tab Set.
- Position the arrow pointer anywhere on the Ruler, click the *right* mouse button, and then click Tab Set.
- Double-click a tab icon on the Ruler.
- Double-click any tab code in Reveal Codes.

8.8 Tab Set Dialog Box

If the display of the Ruler is on, the Ruler can be seen above the Tab Set dialog box. This is helpful when determining tab settings.

Clearing Tabs

At the Tab Set dialog box, you can clear an individual tab or all tabs. To clear all tabs from the Ruler, click the Clear All button. To clear an individual tab, display the Tab Set dialog box, and then select the current measurement in the Tab position text box. Key the measurement of the tab to be cleared and then click the Clear button. You can also click the up-pointing triangle at the right side of the Tab position text box until the desired measurement displays and then click the Clear button.

Tabs in the Tab Set dialog box are, by default, relative tabs. Relative tabs are measured from the left margin. The Ruler displays absolute tabs, which are measured from the left edge of the page. With tabs that are measured relative to the left margin, the left margin measurement is 0 inches (rather than 1 inch). Positions to the right of the left margin are positive numbers and positions to the left of the left margin are negative numbers. With relative tabs that are measured from the left margin, the distance between tab settings and the left margin remains the same regardless of what changes are made to the document.

Absolute tabs are measured from the left edge of the page. The left edge of the page is 0 inches. Tabs that are set from the left edge of the page remain at the fixed measurement regardless of what changes are made to the document.

Setting Tabs

All the tab types available with the Tab drop-down menu are available with the Tab type option from the Tab Set dialog box. To change the type of tab at the Tab Set dialog box, display the dialog box, click the Tab type button, and then click the desired tab at the drop-down menu.

The Tab position text box at the Tab Set dialog box is used to identify the specific measurement where the tab is to be set. To set a tab, select the current measurement in the Tab position text box, key the desired measurement, and then click the Set button. The measurement that you key is a relative measurement. For example, if you set a tab at 3 inches, the tab will appear at the 4-inch mark on the Ruler (if the left margin is at the default setting of 1 inch). In Reveal Codes, the tab would display as Tab Set: (Rel)+3"L . As an example of how to clear and set tabs at the Tab Set dialog box, complete exercise 4.

exercise 4

Clearing and Setting Tabs at the Tab Set Dialog Box

1. At a clear editing window, key the document shown in figure 8.9 by completing the following steps:
   a. Key the headings and the first paragraph of the memo and then center and bold the title **TOP TEN CALORIE-BURNING EXERCISES**.
   b. Press Enter twice.
   c. Set tabs at the Tab Set dialog box by completing the following steps:
      1) If necessary, display the Ruler.
      2) Double-click a tab icon on the Ruler. (This displays the Tab Set dialog box.)
      3) At the Tab Set dialog box, click the Clear All button.
      4) Make sure the tab type is Left. (If not, click the Tab type button and then click *Left* at the drop-down list.)
      5) Select the *0"* in the Tab position text box.
      6) Key **1.25**.
      7) Click the Set button.
      8) Click the Tab type button and then click *Right* at the drop-down list.
      9) Select the *1.25"* in the Tab position text box.
      10) Key **5.25**.
      11) Click Set.
      12) Click Close.

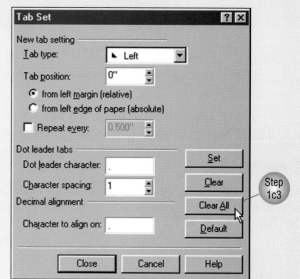

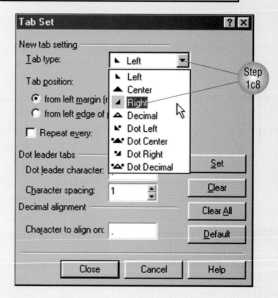

d. Key the text in columns as shown in figure 8.9. Bold the text as indicated. Press the Tab key before keying each column entry. (Make sure you press Tab before keying the text in the first and second columns.)
2. Key the remaining text in the memo.
3. Save the document and name it Ch 08, Ex 04.
4. Print and then close Ch 08, Ex 04.

FIGURE

8.9 **_Exercise 4_**

DATE: February 10, 2003

TO: Paula Kerns, Editor, _Hospital Happenings_

FROM: Steve Ayala

SUBJECT: MARCH NEWSLETTER

At the last department meeting, you told us that the theme for the March _Hospital Happenings_ newsletter was exercise. Just last week, I ran across this information about the efficiency of common exercises.

TOP TEN CALORIE-BURNING EXERCISES

Activity	**Cal. per hr.**
Skiing (cross-country)	1,000
Running	950
Bicycling (stationary)	850
Bicycling (12 mph)	650
Swimming	640
Rowing machine	600
Tennis	600
Handball/Racquetball	577
Jogging (12-minute mile)	570
Aerobic dance	525

I thought this information would be interesting to the readers of the newsletter. Let me know if you decide to publish it.

xx:Ch 08, Ex 04

When tabs are set, a tab set code is inserted in the document at the beginning of the paragraph where the insertion point is positioned. The tab set code displays the relative measurement of the tab as well as the type of tab. Tab codes take effect from the location of the code to the end of the document or until another tab set code is encountered. This code can be viewed in Reveal Codes.

exercise 5

Creating a Table of Contents with a Dot Leader Tab

1. At a clear editing window, create the document shown in figure 8.10 by completing the following steps:
   a. Change the font to 12-point Garamond (or another serif typeface).
   b. Change the line spacing to double (2).
   c. Center and bold the title **TABLE OF CONTENTS**.
   d. Press Enter twice.
   e. Set tabs at the Tab Set dialog box by completing the following steps:
      1) Click Format, point to Line, and then click Tab Set.
      2) At the Tab Set dialog box, click the Clear All button.
      3) Select the *0″* in the Tab position text box.
      4) Key **1**.
      5) Click the Set button.
      6) Click the Tab type button and then click *Dot Right* at the drop-down list.
      7) Select the *1″* in the Tab position text box.
      8) Key **5.5**.
      9) Click Set.
      10) Click Close.
   f. Key the text in columns as shown in figure 8.10. Press the Tab key before keying each column entry. (Make sure you press Tab before keying the text in the first and second columns.)
2. Save the document and name it Ch 08, Ex 05.
3. Print and then close Ch 08, Ex 05.

FIGURE

TABLE OF CONTENTS

Setting Evenly Spaced Tabs

With the Repeat every option from the Tab Set dialog box, you can set tabs at regular intervals. To do this, clear all previous tabs. Select the current measurement in the Tab position text box, key the measurement where the first tab set is to occur, and then click the Set button. Click the Repeat every check box and then select the current measurement in the Repeat every text box. Key the desired interval measurement, click Set, and then Close.

Returning to Default Tabs

If you make changes to the tab settings and then want to return to the default tabs, use the Default button at the Tab Set dialog box. Clicking this button returns the tabs to the default of a tab set every 0.5 inch. Another method for returning to default tab settings is to position the arrow pointer on a tab icon on the Ruler, click the *right* mouse button, and then click Default Tab Settings at the pop-up menu.

Changing Tab Position

As mentioned earlier, tabs can be set that are measured from the left margin or the left edge of the page. Tabs that are measured from the left margin are called relative tabs and tabs set from the left edge of the page are called absolute tabs. By default, tabs are measured from the left margin.

The Tab Set dialog box contains a from left <u>m</u>argin (relative) option and a from left <u>e</u>dge of paper (absolute) option. The default option is from left <u>m</u>argin (relative).

exercise 6

Creating Columns with Absolute Tabs

1. At a clear editing window, key the document shown in figure 8.11 by completing the following steps:
   a. Turn on page numbering at the bottom right corner of all pages.
   b. Change the line spacing to double (2).
   c. Center and bold the title **THE ROLE OF TRANSMISSION IN TELECOMMUNICATIONS**.
   d. Press Enter and then bold the heading **Receiving**.
   e. Press Enter and then key the first paragraph.
   f. After keying the paragraph, press Enter once and then change the line spacing to single (1).
   g. Clear all tabs and set absolute left tabs at 2.8 and 4.5 by completing the following steps:
      1) Display the Tab Set dialog box.
      2) At the Tab Set dialog box, click the Clear <u>A</u>ll button.
      3) Click in the circle before the from left <u>e</u>dge of paper (absolute) option.
      4) Select *0"* in the Tab <u>p</u>osition text box.
      5) Key **2.8**.
      6) Click the <u>S</u>et button.
      7) Select *2.80"* in the Tab <u>p</u>osition text box.
      8) Key **4.5**.
      9) Click the <u>S</u>et.
      10) Click Close.

   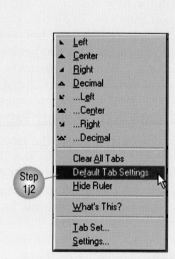

   h. Key the text in columns. After keying the last entry in the second column, press Enter twice.
   i. Change the line spacing to double.
   j. Return the tabs to the default settings by completing the following steps:
      1) Position the arrow pointer on a tab icon on the Ruler and then click the *right* mouse button.
      2) At the pop-up menu that displays, click De<u>f</u>ault Tab Settings.
      3) Key the remaining text in the document.
2. Save the document and name it Ch 08, Ex 06.
3. Print and then close Ch 08, Ex 06.

THE ROLE OF TRANSMISSION IN TELECOMMUNICATIONS

Receiving

Information is sent through the atmosphere as an electromagnetic signal (a signal with magnetic properties resulting from being passed through electrical current). At the intended destination, the electromagnetic signal must be recognized and captured by an antenna system. Antenna systems must accept only those signals we want them to receive and ignore the rest. Some common receiving devices include:

TV Antenna	Satellite Dish
Tuner	Amplifier
Modem	VSAT

The typical home satellite earth station has a number of electromagnetic signals that may strike it. These signals may come from AM (amplitude modulation) or FM (frequency modulation) radio towers, a variety of television stations, ham radio operators, CB radio operators, or microwave signals used for telephone or other telecommunications services. One task of the antenna is to sort out which signal to accept and which to ignore.

Receiving Information Sent through Physical Channels

If we look at the physical channels used for transmitting information, we can see the need to design devices that allow for the physical interconnection of the channel to the transmitter and receiver. This may take a simple form, such as fastening a copper wire to a screw on the back of the receiver, or a quite complicated form, such as splicing a fiber optic cable. Unfortunately, there is little standardization of the physical interconnection of channels to the receiving device. Whether voice, data, or video system, the methods for physical connection are numerous and varied.

CHAPTER summary

➤ By default, left tabs are set every 0.5 inch.

➤ At the Ruler or the Tab Set dialog box, tabs can be deleted, reset, or moved.

➤ The four types of tabs are Left (the default), Center, Right, and Decimal. Any type of tab can be set with dot leaders (periods).

➤ To display the types of tabs available to set on the Ruler, position the arrow pointer on any tab icon on the Ruler, and then click the *right* mouse button. The tab type can also be changed at the Tab Set dialog box.

➤ By default, the Tab Set dialog box displays relative tabs—tabs that are measured from the left margin. The Ruler displays absolute tabs—tabs that are measured from the left edge of the page.

➤ When tabs are set, a tab set code is inserted in the document at the beginning of the paragraph where the insertion point is positioned. Tab codes take effect from the location of the code to the end of the document or until another tab set code is encountered.

➤ At the Tab Set dialog box you can set new tabs at regular intervals or return to the default tabs.

COMMANDS summary

Command	Mouse	Keyboard
Display the Ruler	View, Ruler	Alt + Shift + F3
Display the Tab Set dialog box	Click Format, Line, Tab Set; or position the arrow pointer anywhere on the Ruler, click the *right* mouse button, and then click Tab Set, or double-click a tab icon on the Ruler, or double-click any tab code in Reveal Codes	

CONCEPTS check

Completion: On a blank sheet of paper, indicate the correct term, command, or number for each item.

1. How far apart are tabs set by default?

2. What are the four types of tabs?

3. What type of tab is the default?

4. Relative tabs are measured from here.

5. When tabs are set, a tab set code is inserted in the document at this position.

6. This is the name for the line of periods that can run between columns.

SKILLS check

Assessment 1

1. At a clear editing window, key the document shown in figure 8.12. Before keying the text in columns, display the Tab Set dialog box, clear all tabs, and then set a left tab 0.5 inch from the left margin and a decimal tab with dot leaders 5.5 inches from the left margin.
2. Save the document and name it Ch 08, SA 01.
3. Print and then close Ch 08, SA 01.

FIGURE

8.12   *Assessment 1*

DATE: February 10, 2003

TO: Maxine Paulson, Editor

FROM: Barbara Essex, Investment Coordinator

SUBJECT: PORTFOLIO INFORMATION

Several clients have indicated that the "sample portfolio" helps them understand how and where our company invests their money. Would you please include the following information in the next client newsletter:

PORTFOLIO ACCUMULATION

Direct loans to business . . . . $ 60,453.20
Public debt securities 87,540.00
Mortgage loans 108,540.32
Real estate investments 55,490.90
All others 9,904.50

If you want more information about this sample portfolio, call me at extension 564.

xx:Ch 08, SA 01

Assessment 2

1. At a clear editing window, key the table shown in figure 8.13. Set a left tab for the first column, a right tab for the second and fourth columns, and a center tab for the third column. You determine the location for the tabs.
2. Save the document and name it Ch 08, SA 02.
3. Print and then close Ch 08, SA 02.

FIGURE

8.13 *Assessment 2*

COLOR CODES BY DEPARTMENT

IC Unit	Red	CC Unit	Purple
Surgical Unit	Green	Medical	White
Pediatrics	Blue	Finances	Gray
Payroll	Brown	Admitting	Beige

PERFORMANCE
Assessments

MANAGING AND ENHANCING DOCUMENTS

INTEGRATING SKILLS

In this unit, you have learned how to manage and enhance WordPerfect 10 documents using file management techniques; document properties options; font features; Spell Checker, Thesaurus, and Grammatik features; find and replace options; and tab setting features.

Assessment one

1. At a clear editing window, key the text shown in figure U2.1 in an appropriate business letter format with the following specifications:
   a. Change the font to 12-point Garamond (or a similar serif typeface).
   b. Set a left tab 1 inch from the left margin for the first column.
   c. Set a center tab at 3.5 inches for the second column.
   d. Set a right tab at 5.5 inches for the third.
2. Complete a spell check on the letter.
3. Proofread and correct any grammar errors.
4. Save the letter and name it U02, PA 01.
5. Print and then close U02, PA 01.

March 18, 2003

Mrs. Darlene Frye
Public Works Department
2105 South 42nd Street
Tampa, FL 33613

Dear Mrs. Frye:

The third meting of the members of the Outcomes Assesment Project (OAP) were held yesterday, march 17. The following items were discused:

Continued on next page

1. Survey: Each member shared the current status of the section of the survey for which he or she is responsible.

2. Survey Instruments: Members modified and prioritized items on the first draft of the survey questionnaire.

3. Meeting Dates and Times: The next three meeting days and times were determined as follows:

Tuesday, April 1	3:00 p.m.	Room 420
Wenesday, April 23	11:30 a.m.	Room 100A
Tusday, May 13	3:00 p.m.	Room 420

Hopefully, these days and times are convenient for your. If you want to discuss this meeting farther, give me a call.

Very truly yours,

Dawn Martin, Coordinator
Outcomes Assesment Project

xx:U02, PA 01

FIGURE U2.1 • Assessment 1

Assessment **two**

1. At a clear editing window, key the text shown in figure U2.2 in an appropriate memo format with the following specifications:
   a. Change the font to Arial, 11 point.
   b. Before keying the bulleted text, set a left tab at the 1.25-inch mark on the Ruler.
   c. Insert the bullets as indicated.
   d. Determine the position and type of tabs and then set tabs for the text in columns.
2. Complete a spell check on the memo. Proofread the memo.
3. Save the memo and name it U02, PA 02.
4. Print and then close U02, PA 02.

WRITING SOLUTIONS

The following activities give you the opportunity to practice your writing skills along with demonstrating an understanding of some of the important WordPerfect features you have mastered in this unit. In planning the documents, remember to shape the information according to the writing purpose and the audience. Use correct grammar, appropriate word choices, and clear sentence constructions.

Assessment five 5

Situation: You work in the Training and Development Department of a large business. One of your job responsibilities includes preparing notices for upcoming training sessions. Prepare a notice of an upcoming training session titled *Searching the Internet, Discovering Business Resources*. The training will be held Wednesday, March 12, 2003, in the Computer Resource Room, from 1:30 to 4:00 p.m. Anyone interested in attending this training must contact you by March 10 at extension 459. When preparing the notice, change the font and font size for the text and position the information attractively on the page. Save the notice and name it U02, PA 05. Print and then close U02, PA 05.

Assessment six 6

Situation: You are Jocelyn Cook, assistant superintendent for the Omaha City School District. Compose a memo to all elementary school principals informing them that the members of the site selection committee will be visiting their schools on the following dates and times:

Carr Elementary School	February 18	10:00 - 11:30 a.m.
Leland Elementary School	February 18	1:30 - 3:00 p.m.
Sahala Elementary School	February 22	9:30 - 11:00 a.m.
Young Elementary School	February 22	1:00 - 2:30 p.m.
Armstrong Elementary School	February 25	10:00 - 11:30 a.m.
Bothell Elementary School	February 25	1:30 - 3:00 p.m.

You determine the tab settings for the columns of text (this includes columns for the school names, days, and times). Save the memo and name it U02, PA 06. Print and then close U02, PA 06.

UNIT three

MANIPULATING AND ORGANIZING TEXT

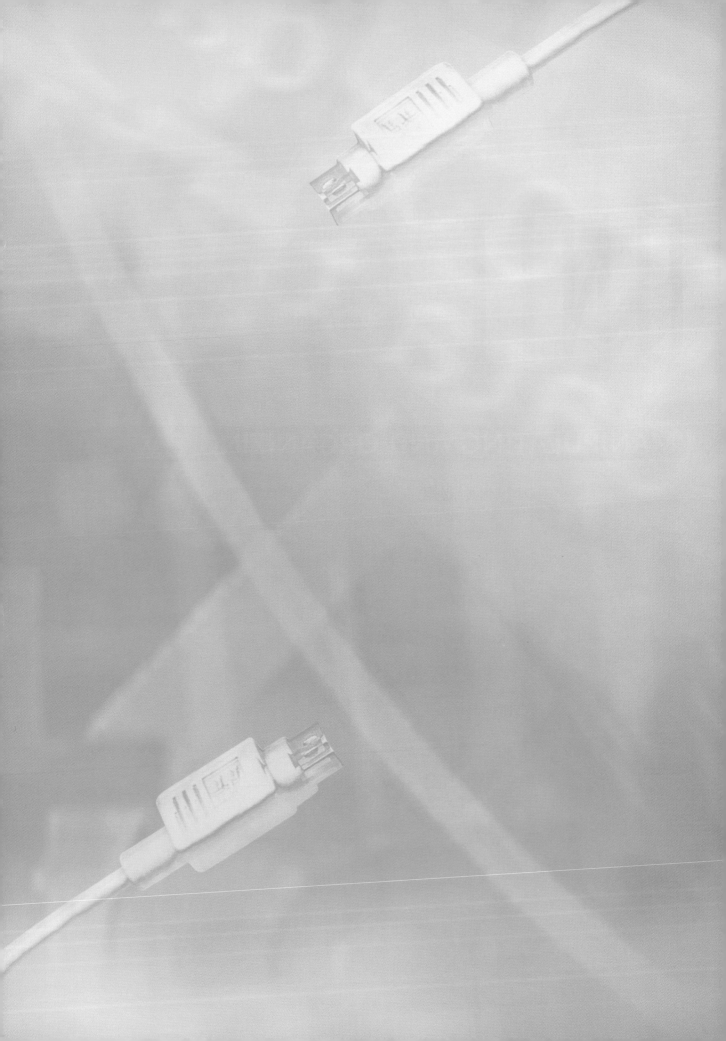

Creating Headers and Footers and Footnotes and Endnotes

PERFORMANCE OBJECTIVES

Upon successful completion of chapter 9, you will be able to:
- **Insert headers and footers**
- **Edit and format headers and footers**
- **Insert footnotes and endnotes**
- **Edit and format footnotes and endnotes**

Chapter 09

In a WordPerfect document, you can create headers and footers. Text that appears at the top of pages is called a header, and text that appears at the bottom of pages is called a footer. When text is identified as a header or footer, it needs to be keyed only one time. After that, WordPerfect prints the text on each page. Headers and footers are common in manuscripts, textbooks, reports, and other publications. Typically, they are used to identify the chapter or section number and/or title.

Creating a Header or Footer

A maximum of two headers and/or two footers can be created in a WordPerfect document. WordPerfect refers to them as Header A, Header B, Footer A, and Footer B. Headers and footers have the following characteristics:

- A header or footer can contain as many lines as needed, up to one page. Generally, however, most headers and footers are only a few lines in length.

- Headers and footers can be created in various forms. They can appear on every page or can be identified as alternating headers or footers. With alternating headers or footers, text is printed only on even-numbered or odd-numbered pages.

- A header or footer can be turned off or discontinued in a document. For example, you can have a header printed on the first and second pages of a document and not printed on the remaining pages. You can also turn a header or footer off on specific pages.

- A header or footer can be created in any of the viewing modes. However, only the Page and Two-Pages viewing modes will display headers or footers in a document.
- When a header or footer is created, the header or footer code is inserted at the beginning of the page where the insertion point is positioned. For example, if you want a header to begin printing on page 1, make sure the insertion point is positioned somewhere in the first page.

To create a header or footer, you would complete the following steps:

1. Position the insertion point anywhere in the page where you want the header or footer to begin.

2. Click Insert and then Header/Footer.

3. At the Headers/Footers dialog box, shown in figure 9.1, select the header or footer desired and then click the Create button.

4. At the Header or Footer window, key the text for the header or footer.

5. Click the Close button on the Header/Footer property bar (shown in figure 9.2).

FIGURE

9.1 **Headers/Footers Dialog Box**

FIGURE

9.2 **Header/Footer Property Bar**

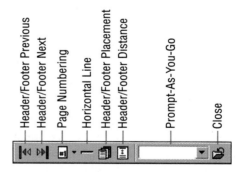

When you click the Create button at the Headers/Footers dialog box, the document displays with a Header window or a Footer window (depending on what you selected at the Headers/Footers dialog box). The Header or Footer window area displays as a rectangular box surrounded by gray dotted lines in the Page viewing mode.

When a Header or Footer window is displayed, the Main property bar changes to the Header/Footer property bar. Figure 9.2 identifies the buttons on the Header/Footer property bar. Use buttons on this property bar to insert page numbering and specify the pages and location of headers or footers, and to close the Header or Footer window.

exercise

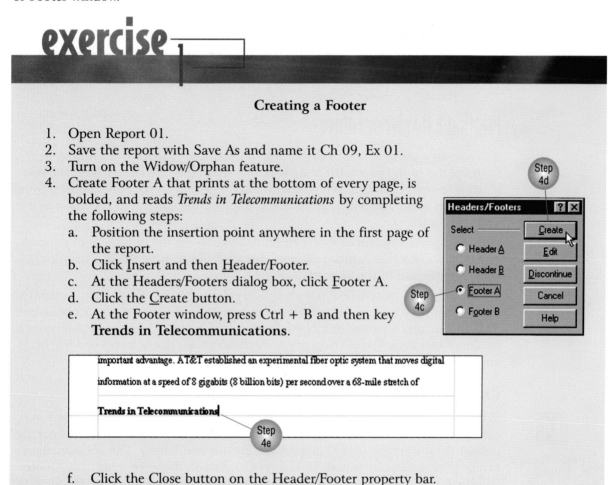

Creating a Footer

1. Open Report 01.
2. Save the report with Save As and name it Ch 09, Ex 01.
3. Turn on the Widow/Orphan feature.
4. Create Footer A that prints at the bottom of every page, is bolded, and reads *Trends in Telecommunications* by completing the following steps:
   a. Position the insertion point anywhere in the first page of the report.
   b. Click Insert and then Header/Footer.
   c. At the Headers/Footers dialog box, click Footer A.
   d. Click the Create button.
   e. At the Footer window, press Ctrl + B and then key **Trends in Telecommunications**.

   Step 4d

   Step 4c

   Headers/Footers
   Select
   ○ Header A
   ○ Header B
   ● Footer A
   ○ Footer B
   Create
   Edit
   Discontinue
   Cancel
   Help

   important advantage. AT&T established an experimental fiber optic system that moves digital information at a speed of 8 gigabits (8 billion bits) per second over a 68-mile stretch of

   Trends in Telecommunications

   Step 4e

   f. Click the Close button on the Header/Footer property bar.
5. Save, print, and then close Ch 09, Ex 01.

Beginning a Header or Footer on Specific Pages

If the insertion point is positioned in the first page when the header or footer is created, the header or footer code is inserted at the beginning of the document and the header or footer will print on every page.

To specify a different page on which the header or footer is to begin printing, position the insertion point in that page, and then create the header or footer. For example, if you want a header or footer to begin printing on page 2 of a document, position the insertion point anywhere in page 2 and then create the header or footer.

You can also print headers or footers on only even-numbered or only odd-numbered pages. This option is available at the Placement dialog box, shown in figure 9.3. To display this dialog box, click the Header/Footer Placement button on the Header/Footer property bar.

Header/Footer Placement

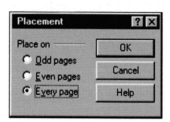

Printing a Header or Footer

A header in a document with default top and bottom margins will print an inch from the top of the page with one blank line separating the header from the text. Unless the bottom margin is changed, the last line of a footer prints an inch from the bottom of the page with one blank line separating the text in the document from the footer.

If you want a header or footer to print closer to the top or bottom of the page, change the top and/or bottom margins. For example, to have the header print 0.5 inch from the top of the page, change the top margin to 0.5 inch.

Headers and footers take the place of regular text lines. By default, a standard piece of paper contains 9 inches of printed text. WordPerfect automatically assigns a blank line after a header or a blank line before a footer. Therefore, if you create a header of two lines, WordPerfect prints the header (two lines), leaves one line blank, and then prints 8.5 inches of text. A footer prints in a similar manner.

Changing the Distance Measurement

Header/Footer
Distance

With the Header/Footer Distance button on the Header/Footer property bar, you can specify the distance between the header and text or the text and the footer. By default the distance is 0.167" (approximately one blank line). This measurement can be decreased or increased. To change the distance between a header or footer and the text in a document, click the Header/Footer Distance button on the Header/Footer property bar. At the Distance dialog box, increase or decrease the distance measurement. The measurement you enter at the Distance dialog box stays in effect for the entire document.

Keying Flush Right Text

When creating headers and/or footers in a document, you may want to key text that prints at the right margin. To create text at the right margin, use the Flush Right command. To do this, click Format, point to Line, and then click Flush Right. You can also access the Flush Right command by pressing Alt + F7. The Flush Right command causes the insertion point to move to the right margin. As text is keyed, the insertion point moves to the left. The Flush Right command is ended when you press the Enter key. To align the next line at the right margin, click Format, point to Line, and then click Flush Right, or press Alt + F7 again. (If you choose the Flush Right command twice in succession, the text you key will be preceded by dot leaders.)

Changing the Distance between a Header and the Body Text

1. Open Report 04.
2. Save the report with Save As and name it Ch 09, Ex 02.
3. Make the following changes to the report:
   a. Turn on the Widow/Orphan feature.
   b. Change the top margin to 0.5 inch.
   c. With the insertion point at the beginning of the document, press Enter twice to move the report title to approximately Line 1.29" (your measurement may vary slightly).
   d. Insert a hard page break at the beginning of the line containing the title *CHAPTER 4: DEVELOPMENT OF TECHNOLOGY, 1950 - 1960.*
   e. Create Header A that prints at the right margin only on odd pages, is separated from the text in the document by 0.334 inch, is italicized, and includes your last name by completing the following steps:
      1) Position the insertion point somewhere in the first page.
      2) Click Insert and then Header/Footer.
      3) At the Headers/Footers dialog box, make sure Header A is selected and then click Create.
      4) At the Header window, access the Flush Right command by clicking Format, pointing to Line, and then clicking Flush Right, or pressing Alt + F7.
      5) Press Ctrl + I and then key **Your Last Name** (insert your last name).
      6) Click the Header/Footer Distance button on the Header/Footer property bar.
      7) At the Distance dialog box, key **0.334**.
      8) Click OK or press Enter.
      9) Click the Header/Footer Placement button on the Header/Footer property bar.
      10) At the Header A Placement dialog box, click Odd pages.
      11) Click OK.
      12) Click the Close button on the Header/Footer property bar.

      Step 3e6

      Step 3e11

      Step 3e10

      Header A Placement

      Place on
      ● Odd pages
      ○ Even pages
      ○ Every page

      OK
      Cancel
      Help

   f. Create Header B that prints at the left margin only on even pages, is separated from the text in the document by 0.334 inch, is bolded, and reads *Technology, 1900 - 1950* by completing the following steps:
      1) Position the insertion point somewhere in the second page.
      2) Click Insert and then Header/Footer.
      3) At the Headers/Footers dialog box, click Header B and then click Create.
      4) At the Header window, Press Ctrl + B and then key **Technology, 1900 - 1950**.
      5) Click the Header/Footer Distance button on the Header/Footer property bar.
      6) At the Distance dialog box, key **0.334**.
      7) Click OK or press Enter.
      8) Click the Header/Footer Placement button on the Header/Footer property bar.
      9) At the Header B Placement dialog box, click Even pages.
      10) Click OK.
      11) Click the Close button on the Header/Footer property bar.
4. Save, print, and then close Ch 09, Ex 02.

Editing a Header or Footer

A header or footer can be edited at the Headers/Footers dialog box, or, if you are in the Page viewing mode, you can click the mouse inside the Header/Footer window and edit the text.

To edit using the Headers/Footers dialog box, click Insert and then Header/Footer. At the Headers/Footers dialog box, select the header or footer (A or B) you want to change and then click the Edit button. Make any changes to the header/footer text and then click the Close button.

Editing a Header

1. Open Ch 09, Ex 02.
2. Save the report with Save As and name it Ch 09, Ex 03.
3. Edit Header B so that it reads *Development of Technology* by completing the following steps:
   a. Click Insert and then Header/Footer.
   b. At the Headers/Footers dialog box, click Header B and then click the Edit button.
   c. At the Header window, delete the existing text and then key **Development of Technology** bolded.

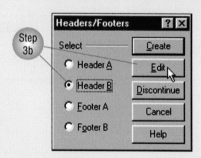

   d. Click the Close button on the Header/Footer property bar.
4. Save, print, and then close Ch 09, Ex 03.

Formatting a Header or Footer

A header or footer that is created in a document does not take on any formatting applied to the document. For example, if the margins and justification are changed in the document, the header or footer text does not conform to these changes. Header or footer text will print at default settings.

If you want formatting changes in a document to also affect header or footer text, insert the formatting codes at the Styles Editor dialog box. To display the Styles Editor dialog box, shown in figure 9.4, click File, point to Document, and then click Current Document Style. Insert formatting codes in this dialog box in the normal manner.

9.4 **Styles Editor Dialog Box**

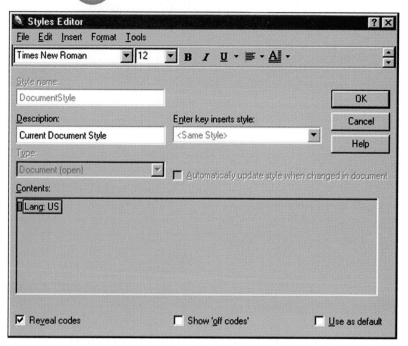

Including Font Changes in a Header or Footer

If you want to change the font for a document and you want the font to also affect header or footer text, select a new font at the Document Default Font dialog box. To display this dialog box, shown in figure 9.5, click File, point to Document, and then click Default Font. At the Document Default Font dialog box, click the desired font in the Face list box and then click OK or press Enter.

9.5 **Document Default Font Dialog Box**

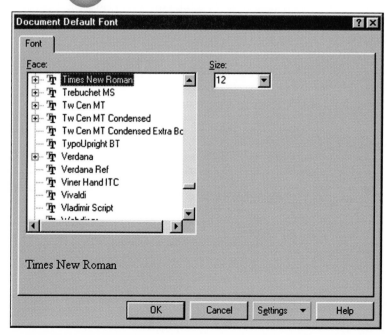

Any changes you make to the Styles Editor dialog box or Document Default Font dialog box affect only the document in which you are working. When you begin a new document, the WordPerfect defaults are in effect. If you want the changes to affect the current as well as future documents, insert a check mark in the Use as default check box at the Styles Editor dialog box.

Inserting Page Numbering in a Header or Footer

Page Numbering

Page numbering can be included in a header or footer with the Page Numbering button on the Header/Footer property bar. When you click the Page Numbering button on the Header/Footer property bar, a drop-down menu displays with numbering choices.

With the options from the drop-down menu, you can insert page numbers, secondary numbers, chapter numbers, volume numbers, or the number of total pages. For example, if you click Page Number at the Page Numbering drop-down menu, a *1* is inserted in the header or footer. This number will change on each subsequent page. (For example, a *2* will display in the header or footer on page 2.)

exercise

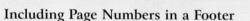

Including Page Numbers in a Footer

1. Open Report 04.
2. Save the report with Save As and name it Ch 09, Ex 04.
3. Display the Styles Editor dialog box, change the left margin to 1.5 inches and the justification to Full, and then close the dialog box.
4. Change the font for the entire document (but not future documents) to 13-point Garamond by completing the following steps:
   a. Click File, point to Document, and then click Default Font.
   b. At the Document Default Font dialog box, click *Garamond* in the Face list box (you will need to scroll up the list to display this font).
   c. Click OK or press Enter to close the Document Default Font dialog box.
5. Create Footer A that prints at the left margin of every page, is bolded, and reads *Development of Technology*.
6. Create Footer B that prints at the right margin of every page, is bolded, and reads *Page #* (where WordPerfect inserts the proper page number) by completing the following steps:
   a. Position the insertion point somewhere in the first page.
   b. Click Insert and then Header/Footer.
   c. At the Headers/Footers dialog box, click Footer B and then click Create.
   d. At the Footer window, click Format, point to Line, and then click Flush Right (or press Alt + F7). (The previous footer text will disappear. The text, however, will display and print properly.)
   e. Press Ctrl + B, key **Page**, and then press the spacebar once.
   f. Click the Page Numbering button on the Header/Footer property bar.
   g. At the Page Numbering drop-down list, click Page Number.
   h. Click the Close button on the Header/Footer property bar.
7. Save, print, and then close Ch 09, Ex 04.

Step 6f

Discontinuing a Header or Footer

Header or footer text can appear at the top or bottom of each page, or it can appear on certain pages and be turned off on others. For example, you can create Header A that prints on the first three pages of a document, and then turn off Header A for the remaining pages of the document. You can do the same for footers. The Discontinue option at the Headers/Footers dialog box turns off the printing of the header or footer from the page where the insertion point is positioned to the end of the document.

Suppressing a Header or Footer

A header or footer can be suppressed on a specific page in a document. This might be useful for a page in a document such as a title page, copyright page, or opening page of a chapter. When a header or footer is discontinued, it is off for the remainder of the document (unless another header or footer is created). With options from the Suppress dialog box, shown in figure 9.6, headers or footers can be suppressed on a specific page. Display the Suppress dialog box by clicking Format, point to Page, and then click Suppress.

FIGURE

9.6 **Suppress Dialog Box**

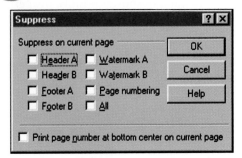

exercise

Suppressing a Footer on One Page

1. Open Ch 09, Ex 04.
2. Save the report with Save As and name it Ch 09, Ex 05.
3. Suppress Footer A on page 3 by completing the following steps:
   a. Position the insertion point anywhere in page 3.
   b. Click Format, point to Page, and then click Suppress.
   c. At the Suppress dialog box, click Footer A.
   d. Click OK or press Enter.
4. Save, print, and then close Ch 09, Ex 05.

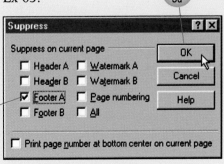

Step 3d

Step 3c

Using Footnotes and Endnotes

A research paper or report contains information from a variety of sources. To give credit to those sources, a footnote can be inserted in the document. A footnote is an explanatory note or reference that is printed at the bottom of a page.

A footnote notation appears in the body of the document as a superscripted number. At the bottom of the page, this same number identifies the footnote containing information about the source. When footnotes are created in a document, WordPerfect determines the number of lines needed at the bottom of the page for the footnote information and adjusts the page endings accordingly.

An endnote is similar to a footnote, except that endnote reference information appears at the end of a document rather than on the page where the reference was made.

Creating Footnotes and Endnotes

Footnotes and endnotes are created in a similar manner with WordPerfect. To create a footnote in a document, move the insertion point to the location in the document where the notation is to appear, click Insert and then Footnote/Endnote. At the Footnote/Endnote dialog box, shown in figure 9.7, make sure the correct footnote number displays in the Footnote Number text box and then click the Create button. At the Footnote window, key the footnote reference information, and then click the Close button that displays on the Footnote/Endnote property bar. The Footnote/Endnote property bar takes the place of the Main property bar.

FIGURE

9.7 *Footnote/Endnote Dialog Box*

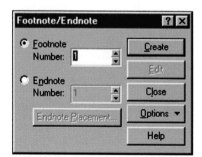

To create an endnote, move the insertion point to the location in the document where the notation is to appear, click Insert and then Footnote/Endnote. At the Footnote/Endnote dialog box, click the radio button preceding Endnote Number, make sure the correct endnote number displays in the text box, and then click the Create button. At the Endnote window, access the Indent command, key the endnote reference information, and then click the Close button on the Footnote/Endnote property bar.

After keying the footnote or endnote reference text, do not press the Enter key. By default, footnotes and endnotes are separated by a blank line. If you press the Enter key after keying the footnote or endnote reference text, an extra blank line is inserted between the notes.

exercise 6

Creating Footnotes

1. Open Report 01.
2. Save the report with Save As and name it Ch 09, Ex 06.
3. Turn on the Widow/Orphan feature.
4. Create the first footnote shown in figure 9.8 at the end of the first paragraph in the *Continued Growth of Photonics (Fiber Optics)* section by completing the following steps:
   a. Position the insertion point at the end of the first paragraph in the *Continued Growth of Photonics (Fiber Optics)* section.
   b. Click Insert and then Footnote/Endnote.
   c. At the Footnote/Endnote dialog box, make sure Footnote Number is selected and then click Create.
   d. At the Footnote window, key the first footnote reference information shown in figure 9.8.
   e. Click the Close button on the Footnote/Endnote property bar.
5. Move the insertion point to the end of the second paragraph in the *Continued Growth of Photonics (Fiber Optics)* section and then create the second footnote shown in figure 9.8 by completing steps similar to those in 4.
6. Move the insertion point to the end of the last paragraph in the *Continued Growth of Photonics (Fiber Optics)* section and then create the third footnote shown in figure 9.8 by completing steps similar to those in 4.
7. Move the insertion point to the end of the last paragraph in the report and then create the fourth footnote shown in figure 9.8 by completing steps similar to those in 4.
8. Check page breaks in the report and, if necessary, insert your own page breaks in more appropriate locations.
9. Save, print, and then close Ch 09, Ex 06.

FIGURE 9.8 Exercise 6

[1]Mitchell, William, Robert Hendricks, and Leonard Sterry, *Telecommunications: Systems and Applications*, Paradigm Publishing, 2001, pages 39-41.

[2]Weik, Robert, "History of Light Wave Technology," *Computer Technologies*, May/June 2002, pages 9-12.

[3]Griffith, Kathleen, "The Importance of Fiber Optics," *Computing in the 90's*, April 2000, pages 2-6.

[4]McKenna, Kelly A., *Telecommunications Innovations*, Princetown Publishing, 2003, pages 44-48.

Printing Footnotes and Endnotes

When a document containing footnotes is printed, WordPerfect automatically reduces the number of text lines on a page by the number of lines in the footnote plus two lines for spacing between the text and the footnote. WordPerfect keeps at least 0.5 inch of footnote text together. If there is not enough room on the page for the 0.5 inch of footnote text, the footnote number and footnote are taken to the next page. WordPerfect separates the footnotes from the text with a 2-inch separator line that begins at the left margin. The footnote number in the document and the footnote number before the reference information print as superscripted numbers (above the text line).

When endnotes are created in a document, WordPerfect prints all endnote references at the end of the document. If you want the endnotes printed on a separate page at the end of the document, move the insertion point to the end of the document, and then insert a hard page break by clicking Insert and then New Page, or by pressing Ctrl + Enter.

Endnotes can also be placed in other locations in the document. For example, in a document containing several sections, you can have the endnotes placed at the end of each section within the document. To position endnotes at a location other than the end of a document, display the Endnote Placement dialog box and then click either Insert endnotes at insertion point or Insert endnotes at insertion point and restart numbering. To display the Endnote Placement dialog box, click Insert and then Footnote/Endnote. At the Footnote/Endnote dialog box, click the radio button preceding Endnote Number, and then click the Endnote Placement button.

Creating Endnotes

1. Open Report 02.
2. Save the report with Save As and name it Ch 09, Ex 07.
3. Make the following changes to the document:
   a. Turn on the Widow/Orphan feature.
   b. Move the insertion point to the end of the document and then insert a hard page break by clicking Insert and then New Page or by pressing Ctrl + Enter.
   c. Key **ENDNOTES**, bolded and centered, and then press the Enter key once. (This will cause the endnotes to print on a separate page with the heading *ENDNOTES*.)
   d. Create the first endnote shown in figure 9.9 by completing the following steps:
      1) Position the insertion point at the end of the first paragraph in the report.
      2) Click Insert and then Footnote/Endnote.
      3) At the Footnote/Endnote dialog box, click the radio button preceding Endnote Number and then click Create.
      4) At the Endnote window, press F7 to access the Indent command and then key the first endnote reference information shown in figure 9.9.

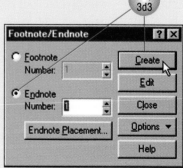

Step
3d3

      5) Click the Close button on the Footnote/Endnote property bar.

  e. Move the insertion point to the end of the first paragraph in the *Contributions of Major Historical Events* section and then create the second endnote shown in figure 9.9 by completing steps similar to those in 3d.

  f. Move the insertion point to the end of the last paragraph in the *Contributions of Major Historical Events* section and then create the third endnote shown in figure 9.9 by completing steps similar to those in 3d.

  g. Move the insertion point to the end of the last paragraph in the document and then create the fourth endnote shown in figure 9.9 by completing steps similar to those in 3d.

4. Check page breaks in the report and, if necessary, insert your own page breaks in more appropriate locations.

5. Save, print, and then close Ch 09, Ex 07.

FIGURE

9.9 *Exercise 7*

1.   Mitchell, William, Robert Hendricks, and Leonard Sterry, *Telecommunications: Systems and Applications*, Paradigm Publishing, 2001, pages 16-19.

2.   Brewer, Ilene, *Industrialization in the U.S.*, City Publishing Services, 2000, pages 43-45.

3.   Morrell, Ashley, *History of Computing*, G. Hardy Publishing, 2002, pages 12-20.

4.   Pang, Yi, *Computing Today*, Pacific Coast Publishing, Inc., 2003, pages 7-13.

Formatting Footnotes and Endnotes

If you want formatting changes to affect footnotes or endnotes as well as the document, insert the formatting codes at the Styles Editor dialog box. If you also change the font in a document and want the new font to apply to footnotes or endnotes, change the font at the Document Default Font dialog box. Otherwise, the footnotes or endnotes will print in the default font of the document.

Any changes you make at the Styles Editor dialog box or the Document Default Font dialog box affect only the document in which you are working. When you begin a new document, the WordPerfect document defaults are in effect.

Editing Footnotes or Endnotes

Changes can be made to a footnote or an endnote that was previously created in a document. You can edit a footnote or an endnote by clicking the footnote or endnote text that displays in the document. (You must be in Page or Two-Pages view for the footnote or endnote text to be visible.) Another method for editing a footnote or an endnote is to display the Footnote/Endnote dialog box, insert the desired number in the <u>F</u>ootnote Number text box or the E<u>n</u>dnote Number text box, and then click the <u>E</u>dit button.

Editing Endnotes

1. Open Ch 09, Ex 07.
2. Save the document with Save As and name it Ch 09, Ex 08.
3. Make the following changes to the document:
   a. Display the Styles Editor dialog box, change the left and right margins to 1.25 inches, and then close the dialog box.
   b. Display the Document Default Font dialog box, and change the font to 12-point Garamond.
   c. Number pages in the document at the bottom center of each page.
   d. Edit the second endnote, changing the year from 2000 to 2002 and changing the page numbers from 43-45 to 21-24, by completing the following steps:
      1) Click <u>I</u>nsert and then <u>F</u>ootnote/Endnote.
      2) At the Footnote/Endnote dialog box, key **2** in the E<u>n</u>dnote Number text box and then click the <u>E</u>dit button.
      3) With the reference text for the endnote displayed in the Endnote window, change the year from *2000* to *2002* and the pages from *43-45* to *21-24*.
      4) Click the Close button on the Footnote/Endnote property bar.
   e. Edit the fourth endnote, changing the title from *Computing Today* to *Perspectives in Telecommunications*.
4. Check page breaks in the report and, if necessary, insert your own page breaks in more appropriate locations.
5. Save, print, and then close Ch 09, Ex 08.

Deleting Footnotes or Endnotes

A footnote or an endnote can be deleted from a document by positioning the insertion point immediately to the left of the footnote or endnote number in the document text and then pressing the Delete key. You can also position the insertion point immediately to the right of the footnote or endnote number and then press the Backspace key. Or, you can use the mouse to drag the footnote or endnote code out of the Reveal Codes window. When a footnote or an endnote is deleted from a document, WordPerfect automatically renumbers any remaining footnotes or endnotes.

exercise 9

Deleting Footnotes

1. Open Ch 09, Ex 06.
2. Save the document with Save As and name it Ch 09, Ex 09.
3. Make the following changes to the document:
   a. Display the Styles Editor dialog box, change the left and right margins to 1.25 inches and the justification to Full, and then close the dialog box.
   b. Select the title *TRENDS IN TELECOMMUNICATIONS* and then change the relative size to Very large.
   c. Select the heading *Continued Growth of Photonics (Fiber Optics)* and then change the relative size to Large.
   d. Select the heading *Microcomputer Trends in the Nineties* and then change the relative size to Large.
   e. Move the insertion point to the end of the second paragraph in the *Continued Growth of Photonics (Fiber Optics)* section and then delete the footnote number.
4. Check page breaks in the report and, if necessary, insert your own page breaks in more appropriate locations.
5. Save, print, and then close Ch 09, Ex 09.

Changing the Beginning Number

When a footnote or an endnote is created in a document, the numbering begins with 1 and continues sequentially. The beginning footnote or endnote number can be changed as well as the numbering style. For example, you can begin footnote numbering with *2* rather than *1*. These kinds of changes are made at the Footnote Number dialog box. The Endnote Number dialog box contains the same options. To display the Footnote Number dialog box, click Insert and then Footnote/Endnote. At the Footnote/Endnote dialog box, click the Options button. At the drop-down menu that displays, click Set Number.

At the Footnote Number dialog box (and Endnote Number dialog box), you can choose to increase or decrease the number by 1 or enter a new number in the New number text box. When a footnote or an endnote number is changed, a code is inserted in the document at the location of the insertion point that can be seen in Reveal Codes.

CHAPTER summary

➤ Text that appears at the top of pages is called a header; text that appears at the bottom of pages is called a footer.

➤ A maximum of two headers and/or two footers can be created in one document. WordPerfect calls them Header A, Header B, Footer A, and Footer B.

➤ A header is created at the Header window and a footer is created at the Footer window.

➤ WordPerfect inserts a header or footer code at the beginning of the page where the insertion point is positioned. If the code is positioned in the first page of the document, the header/footer will print on every page.

➤ When the Header or Footer window is displayed, the Header/Footer property bar displays in place of the Main property bar. Use buttons on this property bar to insert page numbering in a header or footer, change the distance measurement between a header/footer and the text, and specify whether a header/footer is to be printed on all pages or only odd or even pages.

➤ Use the Flush Right command to create text aligned at the right margin.

➤ A header/footer that is created in a document does not take on any formatting applied to the document. If you want formatting changes in a document to also affect header/footer text, insert the formatting codes at the Styles Editor dialog box.

➤ If you use a font in a document other than the default and want this font to apply to the headers/footers, change the font at the Document Default Font dialog box.

➤ When a document is printed, header or footer text occupies the place of regular text lines. By default, a blank line separates the header or footer from the main text.

➤ Header or footer text can be edited by clicking the Edit button at the Headers/Footers dialog box or by clicking in the header/footer text.

➤ A header/footer can be discontinued at the Headers/Footers dialog box or suppressed at the Suppress dialog box.

➤ A footnote is an explanatory note or reference that is printed at the bottom of a page. An endnote is a note or reference printed at the end of a document.

➤ When a footnote or an endnote is created, a superscripted number is inserted in the document where the insertion point is positioned.

➤ Before the footnote/endnote is created at the Footnote/Endnote window, position the insertion point in the document where the notation number is to appear.

➤ A footnote prints at the bottom of the page where the text is referenced; footnotes are separated from the text by a 2-inch line that begins at the left margin.

➤ Endnotes print at the end of the last text in the document. To print endnotes on a separate page, insert a hard page break at the end of the document.

➤ A footnote/endnote that is created in a document does not take on any formatting applied to the document. If you want formatting changes in a document to also affect header/footer text, insert the formatting codes at the Styles Editor dialog box.

➤ If you use a font in a document other than the default and want this font applied to the footnotes/endnotes, change the font at the Document Default Font dialog box.

➤ Footnotes/endnotes can be edited.

➤ A footnote/endnote can be removed by deleting the notation number in the document. WordPerfect will automatically renumber any remaining footnotes/endnotes.

COMMANDS summary

Command	Mouse	Keyboard
Display the Header/Footer dialog box	Insert, Header/Footer	
Key text flush right		Alt + F7
Display the Suppress dialog box	Format, Page, Suppress	
Display the Footnote/Endnote dialog box	Insert, Footnote/Endnote	

CONCEPTS check

Completion: On a blank sheet of paper, indicate the correct term, symbol, or command for each item.

1. Text that appears at the top of every page is referred to as this.

2. This is the maximum number of headers that can be created in the same document.

3. Text that appears at the bottom of every page is referred to as this.

4. A header or footer code will be inserted here when a header or footer is created in a document.

5. This is the shortcut command from the keyboard to align text at the right margin.

6. To print the header in a document on every page except page 3, place this code on page 3.

7. Headers and/or footers will display in these viewing modes.

8. If you want formatting changes in a document to affect any headers or footers in a document, insert the formatting codes at this dialog box.

9. If you use a font in a document other than the default and want this font to apply to any headers or footers in the document, change the font at this dialog box.

10. If you want a header to print 0.5 inch from the top of the page, change the top margin to this measurement.

11. So that the endnotes will print on a separate page, insert this at the end of the document.

12. When a footnote or an endnote is created, this type of number is inserted in the document at the location of the insertion point.

13. If you want formatting changes to affect footnotes or endnotes, insert the formatting codes here.

14. By default, WordPerfect separates footnotes from the text by this.

15. By default, footnotes are printed here.

16. If you use a font in a document other than the default and want this font applied to footnotes, change the font at this dialog box.

SKILLS check

Assessment 1

1. Open Report 02.
2. Save the report with Save As and name it Ch 09, SA 01.
3. Make the following changes to the report:
   a. Turn on the Widow/Orphan feature.
   b. Change the top and bottom margins to 0.5 inch.
   c. Press Enter twice to move the title of the report down to approximately Line 1.29". (Your measurement may vary slightly.)
   d. Display the Styles Editor dialog box, change the left and right margins to 1.25 inches and the justification to Full, and then close the dialog box.
   e. Display the Document Default Font dialog box, change the font to 12-point Garamond, make sure there is no check mark in the Use as default check box, and then close the dialog box.
   f. Create Footer A that prints centered and bolded at the bottom of every page and reads *Telecommunications*.
   g. Create Header A that prints at the right margin on every page except the first, is bolded, and reads *Development of Technology*.
   h. Save, print, and then close Ch 09, SA 01.

Assessment 2

1. Open Report 07.
2. Save the document with Save As and name it Ch 09, SA 02.
3. Make the following changes to the report:
   a. Turn on the Widow/Orphan feature.
   b. Change the line spacing to double (2).
   c. Display the Document Default Font dialog box, change the font to 12-point Garamond, and then close the dialog box.
   d. Display the Styles Editor dialog box, change the left and right margins to 1.5 inches and the justification to Full, and then close the dialog box.
   e. Select the title and then change the relative size to Large.
   f. Create Header A that prints at the right margin of odd pages, is bolded, and includes your last name.
   g. Create Header B that prints at the left margin of even pages, is italicized, and reads *Page #* (where WordPerfect inserts the proper page number).
   h. Create the first footnote shown in figure 9.10 at the end of the last paragraph in the *Industrialization* section of the report.

    i.   Create the second footnote shown in figure 9.10 at the end of the last paragraph in the *Development of a World Market* section of the report.

    j.   Create the third footnote shown in figure 9.10 at the end of the last paragraph in the report.

4. Check page breaks in the report and, if necessary, insert your own page breaks in more appropriate locations.

5. Save, print, and then close Ch 09, SA 02.

FIGURE

9.10 *Assessment 2*

[1]Mitchell, William, Robert Hendricks, and Leonard Sterry, "Contributions of Major Historical Events," *Telecommunications: Systems and Applications*, Paradigm Publishing, 2001, pages 16-17.

[2]Reynolds, Susan, "The World Market in the 1850s," *Communicating in the World Market*, Lowell & Howe Publishing, 2002, pages 25-28.

[3]Boronat, Walter, "Impact of the 1870s Depression on Technology," *Computer Technology*, Holstein/Mann Publishing, 2001, pages 55-78.

Assessment 3

1. Open Ch 09, SA 02.
2. Save the document with Save As and name it Ch 09, SA 03.
3. Edit Header A by making the following changes:
    a.   Change the text from your last name to your first initial and last name.
    b.   Remove the bold and add italics.
4. Edit the first footnote, changing the page numbers from 16-17 to 17-20.
5. Delete the second footnote.
6. Save, print, and then close Ch 09, SA 03.

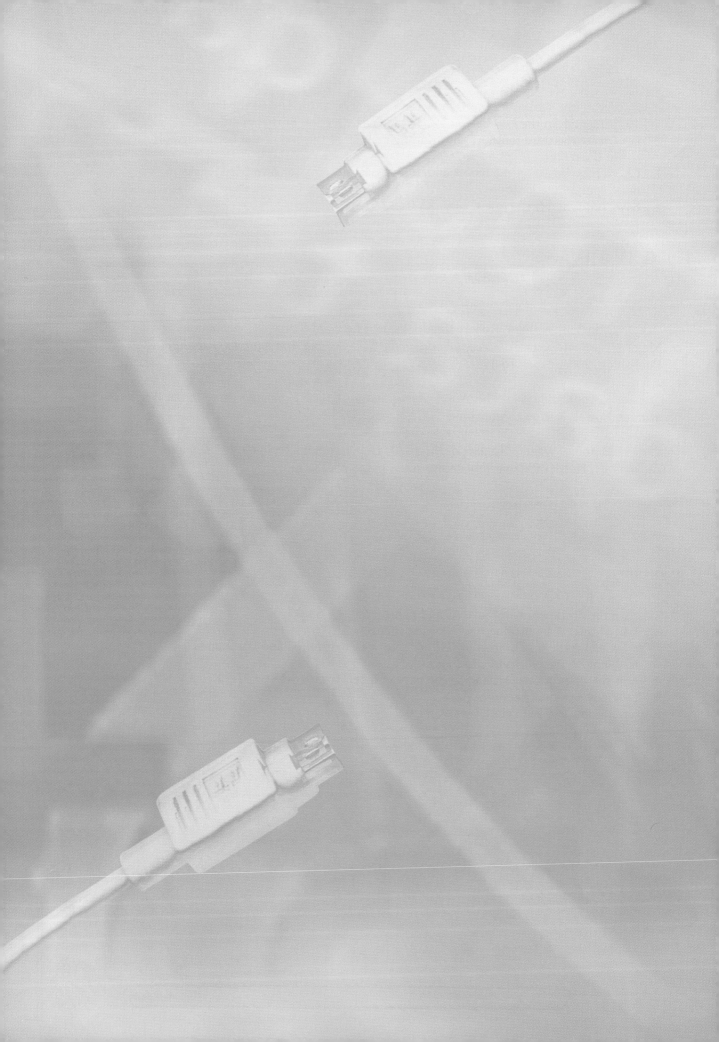

Manipulating Text

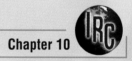

Chapter 10

Some documents may need to be heavily revised, and these revisions may include deleting, moving, copying, or pasting blocks of text. This kind of editing is generally referred to as *cut and paste*. In this chapter, you will learn to cut, copy, and paste text within and between documents.

Corel WordPerfect 10 operates within the Windows environment. When working in WordPerfect, a *window* refers to the editing window plus the scroll bars. Windows creates an environment in which various software programs are used with menu bars, scroll bars, and icons to represent programs and files. With Windows, you can open several different software programs and move between them quickly. Similarly, using windows in WordPerfect, you can open several different documents and move between them quickly. In this chapter, you will learn to open multiple documents, tile and cascade documents, move and copy text between open documents, and use various print options.

Working with Blocks of Text

When cutting and pasting, you work with blocks of text. A block of text is a portion of text that you have selected. (Chapter 2 explained the various methods for selecting text.) A block of text can be as small as one character or as large as an entire page or document.

Once a block of text has been selected, it can be:

- deleted
- moved to a new location
- copied to a new location

The last two operations involve using WordPerfect's Cut, Copy, and Paste features.

Deleting a Block of Text

WordPerfect offers different methods for deleting text from a document. To delete a single character, you can use either the Delete key or the Backspace key. To delete more than a single character, select the portion of text to be deleted, and then choose one of the following options:

Cut

- Press the Delete key.
- Click the Cut button on the Toolbar.
- Click Edit and then Cut.
- Press Ctrl + X.
- Click the *right* mouse button and then click Cut.

Undo

If you press the Delete key, the text is deleted permanently. (You can, however, restore deleted text by clicking the Undo button on the Toolbar.) Shift + Delete, the Cut button on the Toolbar, Cut from the Edit menu, Ctrl + X, and the Cut option from the shortcut menu will delete the selected text and store it in temporary memory. Text stored in temporary memory can be reinserted in a document at a later time.

Selecting and Deleting Text

1. Open Report 01.
2. Save the document with Save As and name it Ch 10, Ex 01.
3. Delete the following text in the report:
   a. Delete the fourth sentence (beginning *The US Sprint Network*) in the second paragraph of the *Continued Growth of Photonics (Fiber Optics)* section of the report by completing the following steps:

1) Select the sentence.
2) Click the Cut button on the Toolbar.

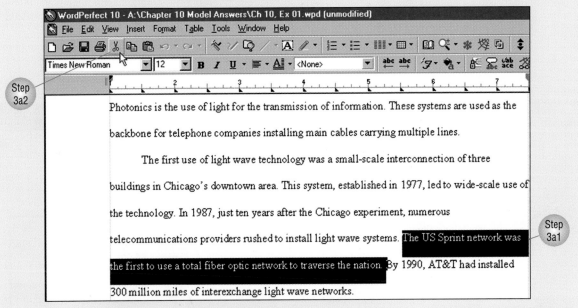

Step
3a2

Photonics is the use of light for the transmission of information. These systems are used as the

backbone for telephone companies installing main cables carrying multiple lines.

The first use of light wave technology was a small-scale interconnection of three

buildings in Chicago's downtown area. This system, established in 1977, led to wide-scale use of

the technology. In 1987, just ten years after the Chicago experiment, numerous

telecommunications providers rushed to install light wave systems. The US Sprint network was

the first to use a total fiber optic network to traverse the nation. By 1990, AT&T had installed

300 million miles of interexchange light wave networks.

Step
3a1

b. Delete all the bulleted items on the first page and the line of text above the items
   by completing the following steps:
   1) Select from *The advantages of light wave systems are many and include* through the
      bulleted item *relative low cost*.
   2) Press the Delete key.
c. Delete the second bulleted item, *increased disk storage (erasable optical disks)*, in the
   Microcomputer Trends in the Nineties section of the report.
d. Delete the fifth bulleted item, *increased cycle speeds (in excess of 100 million)*, in the
   Microcomputer Trends in the Nineties section of the report.
4. Save, print, and then close Ch 10, Ex 01.

Moving a Block of Text

WordPerfect offers multiple methods for moving text within a document. After you
have selected a block of text, you can use the Cu̲t and P̲aste options from either the
E̲dit drop-down menu or the shortcut menu, Ctrl + X to cut or Ctrl + V to paste, or
the Cut and Paste buttons on the Toolbar to move text from one location to another.
The Cu̲t option from the E̲dit drop-down menu or the shortcut menu, Ctrl + X,
or the Cut button on the Toolbar deletes text to temporary memory. The text in
temporary memory can be inserted in a document with the P̲aste option from the
E̲dit drop-down menu or the shortcut menu, Ctrl + V, or the Paste button on the
Toolbar.

Paste

A block of selected text can also be moved with the mouse. To do this, you
would complete the following steps:

1. Select the text.
2. Move the arrow pointer inside the selected text.
3. Hold down the left mouse button, drag the arrow pointer to the location
   where you want the selected text inserted, and then release the button.
4. Turn off Select by clicking anywhere in the editing window (outside the
   selected text) or pressing F8.

When you hold down the left mouse button and drag the arrow pointer, the arrow pointer turns into an arrow connected to a box. The box represents the text that is being moved. When you move the arrow pointer to the desired location and release the mouse button, the selected text is removed from its original position and inserted in the new location.

Selecting and Moving Text

1. Open Para 03.
2. Save the document with Save As and name it Ch 10, Ex 02.
3. Move the following text in the document:
   a. Move the second paragraph above the first paragraph by completing the following steps:

   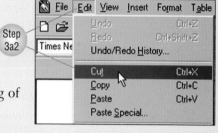

   1) Select the second paragraph including the blank line below the paragraph.
   2) Click Edit and then Cut.
   3) Position the insertion point at the beginning of the first paragraph.
   4) Click Edit and then Paste.
   b. Move the fourth paragraph above the third paragraph by completing the following steps:
   1) Select the fourth paragraph including the blank line below the paragraph.
   2) Click the Cut button on the Toolbar.
   3) Position the insertion point at the beginning of the third paragraph.
   4) Click the Paste button on the Toolbar.
   c. Move the fourth paragraph to the end of the document using the mouse by completing the following steps:
   1) Select the fourth paragraph including the blank line below the paragraph.
   2) Position the arrow pointer inside the selected text area.

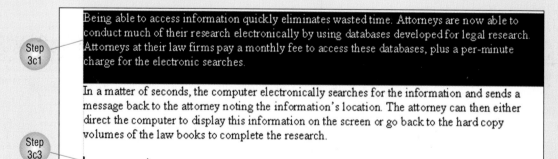

   3) Hold down the left mouse button, drag the arrow pointer a double space below the last paragraph, and then release the mouse button.
   4) Deselect the text.
   d. Save, print, and then close Ch 10, Ex 02.

Copying a Block of Text

WordPerfect's Copy option can be useful in documents that contain repetitive portions of text. You can use this function to insert duplicate portions of text instead of rekeying the text. You can copy text in a document with any of the following methods:

- Click Edit and then Copy.
- Ctrl + C.
- Click the Copy button on the Toolbar.
- Click the *right* mouse button and then click Copy.

Copy

The mouse can also be used to copy a block of text in a document and insert the copy in a new location. To do this, you would complete the following steps:

1. Select the text.
2. Move the arrow pointer inside the selected text.
3. Hold down the left mouse button and the Ctrl key.
4. Drag the arrow pointer to the location where a copy of the selected text is to be inserted, release the mouse button, and then release the Ctrl key.
5. Deselect the text.

With the Ctrl key down, the box with the arrow pointer displays with a page icon. There is a plus sign (+) in the middle of the page icon. When text is copied, the text remains in the editing window and a copy is inserted in temporary memory. Once text has been cut or copied to temporary memory, it can be inserted in a document any number of times without deleting or copying it again. The text will remain in temporary memory until other text is cut or copied to temporary memory or until you exit WordPerfect.

If you select a block of text and then decide you selected the wrong text or you do not want to do anything with the block, you can deselect it. If you are using the mouse, click the left mouse button outside the selected text. If you are using the keyboard, press F8 to turn off Select.

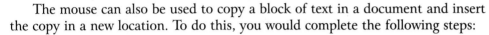

Copying Selected Text

1. Open Block 01.
2. Save the document with Save As and name it Ch 10, Ex 03.
3. Change the font to 20-point Rockwell. (If Rockwell is not available, choose a decorative typeface.)
4. Copy all the text to the end of the document by completing the following steps:
   a. Select the entire document (four lines of text plus two blank lines below the text) by clicking Edit, pointing to Select, and then clicking All.

b. Click the Copy button on the Toolbar.

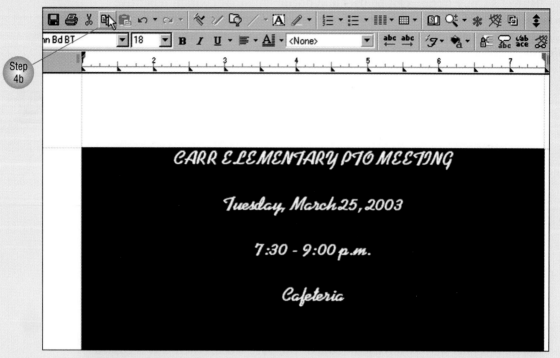

Step 4b

CARR ELEMENTARY PTO MEETING

Tuesday, March 25, 2003

7:30 - 9:00 p.m.

Cafeteria

    c. Deselect the text.

    d. Move the insertion point to the end of the document.

    e. Click the Paste button on the Toolbar.

5. Insert the text again by pressing Ctrl + V.

6. Save, print, and then close Ch 10, Ex 03.

Working with Columns of Text

Text set up in columns and separated by tabs can be selected and then deleted, moved, or copied within the document. (Refer to chapter 8 for a review of setting tabs and entering text into columns.) To select a column of text, you would complete the following steps:

1. Move the insertion point or the I-beam pointer to any character in the first entry of the column.

2. If you are using the mouse, hold down the left mouse button, drag the I-beam pointer to the last entry of the column, and then release the mouse button. (More than the one column will be selected, as shown in figure 10.1.) If you are using the keyboard, press F8 to turn on Select, and then move the insertion point to any character in the last entry of the column.

10.1 **Selected Text in Columns**

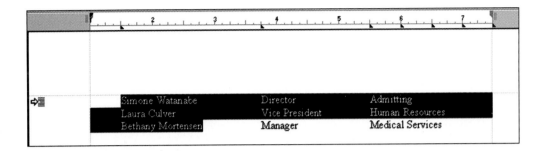

3. To select just the column, click <u>E</u>dit, point to Se<u>l</u>ect, and then click Tabular <u>C</u>olumn. The column plus any tab code before or after the column is selected as shown in figure 10.2.

10.2 **Selected Column**

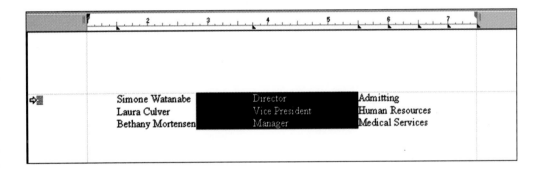

When you click Tabular <u>C</u>olumn, the selected text changes. The column and any tab before or after the column are selected. With the column selected, it can be deleted, moved, or copied.

Moving a Column

To understand how to move a column, look at the columns shown in figure 10.3. The three columns were keyed with left tabs set at the 2-inch mark, the 3.75-inch mark, and the 5.5-inch mark on the Ruler. The Tab key was pressed to move from one column to the next when entering the text. To move the second column to the right of the third column, you would complete the following steps:

1. Move the insertion point or the I-beam pointer to any character in the first entry of the second column (somewhere on *Director*).

2. If you are using the mouse, hold down the left mouse button, drag the I-beam pointer to any character in the word *Manager*, and then release the button. If you are using the keyboard, press F8 to turn on Select, and then move the insertion point to any character in the word *Manager*.

3. Click Edit, point to Select, and then click Tabular Column.

4. Click the Cut button on the Toolbar.

5. Position the insertion point on the space immediately after the first column entry in the second column (*Admitting*).

6. Click the Paste button on the Toolbar. The columns will appear as shown in figure 10.4.

As with selected blocks of text, selected columns of text can be moved with the mouse. This is referred to as "drag-and-drop" editing.

F I G U R E

10.3 *Columns Before Moving*

Simone Watanabe	Director	Admitting
Laura Culver	Vice President	Human Resources
Bethany Mortensen	Manager	Medical Services

F I G U R E

10.4 *Columns After Moving*

Simone Watanabe	Admitting	Director
Laura Culver	Human Resources	Vice President
Bethany Mortensen	Medical Services	Manager

Moving Columns

1. Open Tab 01.
2. Save the document with Save As and name it Ch 10, Ex 04.
3. Reverse the order of the columns by completing the following steps:
   a. Position the I-beam pointer on any character in the column heading of the first column (somewhere on *California*).
   b. Hold down the left mouse button, drag the I-beam pointer to any character in the words *Palm Springs*, and then release the button.
   c. Click Edit, point to Select, and then click Tabular Column. Your screen should look similar to the screen shown below.

WESTERN SHORES RESORTS

California	Oregon
Yosemite/Oakhurst	Portland Airport
Mammoth Lakes	Portland Lloyd Center
Pomona/Diamond Bar	Tigard/Washington Square
Corcoran	Wood Village/Gresham
Palm Springs	Troy Wilderness Resort

---

   d. Click the Cut button on the Toolbar.
   e. Position the insertion point at the space immediately following *Oregon*.
   f. Click the Paste button on the Toolbar.
4. Save, print, and then close Ch 10, Ex 04.

Copying a Column

Copying a column of text is very similar to moving a column. The main difference is that you click Copy (or click the Copy button) rather than Cut at the Edit drop-down menu. You can also use the drag-and-drop feature to copy selected columns.

Deleting a Column

To delete a column of text, select the column, and then click Edit and then Cut; press Ctrl + X; click the Cut button on the Toolbar; or click the *right* mouse button and then click Cut. When a column is removed from the editing window, any columns to the right move over to fill in the gap.

Deleting Columns

1. Open Tab 03.
2. Save the document with Save As and name it Ch 10, Ex 05.
3. Delete the second column by completing the following steps:
   a. Position the I-beam pointer on any character in the word *Semi*.
   b. Hold down the left mouse button, drag the I-beam pointer to any character in the number *42.00*, and then release the mouse button.
   c. Click Edit, point to Select, and then click Tabular Column.
   d. Click the Cut button on the Toolbar.
4. Display Reveal Codes and then move the insertion point to the line containing the Tab Set code.
5. Display the Tab Set dialog box, clear previous tabs, and then set a left tab at position 1.5 and a right tab at position 4.9. Turn off the display of Reveal Codes.
6. Save, print, and then close Ch 10, Ex 05.

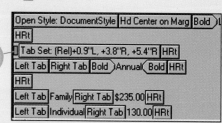

Working with Documents

Some documents may contain standard information—information that remains the same. For example, a legal document, such as a will, may contain text that is standard and appears in all wills. Repetitive text can be saved as a separate document and then retrieved into an existing document whenever needed.

Two methods can be used for saving text into a separate document. The first is to save a document just as you have been doing. The other method is to select standard text within a document and save it as a separate document.

Saving Standard Text

Save

If you know in advance what information or text is standard and will be used again, you can save it as a separate document. You should determine how to break down the information based on how it will be used. After deciding how to break down the information, key the text at a clear editing window, and then save it in the normal manner.

Saving Selected Text

When you create a document and then realize that a portion of the text in the document will be needed for future documents, you can save it as a separate document by selecting the text first. For example, to save a paragraph as a separate document, you would complete the following steps:

1. Select the paragraph.

2. Click File and then Save; or click the Save button on the Toolbar.

3. At the Save dialog box shown in figure 10.5, click Selected text and then click OK or press Enter.

4. At the Save File dialog box, key a name for the document.

5. Click the Save button or press Enter.

FIGURE

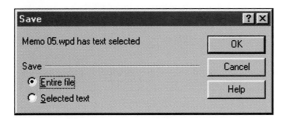

10.5 **Save Dialog Box**

These steps save the paragraph as a separate document while retaining the paragraph in the original document.

Inserting a Document

A document containing standard text can be inserted into an existing document with the File option from the Insert menu. For example, suppose you are keying a will and want to insert a standard document into the current will document. To do this, you would complete the following steps:

1. Position the insertion point in the will document at the location where you want the standard text.

2. Click Insert and then File.

3. At the Insert File dialog box, double-click the document name to be inserted, or key the document name, and then press Enter or click the Insert button.

WordPerfect brings the entire document to the screen including any formatting codes. If you want standard text to conform to the formatting of the current document, do not insert any formatting codes in the standard document.

Inserting a Document into Another Document

1. Open Report 01.
2. Select the bulleted items on the second page and then save them to a separate document named *Hardware* by completing the following steps:
   a. Select the six bulleted items on the second page.
   b. Click the Save button on the Toolbar.

c. At the Save dialog box, click Selected text and then click OK or press Enter.
d. At the Save File dialog box, key **Hardware**.
e. Click Save or press Enter.
f. Deselect the text.

Step 2c

3. Close Report 01.
4. At a clear editing window, key the memo headings and the first paragraph of the text shown in figure 10.6. Use an appropriate memo format. After keying the first paragraph, press Enter twice and then insert the Hardware document by completing the following steps:
   a. Click Insert and then File.
   b. At the Insert File dialog box, double-click *Hardware* in the list box.
5. Move the insertion point a double space below the bulleted items and then key the last paragraph. Include your initials and the document name a double space below the last line of the paragraph.
6. Save the memo and name it Ch 10, Ex 06.
7. Print and then close Ch 10, Ex 06.

FIGURE

10.6 *Exercise 6*

DATE: March 24, 2003; TO: Heath Brewer; FROM: Sonya Roth; SUBJECT: HARDWARE

The microcomputers at the two high schools need to be upgraded or replaced. This past quarter, I completed a telecommunications class at the local community college. During this class, I learned that new hardware should include the following:

[Insert Hardware document here.]

We need to get together in the next week or so to put together our equipment request for the next school year. Please call me to schedule a meeting.

xx:Ch 10, Ex 06

Working with Windows

In WordPerfect, multiple documents can be open at the same time. With multiple documents open, you can move or copy information between documents or compare the contents of several documents.

Opening Windows

With multiple windows open, you can move the insertion point between them. The maximum number of documents (windows) that you can have open at one time depends on the memory of your computer system and the amount of text in each document. When you open a new window, it is placed on top of the original window. Once multiple windows are opened, you can resize the windows to see all or a portion of them on the screen.

A single document can be opened at the Open File dialog box or you can open multiple documents at the same time. To do this, display the Open File dialog box, and then click the first document to be opened. Hold down the Ctrl key while clicking the remaining desired document names. Release the Ctrl key and then click the Open button. (Note: Some virus protection software will let you open only one document at a time.) The documents will be opened in the order in which they are selected.

When you are working in a document, the document fills the entire editing window. If you open another document without closing the first, the newly opened document will fill the editing window. The first document is still open, but it is covered by the new one. To see what documents are currently open, check the Application bar located toward the bottom of the screen. The name of an open document displays on a button that is positioned at the left side of the Application bar. Figure 10.7 shows the Application bar with three documents opened—Letter 01, Memo 01, and Report 01. The name of the active document displays with a lighter background on the Application bar.

FIGURE

10.7 Application Bar with Open Documents

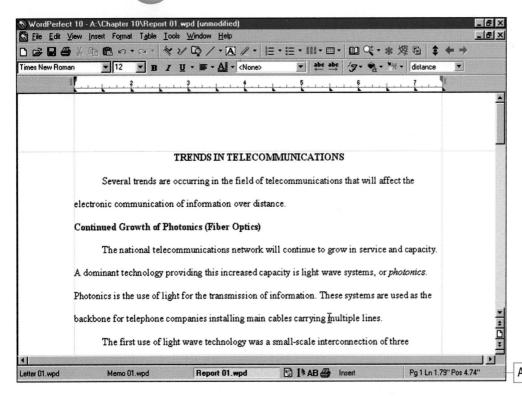

To move between open documents, click the desired document name on the Application bar. Moving between open documents using the Application bar is similar to moving between open programs using the Taskbar.

You can also move between open documents by clicking the <u>W</u>indow option on the Menu bar, and then clicking the desired document name at the drop-down menu. The open document names are displayed at the bottom of the drop-down menu. The document name with the check mark in front of it is the active document. The active document is the document containing the insertion point.

To make one of the other documents active, move the arrow pointer to the desired document, and then click the left mouse button. When you change the active document, the Window menu is removed from the screen and the new active document is displayed.

Closing Windows

To close an open document, make the document active, and then click the Close button on the document title bar. You can also close the active document by clicking <u>F</u>ile and then <u>C</u>lose or by pressing Ctrl + F4. To close the other open documents, repeat these steps.

Opening Multiple Documents

1. At a clear editing window, open several documents at the same time by completing the following steps:
   a. Display the Open File dialog box.
   b. Click the document named *Column 01*. (Be sure to click once and not double-click.)
   c. Hold down the Ctrl key, click *Letter 01*, and then click *Memo 05*.
   d. Release the Ctrl key.
   e. Click the <u>O</u>pen button.
2. Make Letter 01 the active document by clicking the button on the Application bar representing Letter 01.
3. Make Column 01 the active document by clicking <u>W</u>indow on the Menu bar and then clicking *A:\ Chapter 10\Column 01.wpd (unmodified)* at the drop-down menu.
4. Close Column 01.
5. Close Letter 01.
6. Close Memo 05.

Cascading Windows

When you have more than one open document, you can use the <u>C</u>ascade option from the <u>W</u>indow drop-down menu to view portions of all open documents. When open documents are cascaded, they overlap down the window, leaving the Title bar of each open document visible. For example, suppose you have the following three documents open: Letter 01, Memo 01, and Report 01. To cascade these three open documents, you would click <u>W</u>indow and then <u>C</u>ascade. The documents are arranged and displayed as shown in figure 10.8.

10.8 *Cascaded Windows*

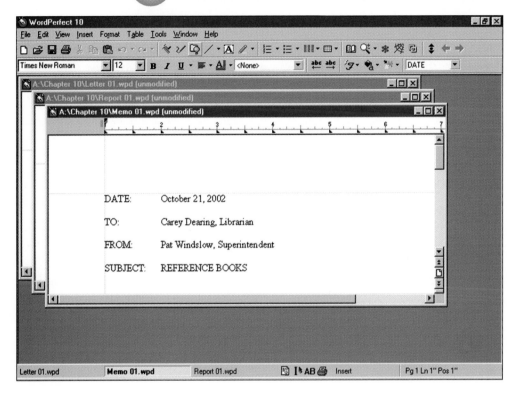

By default, the document closest to the front is the active document. The document name (along with drive and path) is displayed at the top of each open document. The Title bar of the active document displays with a blue background. The Title bar for inactive documents displays with a gray background.

To change the active window with the mouse, position the arrow pointer on the Title bar and then click the left mouse button. This causes the document to move to the front and become active. You can also click the button on the Application bar representing the desired document.

Tiling Windows

The Tile Top to Bottom and Tile Side by Side options from the Window drop-down menu cause each open document to appear in a separate window with no windows overlapping. For example, suppose you have the following three documents open: Letter 01, Memo 01, and Report 01. To tile these three open documents vertically, click Window and then Tile Top to Bottom. The windows display as shown in figure 10.9. Documents can also be tiled horizontally as shown in figure 10.10 by clicking Window and then Tile Side by Side.

F I G U R E

10.9 *Windows Tiled Top to Bottom*

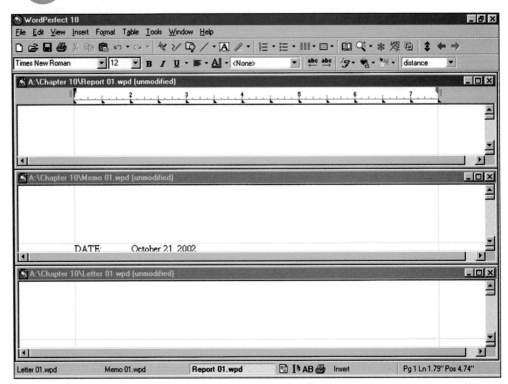

F I G U R E

10.10 *Windows Tiled Side by Side*

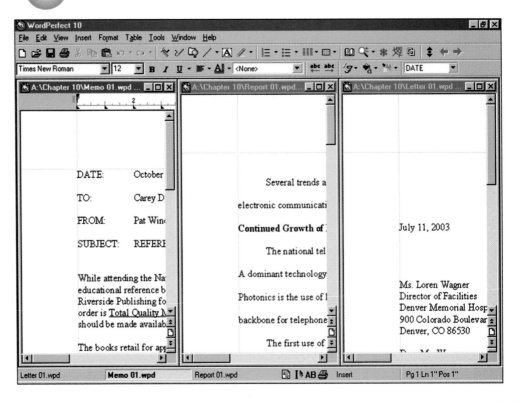

The Title bar in the active document displays with white characters on a blue background. The Title bar for inactive documents displays with light gray characters on a darker gray background. To change the active window, move the arrow pointer to the document you want active and then click the left mouse button. You can also click the button (file name) on the Application bar representing the desired document.

Sizing Windows

You can use the Maximize and Minimize buttons at the right side of the Title bar to reduce or increase the size of the active window. The Maximize button is the button in the upper right corner of the Title bar of the active window with the icon of a square with a thick dark line across the top. The Minimize button is the button in the upper right corner with the icon of a thick underscore character. The Maximize and Minimize buttons display in a document that has been tiled or cascaded.

Maximize

Minimize

Restore

If you cascade or tile open documents and then click the Maximize button in the active document, the active document expands to fill the editing window. If you click the Minimize button in the active document, the document is reduced to a small Title bar that displays along the bottom of the screen. To restore a document that has been reduced to a Title bar, move the arrow pointer to the Title bar, and then click the Restore button (formerly the Minimize button). Figure 10.11 shows an example of a document named *Letter 01* that has been minimized to a Title bar along the bottom left corner of the screen. (Not all of the document name is visible in the Title bar in figure 10.11—only A:\Chapter....) Notice the Minimize button has changed to the Restore button (two squares with thick dark lines across the top). Clicking the Restore button restores the document to its previous size.

F I G U R E

10.11 *Minimized Document*

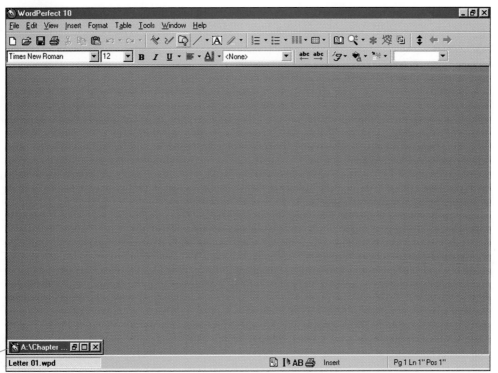

Minimized Document

If only one document is open, two Corel WordPerfect icons display in the upper left corner of the document window. The top Corel WordPerfect icon is called the *Application control button* and is used to change the size of the Windows application window. The second Corel WordPerfect icon is called the *Document control button*. The Document control button is used to change the size of the WordPerfect application window. When documents are tiled or cascaded, the Document control button displays at the left side of the Title bar.

To minimize a document using the Document control button with the mouse, click the Document control button (the second one in the upper left corner of the screen) and then click Mi_n_imize at the drop-down menu that displays. When a document has been minimized, it can be restored or maximized. To maximize a minimized document, click the Maximize button on the Title bar.

Cutting and Pasting Text between Windows

With several documents open, you can easily move, copy, and/or paste text from one document to another. To move, copy, and/or paste text between documents, use the cutting and pasting commands you learned in this chapter together with the information about windows.

In WordPerfect, selected text can be "dragged" to a document in another window using the mouse. For example, to drag selected text from one document to another, you would complete the following steps:

1. Open the document you want to move text from and also the document you want to move text to.

2. Tile the documents.

3. Select the text to be moved.

4. Drag the text to a new location.

You would complete similar steps to copy selected text except you would hold down the Ctrl key while dragging the arrow pointer.

Moving Text between Documents

1. At a clear editing window, change to the Draft viewing mode and then key the memo shown in figure 10.12 in an appropriate memo format. (Press the Enter key four times after keying the first paragraph and before keying the second paragraph.)
2. Save the memo and name it Ch 10, Ex 08.
3. With Ch 10, Ex 08 still open on the screen, open Memo 02 and then change the viewing mode to Draft.
4. Tile the windows side by side by clicking _W_indow and then Tile _S_ide by Side.
5. Copy the first three books listed in Memo 02 by completing the following steps:

a. Select the three paragraphs containing the first three book titles (the paragraphs containing *The ABCs of Integrated Learning*, *Total Quality Management in the Education Environment*, and *Health Education for Today's Child*).

b. Move the I-beam pointer into the selected area until it turns into an arrow pointer.

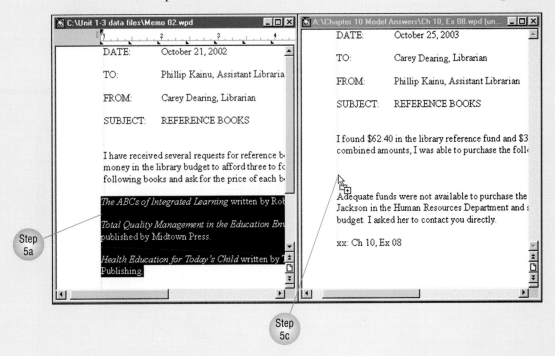

c. Hold down the Ctrl key and the left mouse button. Drag the arrow pointer a double space below the first paragraph in Ch 10, Ex 08 and then release the left mouse button and then the Ctrl key.

d. Maximize Ch 10, Ex 08.

e. Deselect the text.

6. Save, print, and then close Ch 10, Ex 08.

7. Close Memo 02.

IGURE

10.12 *Exercise 8*

DATE: October 25, 2003; TO: Carey Dearing, Librarian; FROM: Phillip Kainu, Assistant Librarian; SUBJECT: REFERENCE BOOKS

I found $62.40 in the library reference fund and $32.50 in the emergency fund. With these combined amounts, I was able to purchase the following books:

Adequate funds were not available to purchase the Grant Writing book. I contacted Anissa Jackson in the Human Resources Department and suggested she purchase the book out of her budget. I asked her to contact you directly.

xx:Ch 10, Ex 08

Using the Print Dialog Box

Print

In chapter 1, you learned to print documents with the Print button on the Toolbar or at the Print dialog box. In this chapter, you will learn to customize a print job with selections from the Print dialog box. To display the Print dialog box shown in figure 10.13, click File and then Print or click the Print button on the Toolbar. You can also display the Print dialog box by pressing Ctrl + P. Your print dialog box may display differently, depending on your default printer.

FIGURE

10.13 *Print Dialog Box*

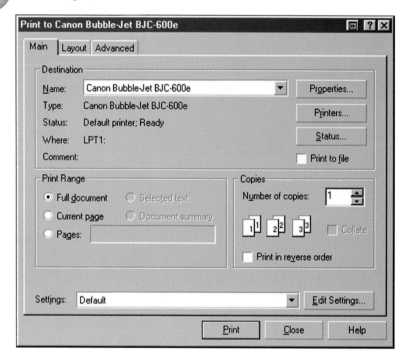

Selecting a Printer

The Name text box in the Print dialog box displays the name of the selected printer. If more than one printer was selected during installation, you can select a different printer. To do this, click the down-pointing triangle at the right side of the Name text box and then click the desired printer at the drop-down list.

Print

The Print Range section of the Print dialog box with the Main tab selected contains options to control printing. Choose the Full document option to print all pages of the open document. This is the default setting. If you want to print only the page where the insertion point is located, choose the Current page option.

Choose the Pages option in the Print Range section to print multiple pages. Key an entry in the text box to indicate the pages to be printed. If you want specific multiple pages printed, use a comma (,) to indicate *and* and use a hyphen (-) to indicate *through*. For example, to print pages 4 and 7, you would key **4,7** in the Pages text box. To print pages 4 through 9, you would key **4-9**. Figure 10.14 illustrates options for printing pages (X, Y, and Z denote page numbers).

10.14 *Multiple Page Entries/Actions*

Entry	Action
X	Page X printed
X,Y	Pages X and Y printed
X-	Pages X to end of document printed
X-Y	Pages X through Y printed
-X	Beginning of document through page X printed
X-Y,Z	Pages X through Y and page Z printed

exercise 9

Printing Specific Pages

1. Open Report 02.
2. Print pages 1 and 3 by completing the following steps:
   a. Display the Print dialog box.
   b. At the Print dialog box, select Pages.
   c. Key **1,3** in the text box next to the Pages option.
   d. Click the Print button to print pages 1 and 3.
3. Close Report 02.

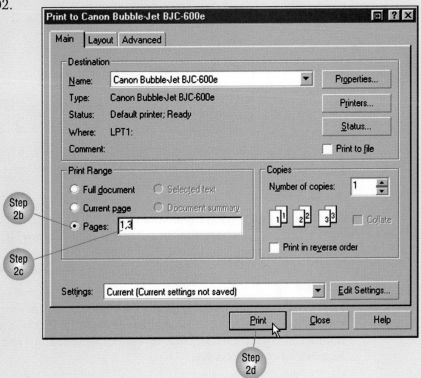

If you wish to print only a selected amount of text, select the desired text before displaying the Print Dialog box. The Selected text option will be automatically selected in the Print section of the Print dialog box. Click the Print button to send the selected text to the printer.

When selected text is printed, it is positioned on the page exactly where it would be if the entire page were printed. For example, if you select a paragraph at the bottom of a page and then print it, the paragraph will print at the bottom of the paper with blank space above it where the other text was that you did not select.

exercise 10

Printing Selected Text

1. Open Report 06.
2. Select and print the last six lines of text in the report by completing the following steps:
   a. Select the last six lines of text in the report.
   b. Display the Print dialog box.
   c. At the Print dialog box, click Print.
   d. Close Report 06.

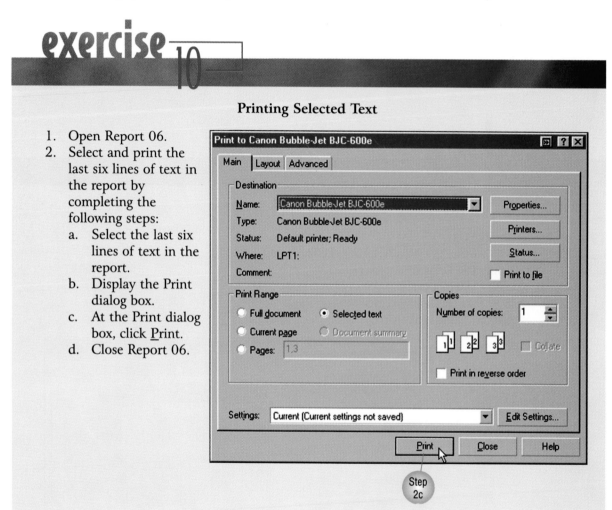

Step 2c

If a document contains a summary, you can print the summary by choosing the Document summary option at the Print dialog box. If a document does not contain a document summary, this option is dimmed.

Copies

Print multiple copies of a document by increasing the number in the Number of copies text box. Select the current number in the text box and then key the desired number of copies. Or, click the up-pointing triangle to increase the number in the Number of copies text box.

Document on Disk

If you click the Advanced tab at the Print dialog box and then insert a check mark in the check box preceding the <u>D</u>ocument on disk option at the Print dialog box, a text box displays followed by a button containing a folder. If you click the folder button, the Open File dialog box appears over the Print dialog box, as shown in figure 10.15 displays. At the Open File dialog box, identify a specific document for printing.

F I G U R E

10.15 *Open File Dialog Box*

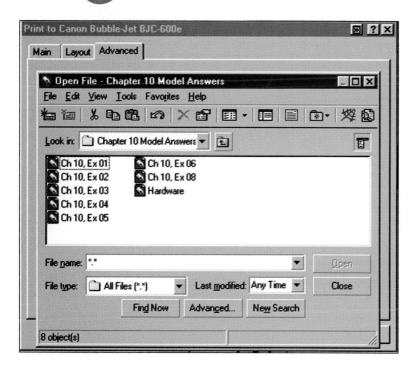

CHAPTER summary

➤ Deleting, moving, copying, or pasting blocks of text within a document is generally referred to as cutting and pasting. A selected block of text can be as small as one character or as large as one page or one document.

➤ Selected text can be deleted permanently with the Delete key, or deleted and stored in temporary memory and reinserted later in a document.

➤ Selected text can be copied one or more times in a document.

➤ Text that has been set up in columns and separated by tabs can be selected and then deleted, moved, copied, or pasted within a document.

➤ Standard blocks of text that will be used repeatedly can be saved as separate documents and then inserted into existing documents. These blocks can be keyed separately and then saved. Or, sections of text within other documents can be selected and then saved as separate documents.

➤ When working in WordPerfect, a window refers to the editing window plus the scroll bars.

➤ With multiple documents open, you can copy or move text between documents or compare the contents of several documents.

➤ Each document you open will fill the entire editing window. Move among the open documents by clicking the button on the Application bar representing the desired document. Or, click the Window option on the Menu bar and then click the desired document name.

➤ Open documents can be cascaded, one over the top of the other; or they can be tiled top to bottom or side by side, each arranged next to the other.

➤ Use the Maximize, Minimize, and Close buttons in the upper right corner of the Title bar of the active window to reduce or increase the size of the window, or to close the document.

➤ The Minimize button will reduce the document to a small title bar that displays at the bottom of the screen. A minimized document can be restored to a normal document by clicking the Maximize button on the Title bar; or to its previous size by clicking the Restore button on the minimized Title bar.

➤ Use the Application control button, the Corel WordPerfect icon in the upper left corner of the document window, to change the size of the Windows application window.

➤ Use the Document control button, the second Corel WordPerfect icon in the upper left corner of the document window, to change the size of the WordPerfect application window.

➤ The options available at the Print dialog box can help to customize a print job.

➤ The printer displayed in the Name text box should be the printer you are using. If other printers were selected during the installation of Corel WordPerfect 10, a different printer can be selected by clicking the down-pointing triangle at the right side of the Name text box.

➤ Five options are available in the Print Range section of the Print dialog box including Full document, Current page, Pages, Selected text, and Document summary.

➤ Selected text can be printed by selecting the text first, displaying the Print dialog box, and then clicking the Print button.

➤ Use the Number of copies option in the Copies section of the Print dialog box to print more than one copy of a document or page(s) of a document.

➤ Use the Document on disk option at the Advanced tab of the Print dialog box to print a document from the Open File dialog box.

COMMANDS summary

Command	Mouse	Keyboard
Cut a block of text	Edit, Cut; or click the Cut button on the Toolbar	Ctrl + X
Copy a block of text	Edit, Copy; or click the Copy button on the Toolbar	Ctrl + C
Paste a block of text	Edit, Paste; or click the Paste button on the Toolbar	Ctrl + V
Select a column of text	Edit, Select, Tabular Column; or select the text area beginning in the first entry in the column to the last entry	
Display Insert File dialog box	Insert, File	
Cascade windows	Window, Cascade	
Tile windows top to bottom	Window, Tile Top to Bottom	
Tile windows side by side	Window, Tile Side by Side	
Display the Print dialog box	File, Print; or click the Print button on the Toolbar	Ctrl + P

CONCEPTS check

Completion: On a blank sheet of paper, indicate the correct term, command, or number for each item.

1. Click this button on the Toolbar to remove selected text from the document and store it in temporary memory.

2. Click this button on the Toolbar to insert text that is stored in temporary memory into the document.

3. To copy, rather than move, selected text, hold down this key on the keyboard while dragging the selected text to the new location.

4. To display the Insert File dialog box, click this option at the Insert drop-down menu.

5. This is the name of the feature that causes each open document to overlap down the window, leaving the Title bar of each document visible.

6. This is the word that describes the document where the insertion point is located.

7. Click this button if you want a previously minimized document to fill the editing window.

8. This is the name of the second Corel WordPerfect button located in the upper left corner of the open document.

9. This is the name of the button containing a thick underscore located in the upper right corner of a tiled or cascaded window.

10. Choose this option at the Print dialog box to print a range of pages.

SKILLS check

Assessment 1

1. Open Report 06.
2. Save the document with Save As and name it Ch 10, SA 01.
3. Make the following changes to the report:
   a. Move the section titled *Continued Growth of Photonics (Fiber Optics)* below the section titled *Microcomputer Trends in the Nineties*.
   b. Delete the first sentence of the last paragraph in the *Continued Growth of Photonics (Fiber Optics)* section (the sentence that begins *The growth of fiber optics has other...*).
   c. Change the relative size of the title to Large.
   d. Change the line spacing to double (2).
   e. Delete extra blank lines so there is only a double space between all lines in the document.
   f. Number pages at the bottom center of each page.
4. Save, print, and then close Ch 10, SA 01.

Assessment 2

1. At a clear editing window, create the document shown in figure 10.16 with the following specifications:
   a. Change the font to 12-point Courier New (or a similar monospaced typeface).
   b. Key the text as shown in figure 10.16. Triple space after the last line in the document. *(Hint: Use Shift + Hyphen to create the lines.)*
   c. Select and copy the text a triple space below the original text.
   d. Copy the text two more times. (There should be a total of four forms when you are done and they should fit on one page.)
2. Save the document and name it Ch 10, SA 02.
3. Print Ch 10, SA 02.
4. Select the second set of text and print the selection.
5. Close Ch 10, SA 02.

FIGURE

10.16 *Assessment 2*

COURSE REGISTRATION

Name:_____

Title:_____ Department:_____

Course:_____

Days:_____ Times:_____

Assessment 3

1. At a clear editing window, create the document shown in figure 10.17. You determine the tab settings for the columns. *(Hint: Use right tabs for the second and third columns.)*
2. Save the document and name it Ch 10, SA 03.
3. Print Ch 10, SA 03.
4. With Ch 10, SA 03 open in the editing window, reverse the second and third columns.
5. Print Ch 10, SA 03.
6. Delete the second column (the 01-02 column).
7. Change the tab settings so the remaining columns are more balanced on the page.
8. Save, print, and then close Ch 10, SA 03.

FIGURE

10.17 *Assessment 3*

ENROLLMENT

Grade	00-01	01-02
K	45	39
1	50	44
2	42	50
3	48	41
4	50	48
5	47	49
6	52	47

Assessment 4

1. Open Policy 01.
2. Complete the following steps:
   a. Select all the text in the *PERSONS INSURED* section (including the title) and then save it as a separate document named *Pol 01*.
   b. Select all the text in the *LIMITS OF LIABILITY* section (including the title) and then save it as a separate document named *Pol 02*.
   c. Select all the text in the *UNINSURED MOTORISTS* section (including the title) and then save it as a separate document named *Pol 03*.
   d. Select all the text in the first *PHYSICAL DAMAGE* section (including the title) and then save it as a separate document named *Pol 04*.
   e. Select all the text in the second *PHYSICAL DAMAGE* section (including the title) and then save it as a separate document named *Pol 05*.
   f. Select all the text in the *SUPPLEMENTAL PAYMENTS* section (including the title) and then save it as a separate document named *Pol 06*.
3. Close Policy 01.
4. At a clear editing window, make the following changes:
   a. Change the top margin to 1.5 inches.
   b. Change the line spacing to double (2).
   c. Turn on the Widow/Orphan feature.

5. Key the information shown in figure 10.18 with the following specifications:
   a. Key the document to the first bracketed item.
   b. Insert the documents as indicated in the brackets.
   c. After inserting Pol 06, move the insertion point to the end of the paragraph, make sure there is a double space after the paragraph, and then change the line spacing back to single.
   d. Key the remaining text as indicated in figure 10.18.
   e. Move the insertion point to the beginning of the document and then create Footer A that prints *Automobile Insurance Policy, Page #* at the right side of each page (where the appropriate page number is inserted at the location of the # symbol).
6. Save the document and name it Ch 10, SA 04.
7. Print and then close Ch 10, SA 04.

FIGURE

10.18 **Assessment 4**

AUTOMOBILE INSURANCE POLICY

Policy #: CR321-03

Name of Insured: Karen Heaberlin

Address of Insured: 1302 Second Street, Vancouver, BC V2Y 3X7

[Insert Pol 01 here.]

[Insert Pol 02 here.]

[Insert Pol 03 here.]

[Insert Pol 06 here.]

———————————————————
KAREN HEABERLIN, Insured

———————————————————
Authorized Representative

Assessment 5

1. Open Report 02.
2. Change the top margin to 1.5 inches.
3. Print pages 1 and 4 of the document.
4. Close Report 02 without saving changes.

Creating and Formatting Tables

PERFORMANCE OBJECTIVES

Upon successful completion of chapter 11, you will be able to:
- **Create a table**
- **Enter and edit text within cells in a table**
- **Format a table by changing column width, inserting and deleting columns and rows, merging and splitting cells, aligning text within cells, and adding borders and fill**
- **Insert formulas in a table**
- **Format a table using SpeedFormat**

Chapter 11

Tables are used to create columns and rows of information. The intersection of a column and row is called a *cell*. Cells can contain text, numbers, formulas, or graphic images.

Creating a Table

WordPerfect offers two ways to create a table. The first method is to use the Table QuickCreate button on the Toolbar and then drag down and across to select the desired number of columns and rows. The second method is to click Table and then Create. At the Create Table dialog box, specify the number of columns and rows in the table. The Create Table dialog box is shown in figure 11.1.

Table
QuickCreate

Centering — Table/Format/
Click on Table/Table Position & page
Change to center

11.1 *Create Table Dialog Box*

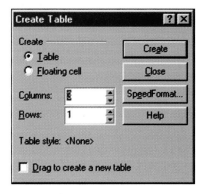

When you click Create at the Create Table dialog box, a table similar to the one shown in figure 11.2 is inserted in the document at the location of the insertion point. As long as your cursor is in a table, the Tables toolbar is displayed in the editing window (figure 11.3).

F I G U R E

11.2 *Table*

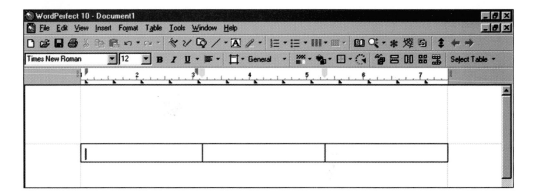

F I G U R E

11.3 *Tables Toolbar*

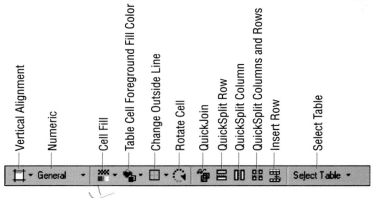

X means nothing

Columns are labeled with letters from left to right. Rows are labeled with numbers from top to bottom. To display the column and row labels, click T<u>a</u>ble and then Ro<u>w</u>/Col Indicators. This will display column letters and row numbers as shown in figure 11.4.

F I G U R E

11.4 **Table with Row/Column Indicators**

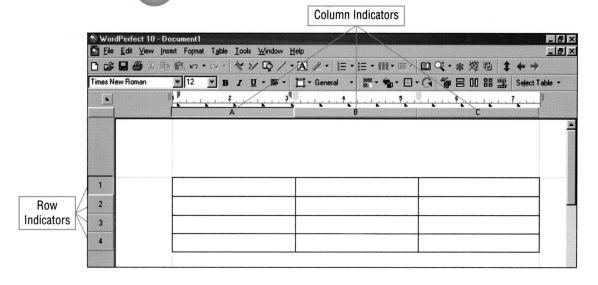

Entering Text in Cells

With the insertion point positioned in a cell, key or edit text as you would normal text. To move the cursor to another cell, click the left mouse button in the cell. If you are using the keyboard, press the Tab key to move to the next cell or press Shift + Tab to move the insertion point to the previous cell. If you want to insert a tab within a cell, use one of the methods displayed in figure 11.5.

F I G U R E

11.5 **Commands to Insert Tabs in Cells**

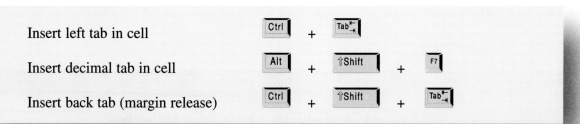

If the text does not fit on one line, it automatically wraps to the next line within the same cell. The cell height will increase to accommodate whatever amount of text you enter. The height of the row is determined by the cell with the most lines of text. You can use the options at the Properties for Table Format dialog box with the Row tab selected to limit the amount of text that can be entered into cells within the row, or to specify a minimum amount of space, regardless of what the cell contains. To display this dialog box, click T<u>a</u>ble and then F<u>o</u>rmat. Changes made at this dialog box affect all cells in the current row.

If the insertion point is in the last cell of the table and you press the Tab key, WordPerfect adds another row to the table. You can insert a page break within a table by pressing Ctrl + Enter. The page break will always be inserted between rows, not within. When you are finished keying information in the table, move the insertion point below the table and continue.

Moving the Insertion Point within a Table

To move the insertion point to a different cell within a table, you can use any of the methods shown in figure 11.6.

FIGURE

11.6 *Commands to Move the Insertion Point in a Table*

Move insertion point within cell in direction indicated	↑ , ← , ↓ , and →
Move insertion point to next cell	Tab
Move insertion point to previous cell	⇧Shift + Tab
Move insertion point one cell down	Alt + ↓
Move insertion point one cell up	Alt + ↑
Move insertion point to first cell in row	Home , Home
Move insertion point to last cell in row	End , End
Move insertion point to top line of multi-line cell	Alt + Home
Move insertion point to bottom line of multi-line cell	Alt + End

exercise

Creating a Table with the Create Table Dialog Box

1. At a clear editing window, create the document shown in figure 11.7 by completing the following steps:
   a. Center and bold *DENVER MEMORIAL HOSPITAL*.
   b. Press Enter twice and then center and bold *Executive Officers*.
   c. Turn off bold, press Enter three times, and then create a table with two columns and five rows by completing the following steps:

1) Click Table and then Create.
2) At the Create Table dialog box, key **2** in the Columns text box.
3) Press the Tab key and key **5** in the Rows text box.
4) Click the Create button.

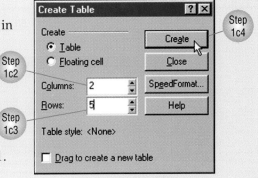

Step 1c4

Step 1c2

d. Key the text in cells as shown in figure 11.7. To indent text within cells, press Ctrl + Tab. Do this for each cell.

Step 1c3

2. Save the document and name it Ch 11, Ex 01.
3. Print and close Ch 11, Ex 01.

FIGURE

 11.7 *Exercise 1*

DENVER MEMORIAL HOSPITAL

Executive Officers

President	Chris Hedegaard
Vice President	Robert Freitas
Vice President	Richard Dudley
Vice President	Glenna Wykoff
Vice President	Laura Culver

Changing the Column Width in a Table

By default, all columns are the same width. You can change the width of columns using the mouse, the Ruler, or the Properties for Table Format dialog box. Each method is explained below.

Changing Column Width with the Mouse

To change column width using the mouse, position the pointer on the line separating columns until it turns into a left- and right-pointing arrow with a vertical line between. Hold down the left mouse button and drag the column line in either direction to the desired location and then release the left mouse button. This will size the one column only. To resize all columns to the right at the same time, hold down the Shift key while performing the steps described above.

Changing Column Width with the Ruler

When the insertion point is positioned in a table, the column widths are displayed on the Ruler as down-pointing block arrows located above the Ruler numbers. These down-pointing block arrows are called *column width markers*. These markers are identified in figure 11.8.

11.8 *Table Markers on the Ruler*

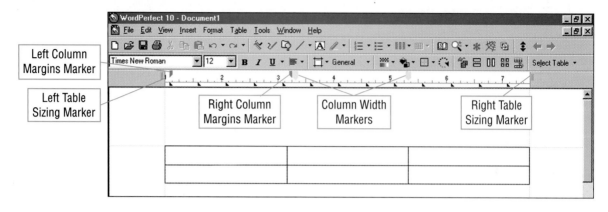

Left Column
Margins Marker

Left Table
Sizing Marker

Right Column
Margins Marker

Column Width
Markers

Right Table
Sizing Marker

Position the arrow pointer on the column width marker to be moved and, while holding down the left mouse button, drag the marker to widen or narrow the column. Release the mouse button when the marker is in the desired position. This will size the one column only. To resize all columns to the right at the same time, hold down the Shift key while performing the steps described above.

Changing Column Width with the Properties for Table Format Dialog Box

If you know the exact measurements for columns in a table, you can change column widths at the Properties for Table Format dialog box. To display this dialog box, click Table, Format, and then select the desired tab. This dialog box is shown in figure 11.9 with the Column tab selected.

11.9 *Properties for Table Format Dialog Box with Column Tab Selected*

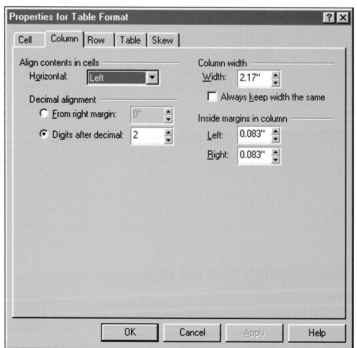

Changing Column Width

1. At a clear editing window, create the document shown in figure 11.10 by completing the following steps:

   a. Change the font to 14-point Century Schoolbook (or a similar serif typeface).

   b. Center and bold *CARIBBEAN CRUISE*.

   c. Change the font size to 12 points and then press Enter twice.

   d. Center and bold *Dining Room Reservations*.

   e. Press Enter three times and then create a table with three columns and five rows.

   f. Change the size of the table by completing the following steps:

      1) Position the tip of the arrow pointer on the right border line of the first column until it turns into a double arrow with a vertical line between.

      2) Hold down the Shift key, click the left mouse button and drag the border marker to the 4-inch mark on the Ruler, and then release the mouse button.

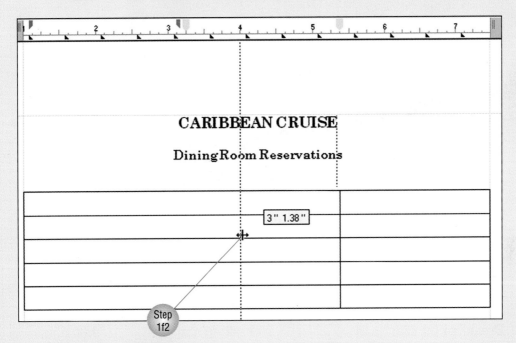

   g. Change the width of the second two columns by performing these steps:

      1) Position the insertion point in any cell in the second column and drag to select the third column.

      2) Click Table and then Format.

3) Click the Column tab, select the current number displayed in the Width text box, and then key **1.6**.

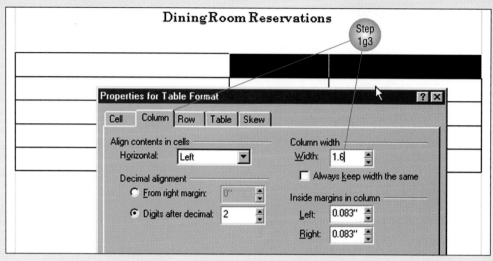

4) Click OK.

   h.   Key the text as indicated in figure 11.10. Center text in the second and third columns. Bold the text in cells B1 and C1.

2.   Save the document and name it Ch 11, Ex 02.

3.   Print and then close Ch 11, Ex 02.

FIGURE 11.10 *Exercise 2*

CARIBBEAN CRUISE

Dining Room Reservations

	Early	Late
Breakfast (in port)	6:45 a.m.	8:00 a.m.
Breakfast (at sea)	7:45 a.m.	9:00 a.m.
Luncheon	12:00 noon	1:30 p.m.
Dinner	6:00 p.m.	8:00 p.m.

Selecting Cells with the Mouse

Select Table ▾

Select Table

A table can be formatted in a variety of ways. To identify the cells that are to be affected by the formatting, the specific cells must be selected first. Using the mouse, click the Select Table button on the Tables toolbar to display a drop-down menu. From this menu, choose Select Table, Select Column, or Select Row.

Another method for selecting cells is to use table selection arrows. To display the horizontal selection arrow, move the arrow pointer to the left border of any cell until it turns into a left-pointing arrow. This arrow is the horizontal selection arrow. To display the vertical selection arrow, move the arrow pointer to the top border of any cell until it turns into an up-pointing arrow. This arrow is the vertical selection arrow. When you see this arrow, double-click to select either the column or row; single-click to select the current cell.

If you want to select all cells within a table, position the arrow pointer in any cell until either the horizontal or vertical arrow is displayed, and then click the left mouse button quickly three times. If you want to select the text in a cell rather than the entire cell, do so in the normal manner.

If row and column indicators are displayed, you can use these indicators to select cells. To select a row, click the row indicator number next to the row to be selected. To select a column, click the column letter above the column to be selected.

Selecting Cells with the Keyboard

The keyboard can be used to select specific cells within a table. Figure 11.11 displays the commands for selecting specific amounts of a table.

F I G U R E

11.11 *Selecting Cells Using the Keyboard*

Current cell	⇧Shift + Ctrl + →
Current row	⇧Shift + Ctrl + →
Current column	⇧Shift + Ctrl + ↑
One cell, row, or column at a time	⇧Shift + →
Beginning of current row	⇧Shift + Home
End of current row	⇧Shift + End
Current table to beginning of document	⇧Shift + Ctrl + Home
Current table to end of document	⇧Shift + Ctrl + End

exercise 3

Selecting Cells and Changing Text Appearance

1. Open Ch 11, Ex 01.
2. Save the document with Save As and name it Ch 11, Ex 03.
3. Select and bold cells A1 and B1 using the mouse by completing the following steps:
   a. Click inside cell A1.
   b. Click the Select Table button on the Tables toolbar and choose Select Row.
   c. With the first row selected, click the Bold button on the Main property bar.
   d. Deselect the row by clicking anywhere outside the selected area.
4. Select and italicize the text in cells A2 through B5 by completing the following steps:
   a. Click in cell A2 and, while holding down the left mouse button, drag through cell B5.

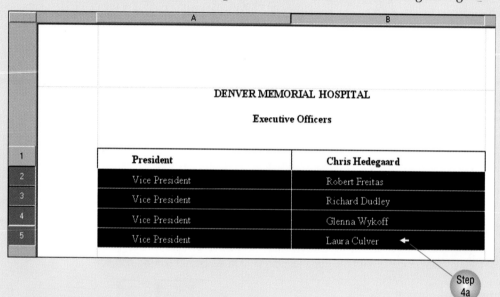

b. Press Ctrl + I to italicize the text.
   c. Deselect the cells by clicking anywhere outside the selected area.
5. Save, print, and then close Ch 11, Ex 03.

Inserting Rows and Columns

By default, rows are added above the insertion point and columns are added to the left of the insertion point. Three methods are available for inserting rows and columns.

Insert Row

1. Click the Insert Row button on the Tables toolbar. A row is added above the insertion point.

2. Click Table and then Insert. This will display figure 11.12. Specify how many rows or columns are to be inserted. You can also specify the placement of the inserted row(s) or column(s) by choosing Before or After. The additional columns or rows will be added in relation to the insertion point.

3. Right-click a cell in the table and then choose Insert from the QuickMenu. The dialog box shown in figure 11.12 will appear.

FIGURE

11.12 *Insert Columns/Rows Dialog Box*

Deleting Rows or Columns

Rows or columns in a document can be deleted with the Delete option from the Table drop-down menu or the Delete option from the QuickMenu. At the Delete Structure/Contents dialog box, shown in figure 11.13, specify whether you want to delete one or more column(s), one or more row(s), the cell contents only, or the formula only. Whichever option you select, it affects the column, row, or cell at the location of the insertion point.

FIGURE

11.13 *Delete Structure/Contents Dialog Box*

Inserting and Deleting Rows in a Table

1. Open Ch 11, Ex 01.
2. Save the document with Save As and name it Ch 11, Ex 04.
3. Add a row in the table between *Glenna Wykoff* and *Richard Dudley* by completing the following steps:

    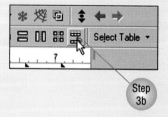

    a. Position the insertion point in any cell in the row for *Glenna Wykoff*.
    b. Click the Insert Row button on the Tables toolbar.
4. Key the following text in the new cells:

    A4 = **Vice President**
    B4 = **Mike Jacobs**

5. Delete the row in the table that contains *Robert Freitas* by completing the following steps:
    a. Position the insertion point in any cell in the row for *Robert Freitas*.
    b. Right-click and then choose Delete from the QuickMenu.

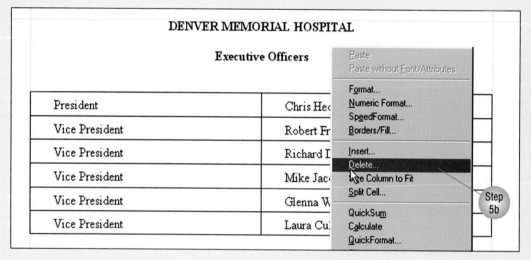

c. Make sure Rows is selected and *1* appears in the text box.
d. Click OK or press Enter.

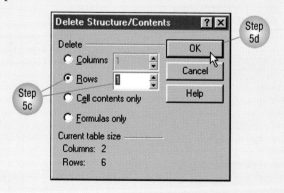

6. Save, print, and then close Ch 11, Ex 04.

Joining and Splitting Cells

Cells can be joined by using the QuickJoin button on the Tables toolbar or with the Join option from the Table drop-down menu. To join using the QuickJoin button, click the QuickJoin button and then drag through the cells you want joined. After joining the cells, click the QuickJoin button again to turn it off. To join cells using the Table drop-down menu, select the cells to be joined, click Table, point to Join, and then click Cell.

QuickJoin

Cells can be split by using the Split option from the Table menu. Select the cell, click Table, point to Split, and then click Cell.

exercise 5

Joining and Splitting Cells

1. At a clear editing window, create the table shown in figure 11.14 by completing the following steps:
   a. Create a table with 3 columns and 10 rows.
   b. Join cells A1 through C1 by completing the following steps:
      1) Click the QuickJoin button on the Tables toolbar.
      2) Position the arrow pointer in cell A1, hold down the left mouse button, drag to cell C1, and then release the mouse button.
      3) Click the QuickJoin button again to turn it off.
   c. Join cells A2 through C2 by completing the following steps:
      1) Select cells A2 through C2.
      2) Click Table, point to Join, and then click Cell.

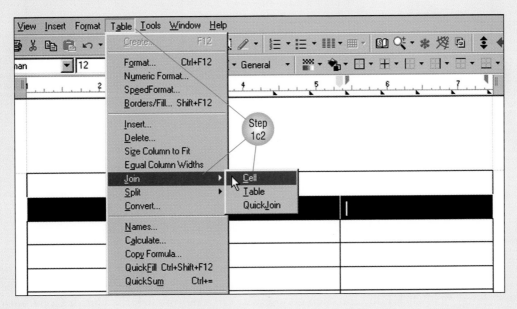

   3) Key the text in the table as shown in figure 11.14. Center and bold the text as indicated. Press Enter once after keying **ACTIVITY LOG**.
2. Save the table and name it Ch 11, Ex 05.

3. Print Ch 11, Ex 05.
4. Split cells B3 through B10 by performing the following steps:
   a. Select cells B3 through B10.
   b. Click Table, point to Split, and then click Cell.
   c. Make sure the Columns option is selected and 2 appears in the text box.
   d. Click OK.
5. In cell C3, key **Duration**, bold and centered.
6. Save, print, and then close Ch 11, Ex 05.

FIGURE

11.14 *Exercise 5*

ACTIVITY LOG		
Training and Education Department		
Client	Activity	Date

Deleting Text

After text has been inserted in a cell, it can be deleted in the normal manner with the Delete or Backspace keys.

Cutting and Pasting

Columns and rows can be moved or copied to a different location within the table using the Cut and Paste commands. To copy or move a row or column, select it first, click Edit, and then choose Cut or Copy (or click the Cut or Copy buttons on the Toolbar). At the Cut or Copy Table dialog box, shown in figure 11.15, choose Selection, Column, Row, or Cell and then click OK.

11.15 *Cut or Copy Table Dialog Box*

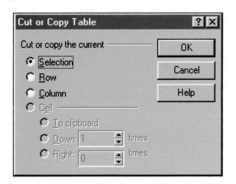

Move your cursor to the desired location and click Edit and then Paste or click the Paste button on the Toolbar. Columns are inserted to the left of the insertion point; rows are inserted above the insertion point.

exercise 6

Moving Columns

1. Open Ch 11, Ex 02.
2. Save the document with Save As and name it Ch 11, Ex 06.
3. Key **Function** in column A, row 1.
4. Move the *Early* and *Late* columns to the left of the *Function* column by completing the following steps:

   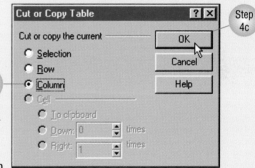
   Step 4c
   Step 4b

   a. Select the *Early* column and then click the Cut button on the Toolbar.
   b. At the Cut or Copy Table dialog box, click the radio button preceding Column.
   c. Click OK.
   d. Position the insertion point anywhere in the *Function* column and click the Paste button.
   e. Using similar steps, move the *Late* column between the *Early* and *Function* columns.
   f. Make adjustments in the column widths to balance the appearance of the table.
5. Save, print, and then close Ch 11, Ex 06.

Changing Alignment

By default, text in a cell is aligned horizontally at the left margin of the cell. This can be changed to *Right, Center, Full, All,* or *Decimal Align*. To change the horizontal alignment, position your cursor in the desired cell, or select multiple cells. Click

Table and then Format. At the Properties for Table Format dialog box, choose the Cell, Column, or Table tab. Click the down-pointing triangle next to the Horizontal text box and choose the desired alignment.

Changing the Horizontal Alignment of Text in Cells

1. At a clear editing window, create the table shown in figure 11.16 by completing the following steps:
   a. Create a table with 3 columns and 10 rows.
   b. Change the column width of the second column to 3 inches.
   c. Join cells A1 through C1.
   d. Join cells A2 through C2.
   e. Change the horizontal alignment of cell A1 to Center by completing the following steps:
      1) Position the insertion point in cell A1 (do not select the cell).
      2) Click Table and then Format.
      3) At the Properties for Table Format dialog box, make sure the Cell tab is selected, click the down-pointing triangle at the right side of the Horizontal text box, and then select *Center*.

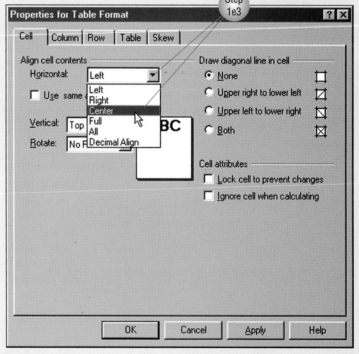

      4) Click OK.
   f. Change the horizontal alignment to *Center* for cell A2 by completing similar steps.
   g. Change the horizontal alignment to *Center* for cells A3 through C3 by completing the following steps:
      1) Select cells A3 through C3.
      2) Click Table and then Format.
      3) Click the Cell tab.
      4) Click the down-pointing triangle at the right side of the Horizontal text box and click *Center*.
      5) Click OK.
   h. Select cells C4 through C10 and change the horizontal alignment to *Center* using similar steps.
   i. Key the text shown in figure 11.16. Bold the text as indicated.
2. Save the table and name it Ch 11, Ex 07.
3. Print and then close Ch 11, Ex 07.

OMAHA CITY SCHOOL DISTRICT		
Technology Advisory Committee		
Name	**Organization**	**Phone**
Barry Vialle	Horizon Broadcasting Company	555-3209
Colonel Gerry Lundstrom	Satler Air Force Base	555-3321
Dr. Jeremy Needham	Omaha Community College	555-4332
Arlene Tommaney	Midwest Banking Institution	555-0091
Kathy Hemphill	Omaha Economic Development	555-8327
Lyle McKeller	Nebraska Health Council	555-1225
Roberta Hughes	Sampson/Kraft Corporation	555-3123

Text Formatting

Text formatting is applied in a table in the same manner as it is in regular text. To format sections of text, select the text first and then apply the desired formatting. Formatting can be applied using the buttons on the property bar or from the Font dialog box.

Creating a Header Row

The Header row option on the Row tab at the Properties for Table Format dialog box is useful in a table that spans more than one page. A header row may contain multiple rows, if necessary, and the header will display at the beginning of the second and all subsequent pages that contain part of the table. The header row will not appear in Draft viewing mode.

Creating a Header Row

1. Open Report 05.
2. Save the report with Save As and name it Ch 11, Ex 08.
3. Create a header row for the table at the end of the first page by completing the following steps:
   a. Position the insertion point in any cell in the first row of the table.
   b. Click Table and then Format.

c. At the Properties for Table Format dialog box, click the Row tab.
d. Click the Header row (repeats on each page) option.
e. Click OK.
4. Save, print, and then close Ch 11, Ex 08.

Step 3c

Step 3d

Step 3e

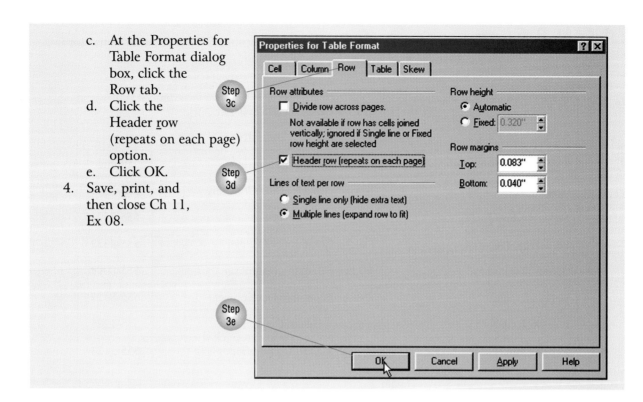

Changing Numeric Format

Numeric

With the Numeric button on the Tables toolbar, you can specify how numbers are used, how many decimal places are displayed, and how numbers are printed in a table. The default numbering type is General. At this setting, numbers display without a thousands separator and no trailing zeroes to the right of the decimal point. To change the numbering type, click the Numeric button and a drop-down list appears with numbering types. Numbering types are described in figure 11.17.

FIGURE

11.17 *Number Types*

Accounting   Up to 15 decimal places display in a number, along with the currency symbol, thousands separator, and the decimal align character. The currency symbol displays at the edge of the column.

Commas   Up to 15 decimal places display in a number along with the thousands separator. Negative numbers are displayed within parentheses.

Currency   Up to 15 decimal places display in a number, the currency symbol, the thousands separator, and the decimal align character.

Date   Converts numbers into the current date and time format.

Continued on next page

Fixed	Up to 15 decimal places display in a number. The thousands separator does not display.
Integer	No trailing zeroes are displayed to the right of the decimal point. Numbers display without the thousands separator.
Percent	Numbers are displayed as percent values (multiplied by 100) with the percent symbol (%) included.
Scientific	Numbers display in scientific notation up to 15 decimal places.
Text	Designates the contents of the cell as text and will not use any numbers in calculations.

To specify which cells are to be affected by the numeric format, click the Numeric button on the Tables toolbar, and select *Other*. At the Properties for Table Numeric Format dialog box, shown in figure 11.18, make your selection.

F I G U R E

11.18 *Properties for Table Numeric Format Dialog Box*

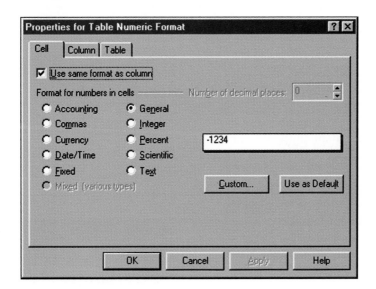

exercise 9

Changing Numeric Format

1. At a clear editing window, create the table shown in figure 11.19 by completing the following steps:

a. Create a table with 3 columns and 10 rows.

b. Change the position of the table to *Center* by completing the following steps:

1) Click Table and then Format.
2) Click the Table tab.
3) Click the down-pointing triangle next to the Table position on page text box and select *Center*.
4) Click OK.

c. Change the width of each column to 1.5 inches.

d. Join cells A1 through C1.

e. Join cells A2 through C2.

f. Select cell A1 and then change the horizontal alignment to *Center*, the appearance to *Bold*, and the relative size to *Very large*.

g. Select cell A2 and then change the horizontal alignment to *Center*, the appearance to *Bold*, and the relative size to *Large*.

h. Select cells A3 through C3 and then change the horizontal alignment to *Center* and the appearance to *Bold*.

i. Change the numbering type to *Currency* for cells B4 through C10 and change the horizontal alignment to *Decimal Align* by completing the following steps:

1) Select cells B4 through C10.
2) Click the Numeric button on the Tables toolbar (contains the word *General*) and then select *Currency* from the drop-down list.

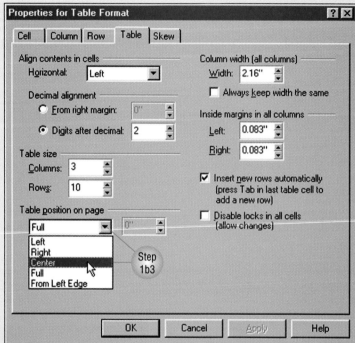

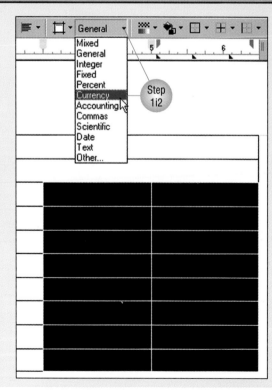

3) With the cells still selected, click T<u>a</u>ble and then F<u>o</u>rmat.
4) At the Properties for Table Format dialog box with the Cell tab selected, change the H<u>o</u>rizontal option to *Decimal Align*.
5) Click OK to close the dialog box.

j. Key the text in the cells as indicated in figure 11.19. Do not key the dollar signs ($) or commas, but do key the decimal points. WordPerfect automatically adds a dollar sign and a comma because the number type is *Currency*. You may not see the dollar sign displayed until you move to the next cell.

2. Save the table and name it Ch 11, Ex 09.
3. Print and then close Ch 11, Ex 09.

FIGURE

11.19 **Exercise 9**

UNITED DISTRIBUTION CENTER		
Sales in Selected States		
State	**Last Year**	**This Year**
Arkansas	$1,204,392.50	$1,139,302.59
California	$3,459,034.20	$3,545,209.65
Delaware	$995,302.85	$1,109,384.22
Florida	$893,410.47	$943,120.87
Montana	$558,329.21	$522,503.40
North Dakota	$421,329.84	$483,204.80
Pennsylvania	$2,298,432.58	$2,103,438.59

Changing Borders and Fill

Table lines and fill can be customized with options from the Properties for Table Borders/Fill dialog box. To display the dialog box shown in figure 11.20, click T<u>a</u>ble and then <u>B</u>orders/Fill. By clicking on either the Cell or Table tab, you can determine which part of the table will be affected by the formatting changes.

11.20 *Properties for Table Borders/Fill Dialog Box*

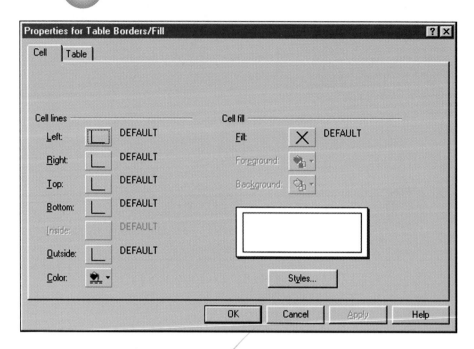

exercise 10

Changing Line Styles

1. Open Ch 11, Ex 07.
2. Save the document with Save As and name it Ch 11, Ex 10.
3. Change the top and bottom lines of cells A3 through C3 to Double by completing the following steps:
   a. Select cells A3 through C3.
   b. Click Table and then Borders/Fill.

c. At the Properties for Table Borders/Fill dialog box with the Cell tab selected, click the Top button in the Cell lines section.

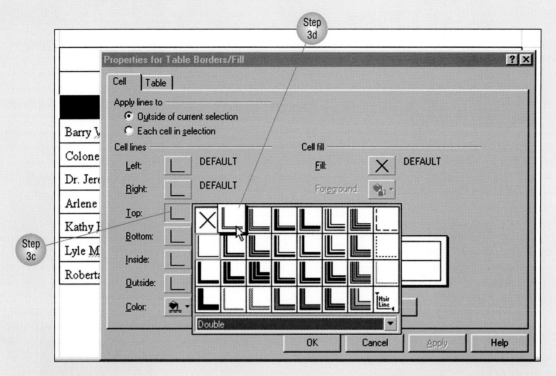

d. At the palette of line choices, click the Double option (second option from the left in the first row).
e. Click the Bottom button and then, at the palette of line choices, click the Double option (second option from the left in the first row).
f. Click OK.
g. Deselect the cells to see the new border.
4. Save, print, and then close Ch 11, Ex 10.

Adding Fill

Add fill to a cell or selected cells with the Cell Fill button on the Tables toolbar or with the Fill option in the Cell fill section of the Properties for Table Borders/ Fill dialog box. A variety of fills are available. Click the Cell Fill button and, at the palette of fill choices, select the desired fill. Change the fill color by selecting the Table Cell Foreground Fill Color button on the Tables toolbar and selecting a color.

Cell Fill

Table Cell Foreground
Fill Color

exercise 11

Changing Cell Fill

1. Open Ch 11, Ex 07.
2. Save the document with Save As and name it Ch 11, Ex 11.
3. Change the fill to Button Fill for cells A3 through C3 by completing the following steps:
   a. Select cells A3 through C3.
   b. Click Table and then Borders/Fill.
   c. At the Properties for Table Borders/Fill dialog box with the Cell tab selected, click the Fill button.

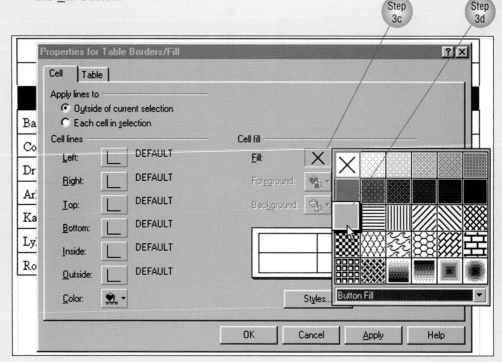

d. At the palette of fill options, click the Button Fill option (first option from the left in the third row).
   e. Click OK.
   f. With cells A3 through C3 still selected, click the Table Cell Foreground Fill Color button on the Tables toolbar and select *Red*.
4. Deselect the cells to see the formatting.
5. Save, print, and then close Ch 11, Ex 11.

Inserting Formulas

A formula can be inserted in a cell that will calculate numbers in rows or columns. To insert a formula, display the Formula toolbar shown in figure 11.21. To display the Formula toolbar, position the insertion point in the table, click the *right* mouse button, and then click Formula Toolbar. With the Formula toolbar displayed, you can enter a formula in a specific cell. If changes are made to cells affected by the formula, the value of the formula can be recalculated.

11.21 *Formula Toolbar*

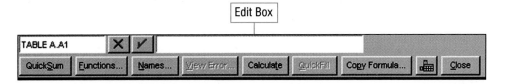

Edit Box

TABLE A.A1	X	✔	
QuickSum	Functions...	Names...	View Error...	Calculate	QuickFill	Copy Formula...		Close

Four basic operators can be used when writing formulas: the plus sign for addition, the minus sign (hyphen) for subtraction, the asterisk for multiplication, and the forward slash (/) for division. Examples of how formulas can be written are shown in figure 11.22.

11.22 *Example Formulas*

Cell E4 is the total price of items.
Cell B4 contains the quantity of items, and cell D4 contains the unit price. The formula for cell E4 is B4*D4. (This formula multiplies the quantity of items in cell B4 by the unit price in cell D4.)

Cell D3 is the percentage of increase of sales from the previous year.
Cell B3 contains the amount of sales for the previous year, and cell C3 contains the amount of sales for the current year. The formula for cell D3 is (C3-B3)/C3*100. (This formula subtracts the amount of sales last year from the amount of sales this year. The remaining amount is divided by the amount of sales this year and then multiplied by 100 to display the product as a percentage.)

Cell E1 is the average of test scores.
Cells A1 through D1 contain test scores. The formula to calculate the average score is (A1+B1+C1+D1)/4. (This formula adds the scores from cells A1 through D1, then divides that sum by 4.) You can also enter the formula as ave(A1:D1). The word "ave" tells WordPerfect to average all entries in cells A1 through D1. The colon is used to indicate a range.

If there are two or more operators in a calculation, WordPerfect calculates from left to right. If you want to change the order of calculation, use parentheses around the part of the calculation to be performed first.

If you want to cancel a formula as you are writing it, click the red X on the Formula toolbar. This removes any formula you have entered so far. If you want to write another formula, position the arrow pointer in the Formula toolbar edit box, click the left mouse button, and then key the formula.

Copying Formulas

Once a formula has been entered in a cell, use options at the Copy Formula dialog box to copy the formula to another cell or to copy a relative version of the formula down or across to other cells. To display the Copy Formula dialog box, shown in figure 11.23, click the Copy Formula button on the Formula toolbar, or click Table and then Copy Formula.

Copy Formula...

FIGURE

11.23 *Copy Formula Dialog Box*

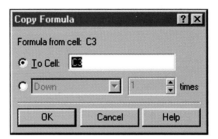

The Copy Formula dialog box contains two options—To Cell and a list box from which you can choose a direction to copy (Up, Down, Right, or Left). Use the To Cell option to copy a formula to another cell. When you use this option, the formula is copied exactly to the specified cell. Use the list box options if you want to copy a relative version of the formula to other cells. With either option, you would key the number of times the formula is to be copied and then click OK. When a formula is copied, it is copied relatively. For example, if the formula A1+B1+C1 in cell D1 is copied down, the formula changes to A2+B2+C2 in cell D2.

Calculating Numbers in a Table

When a formula is inserted in a table that contains numbers, the formula is automatically calculated and the answer is inserted in the cell. If changes are made to the numbers in cells, the table should automatically recalculate. If the automatic recalculation option at the Calculate dialog box is not selected, recalculate the formula by clicking the Calculate button on the Formula Toolbar.

Calculate

Inserting a Test Score Formula

1. Open Table 01.
2. Save the document with Save As and name it Ch 11, Ex 12.
3. Insert a formula to calculate test scores in cell F3 by completing the following steps:
   a. Position the insertion point in cell F3.
   b. Turn on the display of the Formula toolbar by right-clicking and selecting Formula Toolbar from the shortcut menu.
   c. Click the left mouse button in the Formula toolbar edit box. (This box is located immediately to the right of the blue check mark.)

d. Key **(B3+C3+D3+E3)/4**. (You can also enter **ave(B3:E3)**.)

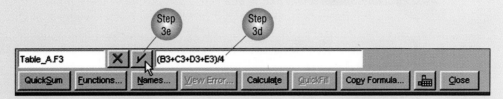

e. Click the blue check mark to accept the formula and calculate the result in cell F3.
4. Copy the formula down five rows by completing the following steps:
   a. With the insertion point still positioned in cell F3 (this cell contains the formula), click the Copy Formula button on the Formula Toolbar.
   b. At the Copy Formula dialog box, click the list box option and then select *Down* from the drop-down list.

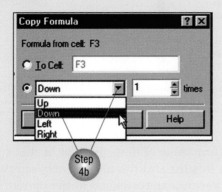

   c. Key **5** in the text box indicating the number of times.
   d. Click OK.
5. Save and print Ch 11, Ex 12.
6. Make the following changes to the test scores:

Devries, Suzanne	#1, change *57* to *70*
	#4, change *58* to *75*
Gaudette, Nicolas	#3, change *62* to *74*
	#4, change *60* to *76*

7. Press the Tab key to move the insertion point to a different cell. This recalculates the average.
8. Save, print, and then close Ch 11, Ex 12.

Formatting with SpeedFormat

WordPerfect has created a feature that provides a variety of table formatting options. This table formatting feature is called *SpeedFormat*. The various formatting options are available at the Table SpeedFormat dialog box shown in figure 11.24. To display this dialog box, position the insertion point in a table, click Table and then SpeedFormat. The dialog box can also be displayed by clicking the *right* mouse button and then clicking SpeedFormat.

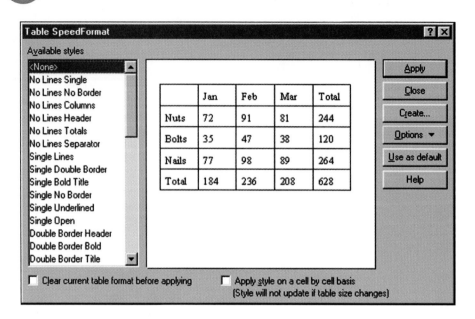

Table SpeedFormat Dialog Box

The list of formatting options displays in the A̲vailable styles list box. Click an option from this list and the preview table in the middle of the dialog box will display the formatting contained in the option. In this way, you can view the various options to find the one that suits you.

If you want to apply formatting to an individual cell, insert a check mark in the Apply s̲tyle on a cell by cell basis check box. Insert a check mark in the C̲lear current table format before applying check box if you want any previous formatting contained by the table to be removed.

exercise 13

Using Table SpeedFormat

1. Open Table 01.
2. Save the document with Save As and name it Ch 11, Ex 13.
3. Apply formatting to the table at the Table SpeedFormat dialog box by completing the following steps:
   a. With the insertion point positioned in any cell in the table, click T̲able and then Sp̲eedFormat.

b. At the Table SpeedFormat dialog box, click *Double Border Totals* in the Available styles list box. (You will need to scroll down the list of styles to display *Double Border Totals*.)

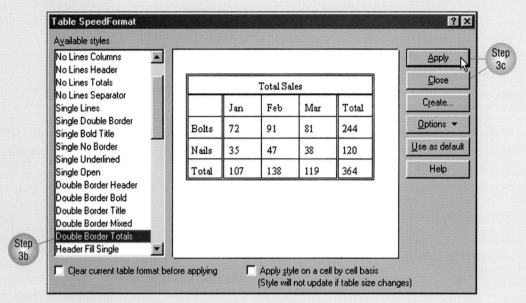

c. Click the Apply button and then click Close.
4. Save, print, and then close Ch 11, Ex 13.

CHAPTER summary

➤ Use the Tables feature to create a form containing boxes of information called cells with customized lines surrounding each cell.

➤ A table can be created with the Table QuickCreate button on the Toolbar or at the Create Table dialog box.

➤ Columns in a table are lettered from left to right, beginning with A. Rows in a table are numbered from top to bottom beginning with 1.

➤ Change the width of columns with the mouse in the table, the Ruler, or options at the Properties for Table Format dialog box with the Column tab selected.

➤ The arrow pointer or the keyboard can be used to select a cell, a row, a column, or an entire table. After cells are selected, alignment or margins can be changed or character formatting can be added.

➤ Insert a row in a table with the Insert Row button on the Tables toolbar. You can also insert rows or columns in a table with the Insert option from the Table drop-down menu or the Insert option from the Tables QuickMenu.

➤ Delete rows or columns in a table with the <u>D</u>elete option from the T<u>a</u>ble drop-down menu or the <u>D</u>elete option from the QuickMenu.

➤ Two or more cells can be joined with the QuickJoin button on the Tables toolbar or the <u>J</u>oin option from the T<u>a</u>ble drop-down menu. A cell or a row or column of cells can be split with buttons on the Tables toolbar or the <u>S</u>plit option from the T<u>a</u>ble drop-down menu.

➤ At the Cut or Copy Table dialog box, columns and/or rows can be moved or copied to a different location within the table.

➤ At the Properties for Table Format dialog box, tabs for Cell, Column, Row, or Table expand the options available for formatting.

➤ Click the Numeric button on the Tables toolbar to display a list of numbering types.

➤ Specify how numbers are used, how numbers are displayed, and how numbers are printed in a table with the Numeric button.

➤ When a table is created, all lines around cells are single lines. These lines can be customized with buttons on the Tables toolbar or with options at the Properties for Table Borders/ Fill dialog box.

➤ At the Formula toolbar, you can insert a formula in a cell that will calculate numbers in rows or columns.

➤ When a formula is inserted in a table containing numbers, the formula is automatically calculated and the answer is inserted in the cell. If changes are made to the numbers in cells, click the Calcula<u>t</u>e button on the Formula toolbar to recalculate the formula.

➤ Use the SpeedFormat feature to apply a variety of formatting options to a table.

COMMANDS summary

Command	Mouse	Keyboard
Create a table	T<u>a</u>ble, <u>C</u>reate; or click the Table QuickCreate button on the Toolbar	F12
Display Properties for Table Format dialog box	T<u>a</u>ble, F<u>o</u>rmat	Ctrl + F12
Display Properties for Table Borders/Fill dialog box	T<u>a</u>ble, <u>B</u>orders/Fill	Shift + F12
Display the Formula toolbar	T<u>a</u>ble, Fo<u>r</u>mula Toolbar; or right-click and select Fo<u>r</u>mula Toolbar	
Display the SpeedFormat dialog box	T<u>a</u>ble, Sp<u>ee</u>dFormat	

CONCEPTS check

Completion: On a blank sheet of paper, indicate the term, command, or number of each item.

1. Press this key on the keyboard to move the insertion point to the next cell.

2. Press these keys on the keyboard to move the insertion point to the previous cell.

3. A table can be created with this button on the Toolbar.

4. Click this button on the Tables toolbar to select the row where the insertion point is positioned.

5. This is the cell that is located immediately below cell D7.

6. To join cells in a table, click this button on the Tables toolbar, and then drag through the cells to be joined.

7. Change the width of columns using the mouse, the Ruler, or options at this dialog box.

8. If you want to move a column width marker and any other column width markers to the right the same distance, hold down this key while dragging the mouse.

9. The Properties for Table Format dialog box with this tab selected includes options for formatting a cell or selected cells.

10. By default, text in a cell is horizontally aligned at this margin of the cell.

11. This option at the Properties for Table Format dialog box with the Row tab selected is useful in a table that spans more than one page.

12. Add fill to cells in a table at this dialog box.

13. The Copy Formula dialog box contains two options—To Cell and a list box with these four options.

SKILLS check

Assessment 1

1. At a clear editing window, create the letter shown in figure 11.25.
2. Save the document and name it Ch 11, SA 01.
3. Print and then close Ch 11, SA 01.

FIGURE

11.25 *Assessment 1*

January 13, 2003

Mr. and Mrs. Phillip Hunter
3120 South 32nd Avenue
Seattle, WA 98104

Dear Mr. and Mrs. Hunter:

The final arrangements have been made for your cruise to the Caribbean. The airfare has been charged to your account. A receipt of this transaction is included in your travel packet. Your itinerary for the cruise is described below:

Day	Port	Arrive	Depart
Saturday, 03/06/03	Miami		4:00 p.m.
Sunday, 03/07/03	At sea		
Monday, 03/08/03	San Juan	6:00 p.m.	
Tuesday, 03/09/03	San Juan		2:00 a.m.
Tuesday, 03/09/03	St. Thomas	8:00 a.m.	5:30 p.m.
Wednesday, 03/10/03	St. Marten	7:00 a.m.	5:00 p.m.
Thursday, 03/11/03	At sea		
Friday, 03/12/03	At sea		
Saturday, 03/13/03	Miami	8:00 a.m.	

I am sure you will have a wonderful time on your cruise. Please stop by our office to pick up your travel packet as soon as possible.

Sincerely,

Judy Peterson

xx:Ch 11, SA 01

Assessment 2

1. At a clear editing window, create the table shown in figure 11.26 with the following specifications:
   a. Change the font to 10-point Arial (or a similar sans serif typeface).
   b. Create a table with 4 columns and 10 rows.
   c. Change the width of the first column to 4 inches.
   d. Join the cells as indicated.
   e. Change the horizontal alignment of cells to *Center* and the appearance to *Bold* as indicated in the figure.
   f. Key the text in the cells as shown in figure 11.26.
   g. Select the text in cell A1 and then change the relative size to *Very large*.
   h. Select the text in cell A2 and then change the relative size to *Large*.
2. Save the table and name it Ch 11, SA 02.
3. Print and then close Ch 11, SA 02.

F I G U R E

11.26 *Assessment 2*

OMAHA CITY SCHOOL DISTRICT			
Technology Study Question #5			
What training do you need to utilize technology?	H.S.	J.H.S.	E.S.
1. Time for hands-on practice and exploration.	4	2	3
2. On-site technical resource to help with problems.	7	3	5
3. Updating of software/hardware.	5	2	6
4. Paid training (money, clock hours, college credits).	3	7	8
5. Training tied to curriculum.	8	4	6
6. Standardized software adoption process.	3	4	2
7. Technical training required for all staff.	2	5	4

Assessment 3

1. At a clear editing window, create the purchase requisition form shown in figure 11.27 by completing the following steps:
   a. Create a table with 5 columns and 11 rows.
   b. Change the width of the first column to 0.5 inch and the second column to 2.5 inches.
   c. Join cells A1 through E1.
   d. Position the insertion point in cell A1 and then change the row height to 2.75 inches.
   e. Select cells A3 through A11 and then change the horizontal alignment to *Center*.
   f. Select cells D3 through E11 and then change the number type to *Currency*.

g. Select cells C3 through E11 and then change the horizontal alignment to *Decimal Align*.

h. Select cells A2 through E2 and then change the lines at the top of the cells and at the bottom of the cells to Double.

i. With cells A2 through E2 still selected, insert 20% Fill.

j. With cells A2 through E2 still selected, change the horizontal alignment to *Center* and the appearance to *Bold*.

k. Insert a double line border around the table.

l. Select cells A3 through A11 and then change the inside lines to *None*.

m. Select cells B3 through B11 and then change the inside lines to *None*.

n. Select cells C3 through C11 and then change the inside lines to *None*.

o. Select cells D3 through D11 and then change the inside lines to *None*.

p. Select cells E3 through E11 and then change the inside lines to *None*.

q. Key the information in the table as shown in figure 11.27. Bold the text in cell A1 as indicated. Press Ctrl + Tab to indent the text in cell A1.

2. Save the table and name it Ch 11, SA 03.

3. Print and then close Ch 11, SA 03.

FIGURE

11.27 *Assessment 3*

DENVER MEMORIAL HOSPITAL
900 Colorado Boulevard
Denver, CO 86530
(303) 555-4400

Purchase Requisition

Name _____ Dept. _____

Purpose of Request _____

Budget Account No. _____

#	Item	Qty.	Price	Total

Merging Documents

PERFORMANCE OBJECTIVES

Upon successful completion of chapter 12, you will be able to:
- Format a data file
- Format a form file
- Use merge to create letters and envelopes
- Input text using the keyboard during a merge
- Merge specific records

WordPerfect includes a merge feature that you can use to create letters, envelopes, labels, and much more, all with personalized information. Generally, there are two documents that need to be created for merging. One document, which WordPerfect calls the *data file*, contains the variable information (information that changes). The second document contains the standard text along with identifiers showing where variable information is to be inserted. WordPerfect refers to this as the *form document*.

Creating a Data File

The data file and the form document required for a merge can be created in any order. However, you might find creating the data file first and then the form document to be the easiest method.

The data file contains the variable information that will be inserted in the form document. Before creating a data file, you need to determine into what type of correspondence you will be inserting the variable information. For example, suppose the sales manager of Sealine Products wants to introduce a new sales representative to all customers in the Spokane, Washington, area. The sales manager decides that a personal letter should be sent to all customers in the greater Spokane area. Figure 12.1 shows one way this letter can be written. The date, body of the letter, and the complimentary close are standard. The variable information—information that will change with each letter—is the name, company name, address, city, state, ZIP Code, and salutation.

12.1 *Sample Letter*

June 9, 2003

Name
Company name
Street address
City, State ZIP

Dear (Name):

At Sealine Products, we are committed to providing quality products and services to our customers. To provide continuing service to you, a new sales representative has been hired. The new sales representative, Ms. Leanne Guile, began her employment with Sealine Products on May 3. She comes to our company with over 10 years' experience in the food industry.

Ms. Guile will be in the Spokane area during the third week of June. She would like to schedule a time for a visit to your company, and will be contacting you by telephone next week.

Sincerely,

Mark Deveau, Manager
Sales Department

Determining Fields

In the letter shown in figure 12.1, the variable information needs to be broken into sections called fields. To determine the variable fields, you need to decide how, and in what form, the information will be used. The following is a name and address of a customer of Sealine Products:

> Mr. Albert Rausch
> Lobster Shoppe
> 450 Marginal Way
> Spokane, WA 98012

The name *Mr. Albert Rausch* could be identified as an entire field. However, the salutation for this letter should read *Dear Mr. Rausch*. If the name is left as one field, the salutation will read *Dear Mr. Albert Rausch*. In this example, then, the name should be broken into three fields: title (Mr.), first name, and last name.

In this example, there is no need for the company name, *Lobster Shoppe*, to be broken into smaller parts. Therefore, it can be identified as one field. The street address, *450 Marginal Way*, can also remain as one field.

The city, state, and ZIP Code in this example can also be considered as one field. However, if you decide that you need the city, state, or ZIP Code separated, you need to make separate fields for each item.

After all fields have been determined, the next step is to determine field names. (This step is optional. If you do not include field names, WordPerfect numbers the fields.) There is no limit to the number of fields a data file can contain. The following list shows one way the fields can be named:

> title
> first name
> last name
> company name
> street address
> city, state ZIP

A field name can be up to 80 characters in length and can include spaces. You can use either uppercase or lowercase letters.

Variable information in a data file is saved as a record. A record contains all the information for one unit (for example, a person, family, customer, client, or business). A series of fields make one record, and a series of records make a data file.

In the data file for the example letter in figure 12.1, each record will contain six fields of information: title; first name; last name; company name; address; and city, state ZIP. Each record in the data file must contain the same number of fields. If the number of fields is not consistent, information will not be inserted correctly during the merge.

WordPerfect offers two methods for creating a data file. You can create a data file as a normal text file, or you can create a data file in the Table format.

Keying a Data File

Remember that the data file contains the variable information that will be inserted into a form document. When you create a data file, name the fields consistent with the field names in the form document. To create a data file for the example letter in figure 12.1, you would complete the following steps:

1. At a clear editing window, display the Merge dialog box, shown in figure 12.2, by clicking Tools and then Merge.

12.2 *Merge Dialog Box*

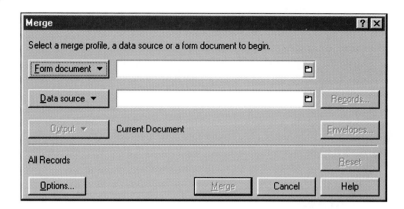

2. At the Merge dialog box, click the <u>D</u>ata source button and then select C<u>r</u>eate Data File from the drop-down menu.
3. At the Create Data File dialog box, shown in figure 12.3, key **title** in the <u>N</u>ame a field text box, and then press Enter or click the <u>A</u>dd button. (This inserts *title* in the <u>F</u>ields used in merge list box.)

12.3 *Create Data File Dialog Box*

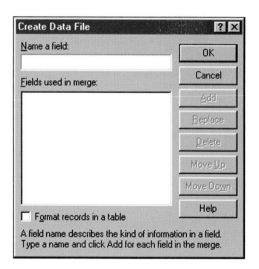

4. Key **first name** and then press Enter.
5. Key the other field names—**last name**; **company name**; **street address**; and **city, state ZIP**. Press Enter after each field name.
6. When all field names have been keyed, click OK.
7. When you click OK at the Create Data File dialog box, the Quick Data Entry dialog box is displayed as shown in figure 12.4. Key the title of a customer to receive the letter and then press Enter. Continue keying the information in each of the fields in the dialog box.

12.4 *Quick Data Entry Dialog Box*

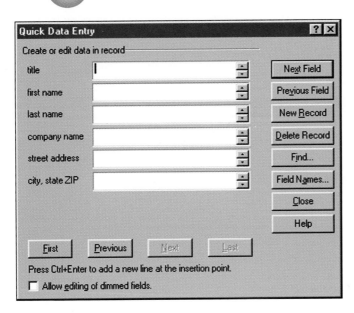

8. After keying the last field for the last customer, click the <u>C</u>lose button.
9. At the query *Save the changes to disk?*, click <u>Y</u>es.
10. At the Save File dialog box, key a name for the data file (such as **Sales rep**) and then press Enter or click the <u>S</u>ave button.
11. Close the file.

When entering text in the Quick Data Entry dialog box, you can use the Tab key to move the insertion point to the next field or press Shift + Tab to move the insertion point to the previous field.

When you save the document in step 10, the data file displays in the editing window. The Data File property bar displays below the Ruler. Figure 12.5 shows an example of how a data file might display for customers of Sealine Products.

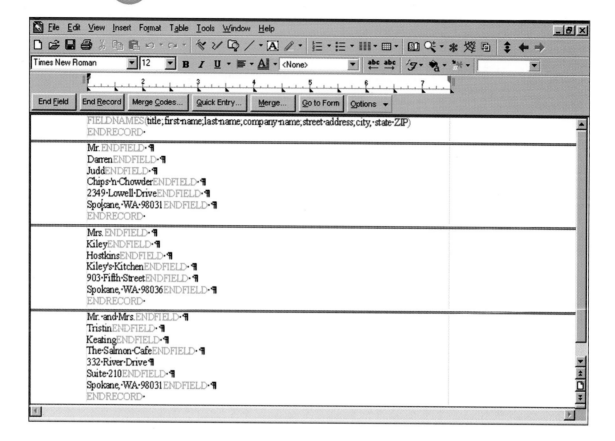

In the data file shown in figure 12.5, each field takes up one line. A field can contain more than one line, however. For example, the record for Mr. and Mrs. Keating could include the following:

> Mr. and Mrs.**ENDFIELD**
> Tristin**ENDFIELD**
> Keating**ENDFIELD**
> The Salmon Cafe**ENDFIELD**
> 332 River Drive
> Suite 210**ENDFIELD**
> Spokane, WA 98031**ENDFIELD**

When entering the information in the street address field at the Quick Data Entry dialog box, key the first line (332 River Drive) and then press Ctrl + Enter. This causes the first line to move up in the street address field and it does not display. Key the second line of the field and then press Enter. This moves the insertion point to the next field.

exercise 1

Creating a Data File

1. At a clear editing window, create a data file containing the information shown in figure 12.6 by completing the following steps:
   a. Click <u>T</u>ools and then M<u>e</u>rge.
   b. At the Merge dialog box, click the <u>D</u>ata source button and then select C<u>r</u>eate Data File.
   c. At the Create Data File dialog box, key **title** and then press Enter. (This inserts *title* in the <u>F</u>ields used in merge list box.)
   d. Key **first name** and then press Enter.
   e. Key the other field names— **last name**, **street address**, **city**, **state**, and **ZIP**. Press Enter after each field name.
   f. When all field names have been keyed, click OK.
   g. At the Quick Data Entry dialog box, key **Mr. and Mrs.** in the title field and then press Enter.
   h. Continue keying the information in figure 12.6 in the appropriate field.
   i. After keying the last field of information for the last customer, click the <u>C</u>lose button.
   j. At the query *Save the changes to disk?*, click <u>Y</u>es.
   k. At the Save File dialog box, key **Fund df** and then press Enter or click the <u>S</u>ave button.
   l. Close the Merge dialog box.
2. Print Fund df. (This may be optional. Check with your instructor to see if you should print this document. Each record will print on a separate page.)
3. Close the Fund df document.

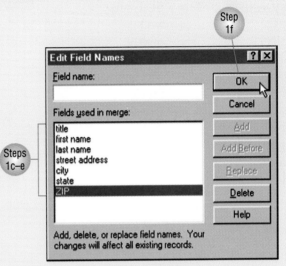

Step 1f

Steps 1c-e

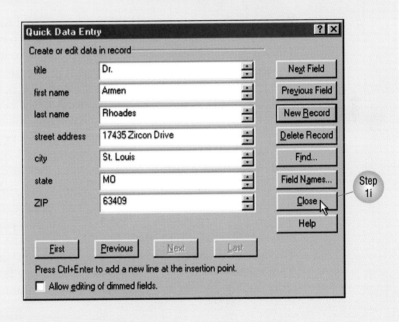

Step 1i

12.6 *Exercise 1*

title	=	Mr. and Mrs.	title	=	Ms.
first name	=	Marcus	first name	=	Jeanne
last name	=	Olsen	last name	=	Hillesland
street address	=	408 Highland Drive	street address	=	1321 North Orchard
city	=	St. Louis	city	=	St. Louis
state	=	MO	state	=	MO
ZIP	=	63409	ZIP	=	63401
title	=	Mr. and Mrs.	title	=	Dr.
first name	=	Patrick	first name	=	Armen
last name	=	Dusek	last name	=	Rhoades
street address	=	3740 South Thompson	street address	=	17435 Zircon Drive
city	=	St. Charles	city	=	St. Louis
state	=	MO	state	=	MO
ZIP	=	63306	ZIP	=	63409

Creating a Form Document

When you have determined the fields and field names and created the data file, the next step is to create the form document. To create the form document, click Tools and then Merge. At the Merge dialog box, click the Form document button and then select Create Form Document at the drop-down menu. Select the desired data file at the Associate Form and Data dialog box, close the dialog box, and then close the Merge dialog box. Key the form letter in the document window including all fields. To insert a field in the form letter, click the Insert Field button on the Merge property bar. At the Insert Field Name or Numbers dialog box, select the field and then click Insert where the field should be inserted. Once all of the desired fields have been inserted, close the dialog box and finish keying the letter.

Insert Field...

When the form letter for our example company, Sealine Products, is completed and the fields have been keyed in the proper locations, it will look like the letter in figure 12.7. Notice that there is a space between the fields. Spaces are inserted between fields as if there were text; then, when the variable information is inserted, it is spaced correctly. This is also true for punctuation. Insert punctuation in a form document as you would in a normal file. For example, place the colon (:) immediately after FIELD(last name) in the salutation.

June 9, 2003

FIELD(title) **FIELD**(first name) **FIELD**(last name)
FIELD(company name)
FIELD(street address)
FIELD(city, state ZIP)

Dear **FIELD**(title) **FIELD**(last name):

At Sealine Products, we are committed to providing quality products and services to our customers. To provide continuing service to you, a new sales representative has been hired. The new sales representative, Ms. Leanne Guile, began her employment with Sealine Products on May 5. She comes to our company with over 10 years' experience in the food industry.

Ms. Guile will be in the Spokane area during the third week of June. She would like to schedule a time for a visit to your company, and will be contacting you by telephone next week.

Sincerely,

Mark Deveau, Manager
Sales Department

The title and last name fields were used more than once in the form document in figure 12.7. Fields in a form document can be used as often as needed. Now you will create your own form document for the data file you created in exercise 1.

Creating a Form Document

1. At a clear editing window, create the form document shown in figure 12.8 by completing the following steps:
   a. Click Tools and then Merge.
   b. At the Merge dialog box, click the Form document button and then select Create Form Document at the drop-down menu.

c. At the Associate Form and Data dialog box, key **Fund df** in the Associate a data file text box (the name of the data file), and then click OK.
d. Close the Merge dialog box.
e. At the editing window with the Merge property bar displayed, key the letter shown in figure 12.8 to the point where the first field code (the field for title) is to be inserted.
f. Click the Insert Field button on the Merge property bar. This causes the Insert Field Name or Number dialog box to display.
g. At the Insert Field Name or Number dialog box, make sure *title* is selected in the Field Names list box, and then click the Insert button. (This inserts *FIELD(title)* in the document.)
h. Press the spacebar once, click *first name* in the Insert Field Name or Number dialog box, and then click the Insert button.
i. Continue creating the fields and text shown in figure 12.8 following steps similar to those in steps 1f and 1g. (Leave on the display of the Insert Field Name or Number dialog box until you have inserted all fields in the form document.)
j. After inserting the fields in the letter, close the Insert Field Name or Number dialog box, and then key the remainder of the letter in figure 12.8.
2. When the form document is completed, save it in the normal manner and name it Fund ltr.
3. Print and then close Fund ltr.

FIGURE

12.8 *Exercise 2*

September 22, 2003

FIELD(title) **FIELD**(first name) **FIELD**(last name)
FIELD(street address)
FIELD(city), **FIELD**(state) **FIELD**(ZIP)

Dear **FIELD**(title) **FIELD**(last name):

Thank you for your support of the financial aid and scholarship programs at Manorwood School District. Each year, we budget nearly $50,000 for deserving students needing financial assistance to attend school in the Manorwood School District. During the next school year, we will depend on people like you to help us raise that amount of money.

At present, over $30,000 has been pledged or given as a result of the Scholarship Fund Drive. Your scholarship investment will be a key part in the success of our ability to raise the necessary funds. Because of your support, we can continue our strong academic program.

Continued on next page

Very truly yours,

MANORWOOD SCHOOL DISTRICT

Sharon Sibrel
Superintendent

xx:Fund ltr

Merging Files

Once the data file and the form document have been created and saved, they can be merged. To merge a form document with a data file, click Tools and then Merge. At the Merge dialog box, click Form document and then select File on Disk. At the Select Form File dialog box, double-click the form file for your merge. The associated data file will appear in the Data source text box; click the Merge button.

When the merge is complete, the merged letters are displayed on the screen and the insertion point is positioned at the end of the last letter. The number of letters is determined by the number of records in the data file. Each letter appears on a separate page.

Merging a Data File and a Form Document

1. At a clear editing window, merge Fund ltr with Fund df by completing the following steps:
   a. Click Tools and then Merge.
   b. At the Merge dialog box, click Form document and then File on Disk. At the Select Form File dialog box, double-click *Fund ltr*. The associated data file (Fund df) should appear in the Data source text box.

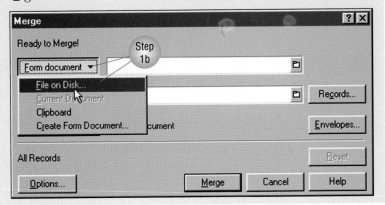

c. Click the Merge button.
2. Save the merged document and name it Ch 12, Ex 03.
3. Print and then close Ch 12, Ex 03.

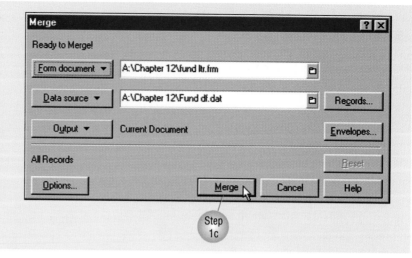

Step 1c

Changing the Merge Output

By default, WordPerfect merges the data file and the form document and inserts the merged documents into the current document. At the Merge dialog box, you can control the output of the merged documents. If you click the down-pointing triangle in the Output button, a drop-down menu displays with the options Current Document, New Document, Printer, File on Disk, and E-mail. Figure 12.9 lists what each of these options does.

FIGURE

12.9 *Merge Output Options*

Click this	For this
New Document	Merges the file to a new document.
Printer	Sends the merged files directly to the printer without displaying them in the editing window.
File on Disk	Displays the Select Output File dialog box. You can choose to save the merged files to an existing document or key a name for the merged files.
E-mail	Allows you to send the merged files through your e-mail system.

Changing Merge Options

By default, WordPerfect merges each record in the data file once with the form document and inserts a hard page break between records. You can change these default settings at the Merge Options dialog box, shown in figure 12.10. To display this dialog box, click the Options button at the Merge dialog box.

12.10 Merge Options Dialog Box

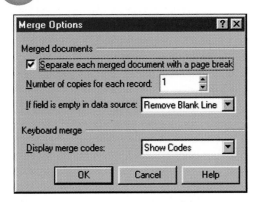

By default, a hard page break separates each merged document. If you do not want a hard page break between merged documents, remove the check mark from the Separate each merged document with a page break option. If you want to merge each record in the data file more than once, increase the number in the Number of copies for each record text box.

The If field is empty in data source option has a default setting of *Remove Blank Line*. At this setting, WordPerfect will remove the blank line if a record does not contain a field entry. For example, the records in the sample data file shown in figure 12.5 each include six fields. If one of the records did not include a company name, the **ENDFIELD** code for that field must still be included in the data file. This is because each record must contain the same number of fields. If one of the records does not contain a company name entry, leave the setting at Remove Blank Line. This will cause the street address to move up just below the title, first name, and last name. The If field is empty in data source option can be changed to *Leave Blank Line*. At this setting WordPerfect will leave a blank line if the field is empty.

When records in a data file are merged with a form document, the merged documents display in the current document with merge codes. If you do not want merge codes to display in merged documents, click the down-pointing triangle at the right side of the Display merge codes text box at the Merge Options dialog box. This causes a drop-down list to display with the options *Show Codes* (the default), *Hide Codes*, and *Show as Markers*. Click *Hide Codes* if you do not want merge codes to display in the merged document. Or, click *Show as Markers* if you want the merge codes to display as markers in the merged document.

Creating a Table Data File

Fields in a data file can be entered in cells within a table. In this manner, each field in a cell is easily identified. To create a table data file, you would follow the same steps for creating a normal text data file, except that you click the Format records in a table check box at the Create Data File dialog box (shown in figure 12.3).

Figure 12.11 shows an example of a table data file containing the same records as the data file in figure 12.5. Notice that some of the cells in figure 12.11 show text wrapping to a second line. Do not worry when text wraps within a table data file since the spacing of the text is determined by the placement of the field codes in the form document. In exercises 4 and 5 you will create a similar table data file and merge it with the form document you created in exercise 2.

12.11 *Sample Table Data File*

title	first name	last name	company name	street address	city, state ZIP
Mr.	Darren	Judd	Chips 'n Chowder	2349 Lowell Drive	Spokane, WA 98031
Mrs.	Kiley	Hostkins	Kiley's Kitchen	903 Fifth Street	Spokane, WA 98036
Mr. and Mrs.	Tristin	Keating	The Salmon Cafe	332 River Drive	Spokane, WA 98031

exercise 4

Creating a Table Data File

1. At a clear editing window, create the table data file shown in figure 12.12 by completing the following steps:
   a. Display the Merge dialog box.
   b. At the Merge dialog box, click the Data source button and then select Create Data File from the drop-down menu.
   c. At the Create Data File dialog box, click the Format records in a table check box.
   d. Click in the Name a field text box, key **title**, and then press Enter. (This inserts *title* in the Fields used in merge list box.)
   e. Key **first name** and then press Enter.
   f. Key the other field names—**last name**, **street address**, **city**, **state**, and **ZIP**. Press Enter after each field name.
   g. Click OK to close the dialog box.
   h. At the Quick Data Entry dialog box, key **Mr. and Mrs.** in the title field and then press Enter. Continue keying the information in each of the fields identified as shown in figure 12.12.
   i. After keying the last field of information for the last customer, click the Close button.
   j. At the query *Save the changes to disk?*, click Yes.
2. At the Save File dialog box, key **Fund2 df** and then press Enter or click the Save button.
3. Print and then close Fund2 df. (This may be optional. Check with your instructor.)

title	first name	last name	street address	city	state	ZIP
Mr. and Mrs.	James	Ricardo	16304 12th Avenue	St. Charles	MO	63306
Mr.	Glenn	Neigel	2223 East Wright	St. Louis	MO	63404
Ms.	Ruby	Marttala	4566 South Oakes	St. Charles	MO	63306
Mr. and Mrs.	Nicholas	Kobe	3348 34th Court East	St. Louis	MO	63402

exercise 5

Merging Two Files

1. At a clear editing window, merge Fund ltr with Fund2 df to the printer by completing the following steps:
    a. Click Tools and then Merge.
    b. At the Merge dialog box, click Form document and then File on Disk. At the Select Form File dialog box, double-click *Fund ltr*.
    c. Click Data source and then WordPerfect Data File. At the Select Data File dialog box, double-click *Fund2 df*.
    d. Click Output and then select Printer at the drop-down menu.
2. Click the Merge button and the merged documents are sent directly to the printer.

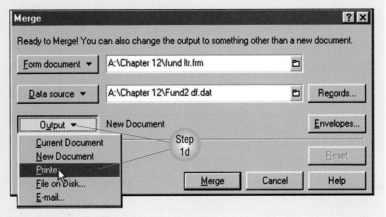

Canceling a Merge

If, during the merge, you want to stop it, press the Esc key or press Ctrl + Break. To begin the merge again, you will need to repeat the steps for completing a merge.

Formatting a Form Document

Any formatting codes you want applied to the merged documents should be inserted at the Styles Editor dialog box in the form document. To display the Styles Editor dialog box, click File, point to Document, and then click Current Document Style. You can also use the Document Default Font dialog box if you want to change the font for the merged documents.

Editing the Format of a Form Document

1. Open Fund ltr.
2. Make the following changes to the document:
   a. Display the Styles Editor dialog box, change the left and right margins to 1.5 inches, and then close the dialog box.
   b. Display the Document Default Font dialog box, change the font to 12-point Garamond, and then close the dialog box.
3. Save and close Fund ltr.
4. Merge Fund ltr with Fund df into the current document. (Make sure that the Output option at the Merge dialog box is set at Current Document.)
5. Save the merged document and name it Ch 12, Ex 06.
6. Print and then close Ch 12, Ex 06.

Creating Envelopes

There are two methods you can use to create envelopes with a data file. You can create a form document to print envelopes, or you can create envelopes while merging a letter or other form document.

Merging Envelopes Only

You can create a form document for printing envelopes that you will merge with a data file. Exercise 7 shows you how to create the form document.

exercise 7

Creating an Envelope Form Document

1. At a clear editing window, create an envelope form document to be merged with the Fund df data file by completing the following steps:
    a. Display the Merge dialog box.

    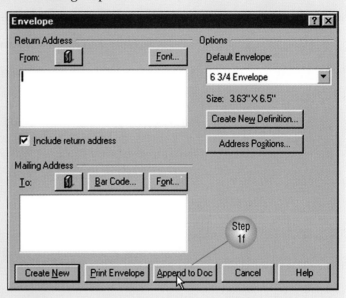

    b. At the Merge dialog box, click the Form document button and then click Create Form Document.
    c. At the Associate Form and Data dialog box, key **A:\chapter 12\Fund df** in the Associate a data file text box and then click OK.
    d. Close the Merge dialog box.
    e. At the clear editing window (with the Merge property bar displayed), click Format and then Envelope.
    f. At the Envelope dialog box, click Append to Doc.
    g. Click the Insert Field button located on the Merge property bar. This causes the Insert Field Name or Number dialog box to display.
    h. At the Insert Field Name or Number dialog box, make sure *title* is selected in the Field Names list box, and then click the Insert button. (This inserts the *title* field in the Mailing Address text box at the Envelope dialog box.)
    i. Press the spacebar once and then click the Field button.
    j. At the Insert Field Name or Number dialog box, double-click *first name* in the Field Names list box.
    k. Press the spacebar once and then click the Field button.
    l. At the Insert Field Name or Number dialog box, double-click *last name* in the Field Names list box.
    m. Press the Enter key once and then click the Field button.
    n. At the Insert Field Name or Number dialog box, double-click *street address* in the Field Names list box.
    o. Continue inserting field names in the Mailing Address text box at the Envelope dialog box. Insert the field names in the appropriate location. Add punctuation, press the spacebar, and press Enter where appropriate.
    p. After all field names have been entered in the Mailing Address text box at the dialog box, click the Close button on the Insert Field Name or Number Dialog Box.
    q. At the editing window containing the envelope fields, save the document in the normal manner and name it Env fd.
    r. Close Env fd.
2. Merge Env fd with Fund df to the current document.
3. Save the merged document and name it Ch 12, Ex 07.
4. Print and then close Ch 12, Ex 07.

Creating Envelopes during Merging

Envelopes can be created for the form document during the merge. When you create envelopes during the merge, you do not have to create a separate form document. When the merge is completed, an envelope for each record in the data file is created and positioned at the end of the document separated by page breaks.

Creating Envelopes during a Merge

1. At a clear editing window, create envelopes when merging Fund ltr with Fund2 df by completing the following steps:
   a. Display the Merge dialog box.
   b. At the Merge dialog box, click Form document and then File on Disk. At the Select Form File dialog box, double-click *Fund ltr*.
   c. Select the file name displayed in the Data source text box and then key **Fund2 df**.
   d. Click the Envelopes button.
   e. At the Envelope dialog box, insert the fields in the Mailing Address text box as described in exercise 7.
   f. After all necessary fields have been inserted in the Mailing Address text box, click Continue Merge.
   g. At the Merge dialog box, click the Merge button.
2. When the merge is completed, save the merged document and name it Ch 12, Ex 08.
3. Print and then close Ch 12, Ex 08. (Check with your instructor to see if you should print the entire document or just the envelopes.)

Merging at the Keyboard

WordPerfect's Merge feature contains a large number of merge codes and merge programming commands that can be inserted in a form document. One of the most commonly used merge codes is KEYBOARD. This merge code can be accessed on the Merge property bar by clicking Insert Merge Code. This displays the Insert Merge Codes drop-down list of merge codes. The steps to insert a KEYBOARD code are explained in the following section. For a detailed list of the merge formatting commands, please refer to the help menu.

Insert Merge Code ▼

Situations may arise in which you do not need to keep variable information in a data file. WordPerfect lets you input variable information directly from the keyboard. You can create a form document with fields and keyboard entry, or you can create a document that requires just keyboard entry.

To insert a KEYBOARD code in a form document, display the Merge dialog box, click the Form document button, and then click Create Form Document.. At the Associate Form and Data dialog box, click No association and then click OK. This tells WordPerfect that there is no data file associated with the form document. At the editing window, key the text of the form document to the point of the first KEYBOARD code. To insert the KEYBOARD code, click Insert Merge Code on the Merge property bar and then select Keyboard. At the Insert Merge Code dialog box, key a message specifying what is to be entered at the keyboard and then click OK. Continue in this manner until all text and KEYBOARD codes have been inserted in the document and then save the document in the normal manner.

To merge a form document containing KEYBOARD codes, display the Merge dialog box, select the form document, and then click the Merge button. WordPerfect merges the form document to the first KEYBOARD code and inserts the message you entered at the bottom of the editing window. Key the required information and then click the Continue button. (The Continue button is located on the Merge property bar.) WordPerfect continues the merge to the next KEYBOARD code and inserts the specified message. Continue inserting the required information and clicking the Continue button until all information has been entered in the merged document.

Performing a Keyboard Merge

1. Open Fund ltr.
2. Save the document with Save As and name it Donate ltr.
3. Position the insertion point on the space between *investment* and *will be* in the second sentence of the second paragraph, press the spacebar once, key **of**, press the spacebar once again, and then insert a KEYBOARD merge code by completing the following steps:

   Step 3b

   Insert Merge Code

   FORMAT: KEYBOARD[[prompt]]
   Enter Prompt:
   amount of donation

   OK   Cancel   Help

   a. Click the Insert Merge Code button on the Merge property bar and then select Keyboard.
   b. At the Insert Merge Code dialog box, key **amount of donation** and then click OK.
4. Save and then close Donate ltr.
5. At a clear editing window, merge Donate ltr with Fund df to the current document by completing the following steps:
   a. Display the Merge dialog box.
   b. Click Form document and then File on Disk.
   c. At the Select Form File dialog box, double-click *Donate ltr* in the list box.
   d. Click the Data source button and then click File on Disk at the drop-down menu.
   e. At the Select Data File dialog box, double-click *Fund df* in the list box.
   f. At the Merge dialog box, click the Merge button.
   g. WordPerfect merges the letter to the KEYBOARD merge code and inserts the message *amount of donation* at the bottom of the editing window. Key **$200** and then click the Continue button.
   h. When WordPerfect stops at the KEYBOARD merge code for the second record, key **$150** and then click the Continue button.
   i. When WordPerfect stops at the KEYBOARD merge code for the third record, key **$300** and then click the Continue button.
   j. When WordPerfect stops at the KEYBOARD merge code for the fourth record, key **$250** and then click the Continue button.
6. When the merge is completed, save the merged document and name it Ch 12, Ex 09.
7. Print and then close Ch 12, Ex 09.

Specifying Records for Merging

With options from the Select Records dialog box, you can specify what records you want merged. This might be useful, for example, to merge only those records containing a certain city or a certain ZIP Code. You can also specify a range of records to be merged. For example, you could specify that only records three through eight be merged.

Marking Records

You can mark specific records in a data file to be merged with the form document. When you specify certain records for merging, you can identify the records by field. To specify certain records for merging, display the Merge dialog box. At the Merge dialog box, key the name of the form document in the Form document text box and then click the Records button.

At the Select Records dialog box shown in figure 12.13, click the radio button preceding Mark records. This causes the Select Records dialog box to change as shown in figure 12.14 Click the down-pointing triangle at the right side of the First field to display text box and then at the drop-down menu that displays, click the field to be used for selecting records. Click the Update Record List button and only the field information for each record displays in the Record list list box. At this list box, click each desired record to mark the record. When all desired records have been selected, click OK. At the Merge dialog box, click the Merge button. When the data file is merged with the form document, only those records marked in the Record list list box are merged.

FIGURE

12.13 *Select Records Dialog Box*

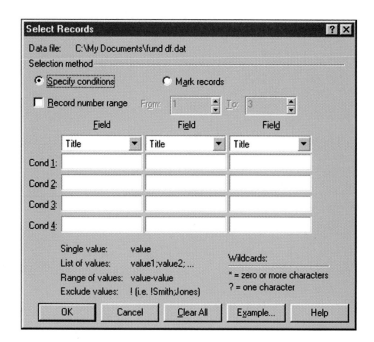

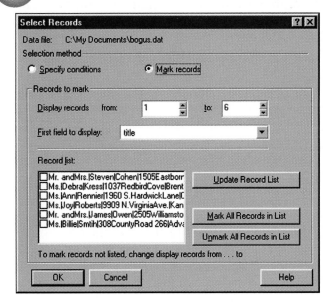

12.14 *Select Records Dialog Box with Mark Records Selected*

exercise 10

Merging Selected Records

1. At a clear editing window, merge Fund ltr with only those records in Fund df containing St. Louis by completing the following steps:
   a. Display the Merge dialog box.
   b. At the Merge dialog box, select *Fund ltr* as the form document.
   c. Select the file name displayed in the Data source text box and then key **Fund df**.
   d. Click the Records button.
   e. At the Select Records dialog box, click the radio button preceding the Mark records option.
   f. Click the down-pointing triangle at the right of the First field to display text box. At the drop-down list that displays, click the down-pointing triangle in the scroll bar until *city* displays, and then click *city*.
   g. Click the Update Record List button and WordPerfect displays only the city for records in the Record list list box.
   h. Mark records with St. Louis as the city. To do this, click the check box before the first record with St. Louis as the city. Repeat the steps for any other records with St. Louis as the city. (This inserts a check mark in the check box before the record.)
   i. When all necessary records have been marked, click OK.
   j. At the Merge dialog box, click the Merge button.
2. When the merge is completed, save the document and name it Ch 12, Ex 10.
3. Print and then close Ch 12, Ex 10.
4. Clear the changes you made to the Select Records dialog box by completing the following steps:
   a. Display the Merge dialog box.
   b. Click the Reset button and then close the Merge dialog box.

Specifying a Range of Records

With the <u>R</u>ecord number range option from the Select Records dialog box, you can identify a range of records to be merged. When the data file and form document are merged, a merged document is created only for the specified records.

Defining Merge Conditions

With options from the Select Records dialog box, you can define conditions for the merge. For example, you may want to select only those records that contain a specific city name. Up to four conditions can be specified. A record is selected if it matches all the conditions.

To specify the first field for which you want to assign a condition, click <u>F</u>ield and then select the desired field from the drop-down list. Click in the Cond <u>1</u> text box and then key the selection condition.

When specifying a condition, you can enter a value (text, amount, number, and so on) and WordPerfect will search for records that contain that value. For example, if you identify *city, state ZIP* as the field and then key **Spokane** in the Cond <u>1</u> text box, WordPerfect will only select those records containing Spokane in the *city, state ZIP* field in the data file. You can also use symbols in conjunction with a value. Figure 12.15 shows what the symbols will perform when used with a value.

FIGURE

12.15 *Condition Symbols*

Symbol	Condition
;	or
-	through
!	exclude
*	wildcard character meaning zero or more characters
?	one character wildcard

Clearing the Select Records Dialog Box

If you make changes to the Select Records dialog box, these changes remain in effect until you make other changes or you exit WordPerfect. If you want to perform a merge on a different document, you will need to clear any conditions established in the Select Records dialog box. To do this, click the <u>C</u>lear All button at the Select Records dialog box.

exercise 11

Specifying Merge Conditions

1. At a clear editing window, select those records in Fund df with St. Louis as the city and 63409 as the ZIP Code, and then merge with Fund ltr by completing the following steps:

    a.   Display the Merge dialog box.

    b.   At the Merge dialog box, identify *Fund ltr* as the form document and *Fund df* as the data source.

    c.   Click the Records button.

    d.   At the Select Records dialog box, click the down-pointing triangle at the right of the first Field text box and then click *city* at the drop-down list.

    e.   Click the down-pointing triangle at the right of the Field text box (the second field) and then click *ZIP* at the drop-down list.

    f.   Click inside the Cond 1 text box below *city* and then key St. Louis.

    g.   Press the Tab key to move the insertion point into the text box below ZIP and then key 63409.

    h.   Click OK.

    i.   At the Merge dialog box, click the Merge button.

2.   Save the merged document and name it Ch 12, Ex 11.

3.   Print and then close Ch 12, Ex 11.

4.   Clear the changes you made to the Select Records dialog box by completing the following steps:

    a.   Display the Merge dialog box.

    b.   At the Merge dialog box, click the Records button.

    c.   At the Select Records dialog box, click the Clear All button.

    d.   Click OK.

    e.   Close the Merge dialog box.

CHAPTER summary

➤ Personalized form documents, such as letters and envelopes, can be created with the Merge feature.

➤ The Merge feature generally requires two documents: the data file that contains the variable information and the form document that contains the standard text.

➤ A data file contains records. A record contains all the information for one unit (a person, family, or business). To be merged with the form document, the information in one record must be divided into fields.

➤ When you create a form document, name the fields consistent with the field names in the data file.

➤ The data for each record can be entered at the Quick Data Entry dialog box.

➤ The form document includes standard text along with identifiers showing where variable information is to be inserted.

➤ Once the data file and form document have been created and saved, they can be merged at the Merge dialog box.

➤ When the merge is complete, the merged letters (or other documents) are displayed in the editing window. These merged letters can then be saved as a separate document.

➤ Control the output of the merged documents at the Merge dialog box.

➤ Another way to create a data file is to enter the fields of the data file in cells within a table. To use this method, click the Format records in a table check box at the Create Data File dialog box.

➤ Any formatting codes you want applied to the merged documents should be inserted in the form document at the Styles Editor dialog box.

➤ Create a form document to print envelopes at the Envelope dialog box, or you can create envelopes while merging a letter or other form document.

➤ Data can be inserted directly from the keyboard during a merge if a KEYBOARD code is inserted in the form document. Other merge codes are available by clicking the Insert Merge Code button on the Merge property bar.

➤ With options from the Select Records dialog box, you can mark specific records or a range of records in a data file to be merged with the form document.

COMMANDS summary

Command	Mouse	Keyboard
Display the Merge dialog box	Tools, Merge	Shift + F9
Display the Merge options dialog box	Tools, Merge, Options button	
Merge envelopes while performing a merge	Tools, Merge, Envelopes button	
Display Insert Field Name or Numbers dialog box	Click the Insert Field button on Merge property bar	
Insert Keyboard Merge Code	Click the Insert Merge Code button on Merge property bar, Keyboard	
Display the Select Records dialog box	Tools, Merge, Records button	

CONCEPTS check

Completion: On a blank sheet of paper, indicate the correct term, command, or number for each item.

1. Creating a personalized form letter with WordPerfect's Merge feature usually requires this number of documents.

2. A data file can be created as a normal text file or in this format.

3. Once the data file and form document have been created and saved, they can be merged at this dialog box.

4. In the Quick Data Entry dialog box, press this key on the keyboard to move the insertion point to the next field.

5. This code will appear at the end of each field created in a data file.

6. This code will appear at the end of each record created in a data file.

7. Any formatting codes you want applied to the merged documents should be inserted in the form document at this dialog box.

8. You can control the output of merged documents at this dialog box.

9. When merging a document containing a keyboard merge code, key the required information, and then click this button on the Merge property bar.

10. When specifying a merge condition, key this symbol to indicate *or*.

11. When specifying a merge condition, key this symbol to indicate *exclude*.

SKILLS check

Assessment 1

1. At a clear editing window, look at the letter in figure 12.17 and the records in figure 12.16. Determine the fields you need for the form document (create a separate field for city, state, and ZIP) and then create a data file for the records in figure 12.16 in a table format.
2. Save the data file and name it Customers df.
3. Print and then close Customers df. (Check with your instructor to see if you should print the document.)

FIGURE

12.16 *Assessment 1*

Ms. Gayle Waymire
14952 Pioneer Way
Toronto, ON M5W 3X9

Mr. and Mrs. LeRoy Huse
1450 Willow Street
Vancouver, BC V3R 2A7

Mr. Douglas Ichikawa
8509 Bayview Drive SW
Calgary, AB T2V 3M1

Mrs. Heather Casey
1409 Wyman Place
Ottawa, ON K1N 8M5

Dr. Holly Bartel
348 Castlegrove Blvd.
Toronto, ON M3A 1L6

Assessment 2

1. At a clear editing window, create the form document shown in figure 12.17 in an appropriate business letter format. Add the Keyboard Merge field as indicated. (At the Associate Form and Data dialog box, identify Customers df as the data file.)
2. Save the form document and name it Refinance ltr.
3. Print and then close Refinance ltr.

F I G U R E

12.17 *Assessment 2*

(current date)

name
address
city, state ZIP

Dear (name):

If you have considered KEYBOARD(action), then take a minute to read this letter. Interest rates have fallen and now is the time to refinance. In addition, real estate prices have appreciated tremendously.

The decline of interest rates lets you refinance your home loan at a lower interest rate, which could save you thousands of dollars or give you extra money to renovate or pay off debts. Northwest Brokers is the largest mortgage broker in Canada. We specialize in portable, blended, and variable-rate loans. We have over 50 lenders to choose from to help find you the lowest rates at no extra cost to you.

If you are curious about the options available to you, the amount you qualify for in a new home, or the amount of equity that is accessible in your current home, then please call me at Northwest Brokers. The information is free and I guarantee the best rates and service available.

Sincerely,

NORTHWEST BROKERS

Anthony Masela
Loan Officer

xx:Refinance ltr

Assessment 3

1. At a clear editing window, select those records in Customers df with Toronto as the city, and then merge with Refinance ltr.
2. When WordPerfect stops at the KEYBOARD merge codes, key the following information:
   a. Ms. Gayle Waymire is interested in *refinancing your current home*.
   b. Dr. Holly Bartel is interested in *buying a new home*.
3. Save the merged document and name it Ch 12, SA 03.
4. Print and then close Ch 12, SA 03.

Assessment 4

1. Create an envelope form document named *Envelope2* with fields to create envelopes for all records in Customers df.
2. Merge Envelope2 with Customers df to the current document.
3. Save the merged document and name it Ch 12, SA 04.
4. Print and then close Ch 12, SA 04.

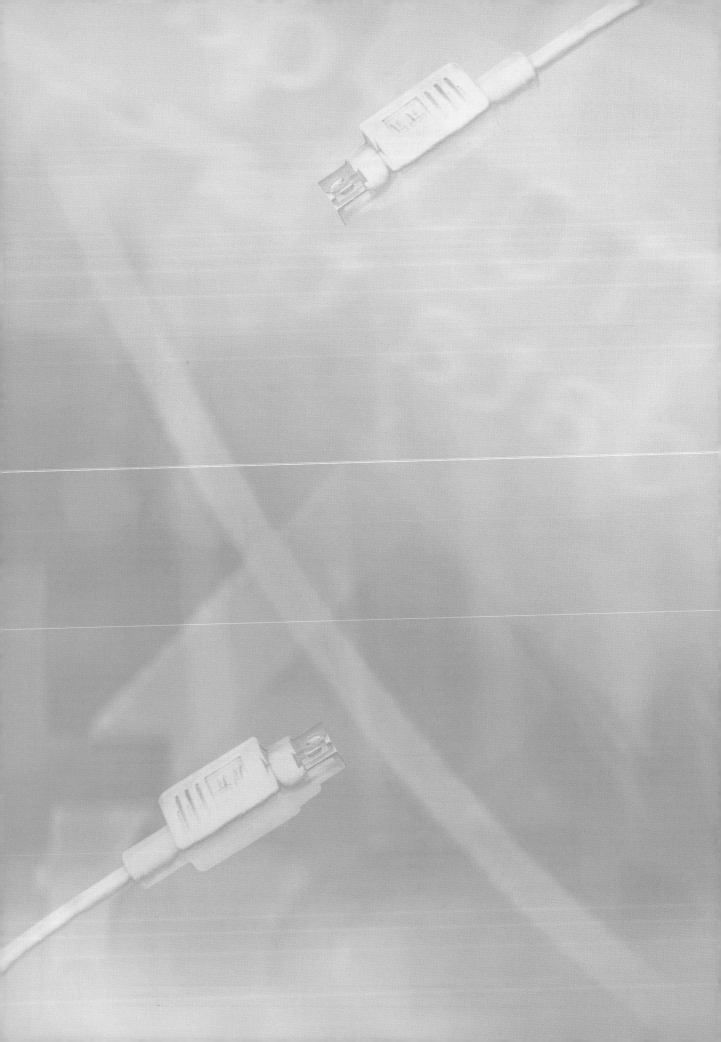

PERFORMANCE
Assessments

MANIPULATING AND ORGANIZING TEXT

INTEGRATING SKILLS

In this unit, you have learned to create and edit headers and footers, as well as footnotes and endnotes, manipulate blocks of text, save selected text as a separate document, move and copy text between documents, use the Print dialog box, create and format tables, insert formulas in a table, create a data file, create a form file, and merge documents.

Assessment 1

1. Open Loan doc.
2. Complete the following steps:
   a. Select the first paragraph and save it as a separate document named *Loan Pr 01*.
   b. Select the second paragraph and save it as a separate document named *Loan Pr 02*.
   c. Do the same with the other paragraphs and name them *Loan Pr 03*, *Loan Pr 04*, and *Loan Pr 05*.
3. Close Loan doc.
4. At a clear editing window, create the document shown in figure U3.1 with the following specifications:
   a. Change the top margin to 1.5 inches.
   b. Turn on the Widow/Orphan feature.
   c. Change the line spacing to double (2) for the body of the document. Change the line spacing back to single (1) for the signature lines.
   d. Insert the documents as indicated by the bracketed items.
   e. After inserting the documents, renumber the paragraphs.
   f. Insert page numbering at the bottom center of each page.
5. Complete a spell check on the document.
6. Save the document and name it U03, PA 01.
7. Print and then close U03, PA 01.

CONSUMER LOAN AGREEMENT

This Consumer Loan Agreement governs the open-end consumer loan plan issued through State Employees Credit Union. EDWARD G. WALLACE and TARA L. WALLACE, applicants, agree jointly to follow the terms and conditions and all other loan documents related to this Account including any Loan Advance Voucher, Loan Proceeds Check, Power of Attorney, if applicable, given when a loan is made, which collectively shall govern this account.

[Insert Loan Pr 03 here.]

[Insert Loan Pr 01 here.]

[Insert Loan Pr 04 here.]

[Insert Loan Pr 02 here.]

[Insert Loan Pr 05 here.]

6.   **Finance Charge.** When finance charges accrue, EDWARD G. WALLACE and TARA L. WALLACE will pay a finance charge calculated on the daily unpaid balance of all loans under this Account and any loan fee applicable to the Account. The finance charges will begin to accrue as of the date each loan advance is made. The finance charge is based on the outstanding balance.

_____
EDWARD G. WALLACE, Applicant

_____
TARA L. WALLACE, Applicant

FIGURE U3.1 • Assessment 1

Assessment 2

1. At a clear editing window, change the left and right margins to 2 inches and then key *Loan Agreement Outline* as shown in figure U3.2.
2. With the outline still open, open Loan doc.
3. Make the following changes to the document:
   a. Tile the windows side by side.
   b. Copy the paragraphs from Loan doc to the the Loan Agreement Outline document in the order indicated in figure U3.2.
   c. Renumber the paragraphs correctly.
4. Save the document and name it U03, SA 02.
5. Print and then close U03, PA 02.
6. Close Loan doc without saving changes.

LOAN AGREEMENT OUTLINE

(Insert Payment section here)

(Insert Minimum Payment section here)

(Insert Paying Loans section here)

(Insert Overdraft Protection section here)

(Insert Limitations on Credit Advances section here)

FIGURE U3.2 • Assessment 2

Assessment 3

1. Open Report 04.
2. Save the report with Save As and name it U03, PA 03.
3. Insert a page break in the second page at the line containing the title *CHAPTER 4: DEVELOPMENT OF TECHNOLOGY, 1950 - 1960.*
4. Move the insertion point back to the beginning of the document and then make the following changes:
   a. Turn on the Widow/Orphan feature.
   b. Change the left and right margins to 1.5 inches. (Make sure this affects all aspects of the document.)
   c. Change the font to 12-point Garamond. (Make sure this affects all aspects of the document.)
   d. Create Header A that prints on every page except the first, is bolded, and reads *Trends in Telecommunications* at the left margin and inserts the page number at the right margin.
   e. Create the first footnote shown in figure U3.3 at the end of the last paragraph in the *World War I* section of the report.
   f. Create the second footnote shown in figure U3.3 at the end of the last paragraph in the *World War II* section of the report.
   g. Create the third footnote shown in figure U3.3 at the end of the last paragraph in the report.
5. Save, print, and then close U03, PA 03.

[1]Mitchell, William, Robert Hendricks, and Leonard Sterry, "A Brief History of Telecommunications," *Telecommunications: Systems and Applications*, Paradigm Publishing, 2001, pages 20-22.

[2]Rhoads, Katherine, "Technological Advances During World War II," *Communications in America*, TrueLine Publishing Services, 2000, pages 112-119.

[3]Junitti, Carl, "Satellite Technology," *Data Transmission*, Puget Sound Publishing, 2002, pages 43-51.

FIGURE U3.3 • Assessment 3

Assessment four

1. At a clear editing window, look at the letter in figure U3.5 and the records in figure U3.4. Determine the fields you need for the form document and then create a data file, in table form, with the records in figure U3.4.
2. Save the data file and name it New Hope df.
3. Print and then close New Hope df. (Check with your instructor to see if you should complete this step.)

Mrs. Sheila Goldsmith
33 Rosemont Way
Petersburg, VA 23415

Mr. Thomas Dircks
2007 East Harris
Hopewell, VA 22459

Ms. Susan Benford
201 West Point Drive
Hopewell, VA 22459

Dr. Glen Davis
7843 90th Street
Petersburg, VA 23451

Mr. Robert Weisert
29044 East Graham
Hopewell, VA 22459

Mrs. Donna Rudman
4812 South 191st Place
Petersburg, VA 23415

FIGURE U3.4 • Assessment 4

Assessment five

1. At a clear editing window, key the letter shown in figure U3.5 in an appropriate business letter format as a form document. Use the Ruler to set a left tab at 0.25" from the left margin. (At the Associate Form and Data dialog box, identify New Hope df as the data file.)
2. Save the letter and name it New Hope ltr.
3. Print and then close New Hope ltr.

February 11, 2003

(name)
(address)

Dear (salutation):

The Assisted Living Program at New Hope Retirement Center offers an independent and dignified lifestyle for senior adults with modest needs for physical assistance. There is assistance available to each resident at New Hope Retirement Center according to his or her individual needs. This assistance is provided 24 hours a day by trained staff members. The types of assistance provided include:

- storing prescribed medication
- reminders of medical schedule
- assistance with dressing and grooming
- assistance with bathing and hygiene
- supervision of nutritional intake
- arranging transportation for medical appointments

Assisted Living residents are provided three full meals a day plus snacks. Housekeeping is done weekly unless more frequency is required. There is a full schedule of social activities such as games and crafts to hold the interest of each resident.

New Hope Retirement Center is committed to providing a fulfilling lifestyle for each resident. If you would like an informational brochure on Assisted Living, please call (804) 555-9093. A tour of the New Hope Retirement Center facilities can also be arranged.

Sincerely,

Antoinette Moreno
Director, Assisted Living

xx:New Hope ltr

FIGURE U3.5 • Assessment 5

Assessment 6

1. At a clear editing window, merge New Hope ltr with New Hope df.
2. Create envelopes as the letters are merged.
3. After the records are merged, save the document and name it U03, PA 06.
4. Print and then close U03, PA 06.

Assessment 7

1. At a clear editing window, create the table shown in figure U3.6 with the following specifications:
   a. Display the Properties for Table Format dialog box with the Table tab selected and then change the Table position on page option to *Center*.
   b. Change the width of the first column to 2.2 inches and the width of the second and third columns to 1.6 inches.
   c. Join the cells as shown in the figure.
   d. Change the horizontal alignment to *Center* and the appearance to *Bold* for cells A1, A2, A3, B3, and C3.
   e. Insert 10% Fill in cells A3 through C3 and cells A11 through C11.
   f. Change the numeric format to *Accounting* and the horizontal alignment to *Decimal Align* for cells B4 through C11.
   g. After entering the text in the cells, calculate the totals of columns B and C.
2. Save the table and name it U03, PA 07.
3. Print and then close U03, PA 07.

SCHOOL EMPLOYEES ANNUITY ASSOCIATION		
BALANCE SHEET		
Asset	**2002**	**2003**
Bonds	$ 42,334,655.00	$ 44,569,345.00
Stocks	$ 2,454,600.00	$ 3,214,748.00
Mortgages	$ 38,543,187.00	$ 43,256,780.00
Real estate	$ 8,543,675.00	$ 9,564,328.00
Other long-term investments	$ 954,367.00	$ 1,284,660.00
Cash, short-term investments	$ 1,456,322.00	$ 1,675,896.00
Other assets	$ 342,564.00	$ 453,234.00
Total Assets		

FIGURE U3.6 • Assessment 7

WRITING SOLUTIONS

The following activities give you the opportunity to practice your writing skills along with demonstrating an understanding of some of the important WordPerfect features you have mastered in this unit. In planning the documents, remember to shape the information according to the writing purpose and the audience. Use correct grammar, appropriate word choices, and clear sentence constructions.

Assessment 8 eight

Situation: You are Owen Lindal, administrative assistant for Jocelyn Cook, the assistant superintendent for the Omaha City School District. You have been asked by Ms. Cook to compose a letter to the individuals listed below with the following information. They have been selected by the principal of the school where their child or children attend to serve on the Facilities Planning Committee. This committee will be comprised of school district administrators, staff, and teachers, as well as people with a child or children attending school in the Omaha City School District. The committee will be responsible for establishing short- and long-term priorities for facilities planning for the district. The first meeting of the committee will be held from 7:00-9:30 p.m. on Tuesday, February 4, 2003, in room 106 at the school administration building. Approximately five additional meetings will be scheduled for the remainder of the school year.

Create a form document containing this information and create a data file for the names and addresses listed below. You determine the names for the form document and data file. After creating the data file and the form document, merge the documents. Save the merged document and name it U03, PA 08. Print and then close U03, PA 08.

Mr. Paul Jackson
302 East 40th Street
Omaha, NE 45056

Mrs. Elaine Natario
9932 Montgomery
Omaha, NE 45054

Ms. Josefina Valdes
14503 South Mildred
Omaha, NE 45054

Mr. Vance Blumenthal
3712 Del Monte Drive
Omaha, NE 45056

Ms. Vicki Cates
24113 Rembert Court
Omaha, NE 45054

Ms. Sung Lim
2033 Columbia Avenue
Omaha, NE 45056

Assessment 9

Situation: You are Jenna McCormick, financial advisor for the Omaha City School District. You have been asked by Pat Windslow, the superintendent for the school district, to prepare a table showing computer expenditures for each school using the data that follows:

OMAHA CITY SCHOOL DISTRICT

Computer Expenditures, 2002-2003

School	Amount
Leland Elementary School	$59,060
Carr Elementary School	43,230
Sahala Elementary School	15,304
Young Elementary School	20,430
Armstrong Elementary School	39,390
Grant Junior High School	68,405
Washington Junior High School	55,304
Roosevelt Junior High School	49,300
Nylan High School	89,000
Cleveland High School	100,230
Total Amount	(calculate total)

Create a table with the data and insert a formula to calculate the total. Format the table to emphasize the important information. Save this document and name it U03, PA 09. Print and then close U03, PA 09.

UNIT four

Formatting with Special Features

Upon successful completion of chapter 13, you will be able to:
- Hyphenate words in a document
- Change the hyphenation options and hyphenation zones in a document
- Add line numbering to a document
- Insert a hard space in a document
- Insert the date
- Convert the case of letters
- Use the Prompt-As-You-Go feature

Chapter 13

WordPerfect contains a variety of features that can affect the line endings or visual appeal of text in a document such as hyphenation, line numbering, and hard spaces. The date can be inserted in a document as text or a code. The Prompt-As-You-Go feature can help you correct spelling and grammar errors as well as display synonyms for words. You will learn to use these features in this chapter.

Hyphenating Words

In some WordPerfect documents, especially documents with left and right margins wider than 1 inch, the right margin may appear quite ragged. If the justification of the paragraph is changed to Full, the right margin will appear even, but there will be gaps of extra space added throughout the line. In these situations, hyphenating long words that fall at the end of the text line provides the document with a more balanced look.

Changing the Hyphenation Zone

WordPerfect provides a left hyphenation zone and a right hyphenation zone. The default left hyphenation zone is 10% of the typing line before the right margin and the default right hyphenation zone is 4% of the typing line after the right margin. If a word begins after the left hyphenation zone and extends beyond the right hyphenation zone, WordPerfect wraps it to the next line. If a word begins at or before the left hyphenation zone and extends past the right hyphenation zone, it will be hyphenated (if it is located in the Spell Check dictionary and if hyphenation is turned on). The illustration in figure 13.1 shows how the word calculations will be either wrapped to the next line or hyphenated.

13.1 *Word Wrap and Hyphenation*

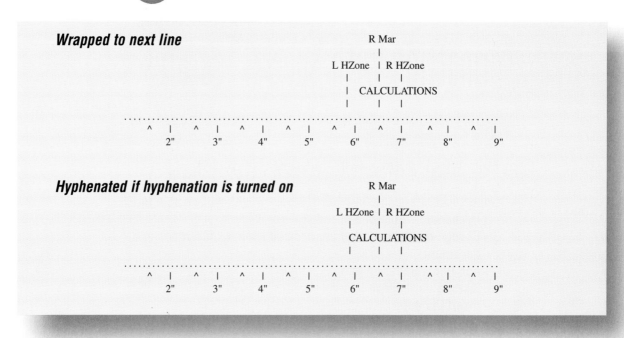

Change hyphenation zones at the Line Hyphenation dialog box shown in figure 13.2. Display this dialog box by clicking Tools, pointing to Language, and then clicking Hyphenation.

F I G U R E

13.2 *Line Hyphenation Dialog Box*

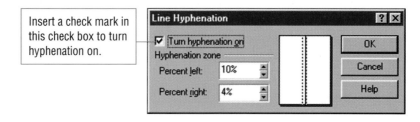

At the Line Hyphenation dialog box, click the up-pointing triangle at the right of the Percent left text box to increase the hyphenation zone or click the down-pointing triangle to decrease the hyphenation zone. Complete the same steps to increase or decrease the percentage in the Percent right text box. You can also select the current percentage in the Percent left or Percent right text box and then key a new measurement.

Turning Hyphenation On

By default, hyphenation is turned off. To turn on hyphenation, click Tools, point to Language, and then click Hyphenation. Once the Line Hyphenation dialog box is displayed, click the Turn hyphenation on check box. To ensure that all text in a document is checked for possible hyphenations, move the insertion point to the end of the document after turning hyphenation on.

If you would like total control over hyphenating words in a document, you can make a change at the Environment Settings dialog box with the Prompts tab selected as shown in figure 13.3. To display this dialog box, click Tools and then Settings. At the Settings dialog box, double-click Environment. At the Environment Settings dialog box, click the Prompts tab.

F I G U R E

13.3 *Environment Settings Dialog Box with Prompts Tab Selected*

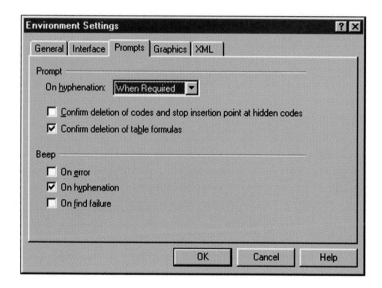

At the Environment Settings dialog box with the Prompts tab selected, change the hyphenation prompt by clicking the down-pointing triangle at the right side of the On hyphenation text box. This causes a drop-down menu to appear with the choices *Always*, *Never*, and *When Required*. These choices behave as follows:

Always	You have total control of the hyphenation decisions.
Never	WordPerfect makes all of the hyphenation decisions.
When Required	This is the default setting and allows WordPerfect to make most of the hyphenation decisions.

If the On hyphenation option is set at *When Required* or *Always*, WordPerfect displays the Position Hyphen dialog box, shown in figure 13.4, during hyphenation.

13.4   *Position Hyphen Dialog Box*

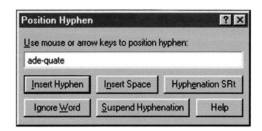

In the box at the top of the Position Hyphen dialog box, the word that WordPerfect wants help hyphenating is displayed. You can move the hyphen to a different location by pressing the left or right arrow keys. When the hyphen is positioned in the desired location, click the Insert Hyphen button or press Enter. You can also move the hyphen with the mouse by positioning the arrow pointer on the word where you want the hyphen and then clicking the left mouse button.

If you do not want to hyphenate the word displayed in the dialog box, click the Ignore Word button. This causes WordPerfect to wrap the entire word to the next line and continue the hyphenation process. WordPerfect will not prompt to hyphenate that word again.

With the Insert Space button, you can insert a space between words. This is useful if you accidentally keyed two words together. During hyphenation, when WordPerfect stops and asks for a hyphenation decision, position the hyphen between the two words and then click the Insert Space button.

Click the Hyphenation SRt button to insert a soft return in the middle of a word rather than a hyphen. This is useful in a situation where you have words divided by a forward slash, such as *problem/conflict*. When WordPerfect presents words with a slash, position the hyphen immediately to the right of the slash and then click the Hyphenation SRt button. This divides the words after the slash if the words fall at the end of the line. If the words do not fall at the end of the line, the soft return is ignored. If you want to stop or suspend hyphenation, click the Suspend Hyphenation button. When hyphenating words, keep in mind the hyphenation guidelines shown in figure 13.5.

Hyphenation Guidelines

Adapted from *The Paradigm Reference Manual* (Paradigm Publishing Inc., 1993)

One-Syllable Words	Do not divide one-syllable words such as length, served, or thoughts.
Multiple-Syllable Words	Divide multiple-syllable words between syllables, as in publish. Note: Some divisions between syllables can confuse a reader, particularly if one or both parts may be read as words by themselves. Examples include coin-sure, reed-ucate, and reap-portion. In such cases, break the word at a different place (co-insure, re-educate, and re-apportion).
Prefixes, Suffixes	Generally, divide *after* a prefix and *before* a suffix. If the root word ends in a double consonant, divide after the double consonant (example bill-ing). If adding a suffix results in a double consonant, divide between the doubled letters, as in refer-ring.
Consecutive Line Ends	Avoid dividing words at the ends of more than two consecutive lines.
Abbreviations, Numbers, Contractions	Do not divide, except for abbreviations already containing hyphens, as in MS-DOS.
Names of People	Avoid dividing a person's name. But if it becomes necessary, hyphenate the name according to the guidelines for common words.
Dash	Do not divide before a dash or between the hyphens if the dash consists of two hyphens.
Dates	Divide date expressions between the day and the year, not between the month and day.
Address	Do not separate the number and the street name. The city, state, and ZIP Code may be divided between the city and the state or between the state and the ZIP Code.
Word Groups Used as Units	Avoid divided word groups such as page and number, chapter and number, or number and unit of measure, as in page 311, chapter 6, and 29 inches.

exercise 1

Changing Hyphenation Zones and Turning On Hyphenation

1. Open Report 01.
2. Save the document with Save As and name it Ch 13, Ex 01.
3. With the insertion point positioned at the beginning of the document, turn on the Widow/Orphan feature.
4. With the insertion point still positioned at the beginning of the document, change the hyphenation zones and turn on hyphenation by completing the following steps:
   a. Click Tools, point to Language, and then click Hyphenation.
   b. At the Line Hyphenation dialog box, click the down-pointing triangle at the right side of the Percent left text box until *5%* displays.
   c. Click the down-pointing triangle at the right side of the Percent right text box until *2%* displays.
   d. Click in the Turn hyphenation on check box.

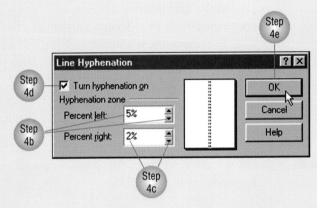

   e. Click OK or press Enter. (Make hyphenation decisions, if required.)
   f. Scroll to the end of the document to make sure that all necessary words are hyphenated.
5. Save, print, and then close Ch 13, Ex 01.

exercise 2

Using Hyphenation Options

1. Open Report 02.
2. Save the document with Save As and name it Ch 13, Ex 02.
3. With the insertion point positioned at the beginning of the report, make the following changes:
   a. Change the hyphenation prompt to *Always* at the Environment Settings dialog box by completing the following steps:
      1) Click Tools and then Settings.
      2) At the Settings dialog box, double-click the Environment option.

3) At the Environment Settings dialog box, click the Prompts tab.

4) At the Environment Settings dialog box with the Prompts tab selected, click the down-pointing triangle at the right side of the On hyphenation text box.

5) At the drop-down menu that displays, click *Always*.

6) Click OK to close the Environment Settings dialog box.

7) Click the <u>C</u>lose button to close the Settings dialog box.

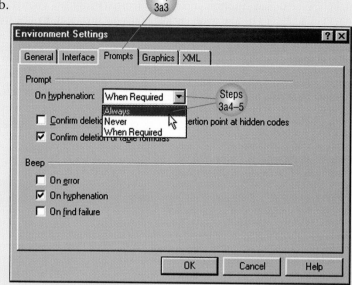

b. Change the left hyphenation zone to 5%, the right hyphenation zone to 2%, and turn hyphenation on.

c. Make hyphenation decisions as required. (Scroll to the end of the document to make sure that all necessary words are hyphenated.)

4. Change the hyphenation prompt back to *When Required* using steps similar to step 3a.

5. Save, print, and then close Ch 13, Ex 02.

Inserting Hyphens

There are several ways that a hyphen is inserted in a document. The type of hyphen in a word like co-worker is called a *regular* hyphen. This hyphen is inserted by keying the minus sign on the keyboard. During hyphenation, WordPerfect will break hyphenated words, if necessary, at the hyphen.

A hyphen that you or WordPerfect inserts during hyphenation is considered a *soft* hyphen. A soft hyphen appears in the editing window and prints only if the word falls at the end of the text line. If text is adjusted and the word no longer falls at the end of the line, the soft hyphen is removed from the editing window and will not print. A soft hyphen is inserted in a word during hyphenation. You can also insert your own soft hyphen in a word by pressing Ctrl + Shift + -. If a word containing a soft hyphen falls at the end of the line, WordPerfect automatically breaks the word at the soft hyphen. If the word does not fall at the end of the line, the hyphen will be ignored.

In some text, such as telephone numbers and Social Security numbers, you may want to insert a *hard* hyphen rather than a regular hyphen. A hard hyphen tells WordPerfect that the text is to be considered a unit and not to break it between lines. A hard hyphen is inserted in text by pressing Ctrl + -.

Deleting Hyphens

A hyphen inserted automatically by WordPerfect displays in Reveal Codes as *Auto Hyphen EOL*. A hyphen you inserted during hyphenation is considered a soft hyphen and displays as *-Soft Hyphen*. A soft hyphen can be easily deleted by deleting the *-Soft Hyphen* code in Reveal Codes or by deleting the hyphen in the document.

A hyphen inserted automatically by WordPerfect cannot be individually deleted. You can, however, delete all *Auto Hyphen EOL* codes in a document by deleting the *Hyph: On* code in Reveal Codes. When this code is deleted, WordPerfect removes all *Auto Hyphen EOL* codes in the document.

Deleting Hyphens

1. Open Ch 13, Ex 02.
2. Save the document with Save As and name it Ch 13, Ex 03.
3. Display Reveal Codes and then delete the *Hyph: On* code. (Leave on the display of Reveal Codes.)
4. Delete the following hyphens:
   a. Delete the hyphen in the first hyphenated word at the end of a text line by completing the following steps:
      1) Position the insertion point immediately to the left of the hyphen (and the *-Soft Hyphen* code) in the first hyphenated word at the end of a text line.
      2) Press the Delete key. (If there is more than one soft hyphen code, delete all soft hyphen codes in the first word.)
   b. Delete the hyphen in the second hyphenated word at the end of a text line.
   c. Delete the hyphen in the third hyphenated word at the end of a text line.
5. Save, print, and then close Ch 13, Ex 03.

Deleting the *Hyph: On* code does not remove soft hyphens. If you want to delete all soft hyphens in a document, you would delete the hyphenation on code, and then use the Find and Replace feature to find all soft hyphen codes.

Removing All Soft Hyphens

1. Open Ch 13, Ex 02.
2. Save the document with Save As and name it Ch 13, Ex 04.
3. Delete all soft hyphens in the document by completing the following steps:
   a. Turn on the display of Reveal Codes, delete the hyphenation on code, and then turn off the display of Reveal Codes.
   b. Click Edit and then Find and Replace.
   c. At the Find and Replace dialog box, click Match and then Codes.

d. At the Codes dialog box, click -*Soft Hyphen* in the Find codes list box.
e. Click the Insert & Close button.
f. At the Find and Replace dialog box make sure there is nothing in the Replace with text box (or the word <Nothing>) and then click the Replace All button.
g. At the message box telling you how many occurrences were replaced, click OK.
h. Click the Close button to close the Find and Replace dialog box.
4. Save, print, and then close Ch 13, Ex 04.

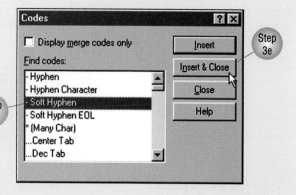

Turning On Line Numbering

With options at the Line Numbering dialog box shown in figure 13.6, you can tell WordPerfect to number each line as it is being printed. To turn on line numbering, click Format, point to Line, and then click Numbering. At the Line Numbering dialog box, click in the Turn line numbering on check box to insert a check mark. Other options available in this dialog box are explained in figure 13.7.

F I G U R E

13.6 *Line Numbering Dialog Box*

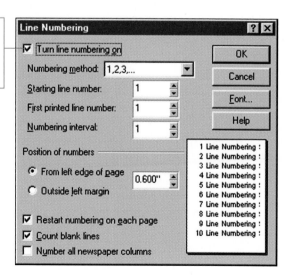

Numbering <u>m</u>ethod	By default, WordPerfect uses Arabic numbers; you can change this by clicking on the down-pointing triangle at the right side of the Numbering <u>m</u>ethod text box and selecting the desired method. Your choices are: a, b, c; A, B, C; i, ii, iii; or I, II, III.
<u>S</u>tarting line number	As a default, line numbering starts with 1. You can select this number and change it to a different number.
F<u>i</u>rst printed line number	This option allows you to specify the first line number that will print. For example, if you don't want the first 10 lines to print, enter 11 in this text box.
<u>N</u>umbering interval	The default numbering interval is 1; change this number to set a different numbering interval.
From left edge of <u>p</u>age	As a default, line numbers print 0.6 inch from the left edge of the page. You can change this number, but you must make sure the left margin is large enough to accommodate whatever measurement you enter.
Outside <u>l</u>eft margin	If you choose this option, you can enter a measurement from the left margin to the line number. In other words, if you enter 0.25 as the measurement, the numbers will print 0.25 inch to the left of the left margin. If you change the left margin, the numbering will still remain the same distance from the left margin.
Restart numbering on <u>e</u>ach page	As a default, WordPerfect starts numbering over at the beginning of each page. Deselect this option to number lines consecutively throughout the document.
<u>C</u>ount blank lines	By default, blank lines are numbered. Deselect this option if you do not want blank lines numbered.
N<u>u</u>mber all newspaper columns	If your document contains newspaper columns, select this option to number the lines in each column.

When line numbering is turned on, line numbers appear in the editing window. In Page or Draft viewing mode, you may need to scroll the text on the screen to the right to see the line numbers.

Adding Line Numbering to a Document

1. Open Legal 01.
2. Save the document with Save As and name it Ch 13, Ex 05.
3. Complete the following find and replaces:
   a. Find *NAME1* and replace with *DAVID R. AMES.*
   b. Find *NAME2* and replace with *SALLY M. ROJAS.*
   c. Find *NUMBER* and replace with *C-7754.*
4. With the insertion point positioned at the beginning of the document, turn on line numbering by completing the following steps:
   a. Click Format, point to Line, and then click Numbering.
   b. At the Line Numbering dialog box, click in the Turn line numbering on check box to insert a check mark.
   c. Click OK.
5. Save and print Ch 13, Ex 05.
6. With Ch 13, Ex 05 still displayed in the editing window, display Reveal Codes, and then delete the *Ln Num: On* code.
7. With the insertion point positioned at the beginning of the document, turn on line numbering with uppercase letters that are 0.3 inch from the left edge of the page by completing the following steps:
   a. Click Format, point to Line, and then click Numbering.
   b. At the Line Numbering dialog box, click the Turn line numbering on check box to insert a check mark.
   c. Click the down-pointing triangle at the right side of the Numbering method text box.
   d. At the drop-down menu that displays, click *A,B,C.*
   e. Make sure the From left edge of page option is selected. (If not, click in the radio button preceding the option.)
   f. Click the down-pointing triangle at the right of the Outside left margin text box until *0.300"* displays.
   g. Click OK.
8. Save, print, and then close Ch 13, Ex 05.

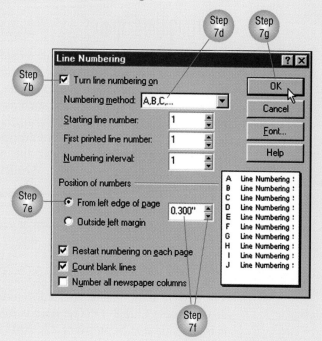

Displaying Symbols

When you press the spacebar, Enter key, Tab key, or a variety of other keys, a symbol is inserted in the document. By default, these symbols are not displayed in the editing window. To turn on the display of symbols, click <u>V</u>iew and then <u>S</u>how ¶. When the display of symbols is turned on, the editing screen will look similar to the one shown in figure 13.8. To turn off the display of symbols, click <u>V</u>iew and then <u>S</u>how ¶.

FIGURE

13.8 **Document with Symbols Displayed**

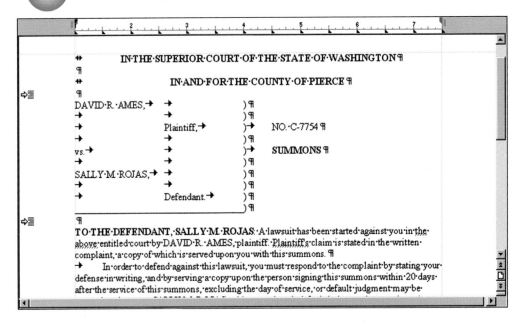

Inserting Hard Spaces

As you key text in a document, WordPerfect makes line-end decisions and automatically wraps text to the next line. Even though word wrap is helpful, there may be times when word wrap breaks up words or phrases that should remain together. For example, a name such as *Katherine L. Brynn* can be broken after, but should not be broken before, the initial *L.* The phrase *World War II* can be broken between *World* and *War* but should not be broken between *War* and *II.* To control what text is wrapped to the next line, a hard space can be inserted between words. When a hard space is inserted, WordPerfect considers the words as one unit and will not divide them.

To insert a hard space, press Ctrl + spacebar. This inserts a code in the document that can be seen in Reveal Codes as *HSpace*.

Inserting the Date

The current date can be inserted in a document as text or a code. To insert the date as text, press Ctrl + D. The date is inserted as month, day, and year. For example, if today's date is September 23, 2003, it will be inserted as September 23, 2003. When you insert the date as text, the date is considered text and can be edited.

If you insert the date as a code, the date the document is opened is inserted in the document. The date displays as text on the screen, but as a code in Reveal Codes. For example, if you insert the date code in a document created on April 21, 2003, that is the date that will appear. If you open the document on May 6, 2003, the date April 21, 2003, is replaced with May 6, 2003. To insert a date as a code in a document, press Ctrl + Shift + D. A date code cannot be edited once it is inserted in a document.

Displaying Symbols and Inserting Hard Spaces

1. At a clear editing window, complete the following steps:
   a. Turn on the display of symbols by clicking <u>V</u>iew and then <u>S</u>how ¶.
   b. Change the left and right margins to 1.75 inches.
   c. Key the memo shown in figure 13.9 in an appropriate memo format.
   d. Insert the date as text by pressing Ctrl + D.
   e. Insert hard spaces between the commands in the memo (for example, between Ctrl + B and Ctrl + I). Insert a hard space by pressing Ctrl + spacebar. Insert a hard space before and after the plus symbol in all the shortcut commands.
2. Save the memo and name it Ch 13, Ex 06.
3. Print and then close Ch 13, Ex 06.
4. Turn off the display of symbols by clicking <u>V</u>iew and then <u>S</u>how ¶.

FIGURE

13.9 *Exercise 6*

DATE: (current date)

TO: All Medical Transcribers

FROM: Debra Wong

SUBJECT: SHORTCUT COMMANDS

As we transition to Corel WordPerfect 10, I will continue offering helpful hints to all medical transcribers.

Character formatting can be applied at the Font dialog box. At this dialog box, you are offered a wide variety of formatting options. To apply formatting quickly, you can use shortcut commands rather than the Font dialog box. For example, use Ctrl + B to bold text. To italicize text such as book and magazine titles, press Ctrl + I. Additional shortcut commands include Ctrl + U to underline text and Ctrl + F to display the Find and Replace dialog box.

xx:Ch 13, Ex 06

Changing the Date Format

The date can be inserted in a document at the Date/Time dialog box shown in figure 13.10. The date format can also be changed at this dialog box. To display the Date/Time dialog box, click Insert and then Date/Time.

FIGURE

13.10 *Date/Time Dialog Box*

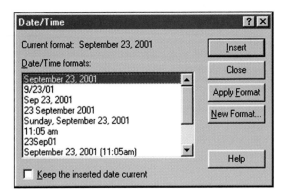

The Date/Time formats list box displays a variety of options for inserting the date and/or time in a document. To make a choice, double-click the desired option or click the desired option and then click Insert.

If the Date/Time dialog box does not contain the option you desire for displaying the date and/or time in a document, you can create your own custom display at the Custom Date/Time Format dialog box shown in figure 13.11. To display this dialog box, click the New Format button in the Date/Time dialog box.

FIGURE

13.11 *Custom Date/Time Format Dialog Box*

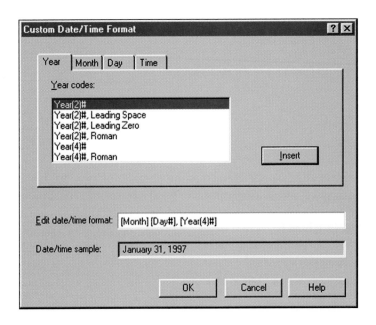

At the Custom Date/Time Format dialog box, you can choose the individual codes you want to use to display the date and/or time. At the bottom of the dialog box, the Date/time sample section shows how the date will display with the codes currently displayed in the Edit date/time format text box. To change the display, add codes to or delete codes from the Edit date/time format text box. As you add or delete codes, the display after the Date/time sample section changes.

To insert a date or time code in the Edit date/time format text box, click the desired tab for Year, Month, Day, or Time. With the desired tab selected, select the required code, and then click the Insert button. When all codes have been added or deleted, click OK.

Inserting a Date Code

1. Open Memo 01.
2. Save the document with Save As and name it Ch 13, Ex 07.
3. Make the following changes:
   a. Delete the date October 21, 2002.
   b. Insert the date as a code by pressing Ctrl + Shift + D.
4. Save and print Ch 13, Ex 07.
5. With Ch 13, Ex 07 still open in the editing window, display Reveal Codes and then delete the *Date* code.
6. Insert the date in the military format by completing the following steps:
   a. Position the insertion point where the date is to be located.
   b. Click Insert and then Date/Time.
   c. At the Date/Time dialog box, click *23 September 2001* in the Date/Time formats list box. (This date will vary.)
   d. Click Insert
7. Save, print, and then close Ch 13, Ex 07.

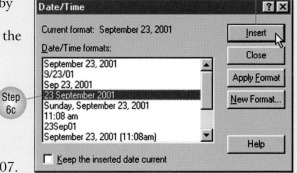

Step 6d

Step 6c

Converting the Case of Letters

With the Convert Case option from the Edit menu, you can convert the case of selected letters to uppercase, lowercase, or initial capitals. Click Edit, point to Convert Case, and then click lowercase and WordPerfect changes selected letters to lowercase except the word *I*, words starting with *I* followed by an apostrophe such as *I've* and *I'm*, and the first letter of the first word of a sentence. You can also change the case of selected text to uppercase letters by clicking the UPPERCASE option or capitalize the first letter of each word by clicking the Initial Capitals option.

WordPerfect also provides the shortcut command, Ctrl + K, to convert the case of selected text. If selected text displays in lowercase letters, pressing Ctrl + K changes the text to uppercase. If selected text displays in uppercase, pressing Ctrl + K changes the text to lowercase.

Converting the Case of Selected Text

1. Open Report 04.
2. Save the document with Save As and name it Ch 13, Ex 08.
3. Make the following changes to the document:
   a. Change the font to 12-point Century Schoolbook (or a similar serif typeface).
   b. Turn on the Widow/Orphan feature.
   c. Convert the heading *World War I* to uppercase letters by completing the following steps:
      1) Select *World War I*.
      2) Click <u>E</u>dit, point to Con<u>v</u>ert Case, and then click <u>U</u>PPERCASE.
      3) Deselect the text.
   d. Convert the heading *World War II* to uppercase letters by selecting *World War II* and then pressing Ctrl + K.
4. Convert the case of the headings *Korean War* and *Cold War and Vietnam* to uppercase letters by completing steps similar to step 3c or 3d.
5. Save, print, and then close Ch 13, Ex 08.

Using the Prompt-As-You-Go Feature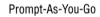

Prompt-As-You-Go

In previous chapters, you have learned about WordPerfect's spell checking, thesaurus, and grammar checking features. WordPerfect offers another method for correcting the spelling of text or grammar in a document as well as displaying synonyms for specific words. This feature, called Prompt-As-You-Go, is available as a button on the Main property bar. When the insertion point is positioned on a misspelled word or a word with a grammar error, click the down-pointing triangle at the right side of the Prompt-As-You-Go button on the Main property bar and a drop-down list of possible corrections displays. Position the insertion point on a word that is spelled correctly, click the down-pointing triangle at the right side of the Prompt-As-You-Go button, and a drop-down list of synonyms displays.

The Prompt-As-You-Go feature is turned on by default. To turn the feature off, click <u>T</u>ools, point to Proof<u>r</u>ead, and then click <u>P</u>rompt-As-You-Go. This removes the check mark from the option. Complete the same steps to turn the feature back on.

exercise 9

Using the Prompt-As-You-Go Feature

1. Open Memo 05.
2. Save the document with Save As and name it Ch 13, Ex 09.
3. Make the following changes to the memo:
   a. Correct the spelling of *Febury* to *February*.

b. Use the Prompt-As-You-Go feature to correct *finel* by completing the following steps:
    1) Click on any letter in the word *finel* (located in the first sentence of the first paragraph).
    2) Click the down-pointing triangle at the right side of the Prompt-As-You-Go button located at the right side of the Main property bar.
    3) At the drop-down list that displays, click *final*.

c. Complete steps similar to those in 3b to correct *establesh* (located in the second sentence of the second paragraph).

d. Complete steps similar to those in 3b to correct *wuld* (located in the last sentence of the second paragraph).

e. Use the Prompt-As-You-Go button on the Main property bar to change *establish* (located in the second sentence of the second paragraph) to *determine*. (If determine is not available, choose *institute*.)

4. Save, print, and then close Ch 13, Ex 09.

CHAPTER summary

➤ Use WordPerfect's hyphenation feature when the right margin of a left-justified document is particularly ragged, or when the lines in a full-justified document include large gaps of extra space.

➤ The default hyphenation zones of 10% and 4% can be changed. If the hyphenation zone is shortened, more words will be hyphenated. If the zone is lengthened, fewer words will be hyphenated.

➤ If the hyphenation zone is changed or if hyphenation is turned on, a code is inserted in the document at the beginning of the paragraph where the insertion point is located.

➤ Keying a minus sign in the document inserts a regular hyphen. A hyphen inserted by you during the hyphenation process is called a soft hyphen. Insert a hard hyphen in words or groups of numbers that should be kept together on one line.

➤ At the Line Numbering dialog box, you can tell WordPerfect to number each line as it is being printed.

➤ The display of symbols such as the spacebar and Enter key can be turned on by clicking View and then Show ¶.

➤ When a hard space is inserted between words, WordPerfect considers the words to be one unit and will not divide them.

➤ The current date can be inserted in a document as text or a code. The date format can be changed at the Date/Time dialog box or the Custom Date/Time Format dialog box.

➤ With the Convert Case option from the Edit drop-down menu, you have the options of converting the case of selected letters to uppercase, lowercase, or initial capitals. Use the shortcut command Ctrl + K to convert the case of selected text.

➤ Use the Prompt-As-You-Go button on the Main property bar to correct the spelling or grammar of text in a document as well as display synonyms for specific words.

COMMANDS summary

Command Line	Mouse	Keyboard
Display the Line Hyphenation dialog box	Tools, Language, Hyphenation	
Display the Line Numbering dialog box	Format, Line, Numbering	
Display symbols	View, Show ¶	Ctrl + Shift + F3
Insert date	Insert, Date/Time	Ctrl + D (text)
		Ctrl + Shift + D (code)
Convert case	Edit, Convert Case	Ctrl + K
Turn Prompt-As-You-Go on/off	Tools, Proofread, Prompt-As-You-Go	

CONCEPTS check

Completion: On a blank sheet of paper, indicate the correct term, symbol, or command for each item.

1. This is the default percentage for the left hyphenation zone.

2. This is the default percentage for the right hyphenation zone.

3. This is the command to insert a soft hyphen from the keyboard when hyphenation is off.

4. This is the command to insert a hard hyphen from the keyboard.

5. This is the command to insert a hard space from the keyboard.

6. Press this key to insert a regular hyphen.

7. With this option from the Edit drop-down menu, you can convert the case of selected letters to uppercase, lowercase, or initial capitals.

8. The Prompt-As-You-Go button is located on this bar.

SKILLS check

Assessment 1

1. Open Report 04.
2. Save the document with Save As and name it Ch 13, SA 01.
3. Make the following changes to the document:
   a. With the insertion point at the beginning of the document, turn on the Widow/Orphan feature.
   b. Display the Environment Settings dialog box with the Prompts tab selected and then change the On hyphenation option to *Always*.
   c. Change the left hyphenation zone to 5%, the right hyphenation zone to 0%, and turn on hyphenation. Hyphenate words in the document as required. Scroll to the end of the document to ensure that all necessary words are hyphenated.
4. Display the Environment Settings dialog box with the Prompts tab selected and then change the On hyphenation option back to *When Required*.
5. Save, print, and then close Ch 13, SA 01.

Assessment 2

1. Open Legal 02.
2. Save the document with Save As and name it Ch 13, SA 02.
3. Complete the following find and replaces:
   a. Find *NAME1* and replace with *MARY J. SLATER*.
   b. Find *NUMBER* and replace with *C-0334*.
   c. Find *Hd Left/Right Indent* codes and replace with *Hd Left Ind* codes.
4. With the insertion point positioned at the beginning of the document, make the following changes:
   a. Turn on line numbering. (Use the default settings at the Line Numbering dialog box.)
   b. Change the left hyphenation zone to 4%, the right hyphenation zone to 0%, and turn on hyphenation. Scroll to the end of the document to make sure any necessary words are hyphenated.
5. Save, print, and then close Ch 13, SA 02.

Assessment 3

1. At a clear editing window, create the memo shown in figure 13.12. Make the following changes:
   a. Change the left and right margins to 1.5 inches.
   b. Insert hard spaces within the keystroke commands to keep each command together.
   c. Insert the current date as text.
2. Save the memo and name it Ch 13, SA 03.
3. Print and then close Ch 13, SA 03.

DATE: (current date)

TO: All Medical Transcribers

FROM: Debra Wong

SUBJECT: SHORTCUT COMMANDS

As you continue working with Corel WordPerfect 10, you can display dialog boxes with options from the Menu bar or with shortcut commands. For example, you can insert the current date in a document with the command Ctrl + D or you can insert the date with options at the Date/Time dialog box.

Text can be aligned at the right margin with the Flush Right feature. Pressing Alt + F7 moves the insertion point to the right margin. You can also click the Flush Right option from the Format Line drop-down menu. You can convert the case of letters to uppercase, lowercase, or initial caps by clicking the Convert Case option from the Edit menu. Pressing Ctrl + K will convert between uppercase and lowercase text.

xx:Ch 13, SA 03

14

Presenting Text Using Special Features

PERFORMANCE OBJECTIVES

Upon successful completion of chapter 14, you will be able to:
- **Change the paper size and orientation**
- **Create and print envelopes**
- **Create and print labels**
- **Create a business document with different column styles**
- **Sort information in a properly prepared file**
- **Extract specific groups of information from a larger group**

Chapter 14

When a printer is installed, a standard page size is included. This page size is used to print text on regular-sized stationery (8.5 x 11 inches). In addition to the standard page size, a page size may also be included for legal-sized stationery (8.5 x 14 inches), envelopes, and labels. In this chapter, you will learn to change the paper size and orientation and to print envelopes and labels.

For some business documents, you may want to format text into columns. In WordPerfect, you can create newspaper columns and parallel columns. Newspaper columns contain text that flows up and down in the document while parallel columns contain text that is grouped across the page in rows. You will be creating and formatting documents with newspaper as well as parallel columns in this chapter.

WordPerfect 10 is a word processing program that includes some basic database functions that let you sort information alphabetically, numerically, or by date as well as extract specific records from a larger file. You will learn to use these features in this chapter.

Changing Paper Size

When a printer is selected, a few predesigned paper sizes are available that can be inserted in a document. For example, a wide stationery size or an envelope size can be inserted in a document. To change the paper size, display the Page setup dialog box with the Page

Setup tab selected as shown in figure 14.1. To display this dialog box, click File and then Page Setup. You can also click Format, point to Page, and then click Page Setup. Choose a different paper size by double-clicking the desired size in the list box.

Changing Page Orientation

At the Page setup dialog box with the Page Setup tab selected, the page orientation can be changed from the default of Portrait to Landscape. A preview displays following the two types of orientations visually representing how the page will be printed.

FIGURE

14.1 *Page Setup Dialog Box with Page Setup Tab Selected*

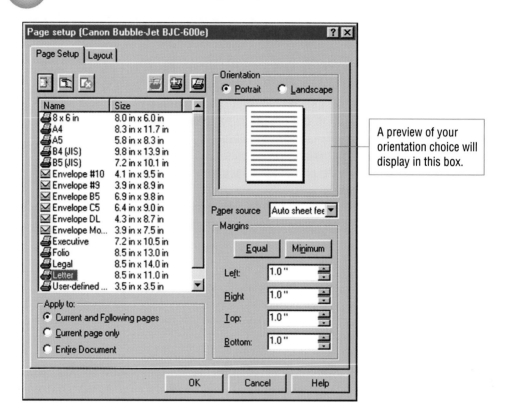

A preview of your orientation choice will display in this box.

exercise

Changing the Page Orientation to Landscape

1. Open Report 01.
2. Save the document with Save As and name it Ch 14, Ex 01.
3. Change the orientation to Landscape by completing the following steps:
   a. With the insertion point positioned somewhere on the first page, click File and then Page Setup.

b. At the Page setup dialog box, make sure the Page Setup tab is selected and then click the radio button immediately preceding the Landscape option.

c. Click OK to close the dialog box.

4. Turn on the Widow/Orphan feature.

5. Move the insertion point to the end of the document to adjust the soft page breaks. Check the location of page breaks to see if they are in desirable locations. If not, you may want to insert your own page break.

6. Save, print, and then close Ch 14, Ex 01. (Before printing, check with your instructor to determine whether the printer you are using is capable of landscape printing.)

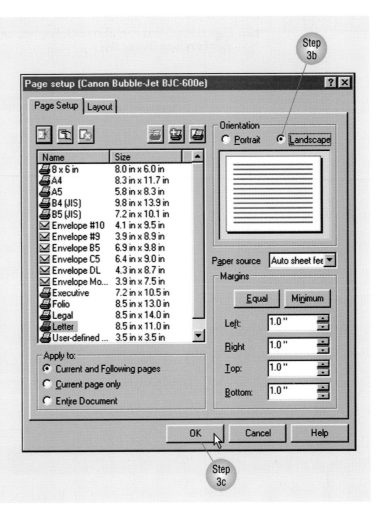

Step 3b

Step 3c

Using the Envelope Feature

You can use the Envelope feature to create an envelope in the current document or create an envelope using a return address and mailing address that you have specified.

Creating an Envelope at a Clear Editing Window

To create an envelope document at a clear editing window using the Envelope feature, click Format and then Envelope. The Envelope dialog box is displayed on the screen as shown in figure 14.2. Key the return address and the mailing address in the text boxes and click Create New to see the envelope or Print Envelope to send it directly to the printer. Follow the instructions given by WordPerfect or your printer.

FIGURE

14.2 *Envelope Dialog Box*

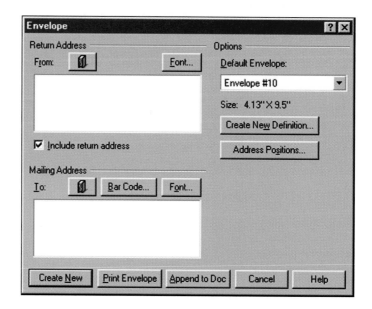

exercise 2

Creating an Envelope

1. At a clear editing window, create an envelope using the Envelope feature by completing the following steps:
   a. Click Format and then Envelope.
   b. In the Envelope dialog box, make sure the insertion point is positioned in the Return Address text box. If it is not, click inside the Return Address text box to position the insertion point. (If the Return Address text box already contains a name and address, select the name and address and then press the Delete key.)
   c. Key the return address shown in figure 14.3. (This is the name and address for Mrs. Michelle Ching.)
   d. Click inside the Mailing Address text box. (If the Mailing Address text box already contains a name and address, select the name and address and then press the Delete key.)
   e. Key the mailing address shown in figure 14.3. (This is the name and address for Mr. Scott Ingram.)
   f. Click Create New.
2. Save the document and name it Ch 14, Ex 02.
3. Print and then close Ch 14, Ex 02.

14.3 **Exercise 2**

Mrs. Michelle Ching
3320 Westside Drive
San Diego, CA 99432

Mr. Scott Ingram
860 South 52nd Street
San Diego, CA 99567

Creating an Envelope in an Existing Document

If you open the Envelope dialog box in a document containing a letter, the inside address in the letter is automatically inserted in the Mailing Address text box. The mailing address in the letter must be located at the left margin and there must be two hard returns following the address.

Click Append to Doc at the Envelope dialog box to add the envelope to the end of the document. WordPerfect automatically inserts a page break separating the envelope from the document.

Formatting Envelopes

To format an envelope, click File and then Page Setup. At the Page setup dialog box with the Page Setup tab selected, click the envelope definition you wish to edit. Click the Edit form button. At the Edit Form dialog box shown in figure 14.4, select from the following choices:

Edit Form

F I G U R E

14.4 **Edit Form Dialog Box**

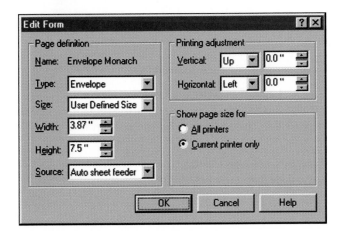

Type: Click the down-pointing triangle in the Type list box to select from various types of envelope stock as well as address labels.

Size: Click the down-pointing triangle in the Size list box to select from several built-in envelope sizes. Click *User Defined Size* if you want to create a new envelope definition.

Width: You can enter a specific envelope width in this text box by selecting the current value and entering a new value. The width of the currently selected envelope is automatically displayed in this box.

Height: You can enter a specific envelope height in this text box by selecting the current value and entering a new value. The height of the currently selected envelope is automatically displayed in this box.

Source: Click the down-pointing triangle to specify how the envelope will be fed into the printer. If you have an automatic envelope feeder, it should be listed here.

Printing adjustment: The two options available in this section, Vertical and Horizontal, allow you to control how much space to allocate for printing adjustment. Review your printer documentation to determine how much you should leave for printer adjustment.

Show page size for: If you are able to print to more than one printer, you can control whether WordPerfect displays envelope sizes for All printers or for the Current printer only.

Once you have set these options, click OK to close the Edit Form dialog box. When you have an envelope in the editing window, the Envelope property bar, as shown in figure 14.5, appears below the Toolbar.

FIGURE

14.5 *Envelope Property Bar*

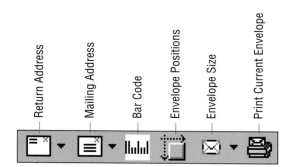

Return Address: Click this button to specify *No Return Address* or *Address Book*. If you select Address Book, you are taken to the CorelCENTRAL Address book where you can select an address to be inserted in the return address section of the envelope.

Mailing Address: Click this button to go to the CorelCENTRAL Address book to select a mailing address for the envelope.

Bar Code: Selecting this button displays the dialog box shown in figure 14.6. Use this dialog box to determine bar code position and ZIP Code (five-, nine-, or eleven-digit).

Envelope Positions: Select this option to display the dialog box shown in figure 14.7. This dialog box allows you to adjust the return address and mailing address positions on the envelope.

Envelope Size: Selecting this button displays the current envelope definitions for your printer. You can also access the Page setup dialog box from the list.

FIGURE 14.6 *POSTNET Bar Code Dialog Box*

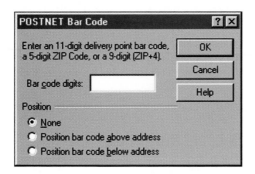

FIGURE 14.7 *Envelope Positions Dialog Box*

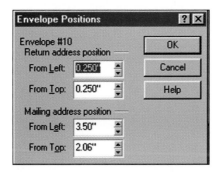

exercise 3

Creating an Envelope with a POSTNET Bar Code

1. Open Letter 01.
2. Create an envelope for the letter with a POSTNET Bar Code using the Envelope feature by completing the following steps:
   a. Click Format and then Envelope.
   b. In the Envelope dialog box, make sure the mailing address is inserted properly in the Mailing Address text box. (The Return Address text box should be empty.)
   c. Click the Bar Code button in the Mailing Address section.
   d. At the POSTNET Bar Code dialog box, select Position bar code below address.
   e. Click OK to close the POSTNET Bar Code dialog box.
   f. Click Append to Doc.

3. WordPerfect inserts a hard page break at the end of the letter and then inserts the envelope definition, name, address, and the POSTNET Bar Code. Change the zoom to Full Page to see how the address will print on the envelope and then change the zoom back to 100%.
4. Save the document and name it Ch 14, Ex 03.
5. Print only the page containing the envelope.
6. Close Ch 14, Ex 03.

Creating Labels

Use the Labels feature to print text on mailing labels, file labels, disk labels, or other types of labels. Corel WordPerfect 10 includes approximately 340 definitions for labels that can be purchased at an office supply store. If none of the predefined label definitions meet your requirements, you can create your own label definition.

Using a Predefined Label Definition

To use a predefined label definition in a document, click Format and then Labels. At the Labels dialog box shown in figure 14.8, click the desired label form in the Labels list box and then click the Select button. As you click different label forms in the Labels list box, details of the label form appear below the Labels list box. The Label details section includes information on the label form such as the sheet size, label size, number of labels, and the label type.

F I G U R E

14.8 **Labels Dialog Box**

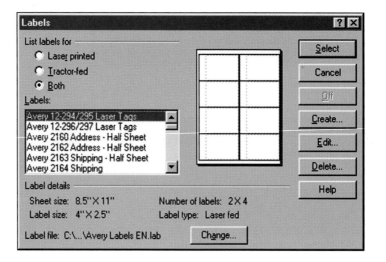

Entering Text in Labels

After inserting a label definition in a document, key the text for the labels. When entering text for labels, use the keys shown in figure 14.9 to perform the actions described.

14.9 *Key Combinations in Labels*

Ends text of current label and moves insertion point to next label. = Ctrl + ← Enter

Ends a line within a label. = ← Enter

Moves insertion point to next label. = Alt + Page Down

Moves insertion point to previous label. = Alt + Page Up

Moves insertion point to label number entered. = Edit, Go To, #

When entering text in a label, press Ctrl + Enter to insert a hard page break. The hard page break moves the insertion point to the next label. In a labels form, a page created with Ctrl + Enter is called a *logical page*, while the entire sheet is called the *physical page*. Each label is considered a separate page. Formatting features that affect a page such as page numbering or headers and footers will print on each label.

In a labels document, you may want to change the font to a smaller point size to ensure that all text fits on the label. You may also want to insert a code to center text on the current page and subsequent pages. This will vertically center the text on the label.

At the Page viewing mode, the label will display in white in the editing window surrounded by gray lines. When you press Ctrl + Enter, the insertion point moves to the next label. At the Draft viewing mode, you will not see the label. When you press Ctrl + Enter, a double line is inserted in the editing window, and the insertion point is moved below the double line. Change the zoom to full page to see how the labels will print on the page.

exercise *4*

Creating Labels

1. At a clear editing window, create mailing addresses using a predefined label definition by completing the following steps:
   a. Click Format and then Labels.

b. At the Labels dialog box, click the down-pointing triangle at the right of the <u>L</u>abels list box until *Avery 5160 Address* is visible and then click *Avery 5160 Address*. (This label is quite far down the labels list. Check with your instructor to see whether your printer will print this label form size. If not, use a different label form size.)

c. Click the <u>S</u>elect button.

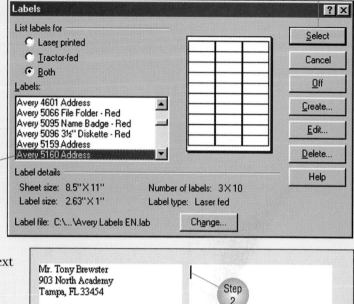

2. At the editing window, key the addresses shown in figure 14.10. Press Ctrl + Enter to end a label and move the insertion point to the next label.

3. After keying all the label addresses, press Ctrl + Home to move the insertion point to the beginning of the document and then insert a code to center current and subsequent pages.

4. Save the document and name it Ch 14, Ex 04.

5. Print and then close Ch 14, Ex 04. (Before printing, check with your instructor to make sure that the printer you are using can print a document with this label definition.)

F I G U R E

14.10 *Exercise 4*

Mr. Tony Brewster 903 North Academy Tampa, FL 33454	Dr. Dione Teague Madison Clinic 100 Madison Avenue Tampa, FL 33422	Ms. Lona Schauffer Southside Shipping 9873 Parker Road Tampa, FL 33512
Mrs. Elana Steffan 15403 South 42nd Street Tampa, FL 33541	Mr. Rodney Marlow 6320 South 32nd Tampa, FL 33453	Professor Lea Steele Bayside Community College 2300 North 51st Tampa, FL 33422

Printing Specific Labels

When you print a label page, the entire page is printed. You can, however, print individual labels. In chapter 10, you learned how to print individual pages in a document or a range of pages. You can do the same with labels.

To print consecutive labels, display the Print dialog box. At the Print dialog box, with the Main tab selected, click the radio button before Pages. Key the label numbers in the text box at the right of the Pages option. For example, to print labels 1, 4, 7, and 10, you would key **1,4,7,10** in the Pages text box. To print labels 14 through 22 and label 26, you would key **14-22,26**.

Creating a Form Document for Labels

A form document can be created for labels and can then be merged with a data file to create the labels. Exercise 5 demonstrates how this is done.

exercise 5

Creating a Label Form Document

1. At a clear editing window, create a label form document for printing mailing labels by completing the following steps:
   a. Click For̲mat and then La̲bels.
   b. At the Labels dialog box, click *Avery 5160 Address* in the L̲abels list box. (You will need to scroll down the list to display this label form. Check with your instructor to see whether your printer will print this label form size. If not, use a different label form size.)
   c. Click the S̲elect button.
   d. At the editing window (with the empty label displayed), click T̲ools and then Me̲rge.
   e. At the Merge dialog box, click the F̲orm document button and then C̲reate Form Document.
   f. At the Data File Source dialog box, make sure the U̲se file in active window option is selected and then click OK.
   g. At the Associate Form and Data dialog box, key **a:/Chapter 14/Customer df.dat** in the A̲ssociate a data file text box and then click OK.
   h. At the editing window, click the I̲nsert Field button on the Merge property bar.
   i. At the Insert Field Name or Number dialog box, double-click *title* in the F̲ield Names list box.

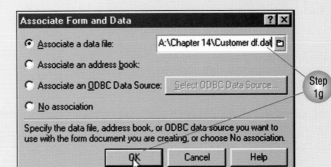

j. Continue inserting field names (*first name, last name, address*) in the appropriate location in the label. (The fields may wrap down a line and to the next label; this is okay. The *address* field contains the street address as well as the city, state, and ZIP.)

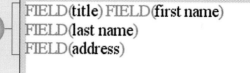

Step 1j

FIELD(title) FIELD(first name)
FIELD(last name)
FIELD(address)

k. When all field names have been inserted, click the <u>C</u>lose button to close the Insert Field Name or Number dialog box.

l. Close the Merge dialog box.

m. Save the labels form document in the regular manner and name it Labels fd.

2. With Labels fd still open, merge the labels to the printer by completing the following steps:

a. Click the <u>M</u>erge button on the Merge property bar.

b. At the Merge dialog box, click the O<u>u</u>tput button and then click <u>P</u>rinter at the drop-down menu.

c. Click the <u>M</u>erge button.

3. After the labels print, close Labels fd.

Creating Columns

When creating some business documents, you may want to set up the text in columns. In WordPerfect, you can create newspaper columns and parallel columns. Newspaper columns contain text that flows up and down in the document. When the first column on the page is filled with text, the insertion point moves to the top of the next column on the same page. When the last column on the page is filled with text, the insertion point moves to the beginning of the first column on the next page. Figure 14.11 illustrates newspaper columns.

FIGURE

14.11 *Newspaper Columns*

Text flows from top to bottom in the first column…

…then to the top of the next column and so on.

Creating Newspaper Columns with the Columns Button

The Toolbar contains a Columns button for creating newspaper columns. To use this button, click the Columns button on the Toolbar and then click the desired number of columns at the drop-down list that displays.

Columns

Newspaper columns can be defined before keying the text, or the columns can be defined in existing text. If you are defining newspaper columns in existing text, position the insertion point at the location where the columns are to begin, and then define the columns.

Editing Text in Columns

To edit text set up in columns, move the insertion point with the mouse or insertion point movement keys and commands either within columns or between columns.

Moving the Insertion Point within Columns

To move the insertion point in a document using the mouse, position the arrow pointer where desired and then click the left button. If you are using the keyboard, the insertion point movement keys—up, down, left, and right arrows—cause the insertion point to move in the direction indicated.

Moving the Insertion Point between Columns

You can use the mouse or the keyboard to move the insertion point between columns. If you are using the mouse, position the arrow pointer where desired, and then click the left button. If you are using the keyboard, use the insertion point movement commands shown in figure 14.12.

FIGURE

14.12 *Insertion Point Movement between Columns*

Move insertion point to next column	Alt + →
Move insertion point to previous column	Alt + ←
Move insertion point to last line of column	Alt + End
Move insertion point to top of column	Alt + Home

Creating Newspaper Columns Using the Columns Button

1. Open Report 02.
2. Save the document with Save As and name it Ch 14, Ex 06.
3. Make the following changes to the document:
   a. Display Reveal Codes, delete the *Ln Spacing: 2.0* code that displays toward the beginning of the document, and then close Reveal Codes.
   b. With the insertion point positioned at the beginning of the document, make sure the Ruler is displayed and then set a left tab at the 1.25-inch mark on the Ruler.
   c. Move the insertion point to the beginning of the first paragraph (the paragraph that begins *Most of the major developments...*) and then press the Enter key.
   d. Insert a hard return (by pressing Enter) above each of the following headings:

   > *Contributions of Major Historical Events*
   > *Development of a World Market*
   > *The American Civil War*
   > *Colonization*
   > *The 1870s Depression*

4. Define two newspaper columns by completing the following steps:
   a. Position the insertion point at the left margin of the first paragraph in the document (begins with *Most of the major developments in telecommunications technology...*).
   b. Click the Columns button on the Toolbar.
   c. At the drop-down list that displays, click *2 Columns*.

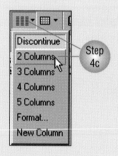

5. Save, print, and then close Ch 14, Ex 06.

Creating Newspaper Columns with the Columns Dialog Box

Newspaper columns can be created with the Columns button and also with options at the Columns dialog box shown in figure 14.13. The Columns dialog box can be used to create newspaper columns that are evenly or unevenly spaced. To display the Columns dialog box, click Fo<u>r</u>mat and then <u>C</u>olumns. You can also display the Columns dialog box by clicking the Columns button on the Toolbar and then clicking *Format* at the drop-down list.

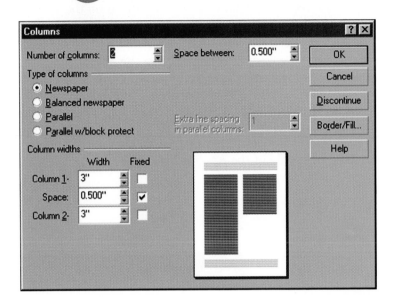

14.13 *Columns Dialog Box*

The Number of columns option has a default setting of 2. This number can be changed by keying a new number or by clicking the up- or down-pointing triangle next to the Number of columns text box. The number of columns is only limited to the space available on the page.

By default, columns are separated by 0.5 inch of space. This space between columns is referred to as the *gutter*. The amount of space between columns can be increased or decreased with the Space between option. At this option, key a new measurement for the spacing or click the up- or down-pointing triangle next to the text box.

The Type of columns section of the dialog box contains four options: Newspaper, Balanced newspaper, Parallel, and Parallel w/block protect. The default setting is Newspaper. The Balanced newspaper option is like the Newspaper option, except each column is adjusted on the page to be as equal in length as possible. To change the type of column, click the radio button preceding the desired option.

If you create parallel columns, WordPerfect automatically inserts a blank line between the longest entry in a row and the first entry of the next row. With the Extra line spacing in parallel columns option, you can increase or decrease this number. You will be creating parallel columns later in this chapter.

WordPerfect automatically determines column widths for the number of columns specified. By default, column widths are the same. If you want to enter your own column widths or change the amount of space between columns, choose the desired column and then key a measurement in the text box or click the up- or down-pointing triangle next to the column text box. These text boxes are located in the Column widths section of the dialog box.

Fixed check boxes are located at the right of the Column widths options. Insert a check mark in a Fixed check box if you want the width of the columns or space between columns to remain fixed regardless of what changes are made to the document margins or other column widths.

Columns that have been defined in a document can be discontinued with the Discontinue button at the Columns dialog box or with the Columns button. To discontinue columns with the Columns button, position the insertion point where columns are to be discontinued, click the Columns button on the Toolbar, and then click *Discontinue* at the drop-down list. To discontinue columns with the Columns dialog box, display the dialog box and then click the Discontinue button.

If you want to end a newspaper column before the end of the page, insert a hard page break by pressing Ctrl + Enter or by clicking Insert and then New Page. When a hard page break is inserted, the insertion point moves to the beginning of the next column on the same page. If the hard page break is inserted in the last column on the page, the insertion point moves to the first column on the next page. When the insertion point is located in a newspaper column, the column number displays toward the right side of the Application bar.

Creating Balanced Newspaper Columns

1. Open Report 08.
2. Save the document with Save As and name it Ch 14, Ex 07.
3. Make the following changes to the document:
   a. Display Reveal Codes, delete the *Ln Spacing: 2.0* code that displays toward the beginning of the document, and then close Reveal Codes.
   b. Insert a hard return (by pressing Enter) above the following headings in the document:

   > *Introduction*
   > *Purpose and Scope*
   > *Application*
   > *Requirements*

   c. Move the insertion point to the beginning of the document, make sure the Ruler is displayed, and then add a left tab at the 1.25-inch mark.
   d. Position the insertion point at the left margin of the line containing *Introduction* and then define three balanced newspaper columns by completing the following steps:
      1) Click Format and then Columns.

2) At the Columns dialog box, key **3** in the Number of <u>c</u>olumns text box.
3) Select <u>B</u>alanced newspaper in the Type of columns section.
4) Change the measurement in the <u>S</u>pace between text box to 0.300" by clicking the down-pointing triangle after the <u>S</u>pace between text box until *0.300"* displays.
5) Click OK.

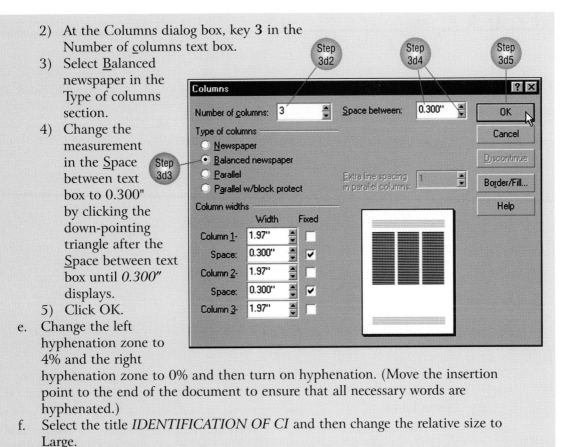

e. Change the left hyphenation zone to 4% and the right hyphenation zone to 0% and then turn on hyphenation. (Move the insertion point to the end of the document to ensure that all necessary words are hyphenated.)

f. Select the title *IDENTIFICATION OF CI* and then change the relative size to Large.

4. Save, print, and then close Ch 14, Ex 07.

Creating Parallel Columns

Parallel columns contain text that is grouped across the page in rows as shown in figure 14.14. The next row begins a double space below the longest column of the previous row. Parallel columns can be used to create documents such as an agenda, itinerary, résumé, or address list.

14.14 *Parallel Columns*

To create parallel columns, display the Columns dialog box, specify the number of columns, click Parallel in the Type of columns section, and then click OK or press Enter.

After parallel columns have been defined, key the text for the first column, and then insert a hard page break. The hard page break moves the insertion point to the next column. To insert a hard page break, press Ctrl + Enter, or click Insert and then New Page. When a hard page break is inserted in the last column in a document, the insertion point moves to the left margin a double space below the longest column entry. When you key text in columns, the word wrap feature will wrap text to the next line within the column.

At the Columns dialog box, parallel columns can be created with block protect. If you click Parallel w/block protect at the Columns dialog box, WordPerfect keeps all columns in a row together. If one column is too long to fit on a page, all the columns in the row are moved to the next page. If you define parallel columns without block protect, a row of columns may be divided between two pages.

As with newspaper columns, the parallel column number where the insertion point is located displays toward the right side of the Application bar.

Creating Parallel Columns

1. At a clear editing window, create the document shown in figure 14.15 by completing the following steps:
   a. Center and bold the title **PATIENT SATISFACTION** and then press the Enter key twice.
   b. Define three parallel columns by completing the following steps:

1) Click Format and then Columns.
2) At the Columns dialog box, key **3** in the Number of columns text box.

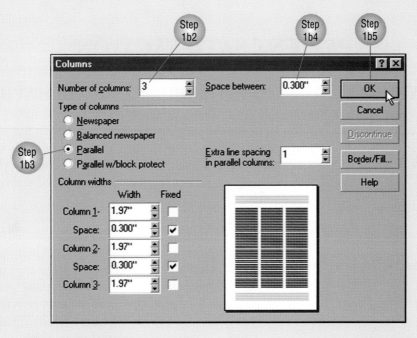

3) Click the radio button immediately preceding the Parallel option in the Type of columns section.
4) Change the Space between measurement to *0.300"*.
5) Click OK.
c. Key the text in columns by completing the following steps:
   1) Center and bold the heading *VALUE* and then press Ctrl + Enter to move the insertion point to the next column.
   2) Center and bold the heading *ATTITUDE* and then press Ctrl + Enter to move the insertion point to the next column.
   3) Center and bold the heading *BEHAVIOR* and then press Ctrl + Enter to move the insertion point to the first column, below *VALUE*.
   4) Key the text **Individualized patient care** and then press Ctrl + Enter.
   5) Continue keying the text in columns as shown in figure 14.15. Press Ctrl + Enter to move from column to column. Let the word wrap feature wrap text within columns (do not press Enter).
d. After keying the text in columns, select the title *PATIENT SATISFACTION* and then change the relative size to Very large.
e. Select the following text and then change the relative size to Large:

   VALUE
   ATTITUDE
   BEHAVIOR

2. Save the document and name it Ch 14, Ex 08.
3. Print and then close Ch 14, Ex 08.

PATIENT SATISFACTION

VALUE	ATTITUDE	BEHAVIOR
Individualized patient care	Concern for the person; recognize that everyone is a unique person; recognize importance of patient's problem	Use patient's name; remember details about the patient's routine; provide personalized service
Respect for individual	Acceptance of physical disabilities, personalities, and cultural differences; tolerance and appreciation of differences	Handle patient situations with respect and tact; prepare personalized care plan; make sure they know you and you know them; provide for patient's individual needs for privacy and respect
Need for control and freedom of choice	Respect for patient competence; understanding patients can take care of themselves	Explain environment; give choices; explain what is happening; involve patient in scheduling when possible
Being treated as a guest	Understand and respect that patient has fear; care for the whole person; treat people as guests	Respond to nonverbal cues; talk about fears; ask patient's opinion; do not rush treatment; maintain respect for family interaction; take time to allow patient to adjust

Changing Column Widths with the Ruler

The options in the Column widths section of the Columns dialog box can be used to change the width of columns as well as determine the space between columns. You can also make these changes using the Ruler. (If the Ruler is not displayed, click View and then Ruler.) Column width and column markers display on the Ruler in a document set in newspaper or parallel columns as shown in figure 14.16.

14.16 *Column Markers on the Ruler*

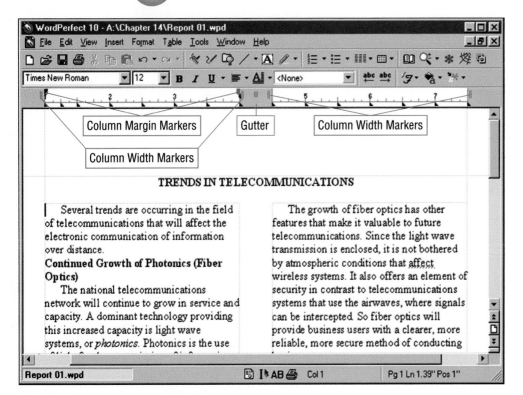

Use the column margin markers shown in figure 14.16 to change left and right column margins. Use the column width markers to change column width. When changing column margins or widths, position the insertion point on the line where the column definition code is located because the change will affect the code. Position the arrow pointer on the desired marker, hold down the left mouse button, drag the marker to the desired position, and then release the mouse button.

The gray space on the Ruler between column markers is referred to as the *gutter*. You can move the gutter along the Ruler. To do this, position the arrow pointer in the gutter, hold down the left mouse button, drag the gutter to the desired position, and then release the mouse button. The tab markers on the Ruler can also be dragged to a new location with the mouse.

Inserting Column Lines and Borders

Text in columns can be separated by a vertical line, or you can insert column borders around all columns in a document. A vertical line can be inserted between columns by clicking Insert, Line, and then Vertical Line. This inserts a solid line from the location of the insertion point to the end of the page. Vertical lines can also be inserted between columns with options from the Column Border/Fill dialog box. Display this dialog box by clicking Format, Columns, and then clicking the Border/ Fill button. When you use this dialog box to insert vertical lines, the lines are solid for newspaper columns but broken for parallel columns.

Figure 14.17 shows a document containing newspaper columns with a vertical line between columns. Figure 14.18 shows the same document with a column border around and between the columns. Figure 14.19 shows a document containing parallel columns with vertical lines inserted between columns. Figures 14.17, 14.18, and 14.19 show a single line between and/or around the columns. The border can be changed to a variety of other styles.

FIGURE

14.17 *Newspaper Columns with Vertical Lines*

FIGURE

14.18 *Newspaper Columns with Borders*

14.19 *Parallel Columns with Vertical Lines*

Inserting a Vertical Graphics Line

A vertical graphics line is inserted at the Create Graphics Line dialog box. The vertical graphics line begins at the position of the insertion point and continues down the page to the bottom margin. This vertical line is inserted between the first and second columns by default. Lines between columns two and three or three and four must be created separately.

Creating Vertical Lines between Columns

1. Open Ch 14, Ex 07.
2. Save the document with Save As and name it Ch 14, Ex 09.
3. Insert a vertical graphics line between the first and second columns by completing the following steps:
   a. Position the insertion point at the left margin of the line containing *Introduction*. (Make sure the insertion point is to the right of the column definition code.)
   b. Click Insert, point to Line, and then click Custom Line.

c. At the Create Graphics Line dialog box, click the radio button immediately preceding the Vertical line option (located toward the top of the dialog box).

d. Click the down-pointing triangle at the right side of the Horizontal text box located in the Position on page section and then click *Column Aligned* at the drop-down menu.

e. Click the down-pointing triangle at the right side of the Vertical text box and then click *Set* at the drop-down menu.

f. Click OK.

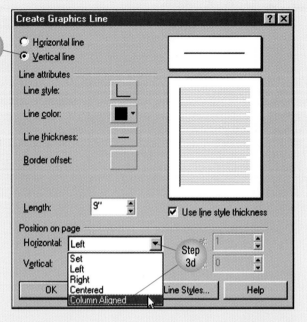

4. Insert a vertical graphics line between the second and third columns by completing the following steps:

a. With the insertion point still positioned at the left margin of the line containing *Introduction*, click Insert, point to Line, and then click Custom Line.

b. At the Create Graphics Line dialog box, click the radio button immediately preceding the Vertical line option.

c. Click the down-pointing triangle at the right side of the Horizontal text box and then click *Column Aligned* at the drop-down menu.

d. Key **2** in the After Col text box.

e. Click the down-pointing triangle at the right side of the Vertical text box and then click *Set* at the drop-down menu.

f. Click OK.

5. Save, print, and then close Ch 14, Ex 09.

Inserting Borders and Fill

Customize columns with options at the Column Border/Fill dialog box shown in figure 14.20. Display this dialog box by clicking the Border/Fill button at the Columns dialog box. The border choices are visually represented in the Available border styles list box. The lines can be customized with different line styles using the Line style button or with different colors using the Color button.

FIGURE

14.20 *Column Border/Fill Dialog Box*

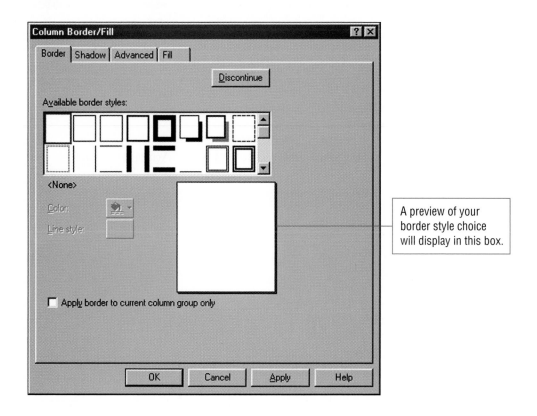

A preview of your border style choice will display in this box.

If you are inserting lines between newspaper columns, the lines will continue down the page to the end of the columns on the page. If you are inserting lines between parallel columns, the lines will be inserted between only one row of columns. If you want the lines inserted between each row of columns, make sure there is no check mark in the Apply border to current column group only option.

Inserting a Border

A border can be inserted around columns of text with the Available border styles option from the Column Border/Fill dialog box. The border option will insert a border around columns but not between columns.

exercise 10

Inserting a Line Border

1. Open Ch 14, Ex 08.
2. Save the document with Save As and name it Ch 14, Ex 10.
3. Insert a border between the parallel columns by completing the following steps:
   a. Position the insertion point on the line containing *Individualized patient care*.
   b. Click Format and then Columns.
   c. At the Columns dialog box, click the Border/Fill button.
   d. At the Column Border/Fill dialog box, scroll to the end of the Available border styles list box, and then click the Column Between option (seventh option from the left in the second-to-the-last row [the sixth option is blank]).
   e. If there is a check mark in the Apply border to current column group only check box, click this option to remove the check mark.
   f. Click OK to close the Column Border/Fill dialog box.
   g. Click OK to close the Columns dialog box.
4. Save, print, and then close Ch 14, Ex 10.

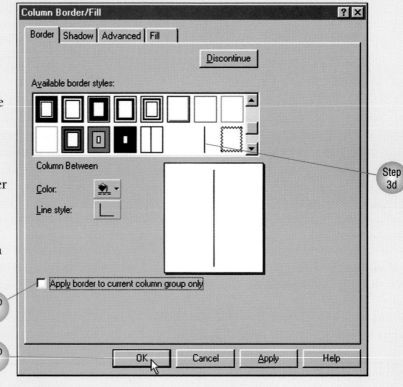

Sorting Text

Text in a line, paragraph, data file, parallel columns, or a table can be sorted alphanumerically (letters and digits), numerically (numbers), or by date. To sort text, click Tools and then Sort. This displays the Sort dialog box shown in figure 14.21.

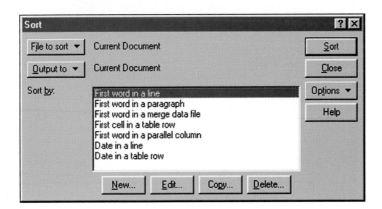

Specifying the Sort Document and the Output Document

At the Sort dialog box, the File to sort option and the Output to option are both set at *Current Document*. At this setting, text in the current document is sorted and the results of the sort replace the current document. To sort text in a document other than the one currently displayed, click the File to sort option at the Sort dialog box. At the drop-down menu, click File on Disk. At the Select Input File dialog box that displays, double-click the desired document in the list box. To specify the output file, click the Output to option at the Sort dialog box and then click File on Disk. At the Select Output File dialog box, key the document name for the output file or click a document name in the list box, and then click the Select button.

Specifying the Type of Sort

Predefined sorts are displayed in the Sort by list box at the Sort dialog box. The kind of sort selected will vary depending on the document to be sorted. For example, if you open a document containing a table, the *First cell in a table row* option is selected. If this is the kind of sort you want to complete, click the Sort button. WordPerfect sorts the contents of the first cell in each table row and rearranges them alphabetically in ascending order (A to Z).

Sorting a List

1. At a clear editing window, key the text shown in figure 14.22 at the left margin.
2. Save the document and name it Ch 14, Ex 11.
3. Sort the list alphabetically by last name by completing the following steps:
   a. Click Tools and then Sort.

b. At the Sort dialog box, make sure *First word in a line* is selected in the Sort by list box and then click the Sort button.

4. Save, print, and then close Ch 14, Ex 11.

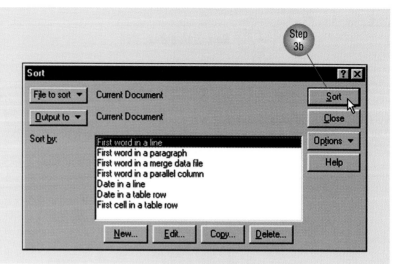

Step 3b

F I G U R E

14.22 *Exercise 11*

Hess, Joanna. *Desktop Publishing Projects*. Seneca, NY: Thousand Pines Publishing, 2002.
Ulrich, Thomas. *Personal Desktop Publishing*. St. Paul, MN: Patterson Publishers, 2001.
Capelino, George. *Desktop Publishing Guidebook*. Arlington, VA: Myers Press, 2003.
Bove, Emil. *Proofreading and Editing Documents*. Miami, FL: Palm West Publishers, 2002.

Creating a New Sort

With the predefined sorts, WordPerfect sorts the first line, paragraph, column, record, or row in a document. If you want to sort on different text, you must either create a new sort or edit an existing sort. To create a new sort, click the New button at the Sort dialog box. This causes the New Sort dialog box to display as shown in figure 14.23.

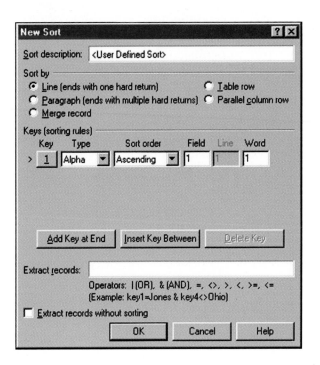

Editing a Sort

If you decide to sort on different text, you can edit an existing sort. To edit a sort, display the Sort dialog box, select the sort listed in the Sort by list box, and then click Edit. This causes the Edit Sort dialog box to display. The Edit Sort dialog box contains the same options as the New Sort dialog box shown in figure 14.23. Make any necessary changes to this dialog box and then click OK.

Naming a Sort

At the New Sort dialog box, key a name for the new sort in the Sort description text box. The name can contain spaces and should be unique from other sort type names.

Determining What to Sort By

At the New Sort dialog box, specify what you want to sort by in the Sort by section. You can choose to sort text in lines, paragraphs, merge records, rows in a table, or text in parallel columns. Figure 14.24 displays the definitions of the sort options.

14.24 *Sort By Definitions*

Sort By	Sort Definition
Line (ends with one hard return)	Text that ends in a hard return.
Paragraph (ends with multiple hard returns)	Text that ends with two or more hard returns.
Merge record	Record that ends with an **ENDRECORD** code.
Table row	A row of cells in a table.
Parallel column row	Each record in a row of columns.

WordPerfect automatically determines the kind of sort based on the sort document. For example, if you sort a document containing text at tab settings, WordPerfect selects the Line (ends with one hard return) option. If you sort a document containing records in a data file, WordPerfect automatically selects the Merge record option. WordPerfect selects Table row if the document to be sorted contains a table. If you sort a document with text in parallel columns, the Parallel column row option is selected.

Defining Keys

With options in the Keys (sorting rules) section of the New Sort dialog box you can define the type of sort. WordPerfect gives key 1 first priority, key 2 second priority, and so on. A sort can be performed on more than one key. For example, you can sort states alphabetically and then sort the last names of individuals alphabetically within each state.

By default, there is one key defined. The settings for key 1 will vary depending on the text in the editing window or in the file identified for sorting.

Defining the Sort Type

The key type can be *Alpha, Numeric,* or *Date. Alpha* is the default setting and will sort numbers and letters together and display numbers first. This is referred to as an alphanumeric sort. Numbers in an alphanumeric sort are treated as regular characters and are read from left to right. For example, in an alphanumeric sort, the number 110 would be sorted before 23. The numbers are read from left to right and the 1 in 110 causes the number to be sorted on that value. In a *Numeric* sort, 23 would be sorted before 110 because 23 has a lesser value. A *Date* sort reads year, month, and then day.

If you are sorting text that contains both numbers and letters, select an alphanumeric sort. You can also complete an alphanumeric sort on numbers of the same length such as ZIP Codes, telephone numbers, and Social Security numbers. You can conduct a numeric sort on text that contains only numbers with values or numbers with varying lengths. You can also perform a date sort on all dates.

Defining the Sort Order

By default, a sort is completed in ascending order. Letters are sorted from A to Z, and numbers are sorted from low to high. This sort order can be changed to *Descending*, which sorts letters from Z to A and numbers from high to low.

Defining Divisions

A sort such as a line sort, a paragraph sort, or a merge record sort is divided into divisions. Use these divisions to specifically identify what you want sorted. The divisions available depend on the kind of sort. The divisions for each sort are shown in figure 14.25.

FIGURE

14.25 *Sort Divisions*

Sort	Divisions
Line	Field, Word
Paragraph	Line, Field, Word
Merge record	Field, Line, Word
Table row	Column, Line, Word
Parallel column	Column, Line, Word

In the line and paragraph sort, a field is text divided by a tab or an indent. With the merge record sort, a field is text that ends in an ENDFIELD code. In all sorts, a word is text that is divided by a space, punctuation, a forward slash (/), or a hard hyphen. In a paragraph sort, a line is text that is divided by a soft or hard return. In a parallel column sort, columns are divided by hard page breaks and are numbered from left to right.

Adding a Key

When the New Sort dialog box is first displayed, there is only one key specified in the Keys (sorting rules) section. This is the active key and is designated by the marker (>) that displays before the key. If you want to sort or extract on more than one key, add a key at the end of the key list by clicking the Add Key at End button. If you want to insert a key between two existing keys, click the Insert Key Between button. Click this button and a key is inserted above the active key. A maximum of nine keys can be defined.

Deleting a Key

A key or keys can be deleted from the Keys (sorting rules) section. To delete a key, make the key active with the mark symbol (>) by clicking the key number and then click the Delete Key button.

Sorting Records in a Data File by Last Name

1. Open Customer df.
2. Save the data file with Save As and name it Ch 14, Ex 12.
3. Sort the records alphabetically by last name by completing the following steps:
   a. Display the Sort dialog box.
   b. At the Sort dialog box, click the New button.
   c. At the New Sort dialog box, change the number in the Field text box to 3.
   d. Make sure the number in the Line and Word text boxes is 1.
   e. Click OK to close the New Sort dialog box.
   f. At the Sort dialog box, click the Sort button.
4. Print Ch 14, Ex 12.
5. Sort the records alphanumerically by Social Security number by completing the following steps:
   a. Display the Sort dialog box.
   b. At the Sort dialog box, click the Edit button.
   c. At the Edit Sort dialog box, change the number in the Field text box to 6.
   d. Click OK.
   e. At the Sort dialog box, click the Sort button.
6. After the records are sorted, save and print Ch 14, Ex 12.
7. Delete *<User Defined Sort>* from the Sort by list box by completing the following steps:
   a. Display the Sort dialog box.
   b. Select *<User Defined Sort>* in the Sort by list box and then click Delete.
   c. At the query *Are you sure you want to delete this item?*, click Yes.
   d. Click the Close button to close the Sort dialog box.
8. Close Ch 14, Ex 12.

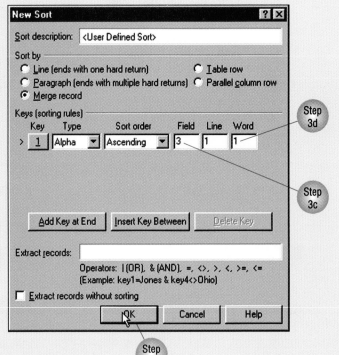

Step 3d

Step 3c

Step 3e

Sorting Considerations

Sorting can be performed on words within lines and fields. When sorting words, WordPerfect reads words within a field or line from left to right. In some situations, consideration must be given to how the sort is conducted. For example, if data file records contain a field with the city, state, and ZIP Code, and you want to sort on the state, you must identify the field number, and then the second word (the city is first and the state is second). The records containing one-word cities would sort correctly, but records containing two-word cities would not. A record containing Dover, Delaware, would sort on Delaware, but a record containing San Diego, California, would sort on Diego.

There are two methods that can be used to ensure that sorting occurs correctly. One method is to enter two-word cities (or any other words that should be kept together) with a hard space (Ctrl + spacebar). The other method is to force WordPerfect to read the line from right to left. If the field contains the city, state, and ZIP Code, you can tell WordPerfect to sort on the second word from the right. This sorts the state correctly. To use this method, key a negative number in the Word text box. For example, to sort on the state when the line contains the city, state, and ZIP Code, key the number **-2** in the Word text box. The hyphen before the 2 tells WordPerfect to read the words from right to left.

When you key a hyphen between hyphenated last names, or use a hyphen in numbers such as Social Security numbers or telephone numbers, the name and numbers are treated as one unit.

Before sorting, save the document. That way, if sorting does not operate the way you intended, you can remove the sorted document from the screen and open the previously saved document.

If you want to sort only a portion of the text in a document, you must select the text first. For example, if you want to sort columns of text that appear within a letter or memo, select the columns of text (including the tab set code) before displaying the Sort dialog box.

Sorting by ZIP Code

1. Open Customer df.
2. Save the data file with Save As and name it Ch 14, Ex 13.
3. Sort the records alphanumerically by ZIP Code by completing the following steps:
   a. Display the Sort dialog box.
   b. At the Sort dialog box, click the <u>N</u>ew button.

c. At the New Sort dialog box, change the number in the Field text box to *4*, the number in the Line text box to *2*, and the number in the Word text box to *-1*.

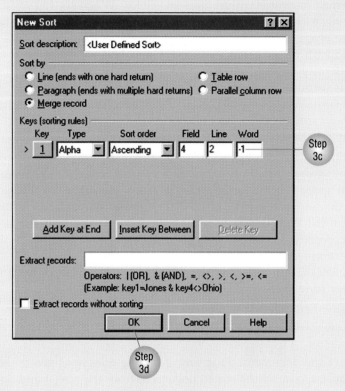

d. Click OK to close the New Sort dialog box.
e. At the Sort dialog box, click the Sort button.
f. After the records are sorted, save and print Ch 14, Ex 13.
4. Delete *<User Defined Sort>* from the Sort by list box by completing the following steps:
  a. Display the Sort dialog box.
  b. Select *<User Defined Sort>* in the Sort by list box and then click Delete.
  c. At the query *Are you sure you want to delete this item?*, click Yes.
  d. Click the Close button to close the Sort dialog box.
6. Close Ch 14, Ex 13.

Extracting Records

With the Extract records option at the New Sort or Edit Sort dialog boxes, you can write an extract equation to extract specific text from a document. This might be useful, for example, in a situation where you want to extract records from a data file of those individuals with a specific ZIP Code. Before extracting records from a document, save the document first. After extracting records, either save the document with the same name (overwriting the original records), or save the document with a new name.

Writing Extract Equations

A variety of operators are available for writing extract equations. The operators and definitions of the operators are shown in figure 14.26.

14.26 *Extract Operators*

=	Equal
<>	Not equal to
&	And
|	Or
>	Greater than
<	Less than
>=	Greater than or equal to
<=	Less than or equal to

The ampersand symbol (&) specifies two conditions and describes "and" situations. With this symbol, the record must contain both conditions—for example, all customers living in a specific state and having a specific area code. The vertical line (|) specifies records that match either one of two conditions and describes "or" situations. For example, with the vertical line you can retrieve all customers who live in Houston or Dallas. The other symbols are mathematical symbols with the conditions shown in figure 14.26. Figure 14.27 shows examples of how extract equations can be written to extract specific records. When keying an extract equation, leave a space before and after the ampersand (&) symbol or the vertical line (|), and leave a space before the key number, but not before or after the mathematical symbol.

FIGURE

14.27 *Extract Equation Examples*

1. Suppose key 1 is the committee assignment, and you want to extract records of individuals serving on the Publicity Committee. The extract equation you would key at the New Sort or Edit Sort dialog boxes is **key 1=Publicity**

2. Suppose key 1 is the software program, and you want to retrieve all records except those customers using PlanPlus software. The extract equation you would key at the New Sort or Edit Sort dialog boxes is **key 1<>PlanPlus**.

3. Suppose key 1 is the company name, key 2 is the state, and you want to extract records of individuals working for CompuPlus in the state of Oregon. The extract equation you would key at the New Sort or Edit Sort dialog boxes is **key 1=CompuPlus & key 2=Oregon**.

4. Suppose key 1 is the Social Security number, and you want to extract records of those individuals with numbers higher than 125-55-7890. The extract equation you would key at the New Sort or Edit Sort dialog boxes is **key 1>125-55-7890**.

Extracting Specific Cities

1. Open Customer df.
2. Save the data file with Save As and name it Ch 14, Ex 14.
3. Extract the records of those individuals living in Bismarck with a Social Security number higher than 330-00-0000 and save the extracted records into a separate document named *Zip df* by completing the following steps:
   a. Display the Sort dialog box.
   b. At the Sort dialog box, click the Output to option and then click File on Disk at the drop-down menu.
   c. At the Select Output File dialog box, key **Zip df** in the File name text box and then press Enter or click the Select button.
   d. At the Sort dialog box, click the New button.

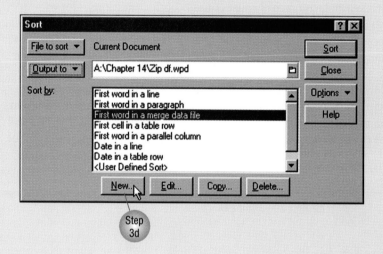

Step 3d

e. At the New Sort dialog box, change the number in the Field text box to *4*, the number in the Line text box to *2*, and make sure the number in the Word text box is *1*. (Make sure the sort type is *Alpha*.)

f. Click the Add Key at End button.

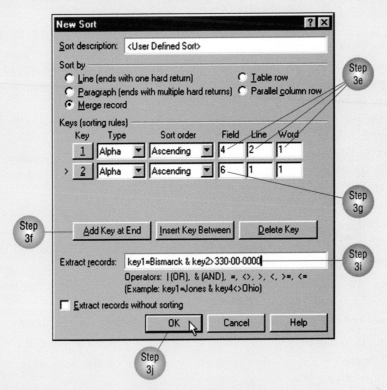

g. For key 2, change the number in the Field text box to *6*.

h. Click in the Extract records text box.

i. Key **key1=Bismarck & key2>330-00-0000**.

j. Click OK to close the New Sort dialog box.

k. At the Sort dialog box, click the Sort button.

4. Delete *<User Defined Sort>* from the Sort by list box by completing the following steps:

a. Display the Sort dialog box.

b. Select *<User Defined Sort>* in the Sort by list box and then click Delete.

c. At the query *Are you sure you want to delete this item?*, click Yes.

d. Click the Close button to close the Sort dialog box.

5. Close Ch 14, Ex 14.

6. Display the Open File dialog box and then print Zip df.

7. Close the Open File dialog box.

CHAPTER summary

➤ When a printer is installed with WordPerfect, a standard page size is generally included in the printer definition menu.

➤ The standard page size is used to print text on stationery that is 8.5 x 11 inches. A page size for printing on legal-sized stationery (8.5 x 14 inches) and a page size for envelopes might also be included.

➤ Change the paper size and orientation at the Page setup dialog box with the Page Setup tab selected.

➤ Use the Envelope feature to create an envelope at a clear editing window or in an existing document. In an existing document, the address is automatically inserted in the mailing address area of the envelope.

➤ Use the Labels feature to print text on mailing labels, file labels, disk labels, and so on. To use a predefined label definition, display the Labels dialog box.

➤ A form document can be created for labels at the Labels dialog box and then merged with a data file to create the labels.

➤ Two types of text columns can be created with WordPerfect's Column feature—newspaper and parallel.

➤ Newspaper columns contain text that flows up and down in the document.

➤ Text keyed into parallel columns flows horizontally across the page in rows.

➤ Format text into columns using the Columns button on the Toolbar or with options at the Columns dialog box.

➤ The Type of columns section of the Columns dialog box contains four options: Newspaper, Balanced newspaper, Parallel, and Parallel w/block protect. The last option keeps all columns in a row together on one page.

➤ Text in columns can be separated by a vertical line, or you can insert column borders around all columns in a document. Insert these lines and borders at the Create Graphics Line dialog box or the Column Border/Fill dialog box.

➤ WordPerfect includes some basic database features such as sorting text alphabetically and numerically and also extracting specific information from a document.

➤ The Sort feature sorts text established in a line, a paragraph, a data file, table, or parallel columns.

➤ By default, text in the current document is sorted and then redisplayed in the editing window. Begin the sort and create or edit a sort type at the Sort dialog box.

➤ With options in the Keys (sorting rules) section of the New Sort or Edit Sort dialog boxes, you can define the type of sort and/or extraction you want performed.

➤ Up to nine keys can be specified, with key 1 given first priority and sorted first. The key is the particular division within the sort type.

➤ With the Extract records option at the New Sort or Edit Sort dialog boxes, you can write an extract equation to extract specific text from a document.

COMMANDS summary

Command	Mouse	Keyboard
Display the Page setup dialog box	File, Page Setup; or Format, Page, Page Setup	
Display the Envelope dialog box	Format, Envelope	
Display the Labels dialog box	Format, Labels	
Display Columns dialog box	Format, Columns	
Format text into columns	Click the Columns button on the Toolbar, select the number of columns	
Display the Create Graphics Line dialog box	Insert, Line, Custom Line	
Display the Column Border/Fill dialog box	Click the Border/Fill button at the Columns dialog box	
Display the Sort dialog box	Tools, Sort	Alt + F9

CONCEPTS check

Completion: On a blank sheet of paper, indicate the correct term, command, or number for each item.

1. This is the width and length, in inches, of standard-sized stationery.

2. Two page orientations, Portrait and this, are usually available at the Page setup dialog box with the Page Setup tab selected.

3. Press these keys on the keyboard to move the insertion point to the next label.

4. This type of column is best suited for creating an agenda, an itinerary, a résumé, or an address list.

5. To ensure that all columns in a row are kept together and not divided between two pages, choose this type of column.

6. When creating parallel columns, press these keys to end the column and move the insertion point to the next column.

7. To create newspaper columns that are approximately equal in length, choose this type at the Columns dialog box.

8. In an alphanumeric sort, which number is sorted first, 235 or 31?

9. When sorting text in columns, the first tab setting is considered this field number.

10. If you sort a document containing records in a data file, WordPerfect automatically selects this sort type in the Sort by list box at the Sort dialog box.

11. If key 1 is the city, this is the extract equation to choose records of people living in Seattle.

12. If key 1 is the city and key 2 is the last name, this is the extract equation to choose people living in Seattle with the last name of Lee.

13. If key 1 is the city and key 2 is the ZIP Code, this is the extract equation to choose all people living in Seattle except those with the ZIP Code of 98101.

SKILLS check

Assessment 1

1. Open Letter 04.
2. Save the document with Save As and name it Ch 14, SA 01.
3. Use WordPerfect's Envelope feature to create an envelope for this letter. Include a POSTNET bar code below the mailing address.
4. Print only the page containing the envelope.
5. Save and close Ch 14, SA 01.

Assessment 2

1. At a clear editing window, create mailing address labels using a predefined label definition. Choose a label definition that can be used by your printer. Depending on the label size, you may need to change the font to a smaller point size to ensure that the text fits on each line.
2. At the editing window, key the addresses shown in figure 14.28. (Press Ctrl + Enter to end a label and move the insertion point to the next label.)
3. After keying all the label addresses, press Ctrl + Home to move the insertion point to the beginning of the document and then insert a code to center current and subsequent pages.
4. Sort the labels by ZIP Code.
5. Save the document and name it Ch 14, SA 02.
6. Print and then close Ch 14, SA 02.

14.28 *Assessment 2*

Mr. Karl Erwin 320 McCutcheon Road Santa Fe, NM 88932	Ms. Patricia Paterno 1008 Valley Avenue Santa Fe, NM 88934	Doug Miyasaki, M.D. Miyasaki & Associates 1102 Lakeridge Drive Santa Fe, NM 88930
Ms. LaDonna Ferraro After-Five Flowers 4302 Third Avenue Santa Fe, NM 88432	Mr. Lloyd Catlin Atwood Fencing 4039 Ridge Street Santa Fe, NM 88043	Mrs. Tamara Butler 9803 Deer Road Santa Fe, NM 88032

Assessment 3

1. Using the Clients df data file, create a label form document using the *Avery 5160* or *Avery 5161 Address* label definition. Save the label form document and name it Mail Labels fd. (The last field in the form document may wrap to the next label. When the form file is merged with the data file, the information will display in the correct location on the label.)
2. Merge Mail Labels fd with Clients df.
3. Save the labels using the name Ch 14, SA 03.
4. Save, print, and then close Ch 14, SA 03.

Assessment 4

1. At a clear editing window, create the document shown in figure 14.29 by completing the following steps:
   a. Change the font to 12-point Century Schoolbook (or a similar serif typeface).
   b. Key the title **PROJECT TIMELINES** centered and bolded.
   c. Press Enter three times and then define three evenly spaced parallel columns.
   d. Key the text in columns as shown in figure 14.29. Center and bold the column headings as shown.
   e. Change the relative size of the title *PROJECT TIMELINES* to Very large.
   f. Change the relative size of the headings *Project*, *Completion*, and *Update* to Large.
   g. Insert a vertical line between columns as shown in figure 14.29.
2. Save the document and name it Ch 14, SA 04.
3. Print and then close Ch 14, SA 04.

FIGURE

14.29 *Assessment 4*

PROJECT TIMELINES

Project	Completion	Update
Engineering building	September - December 2002	Framing underway, roofing begun, masonry going up
Administration annex	October 2002	Expected bid date early spring, permit hearing scheduled
Remodeling of personnel offices	June - September 2003	Mechanical and electrical beginning
East parking lot	September 2003	Soil testing completed, preliminary plans completed

Assessment 5

1. Open Table 03.
2. Save the table with Save As and name it Ch 14, SA 05.
3. Extract the records of those individuals with a quota less than 100,000. (Be sure to change the type of sort to *Numeric*.)
4. Save, print, and then close Ch 14, SA 05.

Inserting Graphics

PERFORMANCE OBJECTIVES

Upon successful completion of chapter 15, you will be able to:
- Insert and format a graphics image in a document
- Insert a text box in a document
- Insert a button box in a document
- Insert a watermark in a document
- Customize and edit a graphics box
- Create a caption for a graphics box

Chapter 15

With WordPerfect's Graphics feature, you can create many different graphics boxes including image, text, figure, table, user, equation, button, watermark, inline equations, OLE box, draw object, draw object text, sticky note text, and inline text. In each of these boxes, you can insert such items as graphics elements, equations, text, or statistical data. Each graphics box has a specific border style, location, and size.

You can insert what you want into any style of graphics box. Generally, however, insert clipart images in an image box; text or quotes in a text box; logos or drawings in a figure box; a table, spreadsheet, or statistical data in a table box; mathematical, scientific, or business equations in an equation box; a keystroke, function key, or icon in a button box; an image that is printed behind text in a watermark box; an equation or expression in a line of text in an inline equation box; and whatever is not addressed here in a user box. Data from other programs can be inserted into an OLE box. OLE is an acronym for Object Linking and Embedding. When an object is inserted into WordPerfect using OLE, the data is linked to the original source. If the data is modified in the original source program, the object is updated automatically in WordPerfect.

In this chapter, you will learn how to create image, text, and button boxes as well as watermark images. For more information on other box types and OLE objects, refer to WordPerfect's help system.

Inserting Clipart into a Document

Corel WordPerfect provides several predesigned clipart images that are included when WordPerfect is installed. You will be using some of these predesigned images in this chapter. You can insert one of the clipart images into a document, or you can retrieve a clipart image created in a different program. In this chapter, you will be using the images provided by WordPerfect.

WordPerfect provides a Graphics toolbar that contains buttons for creating and customizing graphics elements. To display the Graphics toolbar, position the arrow pointer on the current Toolbar, click the *right* mouse button, and then click Graphics at the drop-down menu.

Clipart

The Toolbar as well as the Graphics toolbar contains a Clipart button. Click this button and the Scrapbook dialog box shown in figure 15.1 displays. To insert a clipart image into a document, you can use the drag-and-drop technique, or you can select the desired image and click the Insert button. To use drag and drop, position the arrow pointer on the desired clipart, hold down the left mouse button, drag into the document screen, and then release the mouse button.

F I G U R E

15.1   *Scrapbook Dialog Box*

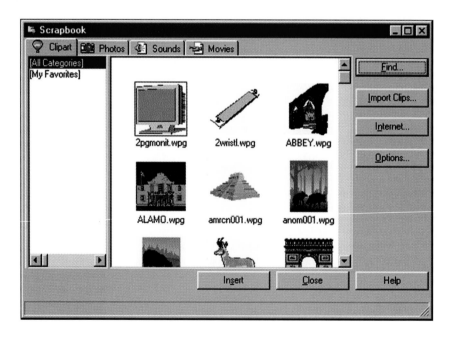

When a clipart image is inserted in a document, it displays in the document in the upper left corner. The width and the height of the image will vary depending on the image. When a clipart image is inserted in the document, two elements are inserted—the graphics box and the clipart. By default, a clipart image is inserted in an image box. An image box, by default, contains no border lines and is 1.5 inches wide. The height is determined by the image.

Sizing and Moving an Image Box

An image box can be moved by positioning the arrow pointer on the image, holding down the left mouse button (this causes the arrow pointer to turn into a four-headed arrow), dragging the outline of the image box to the desired location, and then releasing the mouse button.

The width and height of a clipart image can be changed using sizing handles. To display sizing handles, click once on the image box to select it. This causes black sizing handles to display around the box. To change the size of an image, position the arrow pointer on a sizing handle until the pointer turns into a double-headed arrow, hold down the left mouse button, drag the sizing handle in or out to decrease or increase the size of the image, and then release the mouse button.

Use the middle sizing handles at the left or right side of the image box to make the image wider or thinner. Use the middle sizing handles at the top or bottom of the image to make it taller or shorter. Use the sizing handles at the corners of the image to change both the width and height at the same time.

Inserting, Moving, and Sizing a Clipart Image

1. At a clear editing window, insert the clipart image named *chair2c.wpg* by completing the following steps:
   a. Click the Clipart button on the Toolbar.
   b. At the Scrapbook, drag the *chair2c.wpg* clipart into the document by completing the following steps:
      1) Position the arrow pointer on the *chair2c.wpg* clipart image.
      2) Hold down the left mouse button, drag the image to the right into the document screen (outside the Scrapbook), and then release the mouse button.
      3) Close the Scrapbook by clicking the Close button.
2. Move the clipart image of the chair by completing the following steps:
   a. Position the arrow pointer on the clipart image and then hold down the left mouse button (this changes the arrow pointer into a four-headed arrow).
   b. With the left mouse button held down, drag the outline of the image to approximately the middle of the screen and then release the mouse button. (Black sizing handles will display around the image.)
3. Change the size of the clipart image by completing the following steps:
   a. Make sure that the image is selected (black sizing handles display).
   b. Position the I-beam pointer on the sizing handle located at the bottom right corner of the image until the pointer turns into a diagonally pointing two-headed arrow.
   c. Hold down the left mouse button, drag down and to the right approximately 1 inch, and then release the mouse button.

Step 3c

4. Move the image back to the middle of the document screen between the left and right margins.
5. Click outside the clipart image box to deselect the box.
6. Save the document and name it Ch 15, Ex 01.
7. Print and then close Ch 15, Ex 01.

Creating a Text Box

Generally, you create a text box for quotes or other special text to be set off from regular text in a document. When a text box is created, it is inserted at the right margin, displays with thin border lines on all sides, and is 3.25 inches wide. The height of the text box will vary depending on what is inserted inside.

Text Box

To create a text box, click the Text Box button on the Toolbar or the Graphics toolbar. A text box is inserted in the document with the insertion point positioned inside the box as shown in figure 15.2.

F I G U R E

15.2 **Text Box**

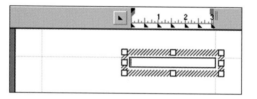

Another method for creating a text box is to click Insert, point to Graphics, and then click Custom Box. This displays the Custom Box dialog box shown in figure 15.3. At the Custom Box dialog box, double-click *Text Box* in the Style name list box. The Custom Box dialog box can also be displayed by clicking the Custom Box button on the Graphics toolbar.

Custom Box

F I G U R E

15.3 **Custom Box Dialog Box**

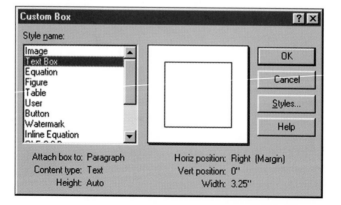

You can key up to one page of text in a text box and can format the text in the normal manner. For example, you can turn on bold or underlining, change the font, or change the justification of paragraphs. You can even include columns in a text box.

Each graphics box is attached to something in the document. A box may be attached to a specific location on the page, a specific paragraph, or a specific character. A text box is attached to a specific paragraph. If you move a text box, a pushpin will display indicating the paragraph to which the box is attached followed by a guideline connecting the text box to the pushpin.

Creating a Text Box

1. Be sure you are in Page view before beginning this exercise.
2. At a clear editing window, display the Graphics toolbar.
3. Create a text box containing the text *DENVER MEMORIAL HOSPITAL*, bolded and centered, by completing the following steps:
   a. Click the Text Box button on the Graphics toolbar.
   b. With the insertion point located inside the text box, complete the following steps:
      1) Press Enter three times.
      2) Press Shift + F7 to access the Center command.
      3) Press Ctrl + B to turn on bold.
      4) Key **DENVER MEMORIAL HOSPITAL**.
      5) Press Ctrl + B to turn off bold.
      6) Press Enter three times.

4. Move the text box by completing the following steps:
   a. Position the arrow pointer on the border of the text box (displays with small, gray, diagonal lines) until the pointer turns into a four-headed arrow.

b. Hold down the left mouse button, drag the outline of the text box to the middle of the screen between the left and right margins, and then release the mouse button. This causes a pushpin and guideline to display.

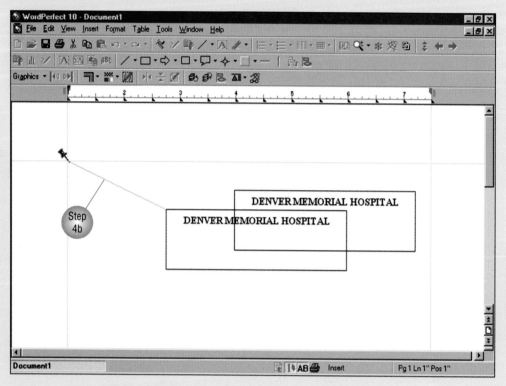

5. Click in the editing window outside the text box to deselect it.
6. Save the document and name it Ch 15, Ex 02.
7. Print and then close Ch 15, Ex 02.

Creating a Button Box

A button box can be created for items such as a keystroke, a function key, or an icon. Unlike text, figure, table, and user boxes, a button box is inserted at the left margin at the location where the insertion point is positioned and is approximately 1 inch wide. Figure 15.4 displays a sample button box. This option is available at the Custom Box dialog box.

FIGURE

15.4 *Sample Button Box*

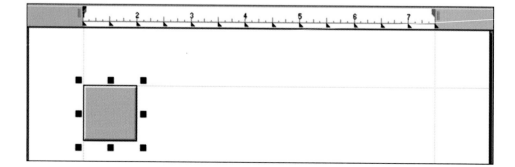

To insert text inside the button box, you would complete the following steps:

1. Position the arrow pointer inside the button box and then click the *right* mouse button.

2. At the QuickMenu that displays, click Co**nt**ent.

3. At the Box Content dialog box, click the **E**dit button. (This positions the insertion point inside the button box.)

4. Key the text you want included in the button box. The height of the button box will increase to accommodate additional text.

Creating Button Boxes in a Memo

1. At a clear editing window, key the top portion of the memo shown in figure 15.5 in an appropriate memo format. After keying the first paragraph of the memo, press Enter twice, then create the button boxes and text by completing the following steps:
   a. Press the Tab key once.
   b. Click the Custom Box button on the Graphics toolbar.
   c. At the Custom Box dialog box, double-click *Button* in the Style name list box.
   d. Position the arrow pointer inside the button box and then click the *right* mouse button.
   e. At the QuickMenu, click Co**nt**ent.
   f. At the Box Content dialog box, click the **E**dit button. (This causes the insertion point to move into the button box.)

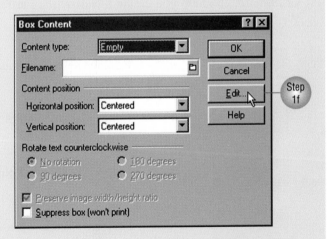

   g. With the insertion point positioned in the button box, complete the following steps:
      1) Change the font size to 10 points.
      2) Press Shift + F7 to move the insertion point to the horizontal center of the button box.
      3) Key **Replace**.
   h. Click in the editing window to the right of the button box to deselect it.
   i. Press the Tab key once and then key the equal sign (=). (The insertion point will display as large as the height of the button box. This is normal and does not mean that the text you key will be as large as the insertion point.)
   j. Press the Tab key once and then key the text after the Replace button as shown in figure 15.5.
   k. Press Enter twice and then create the remaining buttons and text following steps similar to those in 1a through 1j.

2. After creating the last button box and keying the text after the button box, press Enter twice and then key the last paragraph and reference initials and document name for the memo.
3. When the memo is completed, save it and name it Ch 15, Ex 03.
4. Print and then close Ch 15, Ex 03.

FIGURE

15.5 **Exercise 3**

DATE: April 7, 2003

TO: Newsletter Staff

FROM: Tonya Lowe, Editor

SUBJECT: USING GRAMMATIK

As you learn about Corel WordPerfect 10, I encourage you to use the Grammatik feature. Grammatik can help you create a well-written article. Some of the buttons available at the Writing Tools dialog box with the Grammatik tab selected include the following:

Replace	=	Replace selected sentence with the suggested sentence.
Skip Once	=	Ignore the selected phrase for the current occurrence only.
Skip All	=	Ignore the selected phrase for the rest of the document.
Options	=	Display a list of options for customizing Grammatik.

A training session on advanced Corel WordPerfect 10 has been planned for early next month. I will contact all of you before the training to find out your specific needs.

xx:Ch 15, Ex 03

Creating a Watermark

A watermark is a lightened image that displays on an entire page. Text can be inserted on top of the watermark, creating a document with a foreground and a background. The foreground is the text and the background is the watermark image. Figure 15.6 shows an example of a document containing a watermark image. A maximum of two watermarks can be created in a WordPerfect document.

WordPerfect refers to them as Watermark A and Watermark B. A watermark can be discontinued in a document; it can also be suppressed on specific pages. Watermark is another option available at the Custom Box dialog box.

15.6 *Sample Watermark*

> Attention Zoo Friends!!
>
> Annual Picnic
>
> Sunday, May 18, 2003
>
> 12:30 - 4:00 p.m.
>
> Living World Pavilion

In chapter 9, you learned to create headers and footers in a document. A watermark can be created in a manner similar to a header or footer. To create a watermark like a header or footer, you would complete the following steps:

1. Click Insert and then Watermark.

2. At the Watermark dialog box shown in figure 15.7, click the Create button.

3. At the screen displaying the full page, click the Clipart button on the Toolbar or the Graphics toolbar.

4. At the Scrapbook, drag the desired clipart image into the document screen. (You may need to move the Scrapbook to display more of the document.)

5. Close the Scrapbook.

6. Make any changes necessary using buttons on the Watermark property bar.

7. Click the Close button on the Watermark property bar.

15.7 *Watermark Dialog Box*

If you insert a watermark in a multiple-paged document, the watermark will display and print on each page. With options from the Watermark A Placement dialog box, you can choose whether you want the watermark to display on every page, only odd-numbered pages, or only even-numbered pages. To display this dialog box, click the Watermark Placement button on the Watermark property bar.

Watermark
Placement

By default, a watermark displays at 25% shading. You can lighten or darken the watermark image at the Watermark Shading dialog box. To display this dialog box, click the Watermark Shading button on the Watermark property bar. Change the Text shading to increase or decrease the shading of watermark text or change the Image shading to increase or decrease the shading of a watermark image.

Watermark
Shading

exercise 4

Creating a Watermark

1. Open Report 01.
2. Save the document with Save As and name it Ch 15, Ex 04.
3. Create a watermark that prints on both pages by completing the following steps:
    a. Click Insert and then Watermark.
    b. At the Watermark dialog box, click the Create button.
    c. At the screen displaying the full page, click the Clipart button on the Toolbar or the Graphics toolbar.
    d. Scroll down the list of clipart images until *g0186368.wpg* displays.
    e. Position the arrow pointer on the *g0186368.wpg* image, hold down the left mouse button, drag the image into the document, and then release the mouse button. (You may need to move the Scrapbook to display more of the document.)
    f. Close the Scrapbook by clicking the Close button (contains the *X*).
    g. Increase the watermark image shading by completing the following steps:
        1) Click the Watermark Shading button on the Watermark property bar.
        2) At the Watermark Shading dialog box, select *25%* in the Image shading text box and then key **30**.
        3) Click OK to close the Watermark Shading dialog box.
    h. Click the Close button located at the right side of the Watermark property bar.
4. Save, print, and then close Ch 15, Ex 04.

Customizing a Graphics Box with Buttons on the Graphics Property Bar

When a graphics box is selected in a document, the Graphics property bar displays below the Graphics toolbar (or the Toolbar if the Graphics toolbar is not visible). This Graphics property bar contains buttons with options for customizing the graphics box. Figure 15.8 identifies the buttons and describes the function of each.

FIGURE

15.8 *Graphics Property Bar Buttons*

Click this button	Named	To do this
 Graphics ▾	Graphics	Display the Graphics drop-down menu containing options for editing the graphics box.
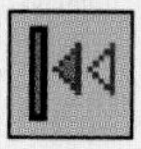 ◄◄	Previous Box	Select the previous graphics box in the document. This option is dimmed if there is only the selected graphics box in the document.
►►|	Next Box	Select the next graphics box in the document. This option is dimmed if there is only the selected graphics box in the document.
 ⬓ ▾	Border Style	Display a palette of border style choices for the graphics box.
 ▦ ▾	Box Fill	Display a palette of fill textures that can be inserted in the graphics box.
 ▧	Caption	Move the insertion point to a position on the graphics box border where a caption can be keyed.
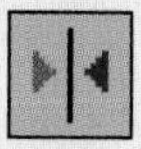 ▐◄	Flip Left/Right	Flip selected object(s) on a vertical axis. This button is dimmed for many graphics boxes.
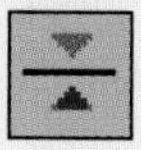 ▼▲	Flip Top/Bottom	Flip selected object(s) on a horizontal axis. This button is dimmed for many graphics boxes.
 ✎	Image Tools	Display the Image Tools dialog box that contains buttons for editing images.

Continued on next page

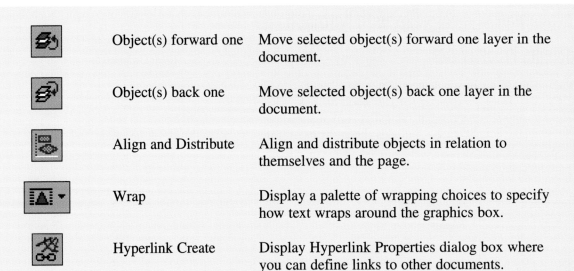

	Object(s) forward one	Move selected object(s) forward one layer in the document.
	Object(s) back one	Move selected object(s) back one layer in the document.
	Align and Distribute	Align and distribute objects in relation to themselves and the page.
	Wrap	Display a palette of wrapping choices to specify how text wraps around the graphics box.
	Hyperlink Create	Display Hyperlink Properties dialog box where you can define links to other documents.

exercise 5

Inserting a Clipart Image and Customizing the Image Box

1. At a clear editing window, insert a clipart image by completing the following steps:
   a. Click the Clipart button on the Toolbar.
   b. At the Scrapbook, drag the *g0127236.wpg* clipart into the document by completing the following steps:
      1) Scroll through the list of clipart images until the image named *g0127236.wpg* is visible.
      2) Position the arrow pointer on the *g0127236.wpg* clipart image.
      3) Hold down the left mouse button, drag the image into the document screen, and then release the mouse button.
      4) Close the Scrapbook by clicking the Close button.
2. Click the clipart image to select it and then use a corner sizing handle to increase the width and height of the image approximately 1 inch.
3. Move the clipart image box to the middle of the document screen between the left and right margins.

4. Customize the image box by completing the following steps:
   a. Make sure the clipart image box is selected (black sizing handles display). If the image box is not selected, click once on the image.
   b. Click the Border Style button on the Graphics property bar.
   c. At the palette of border styles, click the sixth option from the left in the first row.
   d. Click the Box Fill button on the Graphics property bar.
   e. At the palette of box fill textures, click the second option from the left in the fourth row.
   f. Click the Flip Left/Right button on the Graphics property bar.
   g. Click the Caption button on the Graphics property bar. (This moves the insertion point below the graphics box and inserts the text *Figure 1*.)
   h. Press the spacebar once, press Ctrl + B, and then key **Take Off**. Your image should look similar to the one shown at the right.
   i. Click outside the clipart image to deselect the box.

Figure 1 Take Off

5. Save the document and name it Ch 15, Ex 05.
6. Print and then close Ch 15, Ex 05.

Wrapping Text around a Graphics Box

Clicking the Wrap button on the Graphics property bar causes a list of wrapping choices to display. With these choices, you can specify how you want text to wrap around the graphics box. You can also choose a wrapping style at the Wrap Text dialog box shown in figure 15.9. To display this dialog box, position the arrow pointer inside the graphics box, click the *right* mouse button, and then click W*r*ap at the QuickMenu.

Wrap

F I G U R E

15.9 **Wrap Text Dialog Box**

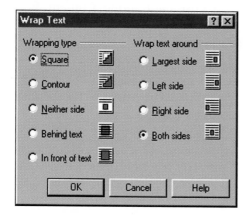

With the options in the Wrapping type section of the Wrap Text dialog box, you can specify whether text in a document wraps around the side of the box (Square), wraps around the contours of the image (Contour), does not wrap on either side of the box (Neither side), wraps behind the text (Behind text), or wraps in front of the text (In front of text). WordPerfect provides a visual representation of each of these options.

The options in the Wrap text around section of the Wrap Text dialog box are used to specify where you want text wrapped in relation to the box. You can choose to wrap text around the Largest side of the box, the Left side, the Right side, or Both sides. These options are also visually represented in the dialog box.

exercise 6

Inserting and Customizing a Clipart Image

1. Open Para 03.
2. Save the document with Save As and name it Ch 15, Ex 06.
3. Insert, move, and change the wrap of a clipart image by completing the following steps:
   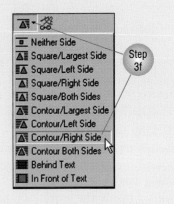
   a. Click the Clipart button on the Toolbar.
   b. At the Scrapbook, scroll down the list until *g0171088.wpg* is visible.
   c. Drag *g0171088.wpg* into the document.
   d. Close the Scrapbook.
   e. Drag the clipart image to the upper left corner of the document.
   f. Wrap the text around the image by clicking the Wrap button on the Graphics property bar and then clicking Contour/Right Side.
4. Save, print, and then close Ch 15, Ex 06.

Editing a Graphics Box with the Graphics Drop-Down Menu

When a graphics box is selected, click the Graphics button located at the left side of the Graphics property bar and a drop-down menu of editing options displays. These options include Size, Position, Caption, Content, Border/Fill, and Style.

Changing the Graphics Box Size

By default, text boxes are one-half the width of the text line. For example, if the left and right margins are set at 1 inch, the graphics box is 3.25 inches wide (one-half the measurement of the text line). The height of the graphics box is automatically determined by WordPerfect and changes depending on what is inserted in the box.

The box size can be changed with options at the Box Size dialog box shown in figure 15.10. To display this dialog box, click the Graphics button located at the left side of the Graphics property bar and then click Size at the drop-down menu. You can also display the Box Size dialog box by positioning the arrow pointer inside the graphics box, clicking the *right* mouse button, and then clicking Size at the shortcut menu.

15.10 *Box Size Dialog Box*

To change the width of a box, select the current measurement in the Set text box (in the Width section) and then key the desired measurement. If you want the box to span the full width of the text line (from margin to margin), click Full. If you want WordPerfect to size the width of the box based on the height of the box, click Maintain proportions.

To change the height of a box, select the current measurement in the Set text box (in the Height section) and then key the desired height measurement. If you want the box to span the full length of the page (from top to bottom margin), click Full. If you want WordPerfect to size the height of the box based on the width of the box, click Maintain proportions.

Changing the Graphics Box Position

If you click the Graphics button on the Graphics property bar and then click the Position option at the drop-down menu, the Box Position dialog box displays as shown in figure 15.11. You can also display the Box Position dialog box by positioning the arrow pointer inside the graphics box, clicking the *right* mouse button, and then clicking Position at the QuickMenu.

F I G U R E

15.11 *Box Position Dialog Box*

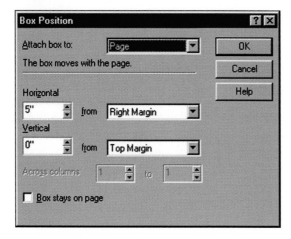

With the Attach box to text box options at the Box Position dialog box, you can determine where the box is attached. The default option is determined by the type of box. For example, a text box is attached to the current paragraph. A button box is attached to a character and a watermark is attached to a page. When a box is attached to a paragraph, the box stays with the paragraph even if text is inserted or deleted. The graphics box is positioned vertically relative to the beginning of the paragraph. If a box is attached to a character, the box is treated like a character in the text line. When text is added before the box, the box moves from left to right as any text character would.

The remaining options in the Box Position dialog box will change depending on the setting selected in the Attach box to text box.

If a box is attached to the paragraph, you can specify the horizontal position of the box from the Left Edge of Page, Left Margin, Right Margin, or Center of Paragraph. You can also specify the vertical distance of the box from the top of the paragraph.

If a box is attached to a character, you can specify where the box is aligned, for example at the top of the text line, centered in the text line, at the bottom of the text line, or at the content baseline. WordPerfect displays examples of each option. The character box, by default, will change the text line height. If you do not want the text line height changed, remove the check mark from the Box changes text line height check box.

If a box is attached to a page, you can specify the horizontal position of the box from the Left Edge of Page, Left Margin, Right Margin, Center of Margins, Left Column, Right Column, or Centered in Columns. You can also specify the vertical distance of the box from the Top of Page, Top Margin, Bottom Margin, or Center of Margins. The Across columns option allows you to span the box across columnar text. This option becomes available after you select a Horizontal position of Left Column, Right Column, or Centered in Columns. Use the Box stays on page option to specify whether the graphics box stays on that page or moves from page to page with surrounding text.

exercise 7

Inserting, Sizing, and Positioning a Graphics Box

1. At a clear editing window, insert *ALAMO.wpg* into a blank document by completing the following steps:
   a. Click Insert, point to Graphics, and then click Clipart.
   b. At the Scrapbook dialog box, double-click *ALAMO.wpg*.
   c. Close the Scrapbook by clicking the Close button.
2. Change the size of the picture by completing the following steps:
   a. With the picture selected, click the Graphics button located at the left side of the Graphics property bar and then click Size at the drop-down menu.
   b. At the Box Size dialog box, select *1.50"* in the Set text box in the Width section and then key **3**.
   c. Click OK to close the dialog box.

3. Change the position of the picture by completing the following steps:
   a. With the picture still selected, position the arrow pointer on the picture, click the *right* mouse button, and then click Position at the QuickMenu.
   b. At the Box Position dialog box, click the down-pointing triangle at the right side of the *from* text box in the Horizontal section and then click *Center of Margins*.
   c. Click the down-pointing triangle at the right side of the *from* text box in the Vertical section and then click *Center of Margins*.
   d. Click OK to close the dialog box.
4. Click outside the picture to deselect it.
5. Save the document and name it Ch 15, Ex 07.
6. Print and then close Ch 15, Ex 07.

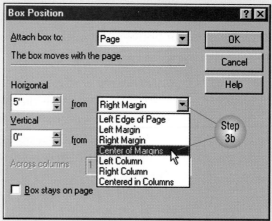

Creating a Caption for a Graphics Box

A caption can be created for a graphics box that displays information such as the box number and a description of the box contents. To create a caption, click the Graphics button on the Graphics property bar and then click Caption at the drop-down menu. This displays the Box Caption dialog box shown in figure 15.12. You can also display the Box Caption dialog box by positioning the arrow pointer inside the graphics box, clicking the *right* mouse button, then clicking Caption at the QuickMenu.

F I G U R E

15.12 *Box Caption Dialog Box*

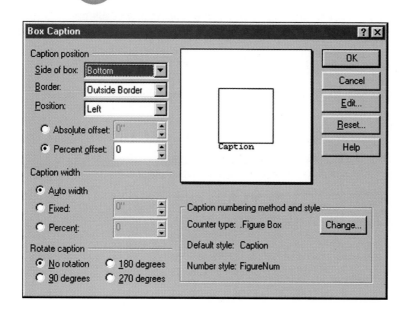

By default, a caption will display and print at the bottom of a figure box, outside the border, and at the left side. Default settings for text, table, and user boxes vary. These default settings for options in the Caption position section of the Box Caption dialog box can be changed.

With the Side of box option, you can insert the caption at the left, right, top, or bottom of the box. The Border option has a default setting of Outside Border. This can be changed to Inside Border. With the Position option, you can determine whether the caption is at the left side of the border, the right side, or the center. The Absolute offset option lets you specify the distance you want to shift the caption from its position. With the Percent offset option, you can specify the percentage distance (0 to 100) that you want to shift the caption text from its position.

WordPerfect automatically determines the width of the caption. If you want to specify the width of the caption, click Fixed in the Caption width section to specify a measurement or click Percent to specify a percentage.

With options in the Rotate caption section of the Box Caption dialog box, you can rotate a caption 90 degrees, 180 degrees, 270 degrees, or stay at the default setting of No rotation.

Each type of box has a different default caption. If you would like to use a different caption type for a box, click the Change button located in the Caption numbering method and style section of the Box Caption dialog box.

If you click the Edit button located at the right side of the Box Caption dialog box, the box in the document displays with the insertion point positioned in the caption. Edit the caption as desired. For example, you can add a descriptive name to the caption, turn on formatting such as italic or bold, and delete or change the caption.

If you make changes to options at the Box Caption dialog box and then want to return to the default settings, click the Reset button. The message *Resetting caption to box style defaults will delete caption* will appear. At this message, click OK.

Inserting a Clipart Image in a Document and Creating a Caption

1. At a clear editing window, insert into the document the clipart image named *g0171142.wpg*.
2. Change the size of the graphics box by completing the following steps:
   a. Click the Graphics button located at the left side of the Graphics property bar.
   b. At the drop-down menu that displays, click Size.
   c. At the Box Size dialog box, click Full in the Width section.
   d. Click OK to close the dialog box.
3. Create a caption for the image by completing the following steps:
   a. Position the arrow pointer inside the clipart image and then click the *right* mouse button.
   b. At the QuickMenu that displays, click Caption.

c. At the Box Caption dialog box, click the down-pointing triangle at the right side of the <u>P</u>osition text box and then click *Center* at the drop-down menu.

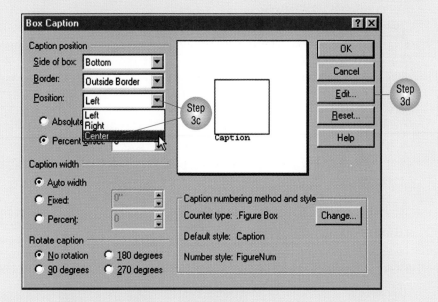

d. Click the <u>E</u>dit button located at the right side of the dialog box.
e. With the insertion point positioned to the right of *Figure 1*, press the spacebar once, press Ctrl + B, and then key **Monitor**.
f. Select *Figure 1 Monitor* and then change the font size to 18 points.
g. Click once on the monitor image. (This redisplays the Graphics property bar.)
4. Click outside the box to deselect it.
5. Save the document and name it Ch 15, Ex 08.
6. Print and then close Ch 15, Ex 08.

Changing Graphics Box Border and Fill Styles

Graphics boxes have varying borders. For example, a button box contains shading and a three-dimensional border. If you click the Border/<u>F</u>ill option from the Gr<u>a</u>phics drop-down menu, the Box Border/Fill dialog box displays as shown in figure 15.13. You can also display this dialog box by positioning the arrow inside the graphics box, clicking the *right* mouse button, and then clicking <u>B</u>order/Fill at the QuickMenu.

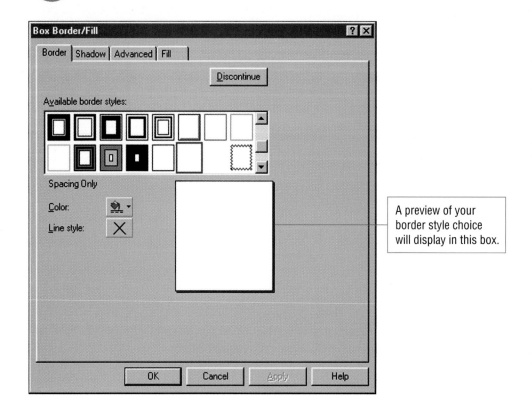

A preview of your border style choice will display in this box.

Changing Border Style: Click the Border tab at the Box Border/Fill dialog box and options display for changing the border style or using a customized style for the border. The Available border styles list box displays various border options such as double lines, thick lines, and shadow lines. To select a border style, click the desired option. When you click an option, the name of the option displays immediately below the Available border styles list box. When a change is made to the Available border styles list box, the change is reflected in the Preview Box located in the lower right corner of the dialog box.

Adding a Shadow: Click the Shadow tab at the Box Border/Fill dialog box and options display for adding a shadow to a graphics box. Various shadow options are available. To choose a shadow type, click the desired option. You can specify the Shadow Height and Shadow Width by clicking in the appropriate text box and entering a value. When you click the Color button, the default color palette opens, allowing you to select the desired color.

Advanced Options: Selecting the Advanced tab allows you to set the spacing Inside or Outside the graphics box by clicking in the appropriate text box and selecting the desired option or entering the appropriate value. If you add fill to the box, the Gradient option will be active. To apply a gradient, select from the linear, circular, or rectangular options in the list box. If you want your graphics box to have rounded corners, click the Rounded corners option. In the Corner radius text box, enter a value or click the arrows to select a value.

Adding Fill: Click the Fill tab at the Box Border/Fill dialog box and options display for adding a fill to a box. WordPerfect provides a wide variety of fills including various shades of gray and designs and patterns such as Checkerboard, Chainlink, Fish Scale, Honeycomb, and so on. The Available fill styles list box contains a variety of fill styles. To select a fill style, click the desired fill style. When a fill style is selected, the Preview Box located in the lower right corner of the dialog box reflects the fill style.

If fill has been added to a box, the foreground and/or background color of the box can be changed. When you add a fill and then click the button after the Foreground, Background, or Pattern options, a palette of options displays. At this palette, click the desired option. When a change is made to the Foreground or Background options, the change is reflected in the Preview Box located in the lower right corner of the dialog box.

Inserting and Customizing a Clipart Image

1. At a clear editing window, insert into the document the clipart image named *BIGBEN.wpg*. Be sure to close the Scrapbook.
2. Make the following changes to the clipart image:
    a. Change the width of the clipart art image box to 3 inches.
    b. Change the horizontal and vertical position of the box to *Center of Margins*.
    c. Add a border and fill to the box by completing the following steps:
        1) With the box selected, click the Graphics button on the Graphics property bar.
        2) At the drop-down menu that displays, click Border/Fill.
        3) At the Box Border/Fill dialog box with the Border tab selected, click the second border option from the left in the second row in the Available border styles list box (Thin Right/Left).
        4) Click the Fill tab.
        5) Click the third fill option from the left in the first row in the Available fill styles list box (10% Fill).
        6) Click the button at the right side of the Foreground option.
        7) At the palette of color choices that displays, click the light green color.
        8) Click OK to close the dialog box.
    d. With the box still selected, click the Flip Left/Right button on the Graphics property bar.
3. Click outside the image box to deselect the box.
4. Save the document and name it Ch 15, Ex 09.
5. Print and then save Ch 15, Ex 09.

Changing the Box Style

If you click the Graphics button on the Graphics property bar and then click the Style option at the drop-down menu, the Box Style dialog box displays. You can change the style of the box in this dialog box by selecting a different type from the list and then clicking OK.

Editing with the Image Tools Dialog Box

Image Tools

WordPerfect provides an Image Tools dialog box that contains a variety of tools you can use to edit or customize the image in a box. To display the Image Tools dialog box shown in figure 15.14, click the Image Tools button on the Graphics property bar. You can also display the Image Tools dialog box by positioning the arrow pointer inside the image box, clicking the *right* mouse button, and then clicking Image Tools at the shortcut menu. Figure 15.15 provides a brief description of the function of each button in the dialog box.

F I G U R E

15.14 *Image Tools Dialog Box*

F I G U R E

15.15 *Image Tools Buttons*

Name	Description
Rotate	Rotate the image around a selected point. To do this, click the button. This causes a point of rotation to display at the middle of the graphics box and handles to appear at each corner. Rotate the box around the middle point by dragging a corner handle to a new location with the mouse.
Move	Move the image within the box. To do this, click the button. This causes the arrow pointer to turn into a four-headed arrow. Position the four-headed arrow on the box image, hold down the left mouse button, then drag the mouse.

Continued on next page

Flip ▶|◀	Flip the image around its vertical axis.
Flip ⊼⊻	Flip the image around its horizontal axis.
Zoom	Zoom in or out or display the image at its actual size. When you click this button a side menu of options displays. The first option allows you to zoom in or out on a section of the image. Click the second option to zoom in or out on the whole image. Click the 1:1 option to return the image to its actual size.
BW threshold	Display the image in black and white only, and set threshold for blackness. When you click the button, a side menu of options displays. Use these options to set the blackness of the image. The darker the option, the darker the image.
Contrast	Set the contrast level for the image. Use this button to change the appearance between light and dark areas of a color. When you click the Contrast button, a side menu of contrast options displays. Choose one of the earlier options to decrease the contrast; choose one of the later options to increase the contrast.
Brightness	Set the brightness level for the image. When you click the Brightness button, a side menu of options displays. Choose one of the earlier options to increase the brightness; choose one of the later options to decrease the brightness.
Fill	Select normal, no fill, or white fill. Use this button to make an image transparent or convert the image to an outline with a white fill. When you click the Fill button, a side menu of options displays. The first option will maintain the normal fill. Click the second option to make the image transparent. Click the third to convert the image to an outline with white fill.
Invert Colors	Change the colors in the image to their complementary colors.
Edit Contents	Edit the object with OLE server. Click this button to display the WordPerfect Draw program.
Edit Attributes	Click the Edit Attributes button to display the Image Settings dialog box, which can be used to move, scale, rotate, set color, fill attributes, and so on. At this dialog box, you can edit all image settings. The options available at this dialog box are the same options available with the buttons at the Image Tools dialog box.
Reset Attributes	Reset all image attributes. This returns the image to its original settings.

Changing Rotation, Contrast, and Brightness of a Clipart Image

1. At a clear editing window, insert into a blank document the clipart image named *bizm0004.wpg*.
2. Make the following changes to the clipart image:
    a. Change the width of the clipart art image box to 2.5 inches.
    b. Change the horizontal and vertical position of the box to *Center of Margins*.
    c. Customize the image box with buttons on the Image Tools dialog box by completing the following steps:
        1) With the box still selected, click the Image Tools button on the Graphics property bar.
        2) At the Image Tools dialog box, click the Flip ▶|◀ button. (This flips the image on its vertical axis.)
        3) Click the Contrast button.
        4) At the side menu of contrast choices that displays, click the first butterfly in the bottom row.

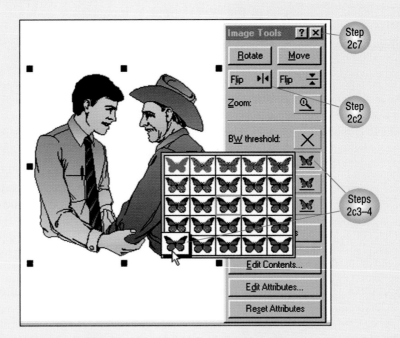

        5) Click the Brightness button.
        6) At the side menu of brightness choices that displays, click the first butterfly from the left in the fourth row.
        7) Click the Close button (contains the *X*).
3. Click outside the image box to deselect the box.
4. Save the document and name it Ch 15, Ex 10.
5. Print and then close Ch 15, Ex 10.

CHAPTER summary

➤ With WordPerfect's Graphics feature, you can insert graphics images into a document. You also have many other graphics boxes available including image, text, figure, table, user, button, watermark, equation, inline equation, OLE, and inline text.

➤ Predesigned clipart images are available at the Scrapbook. Display the Scrapbook by clicking the Clipart button on the Toolbar or Graphics toolbar. At the Scrapbook, use the drag-and-drop technique to insert the clipart image in the document. A clipart image is inserted in an image box.

➤ Move an image box by dragging the image with the mouse.

➤ Increase the size of an image box by dragging sizing handles that display around a selected box.

➤ Create a text box by clicking the Text Box button on the Toolbar or the Graphics toolbar. A text box can also be created by displaying the Custom Box dialog box and then double-clicking *Text Box* in the Style name list box.

➤ Create a button box by displaying the Custom Box dialog box and then double-clicking *Button* in the Style name list box.

➤ To insert text in a button box, display the Box Content dialog box and then click the Edit button.

➤ A watermark is a lightened image that displays on an entire page.

➤ Create a watermark using the Watermark dialog box and customize the watermark image with buttons on the Watermark property bar.

➤ When a graphics box is selected in a document, the Graphics property bar displays below the Graphics toolbar (or the Toolbar if the Graphics toolbar is not visible). The Graphics property bar contains buttons for customizing graphics boxes.

➤ Click the Graphics button located at the left side of the Graphics property bar and a drop-down menu displays with options for customizing a graphics box including Size, Position, Caption, Content, Border/Fill, and Style.

➤ Change the size of a graphics box with options at the Box Size dialog box.

➤ Change the position of a graphics box with options at the Box Position dialog box.

➤ Create a caption for a graphics box by clicking the Caption button on the Graphics property bar or with options at the Box Caption dialog box.

➤ Choose a border and fill style for a graphics box at the Box Border/Fill dialog box.

➤ The Image Tools dialog box contains tools for editing or customizing an image in a graphics box.

COMMANDS summary

Command	Mouse/Keyboard
Display the Scrapbook	Insert, Graphics, Clipart; or click the Clipart button on the Toolbar or Graphics toolbar
Insert a text box	Insert, Graphics, Custom Box; double-click Text Box; or click the Text Box button on the Toolbar or Graphics toolbar
Insert a button box	Insert, Graphics, Custom Box; double-click Button Box
Display the Watermark dialog box	Insert, Watermark

CONCEPTS check

Completion: On a blank sheet of paper, indicate the correct term, command, or number for each item.

1. A clipart image is inserted in this type of graphics box.

2. This toolbar contains buttons for creating and customizing graphics elements.

3. Display the Scrapbook by clicking this button on the Toolbar or the Graphics toolbar.

4. This is the default width of a text box.

5. When a graphics box is selected, this displays below the Graphics toolbar (or the Toolbar if the Graphics toolbar is not displayed).

6. Create this type of graphics box for items such as a keystroke, a function key, or an icon.

7. This is the term for a lightened image that displays on an entire page.

8. Click this button on the Graphics property bar to display a palette of fill textures that can be inserted in a graphics box.

9. Click this button on the Graphics property bar to flip the image on the vertical axis.

10. Specify how text flows around a graphics box at this dialog box.

11. Specify the horizontal and vertical position of a graphics box at this dialog box.

12. Display the Box Border/Fill dialog box by clicking the Graphics button on the Graphics property bar and then clicking this option.

13. Customize a caption at this dialog box.

14. Click this button at the Image Tools dialog box to change the colors in the image to their complementary colors.

SKILLS check

Assessment 1

1. At a clear editing window, create a text box by completing the following steps:
   a. Insert a text box in the document.
   b. Change to a decorative typeface in 18-point size and turn on bold.
   c. Key the following text centered inside the text box:

   FINANCIAL PLANNING SEMINAR

   Planning for Retirement

   Tuesday, January 28, 2003

   Cascade Conference Room

   7:30 - 10:00 p.m.

2. Make the following changes to the text box:
   a. Change the width of the text box to Full.
   b. Display the Box Position dialog box and then make the following changes:
      1) Change the <u>A</u>ttach box to option to *Page*.
      2) Change the horizontal and vertical position of the text box to *Center of Margins*.
      3) Close the Box Position dialog box.
   c. Apply a double border of your choice.
   d. Apply the third fill option from the left in the first row (10% Fill).
3. Save the document and name it Ch 15, SA 01.
4. Print and then close Ch 15, SA 01.

Assessment 2

1. At a clear editing window, turn off the QuickBullets feature by completing the following steps: (If the feature is not turned off, the plus sign in figure 15.16 will be automatically converted to a bullet.)
   a. Click <u>T</u>ools and then QuickCorrect.
   b. At the QuickCorrect dialog box, click the Format-As-You-Go tab.
   c. Click the QuickBullets check box (located in the Format-As-You-Go choices section) to remove the check mark.
   d. Click OK to close the dialog box.
2. Create the document with the button boxes as shown in figure 15.16. *(Hint: The width of the button boxes containing Ctrl is .75 inch and the width of the button boxes containing letters is 0.5 inch.)*
3. Save the document and name it Ch 15, SA 02.
4. Print and then close Ch 15, SA 02.
5. Complete steps similar to those in 1 to turn on the QuickBullets feature.

15.16 *Assessment 2*

FORMATTING SHORTCUT COMMANDS

Ctrl	+	B	=	Bold
Ctrl	+	I	=	Italic
Ctrl	+	U	=	Underline

Assessment 3

1. Open Report 02.
2. Save the document with Save As and name it Ch 15, SA 03.
3. Create a watermark that prints on every page with the following specifications:
   a. Use the clipart image *g0186369.wpg*.
   b. Change the image shading to 15%.
4. Turn on the Widow/Orphan feature.
5. Save, print, and then close Ch 15, SA 03.

Assessment 4

1. At a clear editing window, create the document shown in figure 15.17 by completing the following steps:
   a. Change the page orientation to landscape.
   b. Insert the clipart image named *g0171149.wpg* in the document and then make the following changes to the image:
      1) Change the width of the image box to 4 inches and the height to Full.
      2) Change the horizontal position of the image box to *Left Margin* and the vertical distance from the top margin to 0 inches.
   c. Deselect the image and then complete the following steps:
      1) Change the font to 24-point Goudy Old Style bold (or a similar typeface).
      2) Change the text alignment to Center.
      3) Press Enter two times and then key **IMPORTANT!!**.
      4) Press Enter twice and then key **WORDPERFECT 10 TRAINING**.
      5) Continue until all text has been keyed. (Press Enter twice between each line of text.)
2. Save the document and name it Ch 15, SA 04.
3. Print and then close Ch 15, SA 04.

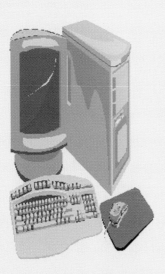

IMPORTANT!

WORDPERFECT 10 TRAINING

Tuesday, May 6, 2003

Thursday, May 15, 2003

1:00 p.m. to 3:00 p.m.

TECH 110

Creating Graphics Elements

PERFORMANCE OBJECTIVES

Upon successful completion of chapter 16, you will be able to:
- Create a paragraph border
- Create a page border
- Create graphics lines
- Create drop caps to enhance a standard business document
- Use the Make It Fit feature
- Draw shapes and insert TextArt into documents

Chapter 16

In the previous chapter, you learned to create graphics boxes with a variety of contents. You learned to create graphics boxes with clipart images, text boxes, button boxes, and watermarks. In this chapter, you will learn to create paragraph and page borders, graphics lines, drop caps, shapes, and TextArt. You will also learn to use the Make It Fit feature.

Creating Borders

In the previous chapter, you learned how to create graphics boxes in a document. These boxes contain a variety of borders including single lines and no lines. In addition to graphics boxes, you can surround text in a document with borders. The borders are similar to the borders of a graphics box. You can customize the border line style as well as the fill style. You can create a border for a paragraph, a page, or a column (as demonstrated in chapter 14).

Inserting a Paragraph Border

With the Paragraph border feature, you can insert a border around the paragraph where the insertion point is located or around the current paragraph plus all subsequent paragraphs. Borders are created at the Paragraph Border/Fill dialog box shown in figure 16.1. Display this dialog box by clicking Format, pointing to Paragraph, and then clicking Border/Fill. The Paragraph Border/Fill dialog box contains the same options as the Box Border/Fill dialog box discussed in chapter 15.

FIGURE

16.1 *Paragraph Border/Fill Dialog Box*

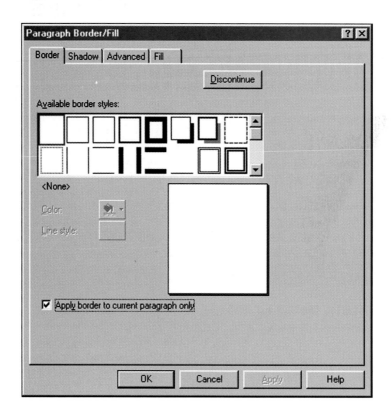

exercise

Inserting a Border around a Paragraph

1. Open Bibliography.
2. Save the document with Save As and name it Ch 16, Ex 01.
3. Insert a single line border around the first paragraph by completing the following steps:
   a. Position the insertion point on any character in the first paragraph.
   b. Click Format, point to Paragraph, and then click Border/Fill.

c. At the Paragraph Border/Fill dialog box, make sure the Border tab is selected.

Step 3c

d. Click the Single option (third option from the left in the first row) in the Available border styles list box.

Step 3d

e. Make sure there is a check mark in the Apply border to current paragraph only check box.

f. Click OK.

4. Complete steps similar to those in 3a through 3f to insert a single line border around each of the remaining paragraphs.

Step 3e

5. Save, print, and then close Ch 16, Ex 01.

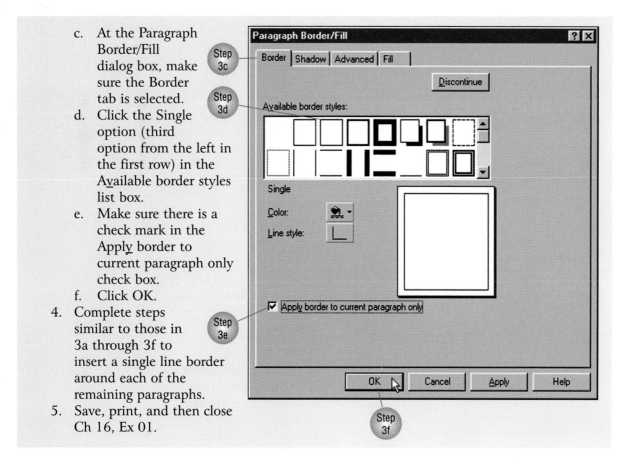

Step 3f

If you want to insert a paragraph border around all paragraphs in the document from the location of the insertion point to the end of the document, remove the check mark in the Apply border to current paragraph only check box. This check box is located at the bottom of the Paragraph Border/Fill dialog box.

Creating a Border around Multiple Paragraphs

1. Open Report 06.
2. Save the document with Save As and name it Ch 16, Ex 02.
3. Change the bottom margin to 0.8 inch.
4. Create a double line border with 10% fill around the last six lines at the end of the report by completing the following steps:
   a. Position the insertion point at the left margin of the line containing *increased random access memory* (toward the end of the document).
   b. Click Format, point to Paragraph, and then click Border/Fill.
   c. At the Paragraph Border/Fill dialog box, make sure the Border tab is selected.

d. Click the Double option (seventh option from the left in the second row) in the Available border styles list box.
e. Remove the check mark in the Apply border to current paragraph only check box.
f. Click the Fill tab.
g. Click the 10% Fill option (third option from the left in the first row) at the Available fill styles list box.

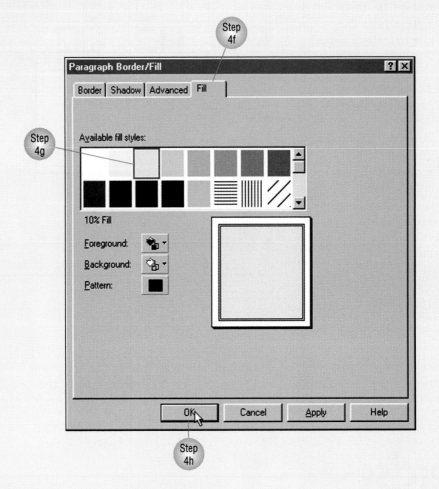

h. Click OK.
5. Save, print, and then close Ch 16, Ex 02.

Inserting a Page Border

Inserting a page border is similar to inserting a paragraph border. A page border will surround the page and all subsequent pages in the document. Display the Page Border/Fill dialog box shown in figure 16.2 by clicking Format, point to Page, and then click Border/Fill.

FIGURE

16.2   *Page Border/Fill Dialog Box*

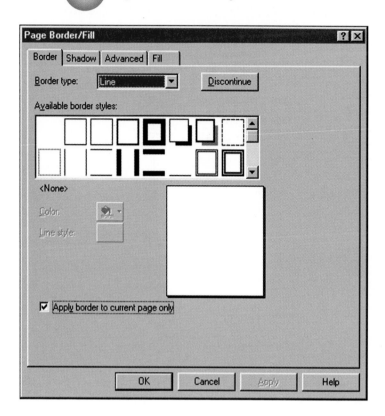

At the Page Border/Fill dialog box, the A̲vailable border styles list box will change depending on whether the B̲order type is set to *Line* or *Fancy*. The Apply̲ border to current page only check box at the bottom of the dialog box contains a check mark. At this setting, a page border will surround only the current page in the document. If you want the page border inserted in all pages, remove the check mark in the Apply̲ border to current page only check box.

Creating a Triple Line Page Border

1. Open Block 01.
2. Save the document with Save As and name it Ch 16, Ex 03.
3. Make the following changes to the document:
   a. Insert a code to center the text vertically on the current page.
   b. Change the font to 24-point Garamond bold (or a similar serif typeface).
   c. Insert a triple line page border by completing the following steps:
      1) Position the insertion point on any character in the page.
      2) Click Fo̲rmat, point to P̲age, and then click B̲order/Fill.

3) At the Page Border/Fill dialog box, make sure the Border tab is selected.
4) Click the Triple option (fifth option from the left in the third row) at the A̲vailable border styles list box. (You will need to scroll down the list to display the third row.)
5) Click OK.

4. Change the zoom to Full Page to see how the border appears around the text and then return the zoom to 100%.

5. Save, print, and then close Ch 16, Ex 03.

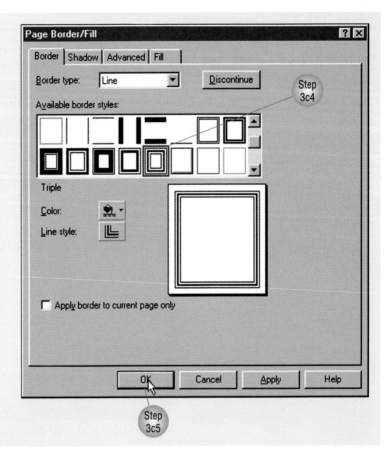

Step 3c4

Step 3c5

Creating Horizontal and Vertical Lines

You can create horizontal and/or vertical lines in a document and adjust the width and shading of the lines. Horizontal and vertical lines can be used in a document to separate sections, create a focal point, separate columns, or add visual appeal.

Creating a Horizontal Line

Horizontal Line

To insert a horizontal line in a document, click I̲nsert, point to L̲ine, and then click H̲orizontal Line; or click the Horizontal Line button on the Graphics toolbar. This inserts a horizontal or vertical line in the document from the left to the right margin at the location of the insertion point.

exercise

4

Inserting Horizontal Lines

1. At a clear editing window, create the document shown in figure 16.3 by completing the following steps:
   a. Change the font to 12-point Garamond (or a similar typeface).
   b. Center and bold the title CARING ACTIONS.
   c. Turn off bold and then press Enter twice.

   d. Key **Reach out**.

   e. Press Enter once and then create a horizontal line by clicking <u>I</u>nsert, pointing to <u>L</u>ine, and then clicking <u>H</u>orizontal Line; or by clicking the Horizontal Line button on the Graphics toolbar.

   f. Press Enter twice, press F7 (the Indent command), and then key the paragraph below *Reach out*.

   g. Press Enter twice.

   h. Create the remaining headings and paragraphs following steps similar to those in 1d through 1g.

2. After keying the document, make the following changes:

   a. Select the title *CARING ACTIONS* and then change the relative size to Very large.

   b. Select *Reach out* and then change the relative size to Very large and the appearance to Bold and Italic.

   c. Select each of the remaining headings *Be friendly, Show courtesy, Demonstrate your competence, Explain what you are doing*, and *Look for an opportunity to serve* separately and then change the relative size to Very large and the appearance to Bold and Italic.

3. Save the document and name it Ch 16, Ex 04.

4. Print and then close Ch 16, Ex 04.

FIGURE

16.3 Exercise 4

CARING ACTIONS

Reach out
_____

Welcome people immediately to your work area. Acknowledge their presence. Make eye contact and smile. Introduce yourself in a pleasant tone of voice.

Be friendly
_____

If you are unsure if someone needs help, ask him/her. Share information willingly and honestly. If you can't help, personally find someone who can. Know what services are available and how to get them.

Show courtesy
_____

Put yourself in the other person's place. Respond quickly. Allow others to go first. Be polite and helpful in person, or on the phone.

Demonstrate your competence
_____

Confidence comes from competence in your job skills and knowledge. Stay current. Express confidence by performing tasks accurately and with ease. Be responsible. While knowing the limits of your practice (job), solve problems within your authority.

Explain what you are doing
_____

Make explanations brief and easy to understand. Answer questions honestly and kindly. Be willing to explain it again. Use language that the other person can understand.

Look for an opportunity to serve
_____

You represent the hospital to every person you encounter. Go out of your way to be helpful to others. Care enough to do your best.

Creating a Vertical Line

Vertical Line

To insert a vertical line in a document, click <u>I</u>nsert, point to <u>L</u>ine, and then click <u>V</u>ertical Line; or click the Vertical Line button on the Graphics toolbar. This inserts a vertical line in the document that extends from the top margin to the bottom margin and is positioned on the line at the insertion point location.

Inserting a Vertical Line

1. At a clear editing window, create the letterhead shown in figure 16.4 (the vertical line in your letterhead will extend to the bottom margin) by completing the following steps:
   a. Create a vertical line by clicking <u>I</u>nsert, pointing to <u>L</u>ine, and then clicking <u>V</u>ertical Line; or by clicking the Vertical Line button on the Graphics toolbar.
   b. Change the font to 14-point Goudy Old Style (or a similar serif typeface).
   c. Press Alt + F7 (the Flush Right command) and then key **CARR ELEMENTARY SCHOOL**.
   d. Press Enter, press Alt + F7, and then key **1098 South Linley**.
   e. Press Enter, press Alt + F7, and then key **Omaha, NE 45034**.
   f. Press Enter, press Alt + F7, and then key **(402) 555-3220**.
2. Save the document and name it Ch 16, Ex 05.
3. Change the zoom to Full Page to see how the document will print and then change the zoom back to 100%.
4. Print and then close Ch 16, Ex 05.

FIGURE

16.4 *Exercise 5*

CARR ELEMENTARY SCHOOL
1098 South Linley
Omaha, NE 45034
(402) 555-3220

Creating Customized Graphics Lines

Custom Line

If you use the Horizontal Line or Vertical Line button on the Graphics toolbar, or click <u>I</u>nsert, point to <u>L</u>ine, and then click <u>H</u>orizontal Line or <u>V</u>ertical Line, a default line is inserted in the document. If you want to create a customized horizontal or vertical line, click <u>I</u>nsert, point to <u>L</u>ine, and then click Custom <u>L</u>ine; or click the Custom Line button on the Graphics toolbar. This causes the Create Graphics Line dialog box shown in figure 16.5 to display.

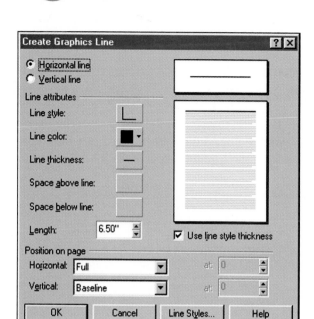

At the Create Graphics Line dialog box, choose whether you want to create a horizontal or vertical line. The default setting is H̲orizontal line. If you want to create a vertical line, click V̲ertical line. This will change some of the options in the dialog box.

Changing Line Attributes

With the options in the Line attributes section of the dialog box, you can choose line style, line color, and line thickness. If you are creating a horizontal line, you can specify the spacing above and below the line, and if you are creating a vertical line, you can specify the border offset. Use the border offset option to specify the amount of white space on either side of the vertical line.

Changing Line Position

If you are creating a horizontal line, the Ho̲rizontal option located toward the bottom of the dialog box has a default setting of *Full*. At this setting, a horizontal line is inserted from the left to the right margin. This can be changed to *Set*, *Left*, *Right*, or *Centered*. Each of these options is explained in figure 16.6.

16.6 *Horizontal Line Positions*

Choose this	For this
Full	The horizontal line is inserted and extends from the left margin to the right margin.
Set	The horizontal line is inserted at the location of the insertion point. Also allows you to enter a number in a text box that represents the distance you want the line to appear from the left margin.
Left	The horizontal line is placed at the left margin.
Right	The horizontal line is placed at the right margin.
Centered	The horizontal line is centered between the left and right margins.

If you are creating a vertical line, the Horizontal option located toward the bottom of the dialog box has a default setting of *Set*. At this setting, a vertical line is inserted at the location of the insertion point. This can be changed to *Left*, *Right*, *Centered*, or *Column Aligned*. Each of these options is explained in figure 16.7.

F I G U R E

16.7 *Vertical Line Positions*

Choose this	For this
Set	The vertical line is inserted at the location of the insertion point. Also allows you to enter a number in a text box that represents the distance you want the line to appear from the left margin.
Left	The vertical line is inserted at the left margin.
Right	The vertical line is inserted at the right margin.
Centered	The vertical line is centered between the top and bottom margins.
Column Aligned	Allows you to insert a vertical line between columns in a document.

Changing Line Length

If the Horizontal line option located toward the top of the dialog box is selected, the Length option has a default setting of 6.50 inches. If the Vertical line option is selected, the Length option has a default setting of 9 inches. If you change the Horizontal option for a horizontal line, you can enter a different measurement in the Length option. For example, if you change the Horizontal option to *Left* rather than *Full* and you want a line drawn 3 inches beginning at the left margin, you would enter **3** in the Length text box.

If you change the Vertical option for a vertical line, you can enter a different measurement in the Length option. For example, if you change the Vertical option to *Top* and you want a 4-inch line beginning at the top margin, you would enter **4** in the Length text box.

Creating a Form with Horizontal Lines

1. At a clear editing window, create the form shown in figure 16.8 by completing the following steps:
    a. Key **PRINTING REQUISITION FORM** centered and bold.
    b. Press Enter twice, key **Name:**, and then press the spacebar once.
    c. Create the horizontal line by completing the following steps:
        1) Make sure the Graphics toolbar is displayed.
        2) Click the Custom Line button on the Graphics toolbar.
        3) At the Create Graphics Line dialog box, click the down-pointing triangle at the right side of the Horizontal option (located in the Position on page section) and then click *Set* at the drop-down list.
        4) Click OK to close the dialog box.
    d. Press Enter twice, key **Department:**, and then press the spacebar once.
    e. Create the horizontal line by completing steps similar to those in step 1c.
    f. Press Enter twice, key **Date Ordered:**, and then press the spacebar once.
    g. Create the horizontal line by completing the following steps:
        1) Click the Custom Line button on the Graphics toolbar.
        2) At the Create Graphics Line dialog box, click the down-pointing triangle at the right side of the Horizontal option (located in the Position on page section) and then click *Set* at the drop-down list.
        3) Select the current measurement in the Length text box and then key **2**.
        4) Click OK to close the dialog box.
    h. Press the Tab key until the insertion point is located on Position 4.5".
    i. Key **Date Required:** and then press the spacebar once.
    j. Create the horizontal line by completing steps similar to those in step 1c.
    k. Press Enter twice, key **Number of Copies:**, and then press the spacebar once.
    l. Create the horizontal line by completing steps similar to those in step 1c.
2. Save the form and name it Ch 16, Ex 06.
3. Print and then close Ch 16, Ex 06.

PRINTING REQUISITION FORM

Name: _____

Department: _____

Date Ordered: _____   Date Required: _____

Number of Copies: _____

Customizing Existing Graphics Lines

To edit a horizontal line, position the I-beam pointer on the line until it turns into an arrow pointing up and to the right, and then click the left mouse button. This causes the line to be selected, sizing handles to display around the line, and the Graphic Line property bar to display. The Graphic Line property bar contains buttons for changing the line style, thickness, and color; buttons for changing to a horizontal or vertical line; and a button that will display the Edit Graphics Line dialog box. The Edit Graphics Line dialog box contains the same options as the Create Graphics Line dialog box shown in figure 16.5.

Line Graphic Edit

To display the Edit Graphics Line dialog box, select the graphic line and then click the Line Graphic Edit button on the Graphic Line property bar. You can also display the dialog box by selecting the graphic line, clicking Edit, and then clicking Edit Graphic Line; or by positioning the mouse pointer on the selected graphic line, clicking the *right* mouse button, and then clicking Edit Horizontal Line (or Edit Vertical Line).

Sizing and Moving Graphics Lines

After a horizontal or vertical line is created in a document, the length, thickness, and location of the line can be changed with the mouse. To make a change, select the line and then use the black sizing handles to increase or decrease the height and/or width of the line. With the line selected, you can drag the line with the mouse to a different location in the document.

exercise 7

Creating Horizontal Lines in a Letterhead

1. At a clear editing window, create the letterhead shown in figure 16.9 (the bottom line and the address and phone number will display in your document and print at the bottom of the page) by completing the following steps:
   a. Open the Scrapbook, drag the clipart image named *bear1.wpg* into the document and then close the Scrapbook.

b. Display the Box Position dialog box for the clipart image box and then make the following changes:
1) Change the horizontal distance from the right margin to zero inches.
2) Change the vertical distance from the top margin to zero inches.
3) Close the Box Position dialog box.
c. Deselect the box.
d. Make sure the insertion point is positioned at the beginning of the document.
e. Change the font to 22-point Goudy Old Style (or a similar serif typeface).
f. Press Enter once and then key **LINCOLN COUNTY ZOO FRIENDS**.
g. Press Enter once.
h. Create a horizontal line by completing the following steps:
1) Click the Custom Line button on the Graphics toolbar.
2) At the Create Graphics Line dialog box, click the Line thickness button.
3) At the palette of line thickness options, click the first option from the left in the fourth row (0.050").
4) Click OK to close the Create Graphics Line dialog box.
i. Press Enter once and then change the font size to 12 points.
j. Press Enter until the insertion point is positioned on approximately Line 9.0" (your measurement may vary).
k. Create a horizontal line by completing the following steps:
1) Click the Custom Line button on the Graphics toolbar.
2) At the Create Graphics Line dialog box, click the Line thickness button.
3) At the palette of line thickness options, click the first option from the left in the third row (0.040").
4) Click OK to close the Create Graphics Line dialog box.
l. Press Enter once, press Alt + F7, and then key **5600 Old Towne Drive**.
m. Press Enter once, press Alt + F7, and then key **Springfield, IL 62702**.
n. Press Enter once, press Alt + F7, and then key **(217) 555-9513**.
2. Save the letterhead and name it Ch 16, Ex 07.
3. Print and then close Ch 16, Ex 07.

FIGURE

16.9 *Exercise 7*

LINCOLN COUNTY ZOO FRIENDS

5600 Old Towne Drive
Springfield, IL 62702
(217) 555-9513

Creating Drop Caps

In publications such as magazines, newsletters, or brochures, a graphics feature called "drop cap" can be used to enhance the appearance of the text. A drop cap is the first letter or group of letters of the first word in a paragraph that is set into a paragraph and set in a larger font size. A drop cap identifies the beginning of major sections or parts of a document. Figure 16.10 shows a few examples of drop caps.

FIGURE

16.10 *Drop Cap Examples*

One obstacle to smooth communications has to do with standards. A procedure becomes standard through common practice. A person can pick up a phone anywhere and call someone nearly anywhere in the world and if both people speak the same language, they can communicate.

One obstacle to smooth communications has to do with standards. A procedure becomes standard through common practice. A person can pick up a phone anywhere and call someone nearly anywhere in the world and if both people speak the same language, they can communicate.

One obstacle to smooth communications has to do with standards. A procedure becomes standard through common practice. A person can pick up a phone anywhere and call someone nearly anywhere in the world and if both people speak the same language, they can communicate.

One obstacle to smooth communications has to do with standards. A procedure becomes standard through common practice. A person can pick up a phone anywhere and call someone nearly anywhere in the world and if both people speak the same language, they can communicate.

A drop cap can be one character as shown in the first, second, and fourth examples or an entire first word as shown in the third example. The four examples in figure 16.10 show only a few ways drop caps can be created. Many other formatting options are available for drop caps.

To display the Drop Caps dialog box as shown in figure 16.11, position the insertion point on any character in the paragraph, and then click Format, point to Paragraph, and then click Drop Cap. Click OK to accept the default Drop Cap in Text; a drop cap is created on the first letter of the paragraph and the letter is three lines high as shown in the first example in figure 16.10.

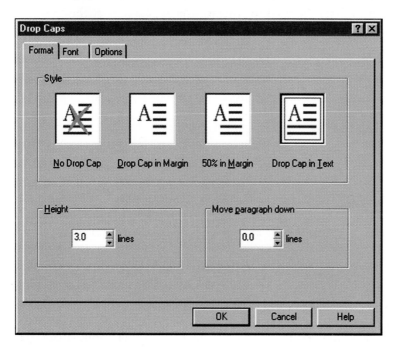

16.11 *Drop Caps Dialog Box*

Inserting Drop Caps

1. Open Para 01.
2. Save the document with Save As and name it Ch 16, Ex 08.
3. Create a drop cap for the first paragraph by completing the following steps:
   a. Position the insertion point anywhere in the first paragraph.
   b. Click Format, point to Paragraph, and then click Drop Cap.
   c. At the Drop Caps dialog box, click OK.
4. Complete steps similar to those in step 3 to create a drop cap for the second paragraph.
5. Save, print, and then close Ch 16, Ex 08.

Customizing a Drop Cap

A drop cap can be customized with buttons on the Drop Cap property bar. To display the Drop Cap property bar, position the insertion point immediately to the left of the drop cap letter. The Drop Cap property bar displays immediately below the Toolbar. Figure 16.12 identifies the buttons and describes the function of each. A down-pointing triangle appears next to some of these buttons. If you click the button, the Drop Caps dialog box displays with the appropriate tab selected. If you click the down-pointing triangle at the right of the button, a drop-down list of choices for that option will appear.

16.12 *Drop Cap Property Bar Buttons*

Use this button	Named	To do this
A	Drop Cap Font	Display the Drop Caps dialog box with the Font tab selected, where you can specify the font for the dropped capital.
A ▼	Drop Cap Style	Display a palette of predefined dropped capitals including No Drop Cap, Drop Cap in Margin, 50% in Margin, and Drop Cap in Text.
A ▼	Drop Cap Size	Display a drop-down list of choices for making the dropped capital two to nine lines in length.
A ▼	Drop Cap Position	Display a drop-down list with the options to specify where the drop cap displays in relation to the margin. Choices include *In Text*, *In Margin*, or *Other*. Click the Other option to display the Drop Caps dialog box with the Options tab selected, where you can specify the number of characters the drop cap will occupy as well as the location of the drop cap in relation to the margin.
⌐	Drop Cap Border/Fill	Display the Drop Cap Border/Fill dialog box. This dialog box contains the same options as the Paragraph Border/Fill dialog box.
A	Drop Cap Options	Display the Drop Caps dialog box with the Options tab selected, where you can specify the number of characters in the drop cap, make the first whole word the drop cap, specify how text wraps around the dropped capital, and position the drop cap in the margin.
A	No Drop Cap	Remove the Drop Cap formatting and return to normal.

Clicking the down-pointing triangle next to the Drop Cap Style button on the Drop Cap property bar displays a palette of predefined dropped capitals. This provides a visual representation of how the dropped capital will display in the document. Use options from the other buttons to apply your own specific formatting to a dropped capital.

By default, the first letter of a paragraph is used for the dropped capital. If you want the entire first word dropped, click the Drop Cap Options button on the Drop Cap property bar. This displays the Drop Caps dialog box with the Options tab selected. In the Characters section, insert a check mark in the <u>M</u>ake first whole word a drop cap check box.

Creating and Customizing Drop Caps

1. Open Para 02.
2. Save the document with Save As and name it Ch 16, Ex 09.
3. With the insertion point positioned at the beginning of the document, change the font to 12-point Goudy Old Style (or a similar typeface).
4. Create a drop cap for the first paragraph by completing the following steps:
   a. Make sure the insertion point is positioned immediately to the left of the first letter of the first paragraph.
   b. Click Fo<u>r</u>mat, point to <u>P</u>aragraph, and then click D<u>r</u>op Cap.
   c. At the Drop Caps dialog box, change the height and font of the drop cap by completing the following steps:
      1) Select the 3 in the <u>H</u>eight text box and key a **2**.
      2) Click the Font tab and then change the font face to Arial Black.
5. Create a drop cap for the second paragraph by completing the following steps:
   a. Make sure the insertion point is positioned immediately to the left of the first letter of the second paragraph.
   b. Click Fo<u>r</u>mat, point to <u>P</u>aragraph, and then click D<u>r</u>op Cap.
   c. Change the height and font of the drop cap by completing the following steps:

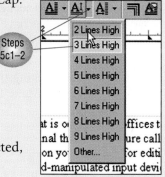

Steps
5c1–2

      1) Click the Drop Cap Size button on the Drop Cap property bar.
      2) At the drop-down list that displays, click *2 Lines High*.
      3) Click the Drop Cap Font button on the Drop Cap property bar.
      4) At the Drop Caps dialog box with the Font tab selected, change the font face to Arial Black.
6. Save, print, and then close Ch 16, Ex 09.

Using Make It Fit

WordPerfect's Make It Fit feature will shrink or expand text in a document to fill a specified number of pages. For example, if a few lines of a business letter display at the beginning of the second page, Make It Fit can be used to shrink the text onto the first page.

To make text fit on a specified number of pages, Make It Fit automatically adjusts font size and line spacing. In addition, margins can be selected to help shrink or expand text in a document. To display the Make It Fit dialog box shown in figure 16.13, open a document containing text you want to shrink or expand, click Fo<u>r</u>mat, and then click Make <u>I</u>t Fit.

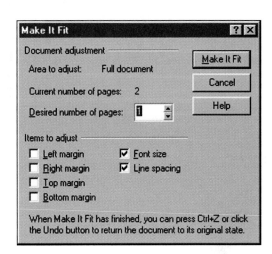

16.13 *Make It Fit Dialog Box*

At the Make It Fit dialog box, the current number of pages in the open document is displayed after the Current number of pages option. Specify the number of pages desired in the Desired number of pages text box. By default, WordPerfect will change fonts and line spacing to shrink or expand text. If you do not want one of these features changed, remove the check mark from the check box before the option. You can also tell WordPerfect to use the left, right, top, or bottom margins to shrink or expand text by inserting a check mark in the check box before the option. When all changes have been made to the Make It Fit dialog box, click the Make It Fit button.

If you use Make It Fit on a document and do not like the changes, you can change the document back to its original state by clicking Edit and then Undo, or by clicking the Undo button on the Toolbar. (You must do this immediately after using Make It Fit.)

Shrinking Text to Fit on One Page

1. Open Policy 01.
2. Save the document with Save As and name it Ch 16, Ex 10.
3. With the insertion point at the beginning of the document, change the line spacing to 1.5.
4. Make the text fit on one page by completing the following steps:
   a. Click Format and then Make It Fit.

b. At the Make It Fit dialog box, make sure *1* displays in the Desired number of pages text box.

c. Click in the Bottom margin check box. (This inserts a check mark in the check box.)

d. Click the Make It Fit button.

5. Save, print, and then close Ch 16, Ex 10.

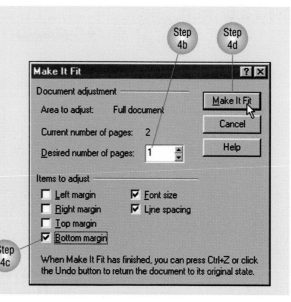

Drawing Shapes

In a Corel WordPerfect 10 document, you can draw shapes such as a rectangle, a circle, or a polygon. You can customize a shape with fill and texture as well as customize the shape border. Corel WordPerfect 10 also includes an application called Corel TextArt 10 that you can use to modify and distort text to conform to a variety of shapes.

A shape can be drawn by clicking Insert, Shapes, and then choosing a particular shape from the Draw Object Shapes dialog box shown in figure 16.14. Shapes can also be drawn in a Corel WordPerfect 10 document by clicking one of the Draw Shape buttons on the Graphics toolbar and then dragging in the document with the mouse to create the shape. The draw objects portion of the Graphics toolbar is shown in figure 16.15. A drawn shape can be enclosed, such as a rectangle or circle, or it can be a line drawing. An enclosed shape will automatically display with fill color while a line drawing will not.

FIGURE

16.14 *Draw Object Shapes Dialog Box*

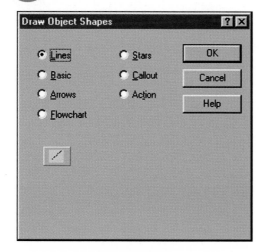

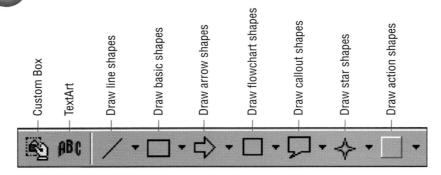

Drawing an Enclosed Shape

To draw a rectangle, click the Draw basic shapes button once. This turns the arrow pointer into crosshairs. Move the crosshairs into the editing window, hold down the left mouse button, drag to create the rectangle, and then release the button. When you release the button, the rectangle is automatically filled with a particular color (usually teal) and displays surrounded by sizing handles. A drawn object is considered a graphics box and can be edited in the same manner you learned to edit graphics boxes in chapter 15.

Size a shape by using the sizing handles that display around the shape. Use the mouse to drag a selected shape in the document. You can also edit a shape with buttons on the Shape property bar, which automatically appears after a shape is inserted or by right-clicking the shape and then choosing an option from the shortcut menu.

With buttons on the Shape property bar, you can customize the shape by changing the foreground and background color and the line color and width, specify the layer where the shape is to reside, and specify how you want text to wrap around the shape. Figure 16.16 provides a brief description of the purpose of each button.

FIGURE

16.16 *Shape Property Bar Buttons*

Click this button	Named	To do this
Graphics ▼	Graphics	Display a drop-down menu of options for customizing the shape such as specifying the layer where the shape is to reside, flipping the shape left/right or top/bottom, and specifying the size and position of the shape.
◄◄	Previous Box	Select previous box in document.

Continued on next page

	Next Box	Select next box in document.
	Shadow	Display a palette of shadow options that can be applied to the shape.
	Shadow Color	Display a palette of shadow color choices.
	Fill Style	Display a palette of fill options including patterns, textures, and gradients.
	Foreground color	Display a palette of foreground color choices.
	Background Color	Display a palette of background color choices.
	Line Pattern	Display a palette of choices for changing the line around the shape.
	Line Width	Display a palette of choices for changing the width of the line around the shape.
	Outline Color	Display a palette of line color choices.
	Object(s) forward one	Move selected shape(s) forward one layer in the document.
	Object(s) back one	Move selected shape(s) back one layer in the document.
	Align and Distribute	Align and distribute objects in relation to themselves and the page.
	Wrap	Display a palette of choices for specifying how text wraps around shape.

Deleting a Shape

If you want to delete a shape from the document, click once on the shape to select it and then press the Delete key.

Drawing and Customizing Enclosed Shapes

1. At a clear editing window, draw a rectangle shape and then customize the shape by completing the following steps:
   a. Click the Draw basic shapes button on the Graphics toolbar.
   b. Move the crosshairs into the editing window.
   c. Hold down the left mouse button, draw a rectangle shape that fills approximately one-third of the editing window, and then release the mouse button.
   d. With the rectangle shape selected, customize the shape by completing the following steps:
      1) Click the Fill Style button on the Shape property bar and then, at the palette that displays, click the last fill choice in the fifth row.
      2) Click the Foreground color button on the Shape property bar and then, at the palette that displays, click the third color from the left in the third row (Baby Blue).
      3) Click the Background Color button on the Shape property bar and then, at the palette that displays, click the fourth color from the left in the fifth row (Light Green).
      4) Click the Line Width button on the Shape property bar and then, at the palette that displays, click the first option from the left in the third row.
      5) Click the Outline Color button on the Shape property bar and then, at the palette that displays, click the third color from the left in the third row (Baby Blue).
   e. Click outside the rectangle shape to deselect it.
2. Draw a circle shape and then customize the shape by completing the following steps:
   a. Click the down-pointing triangle located at the right side of the Draw basic shapes button on the Graphics toolbar.
   b. At the palette of shapes that displays, click the circle shape (third shape from the left on the top row).
   c. Position the crosshairs in the editing window (outside the circle shape), hold down the left mouse button, drag the circle shape, and then release the mouse button.
   d. Make sure the circle shape does not overlap the rectangle shape. If it does, make sure the circle shape is selected, and then drag it to a different location in the document.
   e. Customize the circle shape by completing the following steps:
      1) Click the Shadow button on the Shape property bar and then, at the palette that displays, click the last shadow option.
      2) Click the Shadow Color button on the Shape property bar and then, at the palette that displays, click the last color in the third row (Royal Blue).
      3) Click the Background Color button on the Shape property bar and then, at the palette that displays, click the fourth color from the left in the third row (Light Purple).
   f. Click outside the circle shape to deselect it.
3. Save the document and name it Ch 16, Ex 11.
4. Print and then close Ch 16, Ex 11.

Using TextArt

With Corel's TextArt 10 program, you can distort or modify text to conform to a variety of shapes. This is useful for creating company logos, letterheads, headings, and banners. With TextArt, you can change the font, style, and justification of text. You can also add a shadow to the text, use different fills and outlines, and resize the text. Three-dimensional TextArt can also be created if you selected the 3D TextArt component during a custom installation.

To enter the Corel TextArt 10 program, click Insert, point to Graphics, and then click TextArt; or click the TextArt button on the Graphics toolbar. This causes the TextArt window with the TextArt 10.0 dialog box to display as shown in figure 16.17.

TextArt

FIGURE

16.17 **TextArt 10.0 Window and Dialog Box**

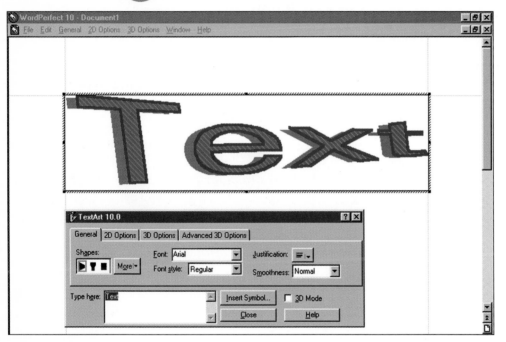

Entering Text

The word *Text* displays toward the top of the TextArt window in a Preview Box. The word *Text* also displays in the Type here text box in the lower left corner of the TextArt 10.0 dialog box. With the word *Text* selected in the Type here text box, key the text you want inserted as TextArt. The text you key is displayed in the Type here text box and also displayed in the Preview Box. The maximum number of characters that can be entered in TextArt varies depending on the size of the characters. Up to three lines of characters can be entered. Press the Enter key to move the insertion point to the next line.

Sizing and Moving a TextArt Graphics Box

TextArt is inserted in the document inside a graphics box. You can edit this graphics box in the same manner as other graphics boxes as you learned in chapter 15. For example, use the sizing handles that display around the TextArt graphics box to increase or decrease the size of the box (and also increase or decrease the size of the TextArt). You can also change the size of the graphics box at the Box Size dialog box. To display this dialog box for the graphics box, position the arrow pointer on the TextArt, click the *right* mouse button, and then click Si*z*e at the shortcut menu.

Change the position of the graphics box containing TextArt by dragging it with the mouse. You can also specify the position of the graphics box at the Box Position dialog box. To display this dialog box, position the arrow pointer on the TextArt, click the *right* mouse button, and then click *P*osition at the shortcut menu.

exercise 12

(Note: Check with your instructor if the TextArt feature is unavailable; it may need to be installed.)

Creating TextArt

1. At a clear editing window, create the heading shown in figure 16.18 by completing the following steps:
   a. Click *I*nsert, point to *G*raphics, and then click Te*x*tArt.
   b. At the TextArt 10.0 dialog box, select *Text* in the Type h*e*re text box, and then key **Bluewater Sports**. (If the shape of your TextArt is not the same as the TextArt shown in figure 16.18, either leave it or change to the shape shown in the figure. To do this, click the M*o*re button in the Sh*a*pes section at the TextArt 10.0 dialog box, and then click the eleventh shape from the left in the top row.)

   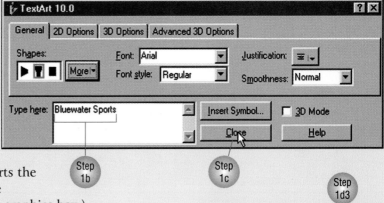

   c. Click the *C*lose button. (This inserts the TextArt text in the document inside a graphics box.)

   Step 1b   Step 1c

   d. Change the size of the TextArt graphics box by completing the following steps:
      1) Position the arrow pointer on the TextArt, click the *right* mouse button, and then click Si*z*e.
      2) At the Box Size dialog box, change the width to 6.5 inches and the height to 2.5 inches.
      3) Click OK to close the dialog box.

   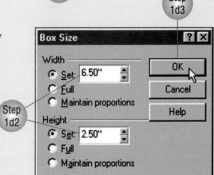

   Step 1d3

   Step 1d2

   e. Change the position of the TextArt graphics box by completing the following steps:
      1) Position the arrow pointer on the TextArt, click the *right* mouse button, and then click *P*osition.
      2) At the Box Position dialog box, change the horizontal and vertical position to *Center of Margins*.

3) Click OK to close the Box Position dialog box.

    f.   Deselect the TextArt graphics box by clicking in the editing window outside the graphics box.

2. Save the document and name it Ch 16, Ex 12.
3. Print and then close Ch 16, Ex 12.

FIGURE

16.18 *Exercise 12*

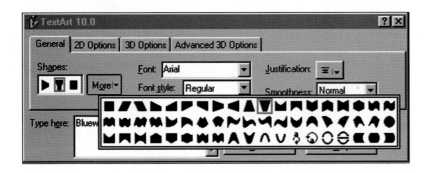

Changing TextArt Shapes

The Shapes section at the TextArt 10.0 dialog box with the General tab selected provides you with a variety of shapes to which you can conform the text. Only three shapes are visible in the Shapes section. To view more shapes, click the More button. A pop-up list of additional shapes will display as shown in figure 16.19. Choose a shape by clicking the desired shape and the text in the Preview Box will conform to the chosen shape.

FIGURE

16.19 *TextArt Shapes*

Changing Fonts

By default, TextArt uses the Arial font (this may vary depending on the selected printer). You can change to a different font with options at the Font list box. To display this list box, click the down-pointing triangle at the right of the Font text box that displays in the TextArt 10.0 dialog box. At the list box, click the desired font. When you change to a different font, the text in the Preview Box reflects the new font.

Change the type style with options from the Font style drop-down list. To display this drop-down list, click the down-pointing triangle at the right of the Font style text box that displays in the TextArt 10.0 dialog box. The default font style is Regular. This will change depending on the font you have selected. For many fonts, you may have only one choice of style. Change the justification and smoothness using steps similar to changing the font style.

 exercise

Creating and Customizing TextArt

1. At a clear editing window, create the letterhead shown in figure 16.20 by completing the following steps:
   a. Click the TextArt button on the Graphics toolbar.
   b. At the TextArt 10.0 dialog box, key **NAES** in the Type here text box.
   c. Change the shape of the text by completing the following steps:
      1) Click the More button in the Shapes section.
      2) At the pop-up list of additional shapes, click the third shape from the right in the first row.

Step 1c2

   d. Change the font by clicking the down-pointing triangle at the right of the Font text box and then clicking *Garamond* (or a similar serif typeface) at the list box.
   e. Click the Close button to close the TextArt 10.0 dialog box.
   f. At the editing window with the TextArt graphics box selected, decrease the width of the box by completing the following steps:
      1) Position the arrow pointer on the middle sizing handle at the right side of the box until the pointer turns into a double-headed arrow.
      2) Hold down the left mouse button, drag to the left until the outline border is located approximately below the 3-inch mark on the Ruler, and then release the mouse button.
   g. Deselect the graphics box by clicking in the editing window, outside the graphics box.
   h. Make sure the insertion point is positioned at the beginning of the document and then key the text in the letterhead in figure 16.20 by completing the following steps:
      1) Change the font to 14-point Garamond bold.

    2) Press Enter once and then press Alt + F7.
    3) Key **National Association of Environmental Safety**.
    4) Press Enter, press Alt + F7, and then key **2300 National Center, Suite 321**.
    5) Press Enter, press Alt + F7, and then key **Washington, D.C. 12029**.
    6) Press Enter, press Alt + F7, and then key **(202) 555-2033**.
    7) Press Enter.
  i. Create the horizontal line by completing the following steps:
    1) Click <u>I</u>nsert, point to <u>L</u>ine, and then click Custom <u>L</u>ine.
    2) At the Create Graphics Line dialog box, click the Line <u>t</u>hickness button and then, at the palette that displays, click the first option from the left in the fourth row (0.050").
    3) Click OK to close the dialog box.
2. Save the document and name it Ch 16, Ex 13.
3. Print and then close Ch 16, Ex 13.

FIGURE

16.20 *Exercise 13*

National Association of Environmental Safety
2300 National Center, Suite 321
Washington, D.C. 12029
(202) 555-2033

Modifying TextArt

The TextArt 10.0 dialog box contains options and buttons for modifying text. With options and buttons in the dialog box with the General tab selected, you can perform such actions as changing the font, font style, and justification. Click the 2D Options tab and you can further modify text with buttons that will change the text pattern, add a shadow, change the outline style of the text, and change the rotation of the text. Figure 16.21 describes the functions of the options and buttons available at the TextArt 10.0 dialog box with the General tab selected and also with the 2D Options tab selected.

TextArt 10.0 Dialog Box with General Tab Selected

Choose this option	To do this
S<u>h</u>apes	Choose a shape to which the TextArt characters will conform.
<u>F</u>ont	Choose a font for the TextArt characters.
Font <u>s</u>tyle	Choose a font style for the TextArt characters.
<u>J</u>ustification	Choose left, right, or center justification for the TextArt characters.
S<u>m</u>oothness	Adjust the smoothness of the curves of the lines. You can select from Normal, High, and Very high. Choosing a higher smoothness greatly increases the size of the file.

TextArt 10.0 Dialog Box with 2D Options Tab Selected

Choose this option	To do this
<u>P</u>attern	Choose a pattern, pattern color, and text color for the TextArt characters.
<u>S</u>hadow	Choose a shadow type, shadow color, and text color. Choosing the center box will turn off the shadow.
<u>O</u>utline	Choose the line width around characters, outline color, and text color. Choose *None* to turn off the outline.
<u>R</u>otation	Drag a rotation handle to rotate TextArt.
Te<u>x</u>t color	Choose a color for the TextArt characters.
Prese<u>t</u>	Choose from a variety of predesigned TextArt styles.

CHAPTER summary

➤ Text in a document can be surrounded with borders at the Paragraph Border/Fill or Page Border/Fill dialog boxes.

➤ Create a horizontal or vertical line in a document with buttons on the Graphics toolbar or by clicking Insert, pointing to Line, and then selecting either Horizontal Line or Vertical Line.

➤ Create a customized horizontal or vertical line at the Create Graphics Line dialog box.

➤ The length, thickness, and location of a line can be changed easily with the mouse. To make a change, position the I-beam pointer on the horizontal or vertical line until it turns into an arrow pointing up and to the right, and then click the left mouse button.

➤ Create a drop cap in a document to enhance the appearance of text.

➤ Create a drop cap on the first letter or group of letters of the first word in a paragraph by clicking Format, pointing to Paragraph, and then clicking Drop Cap.

➤ Customize a drop cap with buttons on the Drop Cap property bar.

➤ The Make It Fit feature will shrink or expand text in a document to fill a specified number of pages.

➤ Draw shapes in a document with any of the Shape buttons on the Toolbar or the Graphics toolbar.

➤ With the Draw Object buttons, you can draw enclosed shapes or draw lines.

➤ Size a shape by using the sizing handles that display around a shape. Use the mouse to drag a selected shape in the document.

➤ Use buttons on the Shape property bar to customize a shape.

➤ Delete a shape by selecting the shape and then pressing the Delete key.

➤ With the TextArt 10.0 program, you can distort or modify characters of text to conform to a variety of shapes.

➤ Other options available with TextArt include the following: changing fonts, adding a pattern, changing the foreground and background color, adding shadow, changing the outline width, changing the justification, and rotating text.

➤ TextArt is inserted in the document inside a graphics box. This box can be edited in the same manner as described in chapter 15.

COMMANDS summary

Command	Mouse	Keyboard
Display the Paragraph Border dialog box	Format, Paragraph, Border/Fill	
Display the Page Border dialog box	Format, Page, Border/Fill	
Insert a horizontal line	Insert, Line, Horizontal Line; or click the Horizontal Line button on the Graphics toolbar	Ctrl + F11
Insert a vertical line	Insert, Line, Vertical Line; or click the Vertical Line button on the Graphics toolbar	Ctrl + Shift + F11
Insert a custom line	Insert, Line, Custom Line	
Display the Drop Caps dialog box	Format, Paragraph, Drop Cap	
Display the Make It Fit dialog box	Format, Make It Fit	
Draw an enclosed shape	Insert, Shapes, and select a shape; or click the appropriate Draw Object button on the Graphics toolbar	
Display the TextArt 10.0 window and dialog box	Insert, Graphics, TextArt; or click the TextArt button on the Graphics toolbar	

CONCEPTS check

Completion: On a blank sheet of paper, indicate the correct term, symbol, or command for each item.

1. Insert a page border in a document with options from this dialog box.

2. Click this button on the Graphics toolbar to display the Create Graphics Line dialog box.

3. By default, a drop cap is created on the first letter of the paragraph and the letter is this number of lines high.

4. Click this button on the Drop Cap property bar to display a palette of predefined dropped capitals.

5. Use this WordPerfect feature to expand or shrink text in a document to fill a specified number of pages.

6. Click this button on the Toolbar to draw a basic shape in the document.

7. Draw a single line in a document by clicking <u>I</u>nsert, pointing to Sh<u>a</u>pes, and then clicking this button.

8. Click this button at the Corel TextArt 10.0 dialog box to display a palette of shape options.

9. Change the font, font style, justification, and/or smoothness of text in TextArt with options from the Corel TextArt 10.0 dialog box with this tab selected.

10. Add or change a pattern, shadow, outline, or text color in TextArt with options from the Corel TextArt 10.0 dialog box with this tab selected.

SKILLS check

Assessment 1

1. At a clear editing window, create the letterhead shown in figure 16.22 by completing the following steps:
   a. Insert the clipart image named *g0127240.wpg* in the document.
   b. Change the horizontal position of the image box to *Left Margin* and the vertical distance from the top margin to 0 inches.
   c. Set the height of the image to 1.5 inches.
   d. Deselect the image.
   e. Change the font to 18-point Bookman Old Style (or a similar typeface) and change the text color to a blue that matches the clipart image.
   f. Key the company name, address, and telephone number as shown in figure 16.22. (Be sure to align the text at the right margin.)
   g. After keying the telephone number, press Enter once, and then create the horizontal line shown in figure 16.22.
2. Save the document and name it Ch 16, SA 01.
3. Print and then close Ch 16, SA 01.

FIGURE

16.22 *Assessment 1*

SEW MANY ALTERATIONS
4300 South Palm Drive
Mesa, AZ 85733
(602) 555-9776

Assessment 2

1. Open Para 03.
2. Save the document with Save As and name it Ch 16, SA 02.
3. Make the following changes to the document:
   a. With the insertion point at the beginning of the document, change the font to 13-point Garamond (or a similar serif typeface).
   b. Create a drop cap for the first letter of each paragraph. Make the drop cap two lines in height and appear 50% in the margin.
   c. Use the Make It Fit option to expand the document to fill the entire page.
4. Create a page border (you determine the border and fill style).
5. Save, print, and then close Ch 16, SA 02.

Assessment 3

1. At a clear editing window, create the letterhead shown in figure 16.23 with the following specifications:
   a. Create the first circle at the left by completing the following steps:
      1) Use the appropriate Shape button on the Graphics toolbar to draw the circle.
      2) Drag the circle so it is positioned in the upper left corner of the editing window (just below the top margin and just to the right of the left margin).
      3) Change the foreground color of the circle to blue.
      4) Change to a thicker line width.
   b. Copy the first circle to the right four times. *(Hint: Use the Ctrl key while dragging the circle.)*
   c. Position the shadow cursor immediately to the right of the circles and then click the left mouse button. (Make sure the insertion point is positioned at the approximate location where you will key *FLOW SYSTEMS LIMITED*.)
   d. Change the font to 22-point Arial bold.
   e. Press Alt + F7 and then key **FLOW SYSTEMS LIMITED**.
   f. Press Enter and then press the Tab key until the insertion point is positioned immediately to the right of the circles just below the company name.
   g. Create a horizontal line at the Create Graphics Line dialog box with the following specifications:
      1) Change the horizontal position to *Set*.
      2) Change the line thickness. (Click the Line thickness button and then click the first thickness option from the left in the fourth row.)
2. Save the document and name it Ch 16, SA 03.
3. Print and then close Ch 16, SA 03.

FIGURE

16.23 *Assessment 3*

Assessment 4

1. At a clear editing window, create the sale notice shown in figure 16.24 with the following specifications:
    a. Display the TextArt 10.0 window and dialog box.
    b. Key **30% Off Sale!** in the Type here text box.
    c. Change the font to Garamond bold (or a similar serif typeface).
    d. Change the shape to match what you see in the figure.
    e. Add a pattern and change the foreground and background colors. (You determine the pattern and the colors.)
    f. Close the TextArt 10.0 dialog box.
    g. Display the Box Size dialog box for the graphics box containing the TextArt, change the width to 6.5 inches, the height to 3.5 inches, and then close the dialog box.
    h. Display the Box Position dialog box for the graphics box, change the horizontal and vertical positions to *Center of Margins*, and then close the dialog box.
2. Save the document and name it Ch 16, SA 04.
3. Print and then close Ch 16, SA 04.

FIGURE

16.24 *Assessment 4*

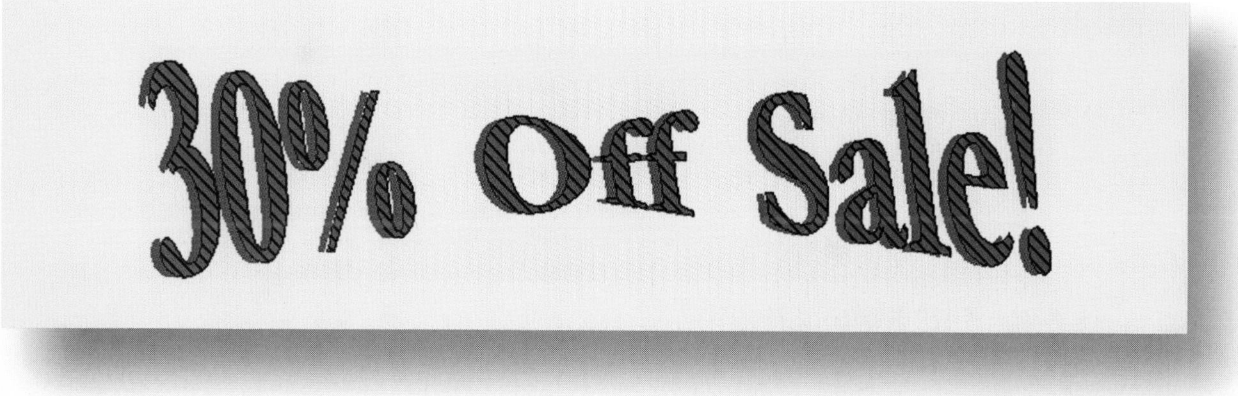

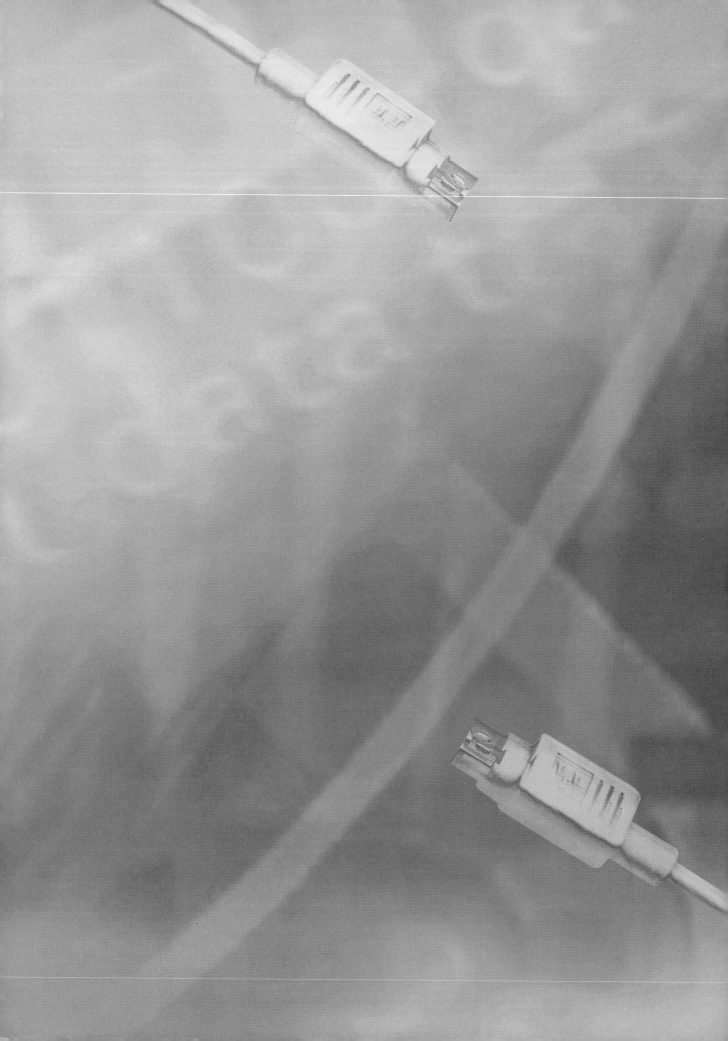

PERFORMANCE Assessments

USING SPECIAL FEATURES AND GRAPHICS ELEMENTS

INTEGRATING SKILLS

In this unit, you have learned to use special features of WordPerfect 10 including formatting columns, formatting envelopes and labels, sorting and extracting information, hyphenating words in a document, line numbering, hard spaces, date codes, converting the case of letters, and the Prompt-As-You-Go feature. In addition, you have learned to use graphic elements such as images, text boxes, button boxes, watermarks, graphic lines, paragraph and page borders, drop caps, drawing features, and TextArt.

Assessment 1 one

1. Open Report 01.
2. Save the document with Save As and name it U04, PA 01.
3. Make the following changes to the document:
    a. Delete the *Ln Spacing: 2.0* code.
    b. Set a left tab at the 1.25-inch mark on the Ruler.
    c. Insert a hard return (by pressing Enter) below the title *TRENDS IN TELECOMMUNICATIONS.*
    d. Change the first heading in the document so it displays as *Continued Growth of Photonics* rather than *Continued Growth of Photonics (Fiber Optics).*
    e. Change the second heading in the document so it displays as *Microcomputer Trends* rather than *Microcomputer Trends in the Nineties.*
    f. Insert a hard return above and below the headings *Continued Growth of Photonics* and *Microcomputer Trends.*
    g. Select the title and then change the relative size to Large.
    h. Position the insertion point at the beginning of the document and then change the page orientation to Landscape.
    i. Position the insertion point at the left margin of the line that begins *Several trends are occurring in the field...* and then define three balanced newspaper columns with 0.3 inch of space between columns.

j. Position the insertion point at the beginning of the document, change the left hyphenation zone to 5%, the right hyphenation zone to 0%, and then turn on hyphenation. Make hyphenation decisions as required.

k. Add a double page border.

4. Save, print, and then close U04, PA 01.

Assessment 2

1. Open Table 03.
2. Save the document using Save As and name it U04, PA 02.
3. Extract the records of those individuals with a quota greater than 100,000.
4. Save, print, and close U04, PA 02.

Assessment 3

1. At a clear editing window, create a text box that contains the following text:

   BROWSING THE WEB WORKSHOP
   Completing Advanced Searches
   Monday, April 21, 2003
   Computer Center
   2:30 - 5:00 p.m.

2. You determine the following for the text and the text box.
   a. Typeface and type size for the text.
   b. Position and size of the text box.
   c. The border and fill for the text box.
3. Save the document and name it U04, PA 03.
4. Print and then close U04, PA 03.

Assessment 4

1. Open Letter 03.
2. Save the document with Save As and name it U04, PA 04.
3. Create a watermark with the following specifications:
   a. Use the clipart image *g0186364.wpg*.
   b. Change the image shading to 20%.
4. Format an envelope including the bar code; but not including a return address. Append to the letter.
5. Save, print (letter and envelope), and then close U04, PA 04.

Assessment 5

1. At a clear editing window, create a letterhead for the company Archway Financial Services. Include the following information in the letterhead:

   Archway Financial Services
   785 Sixteenth Street
   New York, NY 12991
   (914) 555-8770

2. Include the clipart image named *arch.wpg* in the letterhead along with at least one horizontal or vertical line.
3. Save the letterhead and name it U04, PA 05.
4. Print and then close U04, PA 05.

Assessment 6

1. At a clear editing window, create a flyer with the following specifications:
   a. Use TextArt to create the title of the flyer *Spring Carnival*. You determine the shape, formatting, and size of the TextArt.
   b. Include the following information after the title of the flyer:

      Carr Elementary School
      Friday, April 25, 2003
      School Cafeteria
      6:00 p.m. - 9:30 p.m.
      Game tickets: Five for $1.00

2. Save the completed flyer and name it U04, PA 06.
3. Print and then close U04, PA 06.

WRITING SOLUTIONS

The following activities give you the opportunity to practice your writing skills along with demonstrating an understanding of some of the important WordPerfect features you have mastered in this unit. In planning the documents, remember to shape the information according to the writing purpose and the audience. Use correct grammar, appropriate word choices, and clear sentence constructions.

Assessment 7 seven

Situation: You work for COMPUTER CITY, a store that sells computers and peripherals. You have been asked to design a letterhead for the store. When designing this letterhead, include the following information:

> COMPUTER CITY
> 2305 Benson Highway
> Kent, WA 98033
> (206) 555-4422

Save the letterhead and name it U04, PA 07. Print and then close U04, PA 07.

Assessment 8 eight

Situation: You are Cynthia Lakeland, assistant manager for COMPUTER CITY. Write a letter to R & L Suppliers, 903 North Union Street, Seattle, WA 98049, using the letterhead you created in assessment 7. Format an envelope to accompany the letter including the return address and bar code. In the letter, request information on a new line of hard drives you saw advertised in the R & L Suppliers catalog. Ask that a representative of the company visit the store and bring a sample of the drives. You are also interested in any other data storage devices manufactured by the company. Save the letter and name it U04, PA 08. Print the letter and the envelope, and then close U04, PA 08.

Appendix A

Proofreaders' Marks

Proofreaders' Mark	Example	Revised
# Insert space	lettertothe	letter to the
Delete	the commands is	the command is
lc / Lowercase	lc he is Branch Manager	he is branch manager
cap or uc Uppercase	cap Margaret simpson	Margaret Simpson
¶ New paragraph	¶ The new product	The new product
no ¶ No paragraph	the meeting.	the meeting. Bring the
	no ¶ Bring the	
∧ Insert	and pens, clips	pens, and clips
⊙ Insert period	a global search⊙	a global search.
⊐ Move right	⊐ With the papers	With the papers
⊏ Move left	⊏ access the code	access the code
⊐⊏ Center	⊐ Chapter Six ⊏	Chapter Six
∽ Transpose	It is raesonable	It is reasonable
sp Spell out	sp 475 Mill Ave	475 Mill Avenue
⋯ Stet (do not delete)	I am very pleased	I am very pleased
⌢ Close up	regret fully	regretfully
ss Single-space	The margin top ss is 1 inch.	The margin top is 1 inch.
ds Double-space	ds Paper length is set for 11 inches.	Paper length is set for 11 inches.
ts Triple-space	ts The F8 function key turns on Extend	The F8 function key turns on Extend
bf Boldface	bf Boldface type provides emphasis.	**Boldface** type provides emphasis.
ital Italics	ital Use italics for terms to be defined.	Use *italics* for terms to be defined.

Appendix B

Formatting a Memo

There are many memo and business letter styles. This appendix includes one memo and two business letter styles.

At the end of a memo or business letter, the initials of the person keying the document appear. In exercises in this textbook, insert your initials where you see the XX at the end of a document. The name of the document is included after the initials.

Both business letters in this appendix were created with standard punctuation. Standard punctuation includes a colon after the salutation and a comma after the complimentary close.

A business letter can be printed on letterhead stationery, or the company name and address can be keyed at the top of the letter. For the examples in this text, assume that all business letters you create will be printed on letterhead stationery.

↓ *1-inch top margin*

DATE: September 25, 2003
ds
TO: Adam Mukai, Vice President
ds
FROM: Carol Jenovich, Director
ds
SUBJECT: NEW EMPLOYEES
ts

Two new employees have been hired to work in the Human Resources Department. Lola Henderson will begin work on October 1 and Daniel Schriver will begin October 15.
ds
Ms. Henderson has worked for three years as an administrative assistant for another company. Due to her previous experience, she was hired as a program assistant.
ds
Mr. Schriver has just completed a one-year training program at Gulf Community College. He was hired as an Administrative Assistant I.
ds
I would like to introduce you to the new employees. Please schedule a time for a short visit.
ds
XX:Memo

Block-style Letter

2-inch top margin →

December 3, 2003

5 Enters (Returns) →

Mr. Paul Reinke
Iverson Medical Center
1290 South 43rd Street
Houston, TX 77348
ds

Dear Mr. Reinke:
ds

During the entire month of January, our laser printer, Model No. 34-454, will be on sale. We are cutting the original price by 33 percent!
ds

When you purchased your computer system from our store last month, you indicated an interest in a laser printer. Now is your chance, Mr. Reinke, to purchase a high-quality laser printer at a rock-bottom price. Once you have seen the quality of print produced by a laser printer, you will not be satisfied with any other type of printer.
ds

Visit our store at your convenience and see a demonstration of this incredible printer. We are so confident you will purchase the printer that we are enclosing a coupon for a free printer cartridge worth over $100.
ds

Very truly yours,

4 Enters (Returns) →

Gina Cerazzo, Manager
ds

XX: Block Letter
ds

Enclosure

Modified Block-style Letter

2-inch top margin →

December 3, 2003

5 Enters (Returns) →

Mr. Paul Reinke
Iverson Medical Center
1290 South 43rd Street
Houston, TX 77348
ds

Dear Mr. Reinke:
ds

During the entire month of January, our laser printer, Model No. 34-454, will be on sale. We are cutting the original price by 33 percent!
ds

When you purchased your computer system from our store last month, you indicated an interest in a laser printer. Now is your chance, Mr. Reinke, to purchase a high-quality laser printer at a rock-bottom price. Once you have seen the quality of print produced by a laser printer, you will not be satisfied with any other type of printer.
ds

Visit our store at your convenience and see a demonstration of this incredible printer. We are so confident you will purchase the printer that we are enclosing a coupon for a free printer cartridge worth over $100.
ds

Very truly yours,
ds

HOUSTON COMPUTING

4 Enters (Returns) →

Gina Cerazzo, Manager
ds

XX: Modified Block Letter
ds

Enclosure

Index